LIVING LANGUAGE®
U L T I M A T E
SPANISH

REVISED AND UPDATED

Also Available from LIVING LANGUAGE®

ULTIMATE ADVANCED SPANISH. Using the same proven method of the Ultimate Beginner–Intermediate program, Advanced Spanish introduces the finer points of conversation, grammar, and culture and takes your language skills to a new level of ease and sophistication. A special section devoted to business language and etiquette is included in each lesson. Also available in French, German, Inglés, Japanese, Russian, and Italian. Beginner–Intermediate level available in Chinese, French, German, Inglés, Japanese, Portuguese, Russian, and Italian.

ALL-AUDIO SPANISH. This very popular beginner-intermediate level audio program is ideal for learning while you drive, with a Walkman, or anywhere it's convenient. A bilingual narrator guides you through 35 lessons. Just listen, then repeat after the native speakers. Interactive quizzes at the end of each lesson reinforce the learning process. A 96-page listener's guide provides key vocabulary from each lesson plus a brief grammar summary. Includes free access to more practice online. Also available in French, German, and Italian.

SPANISH COMPLETE BASIC COURSE. Whether you're just starting out or want a thorough review, the *Complete Basic Course* is the perfect choice. Developed by U.S. Government experts, the building-block approach used here begins with simple words and phrases and progresses to more complex expressions. Includes a full grammar summary for easy reference. Also available in French, German, Inglés, Japanese, Portuguese, Russian, and Italian.

2000+ ESSENTIAL SPANISH VERBS. No language student should be without this book! This handy reference is the key to mastering what many consider the hardest part of learning a language—verb tenses. It covers more than 2,000 commonly used Spanish verbs with complete verb conjugation charts, a two-way glossary, practice questions, examples, dialogues, and a grammar summary. Plus, 40 flash cards for extra practice. Also available in French.

SPANISH DAILY PHRASE AND CULTURE CALENDAR. This amusing and informative day-by-day desk calendar introduces 365 foreign phrases, cultural tidbits, and trivia. Each page includes the pronunciation and English translation of a Spanish word or phrase. These calendars are ideal for beginners, as well as those who would like to brush up on the fun stuff! They make a perfect gift for students and teachers, co-workers, and family members with a love for foreign languages. Also available in French, Italian, and German.

FODOR'S SPANISH FOR TRAVELERS. From the most respected names in travel and language, this phrasebook/cassette program provides the essential words and phrases you need to communicate in every situation, from changing money to finding a hotel room. The 3,800-word phrasebook includes the most up-to-date vocabulary, all organized by topic. Easy-to-use pronunciation key helps you speak like a native. Loads of Fodor's travel advice, maps, and a 2-way dictionary are also included. The bilingual cassettes or CDs make it easy to learn anywhere. Also available in French, German, and Italian.

LEARN SPANISH TOGETHER: Activity Kits for Kids and Grown-Ups. Easy and fun, the original Learn Together and For the Car activity kits introduce children ages 4–8 (and grown-ups of any age!) to a new language using 16 songs, games, and activities. Each *Adult/Child Activity Kit* includes a 60-minute bilingual cassette, a 48-page, illustrated activity book that doubles as a scrapbook, and 40 play and learn stickers. Also available in French and Italian.

SPANISH WITHOUT THE FUSS. A lighthearted course for anyone who has ever hesitated to learn a language, *Spanish Without the Fuss* is full of naturally spoken Spanish, and features the most commonly used slang terms. A "language coach" guides readers through the lessons, while cartoons in each chapter keep the tone fun and easy. Each 400-page book includes a 60-minute CD containing dialogues spoken by native speakers. Also available in French and Italian.

Available in bookstores everywhere.
Visit our website at: www.livinglanguage.com

ULTIMATE

SPANISH

REVISED AND UPDATED

BASIC–INTERMEDIATE

IRWIN STERN, PH.D.,

DIRECTOR OF LANGUAGE PROGRAMS,

DEPARTMENT OF SPANISH AND PORTUGUESE,

COLUMBIA UNIVERSITY

Previously published as
Living Language® Spanish All the Way™

LIVING LANGUAGE®
A Random House Company

Maps © 2000 Fodors LLC
Fodor's is a registered trademark of Random House, Inc.

Published by Living Language, A Random House Company,
New York, New York. Living Language is a member of the
Random House Information Group.

Random House, Inc., New York, Toronto, London, Sydney, Auckland

www.livinglanguage.com

Living Language and colophon are registered trademarks of Random House, Inc.

Printed in the United States of America

Library of Congress Cataloging-in-Publication Data

Stern, Irwin.
    Ultimate Spanish : basic–intermediate / Irwin Stern.
       p.   cm.
    1. Spanish language—Textbooks for foreign speakers—English.
    2. Spanish language—Grammar.   1. Title.
    PC4129.E5S743   1998
    468.2'421—dc21   97-44325
                                                              CIP

ISBN 0-609-80683-1

10   9   8   7

Second Edition

CONTENTS

Preterite

xiv

INTRODUCTION

Living Language® Ultimate Spanish is a practical and enjoyable way to learn Spanish. The complete course consists of this text and eight hours of recordings. You can, however, use the text on its own if you already know how to pronounce Spanish.

With *Ultimate Spanish,* you'll speak Spanish from the very beginning. Each lesson starts with a dialogue about common situations that you are likely to experience at home or abroad. You'll learn the most common and useful expressions for everyday conversation.

Key grammatical structures introduced in the dialogue are clearly explained in a separate section. The lessons build on one another. The material you've just studied is "recycled," or used again, in later lessons as you are learning new words, phrases and grammatical forms. This method helps you gradually increase your language skills while reinforcing and perfecting material learned previously.

In addition, brief notes on cultural topics will add to your understanding of Spanish and Spanish-speaking people.

COURSE MATERIAL

THE MANUAL

Living Language® Ultimate Spanish consists of 40 lessons, 8 review sections, and 4 reading sections. The review sections appear after every 5 lessons, and the reading sections after every 10 lessons.

Read and study each lesson before listening to it on the recordings.

DIALOGO (DIALOGUE): Each lesson begins with a dialogue presenting a realistic situation in a Spanish-speaking locale. The dialogue is followed by a translation in colloquial English. Note that while there are many regional dialects and accents, we will be using standard Spanish grammar and vocabulary throughout, of course.

PRONUNCIACION (PRONUNCIATION): In lessons 1 through 10, you will learn the correct pronunciation of vowels and diphthongs, as well as those consonants and consonant combinations.

GRAMATICA Y USOS (GRAMMAR AND USAGE): This section explains the major grammatical points covered in the lesson. The heading of each topic corresponds to its listing in the table of contents.

VOCABULARIO (VOCABULARY): In this section you can review the words and expressions from the dialogue and learn additional vocabulary. Most items are arranged thematically.

EXAMEN (QUIZ): These exercises test your mastery of the lesson's essential vocabulary and structures. You can check your answers in the RESPUESTAS *(ANSWER KEY)* section.

NOTAS CULTURALES (CULTURAL NOTES): These brief notes about Spanish and Latin American customs put the language in its cultural context. Cultural awareness will enrich your understanding of Spanish and your ability to communicate effectively.

REPASO (REVIEWS): Review sections appear after every five lessons. These sections are similar to the quizzes in format but integrate material from all the lessons you have studied to that point.

LECTURA (READINGS): The four reading passages are not translated. However, the material covered in the preceding lessons, along with the vocabulary notes that accompany the reading, will enable you to infer the meaning, just as you would when reading a newspaper abroad.

APENDIXES (APPENDIXES): There are three appendixes: a glossary of continents, countries, cities, and languages, verb charts, and a section on letter writing.

GLOSARIO (GLOSSARY): Be sure to make use of the two-way glossary at the back of the manual to check the meanings and connotations of new words.

INDICE (INDEX): The manual ends with an index of all the grammar points covered in the lessons.

The appendixes, the glossary and the index make this manual an excellent source for future reference and study.

RECORDINGS (SETS A & B)

This course provides you with eight hours of audio practice. There are two sets of complementary recordings: the first is designed for use with the manual, while the second may be used without it. Listening to and imitating the native speakers, you'll be able to improve your pronunciation and comprehension while learning to use new phrases and structures.

RECORDINGS FOR USE WITH THE MANUAL (SET A)

This set of recordings gives you four hours of audio practice in Spanish only, with translations in the manual. The dialogue of each lesson, the pronunciation sections of lessons 1 through 10, the vocabulary section, and parts of the grammar section are featured on these recordings. All these words and expressions appear in **boldface** type in your manual.

First, you will hear native Spanish speakers read the complete dialogue at a normal conversational pace without interruption; then you'll have a chance to listen to the dialogue a second time and repeat each phrase in the pauses provided.

Next, listen carefully to learn the sounds from the pronunciation sections. By repeating after the native speakers, you will gradually master the sounds.

You will then have the opportunity to practice some of the most important grammatical forms from the grammar section.

Finally, the most important and commonly used vocabulary words will also be modeled by the native speakers for you to repeat in the pauses provided.

After studying each lesson and practicing with Set A, you can go on to the second set of recordings, Set B. which you can use on the go—while driving, jogging, or doing housework.

RECORDINGS FOR USE ON THE GO (SET B)

The "On the Go" recordings give you four hours of audio practice in Spanish and English. Because they are bilingual, Set B recordings may be used without the manual, anywhere it's convenient to learn.

The 40 lessons on Set B correspond to those in the text. A bilingual narrator leads you through the four sections of each lesson:

The first section presents the most important phrases from the original dialogue. You will first hear the abridged dialogue at normal conversational speed. You'll then hear it again, phrase by phrase, with English translations and pauses for you to repeat after the native Spanish speakers.

The second section reviews and expands upon the vocabulary in the dialogue. Additional expressions show how the words may be used in other contexts. Again, you are given time to repeat the Spanish phrases.

In the third section, you'll explore the lesson's most important grammatical structures. After a quick review of the rules, you can practice with illustrative phrases and sentences.

The exercises in the last section integrate what you've learned and help you generate sentences in Spanish on your own. You'll take part in brief conversations, respond to questions, transform sentences, and occasionally translate from English into Spanish. After you respond, you'll hear the correct answer from a native speaker.

The interactive approach on this set of recordings will teach you to speak, understand and *think* in Spanish.

Now it's time to begin . . .

PRONUNCIATION CHART

While the rules of Spanish pronunciation will be presented and practiced in Lessons 1–10, you can use this chart for a quick reference.

VOWELS

Spanish Sound	Approximate Sound in English	Example
a	(f<u>a</u>ther)	*España*
e	(<u>a</u>ce, but cut off sharply)	*señor*
i	(f<u>ee</u>)	*día*
o	(n<u>o</u>te)	*hotel*
u	(r<u>u</u>le)	*mucho*
y	(f<u>ee</u>t)	*y* (only a vowel when standing alone)

DIPHTHONGS

Spanish Sound	Approximate Sound in English	Example
ai/ay	(<u>ai</u>sle)	*bailar*
		hay
au	(n<u>ow</u>)	*auto*
ei	(m<u>ay</u>)	*peine*
ia	(<u>ya</u>rn)	*gracias*
ie	(<u>ye</u>t)	*siempre*
io	(<u>yo</u>del)	*adiós*
iu	(<u>you</u>)	*ciudad*
oi/oy	(<u>oy</u>)	*oigo*
		estoy
ua	(<u>wa</u>nd)	*cuando*
ue	(<u>we</u>t)	*bueno*
ui/uy	(s<u>wee</u>t)	*cuidado*
		muy

CONSONANTS

The letters *k* and *w* appear in Spanish in foreign words like *kilowatt, kilome-ter*. In some countries, the *k* is spelled with the Spanish equivalent, *qu: quilómetro*. The *w* in Spanish sounds like an English *v: kilowatt*.

Spanish Sound	Approximate Sound in English	Example
b/d/l/m/n/p/s/t	similar to English	
c* (be-fore e/i)	s (<u>c</u>ertain)	*cena*
c (before a/o/u)	k (<u>c</u>atch)	*como*
cc	cks (a<u>cc</u>ent)	*lección*
ch	ch (<u>ch</u>urch)	*mucho*
g (before a/o/u)	hard g (go)	*ganar*
g (before e/i)	hard h (<u>h</u>e)	*gente*
h	always silent	*hasta*
j	hard h (<u>h</u>e)	*jefe*
ll	In Latin America: y (yet) / In Spain: lli (mi<u>lli</u>on)	*pollo*
ñ	ny (canyon)	*caña*
qu	k (<u>k</u>ite)	*que*
r	[in middle of word; single trill] (th<u>r</u>ow)	*pero*
r	[at beginning of word; double trill]	*rosa*
rr	[double trill]	*carro*
v	v (<u>v</u>ote, but softer, almost like <u>b</u>)	*viernes*
x	cks (ro<u>cks</u>)	*taxi*
z*	s	*zona*

* In parts of Spain, *z*—and also *c* before *e* or *i*—is pronounced like English *th*. Examples: *zona, cera, cinco*.

LECCION 1

SALUDOS. Greetings.   PRESENTACIONES. Introductions.

A. DIALOGO (Dialogue)

En una oficina en México, Distrito Federal (D. F.).

MARTA: **Buenos días, señor.**

JULIO: **Buenos días. Mi nombre es Julio Martíncz Vallc. Soy el nuevo abogado.**

MARTA: **Mucho gusto, señor Martínez Valle. ¡Bienvenido! Soy Marta Moreno Vásquez. ¿Es usted de Colombia?**

JULIO: **No, no soy de Colombia, señorita. Soy de Venezuela. Usted es de España, ¿verdad?**

MARTA: **Sí, senor, pero estoy ahora en México. Hay muchos españoles en México.**

JULIO: **Y también hay muchos hispanoamericanos aquí. ¡Hasta luego!**

In an office in Mexico City.

MARTA: Good morning, sir.

JULIO: Good morning. My name is Julio Martínez Valle. I'm the new lawyer.

MARTA: It's a pleasure to meet you, Mr. Martínez Valle. Welcome! I'm Marta Moreno Vásquez. Are you from Colombia?

JULIO: No. I'm not from Colombia. I'm from Venezuela. You're from Spain, right?

MARTA: Yes, sir, but I'm here in Mexico now. There are many Spaniards in Mexico.

JULIO: And there are many Latin Americans here also. See you later.

B. PRONUNCIACION
(Pronunciation)

VOWELS

a (like the "a" in "father"): **a, alta, papa, España**
e (like the "a" in "ace", but cut off sharply): **es, mesa, señor, México**
i/y (like the "ee" in "feet"): **mi, día, Bolivia, y**

The vowel *y* often appears alone as the word *y* meaning "and," or at the end of a word: *hoy,* "today."

C. GRAMATICA Y USOS
(Grammar and Usage)

1. USES OF THE VERB *SER* *

a. The verb *ser,* "to be," and the expression *ser de,* "to be from," are used to express nationality or place of origin.

Soy venezolano.
I am Venezuelan.

Soy de Venezuela.
I am from Venezuela.

¿Es usted venezolana?
Are you Venezuelan?

No, soy de Puerto Rico.
No, I am from Puerto Rico.

b. *Ser* also is used to state professions and jobs and to describe inherent characteristics of persons, places, and things.

Soy el nuevo abogado.
I am the new lawyer.

* See page 28 for the complete conjugation of *ser.*

México, D.F. es la capital.
   Mexico City is the capital.

Mi nombre es Julio.
   My name is Julio.

2. USES OF THE VERB *ESTAR**

The verb *estar* also means "to be," but it has different uses. *Estar* is used to tell location of a person, place, or thing.

Ahora estoy en México.
   I am in Mexico now.

The forms of *ser* and *estar* will be presented in the next two lessons. For now, just try to recognize how and when they are used.

3. *HAY*

The expression *hay* means "there is" and "there are." In questions, it means "Is there. . . ?" or "Are there . . . ?"

¿Hay muchos españoles en México?
   Are there many Spaniards in Mexico?

Si, hay muchos.
   Yes, there are many.

4. SIMPLE NEGATION

The word *sí* means "yes." The word *no* means both "no" and "not." To answer a question negatively in Spanish, *no* is often used twice: first, as the negative response "no," and second, preceding the verb, as the negation of the verb "not." For example:

No, mi nombre no es Juan Carlos.
   No, my name is not Juan Carlos.

No, no soy de Colombia.
   No. I'm not from Colombia.

* See page 18 for the complete conjugation of *estar.*

5. GENDER AND NUMBER OF NOUNS AND ADJECTIVES

Spanish nouns indicate both gender (masculine/feminine) and number (singular/plural). Adjectives agree in gender and number with the nouns they modify.

a. GENDER

Nouns referring to males are masculine; nouns referring to females are feminine:

señor	Mr., sir, gentleman
señora	Mrs., madam
señorita	Miss, miss

In general, nouns and adjectives ending in *-o* are masculine:

libro	book
mucho	a lot, many

Nouns and adjectives ending in *-a, -dad, -ción,* or *-z* are usually feminine:

oficina	office
nacionalidad	nationality
lección	lesson
luz	light (noun)

Nouns and adjectives ending in *-e* can be masculine or feminine:

estudiante	student
inteligente	intelligent

To make a masculine noun or adjective ending in *-o* feminine, change the *-o* to *-a:*

abogado	*abogada*
nuevo	*nueva*

To make a masculine noun or adjective ending in a consonant feminine, add an *-a:*[1] *español, española*

---

[1] Throughout the *Vocabulario* sections, nouns ending in *-o* will be assumed to be masculine and those ending in *-a* will be assumed to be feminine. Other nouns will be preceded by articles indicating gender, since exceptions to the above rules do exist.

b. PLURALS

To pluralize a noun or an adjective ending in a vowel, add an *-s:*

libro	*libros*
oficina	*oficinas*
mucho	*muchos*

To pluralize a noun or adjective ending in a consonant, add *-es:*

señor	*señores*
nacionalidad	*nacionalidades*
español	*españoles*

Nouns and adjectives ending in *-z* are pluralized by dropping the *-z* and adding *-ces:*

feliz	*felices*
luz	*luces*

Nouns ending in *-ción* drop the accent in the plural:

lección	*lecciones*

Masculine plural nouns and adjectives are used to refer to mixed groups of masculine and feminine people or things:

españoles	Spanish men or Spanish men and women; Spanish people
abogados	male lawyers or (a) male and female lawyer(s)
nuevos	new, used for masculine nouns or (a) masculine and feminine noun(s)

As the lessons proceed, you'll see many more examples of masculine and feminine nouns and adjectives. The rules above will become obvious, and any exceptions will be noted as such.

6. PUNCTUATION

Note that questions are preceded by an inverted question mark (¿), and exclamations are preceded by an inverted exclamation point (¡).

VOCABULARIO (Vocabulary)

saludos	greetings
presentaciones	introductions
Buenos días.	Good morning.
Buenas tardes.	Good afternoon.
Buenas noches.	Good evening. Good night.
¡Bienvenido!	Welcome!
¡Hola!	Hello!
¿Qué tal?	How's it going? How are things?
¡Qué hay de nuevo?	What's new?
¡Qué pasa?	What's going on?
¡Mucho gusto![1]	It's a pleasure to meet you.
¿Es usted de . . .?	Are you from . . . ?
¿De dónde es usted?	Where are you from?
Soy de . . .	I am from . . .
Mi nombre es . . .	My name is . . .
señor	Mister, sir, gentleman
señorita	Miss, miss
señora	Mrs., madam
Hasta luego.	See you later.
Hasta mañana.	See you tomorrow.
Adiós.	Good-bye.
ahora	now
mucho	much, many, a lot
y	and
pero	but
aquí	here
también	too, also
en	in

[1] The answer to ¡*Mucho gusto!* is ¡*Mucho gusto!*

NACIONES[1]	NATIONS	NACIONALIDADES	NATIONALITIES[1]
Argentina	Argentina	*argentino, -a*	Argentinian
Canadá	Canada	*canadiense*[2]	Canadian
Chile	Chile	*chileno, -a*	Chilean
Cuba	Cuba	*cubano, -a*	Cuban
El Salvador	El Salvador	*salvadoreño, -a*	Salvadoran
España	Spain	*español, -a*	Spanish/ Spaniard
los Estados Unidos	United States	*estadounidense*[2]	U.S. American
Guatemala	Guatemala	*guatemalteco, -a*	Guatemalan
Inglaterra	England	*inglés, -glesa*	English
México	Mexico	*mexicano, -a*	Mexican
Perú	Peru	*peruano, -a*	Peruvian
Puerto Rico	Puerto Rico	*puertorriqueño, -a*	Puerto Rican
Venezuela	Venezuela	*venezolano, -a*	Venezuelan

EXAMEN (Quiz)

A. *Conteste la pregunta en una oración completa usando la pista.* (Answer the question in a complete sentence using the hint.)

MODELO: *¿Es Ud. de Guatemala? (no)*
   No, no soy de Guatemala.

1. *¿Es Ud. de Venezuela? (sí)*
2. *¿Es Ud. de España? (no)*
3. *¿Hay muchos españoles en México? (si)*
4. *¿Hay muchos hispanoamericanos aqui? (no)*

No, no hay muchos h.a.

per pg14 answers

[1] Be sure to refer to the appendix for a more complete list of nations and nationalities.

[2] *norteamericano, -a* means North Amencan and is used often, to refer to people from the U. S. and Canada.

B. *Relacione una palabra de la columna A con una de la columna B.* (Make a match between a word in column A and column B.)

COLUMNA A

1. *España*
2. *aquí*
3. *¡Hasta luego!*
4. *Soy peruano.*
5. *¿Qué tal?*
6. *¡Bienvenido!*
7. *Soy de . . .*
8. *Mi nombre es . . .*
9. *Buenos días.*
10. *¿De dónde es usted?*

COLUMNA B

a. here
b. How's it going?
c. Where are you from?
d. Spain
e. I am Peruvian.
f. I'm from . . .
g. Good morning.
h. See you later!
i. Welcome!
j. My name is . . .

NOTAS CULTURALES (Cultural Notes)

People in Spain and Latin America are still quite formal when they first meet. Both men and women shake hands. They use the polite form of "you,"—*usted* (abbreviated as *Ud.* or *Vd.*). In informal situations, when greeting family and friends, women kiss each other and men, whereas men shake hands.

Spanish names include the given name, *nombre (de pila),* and the family's compound last name, *apellido,* which includes the father's family name followed by the mother's family name:

   Julio Martínez Valle   *Marta Moreno Vásquez*

If these people were to marry, Marta's new name would be: *Marta Moreno (Vásquez) de Martínez.* Their children would be: *Julio (Julito) Martínez Moreno* and *Marta (Martita) Martínez Moreno.*

The words *latinoamericanos* and *hispanoamericanos* are both used in Spanish to refer to Spanish-speaking peoples of Mexico, Central America, the Caribbean, and South America. In addition, *latinoamericano* is also used when referring to non-Spanish-speaking peoples of Central America, the Caribbean, and South America (e.g., Jamaicans, Haitians, and Brazilians).

RESPUESTAS (Answer Key)

A. 1. *Sí soy de Venezuela.* 2. *No, no soy de España.* 3. *Si, hay muchos españoles en México.* 4. *No, no hay muchos hispanoamericanos aquí.*

B. 1. d; 2. a; 3. h; 4. e; 5. b; 6. i; 7. f; 8. j; 9. g; 10. c.

LECCION 2

INFORMACION.   Asking for information.

A. DIALOGO (Dialogue)

En un centro de turismo de Santiago, Chile.

SEÑORITA FALCON: **Permiso, señor. Necesito información.**

SEÑOR CARRASCO: **Sí, señorita. ¿En qué puedo servirle?**

SEÑORITA FALCON: **¿Dónde está el Hotel Fénix?**

SEÑOR CARRASCO: **No está lejos. La dirección es Calle Once, número ocho dos uno.[1]**

SEÑORITA FALCON: **Ocho, dos . . . ¿Cómo? Repita, por favor.**

SEÑOR CARRASCO: **Ocho, dos, uno, señorita. Aquí hay un mapa, y ésa es la Calle Once.**

SEÑORITA FALCON: **Gracias . . . ¡Estoy cansada! ¿Qué tipo de hotel es?**

SEÑOR CARRASCO: **Es un hotel de primera clase.**

SEÑORITA FALCON: **Bueno . . . ¿Hay un buen restaurante cerca de aquí?**

SEÑOR CARRASCO: **Sí, el restaurante El Dorado está al lado del hotel, a la izquierda. También está el Café Rojas en la esquina de la calle Doce.**

SEÑORITA FALCON: **¿Cuál es el mejor de los dos?**

SEÑOR CARRASCO: **El restaurante El Dorado.**

SEÑORITA FALCON: **Muchas gracias, señor. Le estoy muy agradecida.**

---

[1] This address would be written: *Calle Once, 821.*

At a tourist center in Santiago, Chile.

MISS FALCON: Excuse me, sir. I need some information.

MR. CARRASCO: Yes, miss. How can I help you?

MISS FALCON: Where is the Phoenix Hotel?

MR. CARRASCO: It's not far. The address is 821 Eleventh Street.

MISS FALCON: 8, 2, . . . What? Please repeat that.

MR. CARRASCO: 8, 2, 1, miss. Here's a map, and this is Eleventh Street.

MISS FALCON: Thank you . . . I'm tired! What kind of hotel is it?

MR. CARRASCO: It's a first-rate hotel.

MISS FALCON: Okay . . . Is there a good restaurant near here?

MR. CARRASCO: Yes, the El Dorado restaurant is next door to the hotel, to the left. There's also Café Rojas on the corner of Twelfth Street.

MISS FALCON: Which is the better of the two?

MR. CARRASCO: The El Dorado restaurant.

MISS FALCON: Thank you very much, sir. I'm very grateful to you.

B. PRONUNCIACION
(Pronunciation)

VOWELS

o (like the "o" in "note"): **coma, hotel, cuatro, salvadoreño**
u (like the "u" in "rule"): **usted, luna, una, mucho**

The Spanish vowels *i* and *u* are considered "weak" vowels and, when used in conjunction with other vowels, can only be stressed when a written accent mark appears on them: **filosofía, continúa.**

HOW TO PRONOUNCE WORDS

a. Words ending in a vowel *(a, e, i, o, u)* or *s* or *s* are stressed on the next to last (penultimate) syllable: *una, dicen, cinco, Guatemala, buenas tardes.*
b. Words ending in a consonant other than *n* or *s* are stressed on the last syllable: *hotel, señor, Ecuador, español, por favor.*
c. All other words have a written accent mark to show stress: *aquí, también, Martínez, buenos días, número de teléfono.*
Unlike English, syllables in Spanish are easily defined being made up of either a single vowel or, more commonly, groups of consonants and vowels.

C. GRAMATICA Y USOS
(Grammar and Usage)

1. SUBJECT PRONOUNS

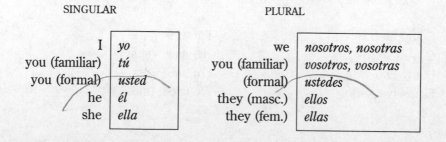

SINGULAR			PLURAL	
I	*yo*	we	*nosotros, nosotras*
you (familiar)	*tú*	you (familiar)	*vosotros, vosotras*
you (formal)	*usted*	(formal)	*ustedes*
he	*él*	they (masc.)	*ellos*
she	*ella*	they (fem.)	*ellas*

These pronouns are used as subjects of the verb. Since the verb ending makes the subject clear, the subject pronouns do not have to be used:

Estoy bien.   I am well.

They are used primarily for clarity (with the *usted, él,* and *ella* verb forms and with the *ustedes, ellos,* and *ellas* verb forms) or for emphasis:

¿Cómo está usted?   How are you?
¿Cómo está él?   How is he?
¿Yo? Yo estoy bien.   Me? I'm fine.

The form usted is abbreviated as *Ud.* (or *Vd.*), and *ustedes* is abbreviated as *Uds.* (or *Vds.*).
Tú is used with family and friends. The plural forms *vosotros, vosotras* are used only in Spain as the familiar plural; in Latin America and other Spanish-speaking areas, use *Uds.* for both the familiar and formal plural "you."

2. THE VERB *ESTAR*

ESTAR TO BE

yo	estoy		nosotros, -as	estamos
tú	estás		~~vosotros, -as~~	~~estáis~~
Ud., él, ella	está		Uds., ellos, ellas	están

As we saw in Lección 1, *estar* means "to be" when talking about the location of a person, place, or thing. It is also used to describe any state of health and well-being, whether mental or physical.

Estoy bien.   I'm well.
Está nervioso.   He is nervous.
Estoy cansada.   I'm tired. (fem.)
Estoy cansado.   I'm tired. (masc.)

Note that when used with *estar,* adjectives must agree with the subject in gender and number, according to the rules explained previously:

Están cansados.   They are tired.
Estamos agradecidos.   We are grateful.
Elena está contenta.[1]   Elena is happy.

These and other adjectives used with *estar* express a state, condition, or a change from the normal state of affairs.

3. INDEFINITE AND DEFINITE ARTICLES

There are two types of articles: indefinite and definite.
a. The indefinite article is equivalent to the English word "a" or "an."

	SINGULAR		PLURAL
masc.	*un número* *un hotel*	masc.	*unos números* *unos hoteles*
fem.	*una dirección* *una calle*	fem.	*unas direcciones* *unas calles*

The plural forms of the indefinite article are equivalent to the English word "some."
b. The definite article is equivalent to the English "the."

	SINGULAR		PLURAL
masc.	*el número* *el hotel*	masc.	*los números* *los hoteles*
fem.	*la dirección* *la calle*	fem.	*las direcciones* *las calles*

[1] Both *contento* and *feliz* (which we saw in *Lección* 1) mean "happy." However, *estar* is always used with *contento,* while either *estar* or *ser* can be used with *feliz (felices).*

Note that the definite article is used when using a title to speak about yourself or someone else:

Soy el señor Carrasco.
   I am Mr. Carrasco.

It is omitted when speaking directly to a person using a title:

En mi opinión, señor Blanco, el Hotel Fénix es el mejor hotel de la ciudad.
   In my opinion, Mr. Blanco, the Phoenix Hotel is the best hotel in the city.

4. THE CONTRACTIONS *DEL* AND *AL*

Contractions facilitate speech. In Spanish, there are only two contractions.

de + el = del	of the, from the
a + el = al	to the, at the

Está al lado del Hotel Fénix.
   It's next door to the Phoenix Hotel.

5. POSSESSION WITH *DE*

To indicate possession, use the verb *ser + de.*

Es el mejor restaurante de la ciudad.
   It's the city's best restaurant.
      (or)
   It's the best restaurant in the city.

¿Cuál es la dirección del hotel?
   What is the hotel's address?
      (or)
   What is the address of the hotel?

Es el libro de Juan.
   It's Juan's book.

6. QUESTION WORDS: *¿QUÉ? ¿CUÁL? ¿CÓMO? ¿DÓNDE?*

Use *¿Qué?* for "What?" when you are asking for a definition, identification, or explanation. Use *¿Qué?* to translate "which" before a noun.

¿Qué es la filosofía?
　What is philosophy?

¿Qué clase de hotel es ése?
　What kind/class of hotel is that?

¿Qué tipo de hotel es?
　What kind of hotel is it?

Use *¿Cuál?* for "Which?" when you are selecting one from among many:

¿Cuál es el mejor de los dos?
　Which is the better of the two?

¿Cuál? can be used to translate "What?" before the verb *ser,* except when asking a definition.

Use *¿Cómo?* for "What?" when you do not understand something said, or when you are asking for a description:

¿Cómo?
　What? (I don't understand.) Pardon me?

¿Cómo está Ud.?
　How are you?

¿Cómo es el hotel?
　What is the hotel like?

Use *¿Dónde?* for "Where?":

¿Dónde está el Hotel Fénix?
　Where is the Phoenix Hotel?

¿Dónde está el restaurante?
　Where is the restaurant?

7. THE NUMBERS 0–12

cero	0	cinco	5	nueve	9
uno, una	1	seis	6	diez	10
dos	2	siete	7	once	11
tres	3	ocho	8	doce	12
cuatro	4				

The number one (and its compound forms, that is, 21, 31, 41, etc.) has both a masculine and feminine form *(uno/una);* it takes the shortened form *un* before masculine singular nouns: *un hotel,* a/one hotel.

VOCABULARIO (Vocabulary)

expresiones de cortesía	polite expressions
Permiso./Con permiso.	Excuse me; Pardon me (to attract attention or ask permission).
Perdón./Perdóneme.	Excuse me; I'm sorry (when you
Disculpe./Dispense.	have caused some harm, confusion or disappointment).
¿En qué puedo servirle?	How can I help you?
Por favor.	Please.
Gracias	Thank you.
De nada.	You're welcome.
Lo siento.	I'm sorry.
Repita, por favor.	Please repeat that.
Le estoy muy agradecido(a).	I'm very grateful to you.
información	information
centro de turismo	tourist center
necesitar	to need
Necesito información.	I need (a piece of/some) information.
el hotel	hotel
¿Dónde está el hotel?	Where is the hotel?
la dirección	address
¿Cuál es la dirección del hotel?	What is the address of the hotel?

¿Qué tipo de hotel es?	What kind of hotel is it?
Es un hotel de primera clase.	It's a first class hotel.
¿Cuál es el número de teléfono?	What is the telephone number?
el restaurante	restaurant
¿Cómo es el restaurante?	What is the restaurant like?
¿Cuál es el mejor de los dos?	Which is the better of the two?
direcciónes	directions
la calle	street
el mapa	map
a la izquierda (de)	to the left (of)
a la derecha (de)	to the right (of)
al lado de	next (door) to
en la esquina	on the corner
enfrente de	across from, opposite
detrás de	behind
delante de	in front of
cerca	near
lejos	far
entre	between
¿Cómo está Ud.?	How are you?
Estoy cansado(a).	I'm tired.
Estoy bien.	I'm fine.
Estoy mal.	I'm ill.
Estoy contento(a).	I'm happy.
Estoy triste.	I'm sad.
con	with
muy	very
Bueno.	Good./Okay.

EXAMEN (Quiz)

A. *Dé el artículo definido en lugar del artículo indefinido.* (Give the definite article in place of the indefinite article.)

MODELO: una esquina/la esquina

1. *un hotel*   *el hotel*
2. *una dirección*   *la d*
3. *una calle*   *la =*
4. *unos señores*   *los s*
5. *unas señoras*   *las*

B. *Escoja la forma correcta de "estar."* (Choose the correct form of *estar.*)

MODELO: Marta (estamos, está, estás) cansada.
        Marta está cansada.

1. *La señorita Falcon (está, estás, estoy) cansada.*
2. *El hotel Palacio (están, estamos, está) al lado del Hotel Fénix.*
3. *Marta y yo (estoy, estamos, estáis) tristes.*
4. *Rosa, ¿tú (estáis, estoy, estás) aquí?*
5. *Yo le (están, estoy, estás) muy agradecido.*

C. *Traduzca las expresiones y oraciones al español.* (Translate the expressions and sentences into Spanish.)

1. twelve young women   *doce mujeres jóvenes*
2. The address is 465 10th Street.   *La dir es*
3. What?   *Qué*
4. I'm well. Are you ill?   *Estoy bien. Tu enfermo?*   *estás*
5. I'm very grateful to you.
6. Where is the Palace Hotel?   *Dondé ese H Pal*
7. I'm tired.
8. What is the telephone number of the hotel?

Estoy cansado

muy agradecio a tu-

Que es el numbre del tel del h-

24

D. *Use las contracciones "del" y "al."* (Use the contractions "del" and "al.")

MODELO: *Marta fue a el concierto.*
        Marta fue al concierto.

1. *Elena toma agua de el jarro.* ~del~
2. *Mi familia y yo vamos a el campo todos los fines de semana.* ~al~
3. *Me gusta el color de el coche.* ~del~
4. *Nosotros somos alumnos de el colegio.* ~del~
5. *El color de el perro es negro.* ~del~
6. *Vamos a el restaurante cubano.* ~al~
7. *Quiero agua de el garrafón.* ~del~

NOTAS CULTURALES (Cultural Notes)

Nouns for professions ending in *a* or *e* have always been used to refer to both men and women; for example: *el/la recepcionista* (the receptionist); *el/la dentista* (the dentist); *el/la estudiante* (the student). In other cases simply changing the masculine noun ending *o* to *a* resolved the problem: for example, *el abogado/la abogada* (the lawyer). Occasionally women reject the feminine form of the noun, believing it to be inferior to the masculine, and rather prefer *la abogado* (the female lawyer), *la médico* (the female doctor), or *la modelo* (the female model).

RESPUESTAS (Answer Key)

A. 1. *el* 2. *la* 3. *la* 4. *los* 5. *las*

B. 1. *está* 2. *está* 3. *estamos* 4. *estás* 5. *estoy*

C. 1. *doce señoritas* 2. *La dirección es calle Diez, número cuatro, seis, cinco.*
  3. *¿Cómo?* 4. *Estoy bien. ¿Está mal?* 5. *Le estoy muy agradecido, -a.*
  6. *¿Dónde está el Hotel Palacio?* 7. *Estoy cansado, -a.* 8. *¿Cuál es el número de teléfono del hotel?*

D. 1. *Elena toma agua del jarro.* 2. *Mi familia y yo vamos al campo todos los fines de semana.* 3. *Me gusta el color del coche.* 4. *Nosotros somos alumnos del colegio.* 5. *El color del perro es negro.* 6. *Vamos al restaurante cubano.* 7. *Quiero agua del garrafón.*

LECCION 3

LA HORA.   Clock time.

A. DIALOGO (Dialogue)

En el teléfono: Haciendo planes para la noche. Buenos Aires, Argentina.

ANITA: **¿Hola?**

GABRIEL: **Buenos días, Anita. Soy yo, Gabriel. ¿Es muy temprano pare llamarte?**

ANITA: **¡No, no! En mi casa somos madrugadores.**

GABRIEL: **Bueno . . . ¿a qué hora es la obra de teatro esta noche?**

ANITA: **Es a las nueve de la noche.**

GABRIEL: **¿Por qué es tan tarde?**

ANITA: **Yo no sé, pero no es una obra muy larga. ¿Qué hora es ahora?**

GABRIEL: **En mi reloj, son las nueve menos veinte. Estoy ocupado en la oficina haste más o menos las siete.**

ANITA: **¿A qué hora estás en el teatro?**

GABRIEL: **A las ocho y media en punto.**

ANITA: **De acuerdo. ¡Hasta luego!**

GABRIEL: **¡Hasta luego!**

On the telephone: Making plans for the evening. Buenos Aires, Argentina.

ANITA: Hello.

GABRIEL: Hello, Anita. It's me (I), Gabriel. Is it too early to call you?

ANITA: No, no! We're early risers in my home.

GABRIEL: Okay . . . at what time is the play tonight?

ANITA: It's at 9:00 in the evening.

GABRIEL: Why is it so late?

ANITA: I don't know, but it's not a very long play. What time is it now?

GABRIEL: My watch says that it's twenty to nine. I'm busy in the office until around 7:00.

ANITA: At what time will you be at the theater?

GABRIEL: At 8:30 sharp.

ANITA: Okay. See you later!

GABRIEL: See you later!

B. PRONUNCIACION
(Pronunciation)

DIPHTHONGS

Diphthongs are two juxtaposed vowels which form one sound. In Spanish one of these two vowels must be an *i* or *u*—the so called weak vowels. (If you have two strong vowels—*a, e, o*—together, you have two separate syllables). Stress in a diphthong is always on the strong vowel *(a, e, o)*. Here are some diphthong sounds:

ai/ay (like the "ai" in "aisle"): **bailar, hay, aire**
au (like the "ow" in "now"): **auto, aurora, restaurante**
ei/ey (like the "ay" in "may"): **peine, veinte, seis, ley**
ia/ya (like the "y" in "yarn"): gracias, estudiar, ya
ie (like the "ye" in "yet"): **siempre, quien, pie**
io/yo (like the "yo" in "yodel"): **adios, nervioso, confusión**

More diphthongs are given in later chapters.

C. GRAMATICA Y USOS
(Grammar and Usage)

1. COGNATES

You have probably noticed that there are many Spanish words that look almost exactly like an English word; these are called "cognates." In many cases they have the same meaning and the same spelling, but a different pronunciation.

motor; idea; gala; radio; similar; hotel

Other cognates vary slightly from their English equivalents. Note the different Spanish spellings of the following words:

agente; atención; centro; diferente; importante; límite; posible; quieto; restaurante; teatro; teléfono; tren; visita.

2. THE VERB *SER*

Here is the complete present tense of the verb *ser;* you already know its uses.

SER TO BE

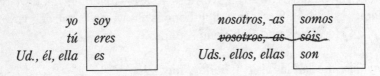

yo	soy	nosotros, -as	somos
tú	eres	~~vosotros, -as~~	~~sóis~~
Ud., él, ella	es	Uds., ellos, ellas	son

Note that adjectives used with *ser* must agree with the subject in gender and number:

La obra de teatro es buena.
The play is good.

Somos nuevas abogadas.
We're new lawyers.

Soy madrugadora.
    I'm an early riser.

3. QUESTION WORDS: *¿CUANDO? ¿POR QUE?*

¿Cuándo? means "when."

¿Cuándo es la obra de teatro?
    When is the play?

¿Cuándo estás ocupado?
    When are you busy?

¿Por qué? means "why."

¿Por qué es tan tarde?
    Why is it so late?

¿Por qué Carlos está en México?
    Why is Charles in Mexico?

4. TELLING TIME

You ask for the time with: *¿Qué hora es?*
For one o'clock, answer: *Es la una (hora).*
For all other clock times, use *son* (the plural of *es):*

Son las ocho.	It's 8:00.
Son las once.	It's 11:00.

Use *y* to add minutes past the hour. For a quarter, use *quince* or *cuarto* (one-quarter). For half past use *treinta* or *media* (half).

Son las once y veinticinco.	It's 11:25.
Es la una y cuarto.	It's 1:15.
Son las dos y treinta.	It's 2:30.
Son las dos y media.	

Past the half hour, traditionally you should subtract from the following hour using the word *menos* (minus).

Son las cuatro menos veinte.   It's 3:40.
Es la una menos cuarto.   It's 12:45.
Es la una menos quince.

    Colloquially you might say:

Son las tres y cuarenta y   It's 3:45.
cinco.
Son las doce y treinta y   It's 12:34.
cuatro.

    To ask "At what time . . . ?", you say *¿A qué hora es . . . ?:*

¿A qué hora es la obra de teatro?
    At what time is the play?

Es a las diez de la noche.
    It's at ten P.M./in the evening.

    As seen above, when you want to refer to "A.M./in the morning" and
"P.M./in the afternoon in the evening," use time + *de la mañana* or time
+ *de la tarde*. When saying "in the morning, afternoon, evening" without
referring to a specific time of day, use the expressions with *por:*

Estoy ocupado por la tarde.
    I am busy in the afternoon.

No estoy ocupado por la noche.
    I am not busy in the evening.

5. THE NUMBERS 13–60

trece	13	veinticinco	25
catorce	14	veintiséis	26
quince	15	veintisiete	27
dieciséis	16	veintiocho	28
diecisiete	17	veintinueve	29
dieciocho	18	treinta	30
diecinueve	19	treinta y uno	31
veinte	20	treinta y dos	32
veintiuno (veinte y uno)	21	cuarenta	40
veintidós (veinte y dos)	22	cincuenta	50
veintitrés (veinte y tres)	23	sesenta	60
veinticuatro	24		

VOCABULARIO (VOCABULARY)

la hora	time of day
¿Qué hora es?	What time is it?
Es la una.	It's one o'clock.
Son las dos.	It's two o'clock.
de la mañana	in the morning, a.m.
de la tarde	in the afternoon, p. m.
de la noche	in the evening, p. m.
la medianoche	midnight
el mediodía	noon
en punto	sharp, on the dot
más o menos las ocho	around 8: 00
cerca (a eso) de las ocho	about 8:00
¿cuándo?	when?
temprano	early
tarde	late
Es tan tarde.	It's so late.
¿por qué?	why?
el reloj	watch, clock
En mi reloj, son las tres.	My watch says that it's three o'clock.
en mi casa	at my house
en casa	at home
Bueno.	Good./Okay

De acuerdo./Bueno.	Okay.
el plan	plan
hasta	until
largo	long
llamar	to call
madrugador	early riser
ocupado	busy
Soy yo.	It's me (I).

EXAMEN (QUIZ)

A. *Conteste la pregunta en una oración completa usando la pista.* (Answer the question in a complete sentence using the hint.)

MODELO: ¿Qué hora es? (las tres de la tarde)
   Son las tres de la tarde.

1. *¿Qué hora es? (las diez de la noche)* Son l A
2. *¿Cuándo está Ud. ocupado? (por la mañana)* Esta oc. por l m
3. *¿A qué hora es la obra de teatro? (a las ocho y media de la noche)*
4. *¿Cuántos teatros hay en Buenos Aires? (sesenta y cinco teatros)*

La o d t es a la f

B. *Escoja la forma correcta de "ser."* (Choose the correct form of *ser*.)

En BA hay s

MODELO: Nosotros (son, soy, somos) portugueses.
   Nosotros somos portugueses.

1. *Juan y yo (son, soy, somos) argentinos.*
2. *Marcos no (eres, es, sois) madrugador.*
3. *(Es, Son, Sois) las tres menos cuarto.*
4. *Talia, tú (son, sois, eres) de Puerto Rico.*
5. *Uds. (somos, sois, son) abogadas.*

C. *Escoja la palabra correcta.* (Choose the correct word.)

1. *La obra de teatro (está, es, estoy) a las nueve de la noche.*
2. *(¿Por qué? ¿Cuándo?) es tan tarde?*
3. *Es la (tres y media, una y cuarto, ocho de la noche) de la mañana.*

4. *Hay (treinta y tres, ocho, veinticuatro) horas en un día.*
5. *(¿Cómo? ¿Qué? Por qué?) está Ud.?*
6. *Hay (veintitrés, sesenta, cuarenta) minutos en una hora.*

D. *Escriba el pronombre sujeto correcto.* (Write the correct subject pronoun.)

MODELO: Ud. y yo
     nosotros/nosotras

1. *Juan y yo* Nos
2. *él y ella* Ellos
3. *nosotros y ellos* Nos
4. *tú y Juan*
     Uds.

NOTAS CULTURALES (CULTURAL NOTES)

"A.M." and "P.M." are occasionally seen in Latin America, hardly ever in Spain. Official schedules (trains, buses, airlines) and radio and television broadcasters in Spain and Latin America, however, use the 24-hour clock: *Son las dieciocho horas.*   It's six P.M. (18:00)

The play might then be at 21:00, or *a las veintiuna.* The quickest way to understand what the time is when using the 24-hour clock is to subtract 12 from the number given.

When first meeting an adult Spaniard or Latin American, you use the formal form *Ud.* for "you." As your acquaintance and friendship grow, you will be told *tutéame,* "talk to me with *tú.*"

RESPUESTAS (ANSWER KEY)

A. 1. *Son las diez de la noche.* 2. *Estoy ocupado por la mañana.* 3. *La obra de teatro es a las ocho y media de la noche.* 4. *Hay sesenta y cinco teatros en Buenos Aires.*

B. 1. *somos* 2. *es* 3. *Son* 4. *eres* 5. *son*

C. 1. *es* 2. *¿Por qué?* 3. *una y cuarto* 4. *veinticuatro* 5. *¿Cómo?*
   6. *sesenta*

D. 1. *nosotros* 2. *ellos* 3. *nosotros* 4. *vosotros/Uds.*

LECCION 4

EL TRABAJO.   Work.

A. DIALOGO (Dialogue)

El trabajo en Guayaquil, Ecuador.

ANDRÉS: ¿Cómo es su trabajo, Isabel?

ISABEL: Es interesante. Trabajo los lunes, martes y miércoles en la oficina, y los jueves y viernes en la fábrica.

ANDRÉS: ¿Quién es su jefe?

ISABEL: El señor González. Es muy simpático.

ANDRÉS: ¿Cuántos empleados hay en la companía?

ISABEL: Hay unos quinientos.

ANDRÉS: Y ¿cuánto gana Ud. por año?

ISABEL: Gano el salario máximo. Mi trabajo no es fácil.

ANDRÉS: Si es difícil, ¿por qué no busca otro trabajo?

ISABEL: Porque me gusta mi trabajo. Además, no es necesario trabajar los fines de semana. Los sábados y los domingos estudio, escucho música, hablo por teléfono . . .

ANDRÉS: ¡Qué bueno! Es importante descansar.

Working in Guayaquil, Ecuador.

ANDRÉS: What is your job like, Isabel?

ISABEL: It's interesting. On Mondays, Tuesdays, and Wednesdays I work in the office and on Thursdays and Fridays in the factory.

ANDRÉS: Who is your boss?

ISABEL: Mr. González. He's very nice.

ANDRÉS: How many employees are there in the company?

ISABEL: There are about 500.

ANDRÉS: And how much do you earn per year?

ISABEL: I earn the maximum salary. My job isn't easy.

ANDRÉS: If it's difficult, why don't you look for another job?

ISABEL: Because I like my work. And moreover, it's not necessary to work weekends. On Saturdays and Sundays I study, listen to music, talk on the phone . . .

ANDRÉS: Great! It's important to rest.

B. PRONUNCIACION
(Pronunciation)

CONSONANTS

The letter *h* is always silent: **hace, hasta, haber, exhibir**
In Spanish, *v* is pronounced more softly than in English, like *b:* **va, bueno, viernes, nombre**

MORE DIPHTHONGS

oi/oy (like the "oy" in "boy"): oigo, estoy, voy
ua (like the "wa" in "wand"): **cuando, cuatro, Juan**
ue (like the "we" in "wet"): **bueno, puerta, nueve**

C. GRAMATICA Y USOS
(Grammar and Usage)

1. THE INFINITIVE

The infinitive is the basic form of the verb. In English "to be," "to rest," "to work," and "to speak" are all infinitives. In Spanish, infinitives also consist of two parts: the root and the infinitive ending. Spanish infinitives belong to three groups determined by these endings: *-ar, -er, -ir.* (Notice that *ser* and *estar,* the two verbs meaning "to be," fall into these categories.) Some new *-ar* verbs in this lesson include *descansar* (to rest); *trabajar* (to work); *estudiar* (to study); see below for others. Infinitives can be used with impersonal expressions, whose implied subject in Spanish is the word "it." [1]

No es necesario trabajar los fines de semana.
It's not necessary to work weekends.
Es importante descansar.
It's important to rest.

2. THE PRESENT TENSE OF REGULAR *-AR* VERBS

In our study of Spanish up to this point, we have seen conjugated verb forms in the present tense: *estoy, soy, está,* etc. A verb is considered conjugated when you drop the infinitive ending *(-ar, -er, -ir)* and add to the root the verb ending (or inflection) appropriate for the subject noun or pronoun. Most verbs in Spanish follow a regular pattern of conjugation. The first group of regular verbs in Spanish are those ending in *-ar.* All verbs in this group are conjugated exactly alike. Add the personal verb ending to the root:

TRABAJAR TO WORK

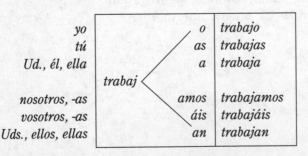

yo	o	trabajo
tú	as	trabajas
Ud., él, ella	a	trabaja
trabaj		
nosotros, -as	amos	trabajamos
vosotros, -as	áis	trabajáis
Uds., ellos, ellas	an	trabajan

[1] See *Lección* 35 for other impersonal expressions.

The ending itself indicates the subject of the *yo, tú, nosotros, -as vosotros, -as* forms of the verbs. But sometimes the subject pronouns *Ud., él, ella* and *Uds., ellos, ellas* must be used to clarify the exact meaning of the verb.

Note the three possible English translations of the Spanish verb:

tú trabajas	you work you are working you do work

The words "are" and "do" are "helping verbs"; they indicate that the main verb follows and that it is in the present tense.

Other regular *-ar* verbs we have seen so far:

buscar	to look for
descansar	to rest
estudiar	to study
escuchar	to listen to
ganar	to earn
hablar	to talk, speak
necesitar	to need
Los sabados descanso.	I rest on Saturdays.
Estudias español.[1]	You're studying Spanish.
Escuchamos música.	We listen to music.
Busca un trabajo.	He's looking for a job.
¿Hablan español?[1]	Do they speak Spanish?
Trabajo mucho pero no gano mucho.	I work a lot but I don't earn a lot.

3. QUESTION WORDS: *¿CUANTO?, ¿CUANTOS?, ¿QUIEN?, ¿QUIENES?*

To ask "how much, how many" followed by a noun, use *¿cuánto?/¿cuánta?* (Sg.) and *¿cuántos? ¿cuántas?* (Pl.):

¿Cuánto tiempo descansas?
   How much time do you rest?

---

[1] Definite articles are not used before languages after the verbs *estudiar* (to study), *hablar* (to talk, speak), *aprender* (to learn), and *enseñar* (to teach), or after *en* or *de*.

¿Cuántos empleados hay?
How many employees are there?

¿Cuánto? is also used before *es* to ask "How much...?"

¿Cuánto es el reloj?
How much is the watch?

Use *¿quién?* for "who?" Note the plural form *¿quiénes?*.

¿Quién es su jefe?
Who is your boss?

¿Quiénes hablan?
Who are speaking?

4. THE WORD ORDER IN QUESTIONS

Interrogative words begin a question: *¿Cuánto tiempo descansas? ¿Qué hora es?* If the subject of a question is a person, the subject pronoun, if necessary, may precede or follow the verb:

¿Ud. estudia muchas horas?
Do you study many hours?

¿Estudia Ud. muchas horas?

5. THE DAYS OF THE WEEK

DÍAS DE LA SEMANA	DAYS OF THE WEEK
los días laborables	workdays
el lunes	Monday
el martes	Tuesday
el miércoles	Wednesday
el jueves	Thursday
el viernes	Friday
el fin de semana	weekend
el sábado	Saturday
el domingo	Sunday

Note that the word *días* is masculine: *el día, los dias.*
To ask, "What day is today?" say: *¿Qué día es hoy?*

The masculine definite article is always used with the day of the week, except after the verb *ser:*

Trabajo el lunes.
I work on Monday.

Hoy es miércoles.
Today is Wednesday.

When making a list of the days of the week, you need to use the article only with the first one: *el lunes, martes, y jueves. El martes* means "Tuesday" and also "on Tuesday."
The workdays are pluralized by using *los: los lunes,* "(on) Mondays."
Sábado and *domingo* have plural forms: *los sábados, los domingos.*

Estudio los sábados.
I study on Saturdays.

Escucho música los domingos.
I listen to music on Sundays.

6. THE NUMBERS 70–1,000,000

setenta	70
ochenta	80
noventa	90
cien	100
ciento uno	101
ciento dos	102
doscientos, *-as*	200
trescientos, *-as*	300
cuatrocientos, *-as*	400
quinientos, *-as*	500
seiscientos, *-as*	600
setecientos, *-as*	700
ochocientos, *-as*	800
novecientos, *-as*	900

mil	1,000
mil novecientos noventa y cinco	1995
cincuenta mil	50,000
novecientos noventa y nueve mil,	
novecientos noventa y nueve	999,999
un millón	1,000,000

Cien is used before a noun: **cien días, cien lecciones.**
Ciento precedes any other number, except for *mil:* **ciento uno; ciento ochenta y ocho; cien mil.**
The hundreds numbers have both masculine and feminine forms.
The word *y* is only used between the tens and the ones.

Trescientos treinta y tres.	333
Mil doscientos cincuenta y siete.	1257

The word *millón* and its compounds *(dos millones,* etc.) are followed by the preposition *de:*

Tres millones de horas.
Three million hours.

VOCABULARIO (VOCABULARY)

trabajo	work
¿Cómo es su trabajo?	What is your job like?
secretario, *-a*	secretary
fábrica	factory
operario, *-a*	factory worker
el jefe/la jefa	boss
¿Quién es su jefe?	Who is your boss?
¿Cómo es su jefe?	What's your boss like?
empleado, *-a*	employee
compañía	company
salario	salary
trabajar	to work
buscar un trabajo	to look for a job
descansar	to rest

ganar	to earn
ganarse la vida[1]	to earn a living
por semana	weekly
por mes	monthly
por año	yearly, per/a year
¿Cuánto gana por año?	How much do you earn a year?
es importante	it's important
es necesario	it's necessary
hoy	today
ayer	yesterday
mañana	tomorrow
pasado mañana	the day after tomorrow
interesante	interesting
aburrido	boring
simpático	pleasant
antipático	unpleasant
difícil	difficult
fácil[2]	easy
buscar	to look for
estudiar	to study
escuchar	to listen
hablar	to talk, speak
música	music

[1] See *Lección* 15 for reflexive verbs.
[2] The feminine and masculine forms of these words are the same.

EXAMEN (QUIZ)

A. *Conteste la pregunta en una oración completa usando la pista.* (Answer the question in a complete sentence using the hint.)

MODELO: *¿Cuándo no trabajas? (el domingo)*
   No trabajo el domingo.

1. *¿Cómo es su trabajo? (difícil)*
2. *¿Cuántas horas trabajas por semana? (40 horas)*
3. *¿Cómo descansa Ud. los sábados? (escuchar música)*
4. *¿Cómo es su jefe? (simpático)*

B. *Escriba los números en palabras.* (Write out the numbers in words).

MODELO: *337 men*
   Trescientos treinta y siete hombres.

1. 944 days
2. 551 hours
3. 892 hotels
4. 1,334,592 lessons
5. 5,543,210 students

C. *Traduzca al español.* (Translate into Spanish.)

1. We work every day of the week: Monday, Tuesday, Wednesday, Thursday, and Friday.
2. He rests on Saturdays and Sundays.
3. Who is studying now?
4. Who is unpleasant?
5. It is difficult to work on Sundays.
6. I don't earn much. I'm looking for another job.

D. *Conteste las siguientes preguntas.* (Answer the following questions.)

MODELO: ¿Cuántos años tienes? (20)
   Tengo veinte años.

1. ¿Cuántos tomates quiere, Señora? (5)
2. ¿Cuánto dinero quiere por ese abrigo? ($45)
3. ¿Quién es ese muchacho? (Mi hermano)
4. ¿Cuántos parientes tienes en EE.UU.? (12)
5. ¿Quiénes son los dueños de este edificio? (No sé)
6. ¿Cuántas páginas tiene ese libro? (564)

[handwritten annotations: "Ese libro tiene", "that", "Quiero cinco t", "Quiero 45 por ese ab", "Ese m. es mi h.", "Tengo doce", "No sé q. s.", "pai. en EU.", "relatives"]

NOTAS CULTURALES (CULTURAL NOTES)

Note that in Spain and Latin America, commas and periods are reversed in the writing of numbers. Compare:

U.S.	SPAIN/LATIN AMERICA
1,000	1.000
25.32	25,32
$394.81	$394,81

[handwritten: "ese that"]

RESPUESTAS (ANSWER KEY)

A. 1. *Mi trabajo es difícil.* 2. *Trabajo cuarenta horas por semana.* 3. *Los sábados escucho música.* 4. *Mi jefe es simpático.*

B. 1. *novecientos cuarenta y cuatro días.* 2. *quinientas cincuenta y una horas* 3. *ochocientos noventa y dos hoteles* 4. *un millón trescientas treinta y cuatro mil quinientas noventay dos lecciones.* 5. *cinco millones quinientos cuarenta y tres mil doscientos diez estudiantes*

C. 1. *Trabajamos todos los días de la semana: el lunes, martes, miércoles, jueves, y viernes.* 2. *Él descansa los sábados y domingos.* 3. *¿Quién estudia ahora?* 4. *¿Quién es antipático?* 5. *Es difícil trabajar los domingos.* 6. *No gano mucho. Busco otro trabajo.*

D. 1. *Quiero cinco tomates.* 2. *Quiero cuarenta y cinco dólares por este abrigo.* 3. *Ese muchacho es mi hermano.* 4. *Tengo doce parientes en Estados Unidos.* 5. *No sé quienes son los dueños de este edificio.* 6. *Este libro tiene quinientas sesenta y cuatro páginas.*

[handwritten: "this", "cinco"]

43

LECCION 5

EL TIEMPO, LOS MESES, LAS ESTACIONES.   Weather, months, seasons.

A. DIALOGO (Dialogue)

En la tienda Paraíso del Paraguas en la Calle Front de Colón, Panamá.

ELENA: **Hace mucho calor en verano en este país. ¿Cuántos grados hace hoy?**

JESUS: **Treinta y dos centígrados, por lo menos. También durante todo el año—el otoño, el invierno, la primavera—hay mucha humedad. Bebemos mucha agua y refrescos.**

ELENA: **Mira, ahora llueve y hace viento. Uds. seguramente venden muchos paraguas en esta tienda.**

JESUS: **Eso es verdad.**

ELENA: **¿Cómo es el tiempo aquí en primavera?**

JESUS: **En esa estación del año el tiempo es menos caliente pero llueve más.**

———————————

In the Umbrella Paradise store on Front Street, Colón, Panama.

ELENA: It's very hot in the summer in this country. What's the temperature today?

JESUS: Thirty-two degrees centigrade, at least. Also, all year long—in fall, winter, spring—it's very humid. We drink a lot of water and soft drinks.

ELENA: Look, it's raining and it's windy. You surely sell many umbrellas in this store.

JESUS: That's true.

ELENA: What is the weather like here in the spring?

JESUS: In that season of the year, the weather is less hot, but it rains more.

B. PRONUNCIACION
(Pronunciation)

MORE CONSONANTS

ch (like the "ch" in "church"): **mucho, ocho, noche**
ll (in Spain, like the "lli" in "million"; in Latin America, like the "y" in "yet"): **pollo, llamar, llover**
ñ (like the "ny" in "canyon"): **año, baño, mañana**
qu (like "k"): **que, quien, quince**

The diacritical mark, ˜, over the *n* is called a *tilde*.

EVEN MORE DIPTHONGS

iu/yu (like the word "you"): **ciudad, yuca**
ui/uy (like the word "we"): **muy, cuidado**

When *i* and *u* come together as a diphthong sound, the stress is always on the second of the two vowels. When you see the letter *í* or *ú (i* or *u* with the accent mark), this indicates that the vowel is a strong vowel and an independent syllable: *filosofía, economía, trilogía*[1]

Once again, if any two strong vowels *(a, e, o)* come together, two separate syllables result: *lee, idea, peor.*

---

[1] Compare *Lección* 2.

C. GRAMATICA Y USOS
(Grammar and Usage)

1. THE PRESENT TENSE OF REGULAR *-ER* VERBS

The second conjugation of regular verbs is the *-er* group. Note the characteristic *e* of the ending:

vender   TO SELL

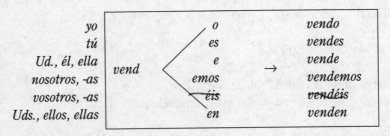

yo		o	vendo
tú		es	vendes
Ud., él, ella	vend	e	vende
nosotros, -as		emos	vendemos
vosotros, -as		éis	vendéis
Uds., ellos, ellas		en	venden

Note again the three possible English translations:

nosotros vendemos

we sell
we do sell
we are selling

Beber (to drink) is another regular *-er* verb we heard in the dialogue:

Bebemos mucha agua y refrescos.

We drink a lot of water and soft drinks.

Other commonly used regular *-er* verbs are:

comer   to eat
comprender   to understand
aprender   to learn
leer   to read
Venden muchos paraguas.   You/They sell a lot of umbrellas.

46

Marcos come ahora.	Mark is eating now.
No comprendemos español.	We don't understand Spanish.
Leo mucho y aprendo.	I read a lot and I'm learning.

2. DEMONSTRATIVE ADJECTIVES

These are the adjectives that point out things: "this book, that hat," etc. As adjectives, they must agree in number and gender with their noun:

This, these:

	SINGULAR	PLURAL
masc.	*este país*	*estos países*
fem.	*esta estación*	*estas estaciones*

That, those:

	SINGULAR	PLURAL
masc.	*ese día*	*esos días*
fem.	*esa tormenta*	*esas tormentas*

OR

	SINGULAR	PLURAL
masc.	*aquel otoño*	*aquellos otoños*
fem.	*aquella tienda*	*aquellas tiendas*

Note that *aquel* and its forms refer to things that are farther away from the speaker:

este libro	this book
esas casas	those houses
aquellos hombres	those men (over there)

3. DEMONSTRATIVE PRONOUNS

If an accent mark is added to the stressed vowel of the demonstrative adjective, it becomes a pronoun:

	MASCULINE	FEMININE	NEUTER
Sg. (this)	éste	ésta	esto
Pl. (those)	éstos	éstas	—
Sg. (that)	ése	ésa	eso
Pl. (those)	ésos	ésas	—
Sg. (that over there)	aquél	aquélla	aquello
Pl. (those over there)	aquéllos	aquellas	—

The three neuter forms refer to concepts or unspecified objects:

Eso es verdad.
That (general concept, unnamed thing) is true.

VOCABULARIO (VOCABULARY)

el tiempo	weather
¿Qué tiempo hace?	What's the weather like?
Hace buen *(mal)* **tiempo.**	It's nice (bad) weather.
Hace calor.	It's hot.
Hace frío.	It's cold.
Hace viento.	It's windy.
Hace sol.	It's sunny.
Nieva.	It's snowing.
Llueve.	It's raining.
lluvioso	rainy
caliente	warm, hot
el/*los* **paraguas**	umbrella(s)
el impermeable[1]	raincoat
el frío	cold (weather)

La gabardina is used for "raincoat" in Spain.

48

el calor	hot (weather)
humedad	humidity
húmedo	humid
¿Cuántos grados hace?	How many degrees is it?
meses	months
enero	January
febrero	February
marzo	March
abril	April
mayo	May
junio	June
julio	July
agosto	August
septiembre	September
octubre	October
noviembre	November
diciembre	December
en julio	in July
¿Cuál es la fecha de hoy?	What is today's date?
estaciones	seasons
primavera	spring
verano	summer
otoño	autumn, fall
invierno	winter
en verano	in summer
el agua	water
beber	to drink
comer	to eat
durante	during
el país	country
leer	to read
refresco	soft drink
seguro, *-a*	sure
seguramente	surely
tienda	store
todo el año	all year long

EXAMEN (QUIZ)

A. *Conteste en una oración completa en español.*

1. *¿Cuáles son los cuatro meses del verano?*
2. *¿Cuántos días hay en marzo?*
3. *¿Cuántos días hay en septiembre?*
4. *¿Cuáles son los cuatro meses de la primavera?*

B. *Escoja la forma correcta.* (Choose the correct form.)

MODELO: Nosotros (comprendes, comprendemos, comprende) todo.
    Nosotros comprendemos todo.

1. Juan y Ana (beben, bebo, bebes) mucha agua.
2. El turista no (comprendéis, comprenden, comprende) por qué siempre llueve y hace calor.
3. Florinda y yo (leen, leemos, lee) el libro.
4. Jesús (venden, vendemos, vende) muchos paraguas.
5. Estudias y (comprendes, comprende, comprendo) español.

C. *Traduzca al español.* (Translate into Spanish.)

1. I drink a lot when it is hot.
2. It is raining and I need an umbrella.
3. He sells umbrellas in that store (over there).
4. In this country it is very cold in winter.
5. Today is July 4, 2000.
6. Do you (pl.) sell those umbrellas?

NOTAS CULTURALES (CULTURAL NOTES)

Remember that in South America, the seasons are the reverse of our own in the northern hemisphere. In most of Latin America and in Spain, temperature is given in *centígrado,* "centigrade" or "Celsius."

Be careful when you consult a calendar in Spain and many Latin American countries. Unlike the U.S. calendar, these calendars begin on Monday, with the last day of the week being Sunday! Also, when writing dates as numbers, Americans follow the order month/day/year (7/28/46). In Spain and in

Latin America the order is day/month/year (28/7/46). Dates in Spanish are written the following way:

¿Cuál es la fecha de hoy?	What is today's date?
Hoy es el veinte de octubre de mil novecientos noventa y cinco.	Today is 20 October, 1995.

RESPUESTAS (ANSWER KEY)

A. 1. *Son junio, julio, agosto y septiembre.* 2. *Hay treinta y un días.* 3. *Hay treinta días.* 4. *Son marzo, abril, mayo, y junio.*

B. 1. *beben* 2. *comprende* 3. *leemos* 4. *vende* 5. *comprendes*

C. 1. *Bebo mucho cuando hace calor.* 2. *Llueve y necesito un paraguas.* 3. *Vende paraguas en aquella tienda.* 4. *En este país hace mucho frío en invierno.* 5. *Hoy es el cuatro de julio del año dos mil (2000).* 6. *¿Venden Uds. esos/aquellos paraguas?*

PRIMER REPASO (FIRST REVIEW)

A. *Dé los plurales.* (Give the plurals.)

MODELO: el libro/los libros

1. *el señor* los señores
2. *feliz* felices
3. *el paraguas* los paraguas
4. *puertorriqueña* s
5. *el mes* los meses

B. *Cambie al artículo indefinido.* (Change to the indefinite article.)

MODELO: la majer/una mujer

1. *la señorita* una s
2. *el estudiante* un est
3. *la dirección* una dir
4. *los números* unos n
5. *los días* unos d

51

C. *Escriba la hora en palabras.* (Write out the time in words.)

MODELO: It's 2:30 p.m.
> *Son las dos y media de la tarde.*

1. It's 11:01 a.m.
2. It's 1:45 p.m.
3. It's 3:15 p.m.
4. At 5:30 a.m.
5. At 12:00 p.m. — *al mediodía*

D. *Complete usando una forma de "estar" o "ser."* (Complete using a form of *estar* or *ser.*)

MODELO: Tú _____ profesora.
> *Tú eres profesora.*

1. *Juan __es__ hispanoamericano.*
2. *Nosotras _____ contentas.* *estamos*
3. *¿Quiénes _____ cansados?* *estan*
4. *Son _____ las seis de la tarde.*
5. *es El film _____ interesante.*
6. *Mercedes y yo _____ maestras.* *somos*
7. *Yo _____ de Nueva York pero ahora _____ en Puerto Rico.*
   soy *estoy*

E. *Escriba nuevamente la oración usando el sujeto entre paréntesis.* (Rewrite the sentence using the subject in parentheses.)

MODELO: Hablo español. (Tú)
> *Tú hablas español.*

1. *Bebo agua.* (Nosotros) N. *bebemos*
2. *¿Vendes paraguas?* (Ellos) *Ellos venden*
3. *Como a la una.* (Tú) *comes*
4. *Trabajamos mucho.* (Yo) T *jo*
5. *¿Descansan?* (Tú) *-sAs*

F. *Traduzca al español.* (Translate into Spanish.)

1. Who is he? *Quiénes es?*
2. Where is that (far away) store?
   Donde es ese *mercado*

52

3. Which days of the week do you (pl.) work?
4. How many umbrellas are there? Five hundred fifty-five.
5. What time does John study?
6. Are they (fem.) drinking a lot?
7. What's the weather like?
8. It's hot in the summer.

G. *Escriba los siguientes números.* (Write out the following numbers.)

MODELO: 253

    doscientos cincuenta y tres

1. 1,258
2. 59,731
3. 64
4. 1,667,042
5. 1,034
6. 589
7. 89,742

RESPUESTAS (ANSWER KEY)

A. 1. *los señores* 2. *felices* 3. *los paraguas* 4. *puertorriqueñas* 5. *los meses*

B. 1. *una señorita* 2. *un estudiante* 3. *una dirección* 4. *unos números*
   5. *unos días*

C. 1. *Son las once y un minuto de la mañana.* 2. *Son las dos menos quince*
   (cuarto) de la tarde. 3. *Son las tres y quince (cuarto) de la tarde.* 4. *A las*
   cinco y media de la mañana. 5. *Al mediodía*

D. 1. *es* 2. *estamos* 3. *están* 4. *Son* 5. *es* 6. *somos* 7. *soy, estoy*

E. 1. *Bebemos agua.* 2. *¿Ellos venden paraguas?* 3. *Comes a la una.*
   4. *Trabajo mucho.* 5. *¿Descansas?*

F. 1. *¿Quién es él?* 2. *¿Dónde está aquella tienda?* 3. *¿Cuáles días de la*
   semana trabajan Uds.? 4. *¿Cuántos paraguas hay? Quinientos cincuenta y*
   cinco. 5. *¿A qué hora/Cuándo estudia Juan?* 6. *¿Beben ellas mucho?*
   7. *¿Qué tiempo hace?* 3. *Hace calor en verano.*

G. 1. *mil doscientos cincuenta y ocho* 2. *cincuenta y nueve mil setecientos*
   treinta y uno 3. *sesenta y cuatro* 4. *un millón seiscientos sesenta y siete*
   cuarenta y dos 5. *mil treinta y cuatro* 6. *quinientos ochenta y nueve*
   7. *ochenta y nueve mil setecientos cuarenta y dos*

LECCION 6

ROPA, COLORES, TALLAS.   Clothing, colors, sizes.

A. DIALOGO

Vamos de compras en Barcelona, España.

FLORINDA: **Voy de compras. ¿Sabes que hay liquidaciones esta semana? Recibimos un descuento de veinticinco por ciento sobre el precio original. El almacén abre a las diez menos cuarto.**

ANTONIO: **Vamos juntos. Hay mucha ropa bonita allí. Necesito comprar un traje de verano de color gris o blanco, y una camisa negra.**

FLORINDA: **¡Hombre! Es la moda actual. ¡Maravilloso!**

ANTONIO: **Sí, lo sé. Necesito una corbata azul, también. ¿Y tú? ¿Qué vas a comprar?**

FLORINDA: **Pues, deseo un vestido verde o amarillo de seda. Debo comprar un cinturón marrón, y también un par de zapatos negros.**

ANTONIO: **¡De acuerdo!**

We're going shopping in Barcelona, Spain.

FLORINDA: I'm going shopping. Do you know that there are closeout sales this week? We receive a discount of 25% off the original price. The department store opens at 9:45.

ANTONIO: Let's go together. There are beautiful clothes there. I need to buy a gray or white summer suit, and a black shirt.

FLORINDA: Wow! It's the latest style! How wonderful!

ANTONIO: Yes, I know. I need a blue tie, too. And what about you? What are you going to buy?

FLORINDA: Well, I want a green or yellow silk dress. I ought to buy a
brown belt, and also a pair of black shoes.

ANTONIO: Okay!

B. PRONUNCIACION

AND MORE CONSONANTS

a
c + *o* (like the sound "k"): **cada, como, cuanto**
u

e
c +   (in Castilian Spanish, like the "th" in "think", in Latin American
i Spanish, like the "s" in "see"):

Castilian	Latin American
cena	**cena**
cinco	**cinco**
dice	**dice**

z (in Castilian Spanish, like the "th" in "think", in Latin American
Spanish, like the "s" in "see"):

Castilian	Latin American
zona	**zona**
zapato	**zapato**
diez	**diez**

The *th* pronunciation of *c* and *z* before *e* and *i,* and the *th* sound of *z* at
the end of a word are characteristic sounds of Castilian Spanish.
Castilian is spoken primarily in the region of Castilla–León and the
Comunidad de Madrid; other areas of Spain use the *s* sound.

C. GRAMATICA Y USOS
(Grammar and Usage)

1. THE PRESENT TENSE OF REGULAR -*IR* VERBS

The third conjugation of regular verbs ends in -*ir.*

ABRIR   TO OPEN

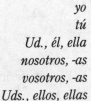
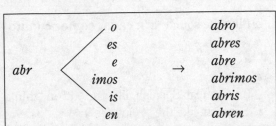

yo	o	abro
tú	es	abres
Ud., él, ella	e	abre
nosotros, -as	imos	abrimos
vosotros, -as	is	abris
Uds., ellos, ellas	en	abren

We also heard the verb *recibir* in this dialogue:

Recibimos un descuento de veinticinco por ciento.
   We receive a 25% discount.

Some other regular -*ir* verbs include:

partir	to leave
vivir	to live
escribir	to write

El almacén abre a las diez.
   The department store opens at 10 o'clock.

Partimos ahora.
   We're leaving now.

Escriben a Verónica.
   They write to Veronica.

56

2. *IR* AND *IR* + *A* + INFINITIVE

The verb *ir* means "to go."

yo voy	*nosotros, -as vamos*
tú vas	*vosotros, -as vais*
Ud., él, ella va	*Uds., ellos, ellas van*

¿Vas al almacén?
Are you going to the department store?

Sí, voy al almacén.
Yes, I'm going to the store.

¿A dónde? (Adónde?) is used instead of *¿dónde?* to indicate motion to a place, as with *ir:*

¿A dónde va Ud.?
Where are you going?

You can talk about a future action using *ir* + *a* + infinitive (to be going + infinitive):

¿Qué vas a comprar?
What are you going to buy?

Voy a comprar un vestido bonito.
I'm going to buy a beautiful dress.

3. THE VERB *SABER*

The verb *saber,* "to know," is used to say that you know facts or general information. Only the first person singular is irregular:

SABER TO KNOW

yo	*sé*	*nosotros, -as*	*sabemos*
tú	*sabes*	*vosotros, -as*	*sabéis*
Ud., él, ella	*sabe*	*Uds., ellos, ellas*	*saben*

¿Sabes que hay liquidaciones esta semana?
   Do you know that there are closeout sales this week?

Sabemos su número de teléfono.
   We know his phone number.

VOCABULARIO

ropa	clothing
sombrero	hat
el traje	suit
el cinturón	belt
abrigo	overcoat
el suéter	sweater
los calcetines	socks
corbata	tie
chaqueta	jacket
un pañuelo	handkerchief
blusa	blouse
camisa	shirt
zapatos	shoes
un par de zapatos	a pair of shoes
las medias	stockings
el pijama	pajamas
los pantalones	pants
falda	skirt
telas	materials
lana	wool
el algodón	cotton
seda	silk
un vestido de seda	a silk dress
colores	colors
negro, -*a*	black
marrón	brown
azul	blue
gris	gray
blanco, -*a*	white

rojo, -*a*	red
verde	green
amarillo, -*a*	yellow
ir de compras	to go shopping
el almacén	the department store
abrir	to open
Deseo probármelo.	I'd like to try it on.
Voy a probármelo.	I'm going to try it on.
llevar/usar	to wear
estar de moda	to be in style
bonito, -*a*	beautiful
feo, -*a*	ugly
comprar	to buy
deber	to need to, must, ought to
desear	to want
escribir	to write
partir	to leave
recibir	to receive
vivir	to live
junto, -*a*	together

EXAMEN

A. *Note la palabra no relacionada con las otras de la categoría.* (Note the word not related to the others in the category.)

MODELO: telas: algodón, lana, pantalones/pantalones

1. *colores: negro, gris, lana*
2. *ropa: marrón, falda, blusa*
3. *ropa: pantalones, algodón, camisa*
4. *telas: lana, ancho, seda*

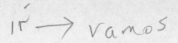

B. *Traduzca al español.*

1. We are going shopping.
2. What are you (pl.) going to buy?
3. I need a cotton dress with a brown belt and a handkerchief.
4. He wants a gray suit and a pair of black shoes.
5. I know that the stores open at ten o'clock in the morning.
6. Are you (familiar sg.) going to write to John?
7. That isn't ugly! It's in style!
8. We know they live here.
9. I'm going to buy a silk shirt.
10. Where are you (fam.) going?

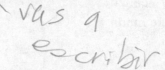

NOTAS CULTURALES

Spaniards and Latin Americans are very fashion conscious. They follow European styles. Cotton fabric and the color white are favored in tropical parts of Latin America due to the heat and humidity. Nonetheless, *el jeans* have become a very popular form of dress. As in most countries around the world, the influence of American culture has permeated the fashion consciousness of Spain and Latin America. You can find designer boutiques and outlet stores such as Calvin Klein, Diesel, and Ralph Lauren in all the major cities of the Spanish-speaking world.

Traditionally Spaniards shop in local stores or in boutiques selling only one group of products. While this is still true today, supermarkets, department stores, and shopping centers—*centros comerciales*—can be found in bigger cities.

RESPUESTAS

A. 1. *lana* 2. *marrón* 3. *algodón* 4. *ancho*
B. 1. *Vamos de compras.* 2. *¿Qué van a comprar Uds.?* 3. *Necesito un vestido de algodón con un cinturón marrón y un pañuelo.* 4. *Él desea un traje gris y un par de zapatos negros.* 5. *Sé que las tiendas abren a las diez de la mañana.* 6. *¿Vas a escribir a Juan?* 7. *¡Eso no es feo! ¡Está de moda!* 8. *Sabemos que viven aquí.* 9. *Voy a comprar una camisa de seda.* 10. *¿A dónde vas?*

LECCION 7

EL CUERPO Y LA SALUD.   The body and health.

A. DIALOGO

Julián y Marisa hablan de la salud y los ejercicios en San Juan, Puerto Rico.

JULIAN: **Hola, Marisa. ¿Estás lista?**

MARISA: **No tengo ganas de correr hoy. Tengo mucho dolor en los brazos, los hombros y las piernas. Es terrible cuando hago ejercicios.**

JULIAN: **¿Tal vez vamos a una clase de yoga?**

MARISA: **No, es que estoy sufriendo de dolores en todo el cuerpo— la espalda, las manos . . .**

JULIAN: **¿Tienes frío? ¿Estás enferma?**

MARISA: **No creo. No tengo fiebre. Me siento fatigada, es todo.**

JULIAN: **Debes tener cuidado; tienes que descansar y seguir una dieta alta en proteínas y carbohidratos.**

MARISA: **Sí, tienes razón. No tengo planes para esta noche; voy a descansar.**

JULIAN: **Es una buena idea. La buena salud es importante.**

Julian and Marisa talk about health and exercise in San Juan, Puerto Rico.

JULIAN: Hi, Marisa. Are you ready?

MARISA: I don't feel like running today. I have pains in my arms, shoulders, and legs. It's terrible when I exercise.

JULIAN: Maybe we'll go to a yoga class?

MARISA: No, (it's that) I'm suffering from pains in my whole body—my
back, my hands . . .

JULIAN: Are you cold? Are you sick?

MARISA: I don't think so. I don't have any fever. I'm feeling fatigued, that's
all.

JULIAN: You must be careful; you have to rest and follow a diet high in
proteins and carbohydrates.

MARISA: Yes, you're right. I don't have plans tonight; I'm going to rest.

JULIAN: That's a good idea. Good health is important.

B. PRONUNCIACION

STILL MORE CONSONANTS

$$g + \begin{matrix} a \\ o \\ u \\ ü \end{matrix}$$ (like the "g" in "go"): **ganar, gordo, guarder, nicaragüense**

Note: *ü* (u with umlaut) means that the *u* sound is pronounced after
the *g*.

$$g + \begin{matrix} e \\ i \end{matrix}$$ (like the guttural "h" in "he"): **gente, gigante**

j (like the guttural "h" in "he"): **jurar, Jorge, mejor**

C. GRAMATICA Y USOS

1. THE VERB *TENER* AND EXPRESSIONS WITH *TENER*

The verb *tener* means "to have" or "to possess." Its present tense conjugation is irregular:

TENER TO HAVE

yo	tengo	nosotros, -as	tenemos
tú	tienes	vosotros, -as	tenéis
Ud., él, ella	tiene	Uds., ellos, ellas	tienen

Tener is used with many nouns to describe physical, mental, and emotional states. In these cases, it is the equivalent of the English "to be." The following is a partial list of some common expressions and idioms with *tener;* be sure to check the glossary for others.

tener frío	to be cold	*tener calor*	to be warm
tener razón	to be right	*no tener razón*	to be wrong
tener prisa	to be in a hurry	*tener cuidado*	to be careful

Tengo mucho dolor en los brazos.[1]
I have pains in my arms.

No tenemos planes para hoy.
We don't have plans today.

Tengo una cita con el médico.
I have an appointment with the doctor.

Tiene prisa; no tiene tiempo.
She's in a hurry; she doesn't have time.

Tienen frío.
They are cold.

[1] Notice that when you speak about parts of the body in Spanish, you use the definite article rather than the possessive adjective.

The expression *tener que* means "to have to"; it is always followed by an infinitive:

Tenemos que correr hoy.   We have to run today.

Tiene que seguir una dieta alta en   You have to follow a high-protein diet.
proteínas.

Tener is also used to ask and state one's age:

¿Cuántos años tienes?   How old are you (How many years
                              do you have)?

Tengo treinta y un años.   I'm 31 years old.

2. THE GERUND

The gerund or present participle is the "-ing" form of the verb (going, being, speaking). In Spanish it is formed as follows:

> *-ar* verbs *(descansar)* . . . drop *ar,* add *-ando: descansando*
> *-er* verbs *(vender)* . . . drop *er,* add *-iendo: vendiendo*
> *-ir* verbs *(abrir)* . . . drop *ir,* add *-iendo: abriendo*

3. THE PRESENT PROGRESSIVE

The gerund is used in the present progressive tense. The present progressive tense stresses the action in progress in the present. It is made up of the conjugated form of the verb *estar* + gerund:

Estoy sufriendo de dolores.
    I'm suffering from pains.

Ellas están haciendo ejercicios.
    They are doing exercises.

Está lloviendo.
    It's raining.

4. THE VERB *HACER*

The verb *hacer* means "to make, to do." Only the first person present is irregular:

HACER   TO MAKE, TO DO

yo	hago	nosotros, -as	hacemos
tú	haces	vosotros, -as	hacéis
Ud., él, ella	hace	Uds., ellos, ellas	hacen

Hago ejercicios todos los días.
  I exercise every day.

Marisa hace una cita con el médico.
  Marisa is making an appointment with the doctor.

¿Qué haces mañana?
  What are you doing tomorrow?

5. TRANSLATIONS OF "TO BE" IN SPANISH

a. To describe states or conditions of people or things, use the verb *estar:*

Están tristes.   They are sad.

b. To describe professions and inherent characteristics, use the verb *ser:*

Soy abogado.   I am a lawyer.

c. To talk about weather or temperature conditions, use *hacer:*

Hace calor en verano.   It is hot in summer.

d. To describe one's age, use *tener:*

Tengo treinta y un años.   I am 31 years old.

65

VOCABULARIO

el cuerpo	body
cabeza	head
pecho	chest
oreja	ear
ojo	eye
la nariz	nose
lengua	tongue
hombro	shoulder
brazo	arm
la mano	hand
dedo	finger
la piel	skin
cuello	neck
cabello	hair
espalda	back
pierna	leg
el pie	foot
boca	mouth
garganta	throat
la salud	health
tener calor	to be hot
tener frío	to be cold
tener fiebre	to have fever
enfermo	sick, ill
dolor	pain
tener dolores en/*de*	to have pains
sufrir	to suffer
sentirse	to feel (health)
Me siento bien.	I feel well.
Me siento fatigada.	I feel fatigued.
una dieta	a diet
seguir[1] **una dieta**	to be on a diet
proteínas	proteins
carbohidratos	carbohydrates
una dieta alta en proteínas y carbohidratos	a diet high in proteins and carbohydrates

(handwritten: "gurgle" written across the garganta/throat line)

[1] See *Lección* 16 for verbs ending in *-guir*, like *seguir.*

ejercicio	exercise
hacer ejercicios	to exercise
correr	to run
una clase de yoga	a yoga class
tener que	to have to
tener ganas de (+ infinitive)	to feel like (doing something)
tener cuidado	to be careful
tener planes	to have plans
tener una cita	to have an appointment, date
tener tiempo	to have time
listo, -a	ready
terrible	terrible
hacer	to do, to make
creer	to believe
No creo.	I don't believe (so). I don't think (so).
tal vez	maybe
Es una buena idea.	It's a good idea.

EXAMEN

A. Conteste la pregunta en una oración completa usando la pista.

MODELO: ¿Estás contenta? (no, triste)
   Estoy triste.

no☑ yes → Tiene que
Tengo que me descansa-

1. ¿Que tiene que hacer cuándo está fatigada? *(descansar)*
2. ¿Julián tiene ganas de hacer ejercicios? *(no, correr)*
3. ¿Qué tipo de dieta necesita seguir Ud.? *(alta en proteínas y carbohidratos)*
4. ¿Tienes planes hoy? *(si, una cita)* *Tengo una cita hoy.*
5. ¿Tienen Uds. tiempo? *(no, tener prisa)*

pl.

B. *Escriba la oración nuevamente. Use el presente progresivo.* (Rewrite the sentence. Use the present progressive.)

MODELO: *Bebe agua todos los días.*
Estoy bebiendo agua todos los días.

1. *Corro todos los días en verano.*
2. *Bebemos mucha agua ahora.* Estamos bebiendo
3. *Hace mucho frío.*
4. *Hago ejercicios por la mañana.*

C. *Traduzca al español.*

1. I am hungry and tired.
2. Do you (familiar) have pains in your legs? las piernas
3. Do you (polite/pl.) feel like doing exercises?
4. They are wrong.
5. She is suffering a great deal.

NOTAS CULTURALES

The exercising fad has taken off in Spain and Latin America in recent years with the growth of other sports. It is common to see joggers in many small towns and in large cities. Jogging is called *el correr, el cooper* or *el jogging*.

RESPUESTAS

A. 1. *Tiene que descansar cuando está fatigada.* 2. *No, Julián tiene ganas de correr.* 3. *Necesito seguir una dieta alta en proteínas y carbohidratos.* 4. *Sí, tengo una cita.* 5. *No, tenemos prisa.*
B. 1. *Estoy corriendo todos los días en verano.* 2. *Estamos bebiendo mucha agua ahora.* 3. *Está haciendo mucho frío.* 4. *Estoy haciendo ejercicios por la mañana.*
C. 1. *Tengo hambre y estoy cansado.* 2. *¿Tienes dolores en las piernas?* 3. *¿Tienen Uds. ganas de hacer ejercicios?* 4. *No tienen razón.* 5. *Ella está sufriendo mucho.*

LECCION 8

PARENTESCOS.   Family relationships.

A. DIALOGO

Una boda limeña tradicional.

DON JOSÉ: **Tu prima favorite, Carmen, acepta nuestra invitación a
la boda de Isabelita.**

DOÑA MARTA: **Vamos a ver, José. Con nuestros dos hijos y sus
esposas y los nietos encantadores somos diez hombres y ocho
mujeres en la iglesia.**

DON JOSÉ: **Sí, y con tus hermanos y sobrinos somos veintiocho
personas.**

DOÑA MARTA: **Invitamos también a los cuatro abuelos queridos de
Arequipa y a los buenos amigos de la familia.**

DON JOSÉ: **¡Y tu tía antipática!**

DOÑA MARTA: **Toda nuestra familia va a estar reunida para la
boda.**

DON JOSÉ: **¡Qué maravilla! ¡Hace mucho tiempo que no estamos
todos juntos!**

A traditional wedding ceremony in Lima, Peru.

DON JOSÉ: Carmen, your favorite cousin, is accepting our invitation to
Isabelita's wedding.

DOÑA MARTA: Let's see, José. With our two sons and their wives and the
charming grandchildren, we'll be ten men and eight women at the
church.

DON JOSÉ: And with your brothers and sisters and nephews and nieces,
we'll be twenty-eight people.

DOÑA MARTA: And we're also inviting the four dear grandparents from Arequipa and good family friends.

DON JOSÉ: And your unpleasant aunt!

DOÑA MARTA: All our family will be together at the ceremony.

DON JOSÉ: How wonderful! It's been a long time since we've been together (that we haven't been together)!

B. PRONUNCIACION,

r (in the middle of a word: like the "r" in "throw"): **pero, caro, hermano**
r (at the beginning of a word) and **rr** (a trilled sound made by tapping the tip of the tongue against the gum ridge of the upper back teeth): **río, rosa, carro**
x (like the "cks" in "rocks"): **taxi, sexto, extra**
The letters *k* and *w* appear in Spanish in foreign words (for example, kilowatt, kilometer). In some countries, the *k* is replaced with the Spanish equivalent, *qu:* **quilómetro.**
w (like the "v" in "venture"): **kilowatt**

C. GRAMATICA Y USOS

1. POSSESSIVE ADJECTIVES

We have seen that to indicate possession you use the word *de* (of):
el paraguas de Juan = John's umbrella (literally, the umbrella of John). Possessive adjectives tell who has something. As adjectives, they must agree in number and gender with the thing possessed, not with the possessor.

	SINGULAR	PLURAL
my	*mi*	*mis*
your (familiar)	*tu*	*tus*
his, her, your	*su*	*sus*
our	*nuestro, -a*	*nuestros, -as*
your	*vuestro, -a*	*vuestros, -as*
their, your	*su*	*sus*

En nuestro país hace mucho calor durante todo el año.
> In our country it's hot all year.

Tus sobrinos son muy simpáticos.
> Your nephews (nieces and nephews) are very nice.

The possessive *su, sus* can mean "his," "her," "your," or "their." In order to clarify the meaning, very often the descriptives *de él* (of him), *de ella* (of her), *de Ud., de ellos, de ellas,* and *de Uds.* follow the definite articles and the noun.

Sus primos aceptan.
> His/her/your/their cousins accept.

Los primos de él aceptan.
> His cousins accept.

Los primos de ella aceptan.
> Her cousins accept.

Los primos de Ud. aceptan.
> Your cousins accept.

Los primos de ellos aceptan.
> Their (masc. pl.) cousins accept.

Los primos de ellas aceptan.
> Their (fem. pl.) cousins accept.

Los primos de Uds. aceptan.
> Your (pl.) cousins accept.

2. THE POSITION OF ADJECTIVES

In Spanish there are two classes of adjectives: limiting and descriptive. Limiting adjectives always precede the noun. These include numbers, demonstratives, possessives, and very common adjectives such as *mucho, poco, buen(o), nuevo, mal(o), gran(de)*.

Tus hermanos están en México.
Your brothers are in Mexico.

Soy el nuevo abogado.
I'm the new lawyer.

La buena salud es importante.
Good health is important.

All other adjectives are descriptive and follow the noun. If two or more descriptive adjectives are used, they follow the noun and are joined by the word *y* (and).

Carmen es tu prima favorita.
Carmen is your favorite cousin.

Invitamos a nuestros nietos queridos y encantadores.
We are inviting our dear, charming grandchildren.

3. SHORTENED FORMS OF ADJECTIVES

Certain adjectives have abbreviated forms before a noun: Before any singular noun, *grande* ("great in importance") becomes *gran*.

una gran mujer	a great woman
un gran actor	a great, grand actor

Before masculine singular nouns, *uno* becomes *un, bueno* becomes *buen,* and *malo* (bad) becomes *mal*.

un buen amigo	a good friend
un mal film	a bad movie

4. *HACE* + TIME + *QUE* + PRESENT TENSE

To express an action begun in the past and continuing into the present, use the structure *"Hace + time + que + present tense"*:

Hace mucho tiempo que no estamos juntas.
 It's been a long time since we've been together.

Hace dos años que deseo estudiar español.
 I've been wanting to study Spanish for two years.

An alternative construction for the same concept is present tense + *hace* + time:

Deseo estudiar español hace dos años.
 I've been wanting to study Spanish for two years.

To ask how long an event has been going on, you say: *¿Cuánto tiempo hace que . . . ?:*

¿Cuánto tiempo hace que está en Colombia?
 How long have you been in Colombia?

5. THE PERSONAL *A*

When the direct object of a verb—the noun that receives the verb's action directly—is a person, you must use the personal *a*.

Invitamos a los abuelos de Arequipa.
 We are inviting the grandparents from Arequipa.

But it is not used after *tener.*

Tenemos veinte amigos en España.
 We have twenty friends in Spain.

6. COLLECTIVE NOUNS

Collective nouns refer to a group but are used with a singular verb form. In Spanish, the words *la familia* (family) and *la gente* (people) fall into this category.

La familia va a estar reunida.
The family is going to be together.

La gente tiene que trabajar mucho en este país.
People have to work a lot in this country.

VOCABULARIO

parentescos	family relationships[1]
familia	family
esposo/esposa	husband/wife
abuelo/abuela	grandfather/grandmother
hermano/hermana	brother/sister
padre/madre	father/mother
hijo/hija	son/daughter
nieto/nieta	grand son/granddaughter
padrino/madrina	godfather/godmother
tío/tía	uncle/aunt
primo/prima	cousin (masc., fem.)
hombre/mujer	man/woman
novio/novia	boyfriend, groom/girlfriend, bride
sobrino/sobrina	nephew/niece
persona	person
amigo/amiga	friend
joven/jóvenes	young person/young people
boda	wedding
bueno/malo	good bad
grande	"great" (before noun); big (after noun)

[1] Keep in mind that the masculine plural form of the noun can refer to groups: *los hijos* = "children" (sons and daughters); *los tíos* = "aunt(s) and uncle(s)"

pequeño	small
querido	beloved, dear
favorito	favorite
encantador	charming
contento[1]	happy
reunido	reunited, together
junto	together
invitar	to invite
aceptar	to accept
Vamos a ver.	Let's see.
cuidar a los niños	to take care of the children.

EXAMEN

A. *Dé el adjectivo posesivo más claro.* (Give the clearest possessive adjective.)

MODELO: los tíos de José
los tíos de él

1. *los hermanos de Juana* ~~ella~~ *sus hermanos*
2. *la amiga de José* ~~su a.~~
3. *mi tío y tu tía* ~~nuestros tíos~~
4. *la abuela de Pedro y el abuelo de Andrés* ~~sus abuelos~~

B. *Añada los adjetivos a la oración.* (Add the adjectives to the sentences.)

MODELO: Bebe leche todos los días. (fresca)
Bebe leche fresca todos los días.

1. *Tengo cinco primos. (favorito)* ~~fav's~~
2. *Vive con sus hermanas. (tres, querido)* ~~sus tres h. queridas~~
3. *Nuestra lección es larga. (difícil)* ~~n. l. d. es l. / l. y d.~~
4. *Invito a los jovenes. (veinte, bueno)*
5. *Tenemos seis amigas. (cansado, contento)*

[1] Remember that the adjective *contento, -a* is only used with verb *estar.* The adjective *feliz* (pl. *felices)* can be used with *estar* or *ser.*

~~los v. j. buenos.~~

~~cas y con's~~

C. *Traducca al español.*

1. The family is big, happy and beloved.
2. Are you inviting your cousins from Mexico?
3. Who is the groom's sister? She is a good friend.
4. I've been working here for three years.
5. What are your favorite aunts like?
6. I need to take care of the children.

NOTAS CULTURALES

The polite forms of address *Don/Doña* are used before the first names of men and women who merit respect owing to their age and/or status in society. The tendency to use these forms of address is slowly dying out.

In the Spanish-speaking world, "family," *la familia,* means parents, siblings, children, aunts, uncles, cousins, grandparents, and godparents, too. Everyone helps to take care of the children, including older siblings. More often than in the U.S., daughters and sons live at home until they marry. Family celebrations are hence often large—and fun!

RESPUESTAS

A. 1. *los hermanos de ella/sus hermanos* 2. *la amiga de él/su amigo*
   3. *nuestros tíos* 4. *los abuelos de ellos/sus abuelos*
B. 1. *Tengo cinco primos favoritos.* 2. *Vive con sus tres queridas hermanas.*
   3. *Nuestra lección es larga y difícil.* 4. *Invito a los veinte buenos jóvenes.*
   5. *Tenemos seis amigas cansadas y contentas.*
C. 1. *La familia es grande, feliz y querida.* 2. *¿Invitas a tus primos de*
   México?/¿Estás invitando a tus primos de México? 3. *¿Quién es la*
   hermana del novio? Ella es una buena amigo. 4. *Hace tres años que*
   trabajo aquí./Trabajo aquí hace tres años. 5. *¿Cómo son tus tías favoritas?*
   6. *Necesito (Tengo que) cuidar a los niños.*

LECCION 9

COMIDA. Food.

A. DIALOGO

Haciendo compras con Doña Elvira en el Supermercado Grandote de Caguas, Puerto Rico.

ELVIRA: **Gracias por venir conmigo, Aurelio. Tengo mi lista aquí . . . Para ti, vamos a comprar carne. Yo no la como. ¿Qué carne deseas?**

AURELIO: **Deseo bistec y chuletas . . . pero Felipe viene este fin de semana y él come jamón.**

ELVIRA: **Bueno, lo compro para él. Vamos ahora al departamento de mariscos.**

AURELIO: **Aquí hay salmón y bacalao frescos. Tenemos que comprar verduras y frutas también.**

ELVIRA: **Sí. Yo las como todos los días. Son buenas para la salud. ¿Cuáles deseas?**

AURELIO: **Para mí, una cajita de fresas, una bolsa de manzanas, y esa piña bonita.**

ELVIRA: **Ya no cabe nada más en el carrito. ¡Muchísimas gracias por tu ayuda!**

AURELIO: **No hay problema. Vengo contigo otra vez.**

Shopping with Doña Elvira at the Grandote Supermarket in Caguas, Puerto Rico.

ELVIRA: Thanks for coming with me, Aurelio. I have my shopping list here . . . For you, we're going to buy meat. I don't eat it. What kind of meat do you want?

AURELIO: I want steak and chops...but Phillip is coming this weekend, and he eats ham.

ELVIRA: Okay, I'll buy it for him. Now let's go to the seafood section.

AURELIO: Here there is fresh salmon and codfish. We have to buy vegetables and fruit also.

ELVIRA: Yes. I eat them every day. They are good for your health. Which do you want?

AURELIO: For me, a box of strawberries, a bag of apples, and that beautiful pineapple.

ELVIRA: Nothing else fits in the cart. Thanks very much for your help!

AURELIO: It's not a problem. I'll come with you again.

B. PRONUNCIACION

THE ALPHABET

a	*a*	j	*jota*	r	*ere*
b	*be grande*	k[1]	*ca*	rr	*erre*
c	*ce*	l	*ele*	s	*ese*
ch	*che*	ll	*elle*	t	*te*
d	*de*	m	*eme*	u	*u*
e	*e*	n	*ene*	v	*ve chica*
f	*efe*	ñ	*eñe*	w[1]	*doble ve*
g	*ge*	o	*o*	x	*equis*
h	*hache*	p	*pe*	y	*i griega*
i	*i*	q	*cu*	z	*zeta*

Learn the names of the letters. When in doubt about the spelling of a word, ask the speaker: *¿Cómo se escribe?* The letters are feminine, *la a, la b, la c.*
Note that *ch* follows *c, ll* follows *l, ñ* follows *n,* and *rr* follows *r* both in the alphabet and in dictionary listings. These digraphs are never separated.

[1] In Spanish *k* and *w* are used only in foreign words.

78

INTONATION

The way you raise and drop your voice is called intonation *(entonación)*. When you make a statement in Spanish, your normal voice is usually at approximately the same pitch, except that you drop the pitch at the end. When you ask a question, you raise your voice at the end of the sentence.

Yo las como todos los días.
I eat them every day.

Aquí hay salmón y bacalao frescos.
Here there is fresh salmon and codfish.

¿Qué carnes vamos a comprar?
What meats are we going to buy?

¿Cuáles deseas?
Which do you want?

C. GRAMATICA Y USOS

1. COMMON PREPOSITIONS

en	in, on
de	of, from
por[1]	by, through, for
a	to, at
para[1]	for, toward, in order to
con	with

Para ti, vamos a comprar carnes.
For you, we're going to buy meats.

Gracias por tu ayuda.
Thank you for your help.

Aurelio hace compras con Elvira.
Aurelio is going shopping with Elvira.

[1] See *Lecciónes* 29 and 30 for more on *por* and *para,* respectively.

2. PREPOSITIONAL OBJECT PRONOUNS

SINGULAR	PLURAL
mí	*nosotros, -as*
ti	*vosotros, -as*
Ud., él, ella	*Uds., ellos, ellas*

These personal pronouns, which are used as objects of prepositions, are the same as the subject pronouns, with the exception of *mí* and *ti:*

Compran frutas para mí.
They are buying fruit for me.

Escriben a ella.
They are writing to her.

Irregular forms of the prepositional object pronouns occur with *con:*

with me	*conmigo*
with you	*contigo*
with him, her, you, them	*consigo*

Gracias por venir conmigo.
Thanks for coming with me.

3. DIRECT OBJECT PRONOUNS

The direct object pronoun *(complemento directo)* takes the place of the direct object (the direct recipient of an action):

I buy the book.
We see John.

I buy it.
We see him.

In Spanish the direct object pronouns are:

me	*me*
you (familiar)	*te*
him, you (formal), it (masc.)	*lo*[1]
her, you (formal), it (fem.)	*la*
us (masc. and fem.)	*nos*
you (pl. familiar)	*os*
them (masc. people and things), you (formal pl. masc.)	*los*
them (fem. people and things), you (formal pl. fem.)	*las*

Yo compro el bistec.	I buy the steak.
Yo lo compro.	I buy it.
Nosotras invitamos a Juan.	We invite John.
Nosotras lo invitamos.	We invite him.
¿Quién vende las manzanas?	Who is selling the apples?
¿Quién las vende?	Who is selling them?

4. THE POSITION OF DIRECT OBJECT PRONOUNS

Direct object pronouns immediately precede the verb in simple sentences:

Nosotros lo hacemos par la mañana.
    We do it in the morning.

Yo no las como.
    I don't eat them.

The object can be attached to an infinitive:

Deseo comprarlas.
    I want to buy them.   comprar + las

Voy a escribirlo aquí.
    I'm going to write it here.   escribir + lo

[1] In Spain only, *le* is sometimes used as a direct object.

The object can precede or be attached to the gerund form:

Lo estoy esperando hace veinticinco minutos.
or
Estoy esperándolo hace veinticinco minutos.
I've been waiting for him for twenty-five minutes.

To keep the stress on the correct syllable when you attach the object to the gerund, you must write an accent mark on the third vowel from the end (the original point of stress in the gerund): *esperándolo.*
To clarify the third person object pronouns, you can use the personal *a* before the prepositional object pronoun:

Estoy esperándolo a Ud.	I am waiting for you.
Estoy esperándolo a él.	I am waiting for him.

5. THE VERB *VENIR*

The verb *venir,* "to come," is irregular. Its forms are:

VENIR TO COME

yo	*vengo*	*nosotros, -as*	*venimos*
tú	*vienes*	*vosotros, -as*	*venís*
Ud., él, ella	*viene*	*Uds., ellos, ellas*	*vienen*

Felipe viene este fin de semana.	Philip is coming this weekend.
Vengo contigo otra vez.	I'll come with you again.
Vienen esta noche.	They are coming this evening.

VOCABULARIO

comida	food
carnes	meats
el bistec	steak
la carne de res	beef

el jamón	ham
chuletas	chops
chorizo	sausage
aves	fowl
pollo	chicken
pato	duck
puerco	pork
cordero	lamb
pescado/mariscos	fish/seafood
el atún	tuna
bacalao	codfish
el salmón	salmon
los camarones	shrimp
verduras/las legumbres	vegetables
el tomate	tomato
lechuga	lettuce
cebolla	onion
patata (Spain)/papa	potato
frutas	fruits
piña	pineapple
fresa	strawberry
naranja	orange
uvas	grapes
manzana	apple
hacer compras	to shop
supermercado	supermarket
lista	list
carrito	shopping cart
nada más	nothing else, nothing more
otra vez	again
No es problema.	It's not a problem.
bolsa	bag
fresco	fresh
cajita	small box

EXAMEN

A. *Conteste afirmativamente. Cambie el sustantivo subrayado a complemento directo.* (Answer affirmatively. Change the <u>underlined</u> object to an object pronoun.)

MODELO: *Compramos <u>la carne.</u>*
       La compramos.

1. *¿Comen <u>chuletas</u>?*
2. *¿Preparamos <u>el salmón</u>?*
3. *¿Deseas <u>el pescado</u> para esta tarde?*
4. *¿Visitamos a <u>los tíos</u>?*

B. *Escoja la palabra no relacionada con las otras.* (Choose the unrelated word.)

MODELO: *bacalao, chuletas, chorizo, came de res / bacalao*

1. *tomate, salmón, lechuga, cebolla*
2. *carne de res, chuletas, chorizo, camarones*
3. *bacalao, camarones, pollo, atún*

C. *Traduzca al español.*

1. They are coming with me today.
2. I know that he is selling it (masc.).
3. You (familiar sing.) have to buy and eat vegetables every day.
4. You (fam.) are coming with me to the supermarket.
5. He is preparing it (fem.) with us.

D. *Conjugue el verbo venir.* (Conjugate the verb *venir.*)

1. *Nosotros (venir) a la escuela todos los días.*
2. *Ella (venir) al restaurante a desayunar.*
3. *Ellos (venir) con nosotros.*
4. *¿Tú (venir) a México cada verano?*
5. *No, yo no (venir) a México todos los veranos.*

NOTAS CULTURALES

Be prepared to encounter a variety of other names for the foods listed here. For example, the common word for the orange in Puerto Rico is *china*, while *naranja* is most common in other Spanish-speaking countries. Also, a great number of fruits and vegetables are not usually seen in the United States other than in Hispanic areas. Here are a few:

yuca	manioc	*plátano*	plantain
chayote	cheyote	*guayaba*	guava
guanábana	bread fruit	*mango*	mango
caña de azúcar	sugar cane	*chirimoya*	cherimoya
nopal	small cactus	*guineo*	sweet banana

RESPUESTAS

A. 1. *Sí, las comen.* 2. *Sí, lo preparamos.* 3. *Sí, lo deseo para esta tarde.* 4. *Sí, los visitamos.*

B. 1. *salmón.* 2. *camarones* 3. *pollo*

C. 1. *Ellos vienen/están viniendo conmigo hoy.* 2. *Sé que él lo vende/está vendiéndolo.* 3. *Tienes que comprar y comer verduras todos los días.* 4. *Tú vienes/estás viniendo conmigo al supermercado.* 5. *Él la prepara/está preparándola con nosotros.*

D. 1. *venimos* 2. *viene* 3. *vienen* 4. *vienes* 5. *vengo*

LECCION 10

GUSTOS.   Likes and dislikes.

A. DIALOGO

En el departamento de aparatos electrónicos del Almacén Todo de Bogotá, Colombia.

SEÑORA MARTINEZ: **Buenas tardes. Deseo comprar algo especial para mi sobrino.**

VENDEDOR: **Si, señora. Hay muchos equipos muy buenos aquí. Le gustaría darle algo especial . . . Aquí hay unos televisores de colores, y ésta es una nueva video-grabadora.**

SEÑORA MARTINEZ: **¡Me parecen caros! ¿Hay equipos de sonido? Me dice que a él le interesa la música moderna.**

VENDEDOR: **Sí, sí . . . los otros vendedores dicen que a los jóvenes les gusta este aparato de discos compactos. Estamos vendiendo muchos de este modelo.**

SEÑORA MARTINEZ: **No sé si él tiene discos compactos. Tal vez le daría un radio-cassette para cintas o un tocadiscos.**

VENDEDOR: **Sin dude un radio-cassette es mejor que un tocadiscos. Tenemos radio-cassettes estereofónicos. Este modelo es portátil, también.**

SEÑORA MARTINEZ: **¡Sí! Ese me gusta. Voy a comprarlo.**

VENDEDOR: **¡Bueno! Le demos a Ud. una garantía de un año. A su sobrino le va a gustar mucho.**

In the electronics department of the Todo department store in Bogotá, Colombia.

MRS. MARTINEZ: Hello. I want to buy something special for my nephew.

SALESMAN: Yes, madam. There's a lot of good equipment here. You'd like to give him something special . . . Here are some color television sets and this is a new video recorder.

MRS. MARTINEZ: They seem expensive (to me)! Do you have stereo equipment? He tells me he's interested in modern music.

SALESMAN: That's good . . . The other salespeople say that the young people like this compact disc player. We're selling many of this model.

MRS. MARTINEZ: I don't know if he has compact discs. Maybe I'll give him a radio/cassette player or a record player.

SALESMAN: Without doubt a radio/cassette player is better than a record player. We have stereo radio/cassette players. This model is portable, too.

MRS. MARTINEZ: Yes! I like that. I'll buy it.

SALESMAN: Good! We are giving you a one-year guarantee. Your nephew is going to like it a lot.

B. PRONUNCIACION

LINKING

There is a tendency in Spanish, as in other languages, to join the vowel ending one word and the vowel beginning the next word as one sound. This is called "linking," *sinalefa*.

La agente entra ahora.   **¿Qué es?**

Even if the next word begins with a different vowel, they appear to be linked in speech:

la otra amiga   **ochenta y uno**

A similar phenomenom occurs with a final consonant followed by a vowel beginning the next word:

el‿amigo

las‿aguas

Es‿hermana‿de‿nuestro‿amigo‿Enrique.

C. GRAMATICA Y USOS

1. THE INDIRECT OBJECT AND INDIRECT OBJECT PRONOUNS

The indirect object is the ultimate recipient of an action; most often it refers to people. In the English sentence "I give the radio to John," "John" is the indirect object. Very often the indirect object in English is preceded by the word "to." However, that same sentence may be written thus: "I give John the radio." By putting the indirect object before the direct object you eliminate the word "to."
The indirect object pronoun substitutes for the indirect object. In the sentence "I give the radio to him," "him" is the indirect object pronoun.

The forms of the Spanish indirect object pronouns are like the direct object pronouns, except for the third persons singular and plural:

me	to/for me
te	to/for you (familiar)
le	to/for you (formal), him, her *(al él, a ella, a Ud.)*
nos	to/for us
os	you (familiar pl.)
les	to/for you (formal pl.), them (masc., fem.) *(a ellos, a ellas, a Uds.)*

The indirect object pronouns are positioned just like the direct object pronouns:

Ella siempre me escribe.
She always writes to me.

Están vendiéndonos los radios.
> They are selling us the radios.

Because *le* and *les* can have several meanings they are usually clarified by using *a* and the prepositional object pronoun.

Le hablo a él todos los días.
> I speak to him every day.

Voy a hablarle a ella mañana.
> I am going to speak to her tomorrow.

Estamos hablándole a Ud. ahora.
> We are talking to you now.

2. *GUSTAR* AND VERBS LIKE IT

The verb *gustar* in Spanish is the equivalent of the English verb "to like." Its literal meaning is "to be pleasing to someone." Thus "I like the radio" in English is equivalent to the Spanish structure "The radio is pleasing to me." The subject of the Spanish sentence is the thing(s) liked; the person becomes an indirect object ("to me").

The verb *gustar* therefore is only used in the forms *gusta* (for liking one thing) and *gustan* (for liking several things). To ask one close friend or family member if they like something, you use the indirect object *te*, "to you":

¿Te gusta la video-grabadora?
> Do you like the video recorder? (Is the video recorder pleasing to you?)

The answer—I like (do not like) the video recorder—requires the use of the indirect object *me*, "to me":

Sí, me gusta la video-grabadora.
> Yes, I like the video recorder.

No, no me gusta la video-grabadora.
> No, I don't like the video recorder.

If you ask a person whom you address as *Ud., él, ella,* "Do you like Spanish songs?" you use the indirect object *le:*

¿Le gustan a Ud. las canciones españolas?

Since *le* can mean "to you, to him, to her," the *a Ud.* (or, as necessary, *a él* or *a ella)* defines to whom the *le* refers. This example has a plural subject, *canciones,* which requires the plural verb, *gustan.* With groups or third person plurals *(Uds., ellos, ellas)* use the word *les* and the descriptives *a Uds., a ellos, a ellas)* as necessary.

¿Les gustan a ellas los aparatos electrónicos nuevos?
Do they like the new electronic appliances?

Notice that the descriptive adjective may come at the very beginning of the sentence, or after the verb *gustar,* or at the end of the sentence. To say "we like" you use *nos gusta(n);* the descriptive *a nosotros* can be used for emphasis.

A nosotros nos gustan los radios modernos.
We like modern radios.

Another verb may be used after *gustar* to tell what one likes to do:

Me gusta ir a los conciertos.
I like to go to concerts.

Note that in the dialogue, the salesman used the form *gustaría:*

Le gustaría darle algo especial . . .
You'd like to give him something special . . .

Keep in mind that *gustaría* translates as ". . . would like . . ." and is used, as in English, for politeness.[1] Compare:

Le gusta darle algo especial.
You want to give him something special.

Le gustaria darle algo especial.
You'd like to give him something special.

[1] *Gustaría is the conditional form, which will be covered in* Lección 30.

Other verbs and expressions like *gustar:*

encantar	to enjoy
faltar	to lack
hacer falta	to lack
interesar	to be interested
parecer	to seem
apetecer[1]	to appeal to

Le falta a ella dinero.
> She lacks money. (Money is lacking to her.)

¡Me encanta la música moderna!
> I enjoy modern music!

Nos hace falta un carro.
> We lack a car.

Parecen importantes.
> They seem important.

¿Te interesan los libros?
> Do the books interest you?

3. THE VERBS *DAR* AND *DECIR*

Both of these verbs are irregular in the present tense:

DAR	TO GIVE		*DECIR*	TO SAY
yo	*doy*		*yo*	*digo*
tú	*das*		*tú*	*dices*
Ud., él, ella	*da*		*Ud., él, ella*	*dice*
nosotros, -as	*damos*		*nosotros, -as*	*decimos*
vosotros, -as	*dais*		*vosotros, -as*	*decís*
Uds., ellos, ellas	*dan*		*Uds., ellos, ellas*	*dicen*

[1] Note that this verb is like *gustar;* the verb agrees with the number of things that are appealing: *Me apetece.* It appeals to me. *Me apetecen.* They are appealing to me.

Both of these verbs take indirect objects, and thus indirect object pronouns:

Le doy una grabadora para cintas a Juana.
I'm giving a cassette recorder to Juana.

Nos dan muchos regalos.
They give us many gifts.

Le digo al vendedor que parece caro.
I'm telling the salesman that it seems expensive.

Dicen que este modelo es el mejor.
They say that this model is the best.

Note that Señora Martínez used the conditional form[1] of *decir, daría* (like *gustaría,* above):

Tal vez le daría un radio-cassette para cintas.
Maybe I'll give (would give) him a radio/cassette player.

Here, this form, along with *tal vez,* shows that Señora Martinez is considering buying a radio/cassette player.

VOCABULARIO

gustos	likes and dislikes, tastes
gustar	to be pleasing to (to like)
A los jóvenes les gusta este modelo.	The young people like this model.
A su sobrino le va a gustar mucho.	Your nephew is going to like it a lot.
Me gusta mucho este modelo.	I like this model a lot.
A ella le gustan ésos.	She likes those.
interesar	to interest
Me interesa el equipo de video.	I'm interested in video equipment.

[1] You will learn more about the conditional in *Lección* 30.

parecer	to seem
parecer caro	to seem, appear expensive
parecer barato	to seem, appear cheap
Me parece moderno.	It appears modern to me.
aparatos electrónicos	electronic equipment
equipo	equipment
televisor	television set
televisor de color	color television set
video	video
equipo de video	video equipment
video-grabadora	video recorder; VCR
máquina	machine (in general)
máquina filmadora	video recorder (lit., filming machine)
equipo de música	music equipment
equipo de sonido	sound (music) equipment
estereofónico	stereophonic; stereo
equipo estereofónico	stereo equipment
disco compacto	compact disc
aparato de discos compactos	compact disc player
modelo	model
el/*la* radio	a radio
el radio-cassette *(pare cintas)*	radio/cassette player
cinta	cassette tape
tocadiscos	record player
grabadora para cintas	cassette recorder
alto-parlantes	loudspeakers
. . . portátil	portable . . .
garantía	guarantee
canción	song
encantar	to enjoy
especial	special
ester seguro	to be sure
faltar	to lack
hacer falta	to lack
moderno	modern
sin duda	without doubt
vendedor	salesman

EXAMEN

A. *Conteste la pregunta en una oración completa usando la pista.*

MODELO: ¿Les decimos la verdad? (siempre)
   Siempre les decimos la verdad.

1. *¿Le gusta o no le gusta? (sí)*
2. *¿Dicen Uds. que el televisor es caro? (sí)*
3. *¿Que le das a él? (una garantía)*
4. *¿Por qué va ella ahora? (le falta tiempo)*

B. *Escriba tantas oraciones lógicas como sea posible relacionando una de la columna A con una o más de la columna B.* (Write out as many logical sentences as possible matching one from Column A with one or more from Column B.)

COLUMNA A	COLUMNA B
1. *Me gusta*	a. *estar en Venezuela?*
2. *¿Le gustan*	b. *las camisas de color azul.*
3. *¿Te gustan*	c. *la máquina a ellas?*
4. *Nos gusta*	d. *a ellas trabajar los domingos?*
5. *¿Les gusta*	e. *el radio-cassette.*
6. *Le gusta*	f. *los nuevos radios?*
7. *Me gustan*	g. *a Uds. las frutas y las verduras.*
8. *¿Te gusta*	h. *escuchar canciones españolas.*

C. *Traduzca al español:*

1. We are giving the appliances to her.
2. She likes the beautiful blue dress.
3. What are you (fam. sg.) saying?
4. Are they (masc.) interested in buying a radio?
5. We are giving them (fem. pl.) the tapes.
6. The CD player is too expensive.
7. I think she's very nice.
8. I need a color television.
9. I'm telling her I don't have money.
10. I'm giving a VCR to my mother.

NOTAS CULTURALES

Electric and electronic appliances were imported into Spain and most of Latin America, and thus were quite expensive, and heavily taxed. In Spain, a member of the EC, and in the large industrial centers of Latin America, multinational corporations and domestic industries have established factories which now produce appliances at more affordable prices, although on a fairly small scale. Furthermore, the EC's attempts to establish free trade and open markets have reduced the import tax burden.

RESPUESTAS

A. 1. *Sí, me gusta.* 2. *Sí, decimos que el televisor es caro.* 3. *Le doy a él una garantía.* 4. *Le falta a ella tiempo.*
B. 1-e/h; 2-f; 3-f; 4-e/h; 5-a/c/d; 6-e/h; 7-b; 8-a.
C. 1. *Le damos los aparatos a ella.* 2. *A ella le gusta el vestido bonito y azul.* 3. *¿Qué dices?/¿Qué estás diciendo?* 4. *¿Les interesa a ellos comprar un radio?* 5. *Les damos a ellas las cintas.* 6. *El aparato de discos compactos está muy caro.* 7. *Ella me cae muy bien.* 8. *Yo necesito una televisión a colores.* 9. *Le digo a ella que no tengo dinero.* 10. *Le doy una videograbadora a my mamá.*

SEGUNDO REPASO

A. *Escriba nuevamente la oración usando el nuevo sujeto en paréntesis.* (Rewrite the sentence using the new subject in parentheses.)

MODELO: Comprenden la lección. (Tú)
   Comprendes la lección.

1. *¿Escribes en español? (Uds.)*
2. *Sabemos la dirección del hotel. (Yo)*
3. *Vivimos en México. (Ella)*
4. *Voy a comprar pantalones. (El)*
5. *¿Quién está de moda? (¿Yo?)*

B. *Termine la oración con una expresión lógica usando "tener."* (Complete the sentence with a logical expression using *tener.*)

MODELO: La clase comienza en dos minutos; tengo _____ para llegar/prisa.

1. *Mañana hay un examen importante; nosotros* _____ *estudiar.*
2. *Vamos a comprar abrigos porque* _____.
3. *No estoy bien.* _____ *en los brazos.*
4. *Sí, dos y dos son cuatro; Ud.* _____.

C. *Traduzca al español.*

1. my fifteen good friends
2. our countries
3. your (polite pl.) aunts
4. a great woman
5. a good man
6. my brother's ten children and my sister's nieces and nephews.
7. They have been here for two weeks.

D. *Responda usando los pronombres directosy las palabras en paréntesis.*
(Answer using direct object pronouns and the words in parenthesis.)

MODELO: ¿A qué hora van? (a las tres)
    Vamos a las tres.

1. *¿Quién nos escribe? (los tíos)*
2. *¿Qué te hace falta? (el tiempo)*
3. *¿Quién las compra? (Ramón)*
4. *¿Cuándo lo abren? (a las nueve)*
5. *¿Quién las vende? (las hermanas)*

E. *Responda con sí o con no y el verbo gustar.* (Answer with *sí* or *no* and the verb *gustar.)*

MODELO: ¿Te gusta el trabajo?
    Sí, (no, no) me gusta el trabajo.

1. *¿Les gusta el radio a Pepe y Gabino?*
2. *¿Te gustan las corbatas de seda?*
3. *¿Le gusta a José hacer ejercicios?*
4. *¿Nos gustan las familias de Enrique y Ana?*
5. *¿Les gustan a ellas las blusas de moda?*

F. *Traduzca las siguientes oraciones.* (Translate the following sentences.)

1. It's been a long time since we've been together.
2. I exercise twice a week.
3. What are you doing Sunday?
4. I'm resting because I'm tired.
5. She's opening the car door.

RESPUESTAS

A. 1. *¿Uds. escriben en español?/¿Escriben Uds. en espanol? 2. Yo sé la dirección del hotel. 3. Ella vive en México. 4. Él va a comprar pantalones. 5. ¿Estoy yo de moda?*

B. 1. *tenemos que* 2. *tenemos frío* 3. *tengo dolores* 4. *tiene razón*

C. 1. *mis quince buenos amigos* 2. *nuestros países* 3. *sus tías/las tías de Ud.* 4. *una gran mujer* 5. *un buen hombre* 6. *los diez hijos de mi hermano y los sobrinos de mi hermana* 7. *Hace dos semanas que están aquí./Están aquí hace dos semanas.*

D. 1. *Los tíos nos escriben.* 2. *Me hace falta el tiempo./El tiempo me hace falta.* 3. *Ramón las compra.* 4. *Lo abren a las nueve.* 5. *Las hermanas las venden.*

E. 1. *Sí, les gusta (No, no les gusta) el radio a Pepe y Gabino. 2. Sí, me gustan (No, no me gustan) las corbatas de seda. 3. Sí, le gusta (No, no le gusta) hacer ejercicios a José. 4. Sí, nos gustan (No, no nos gustan) las familias de Enrique y Ana. 5. Sí, les gustan a ellas (No, no les gustan a ellas) las blusas de moda.*

F. 1. *Hace mucho tiempo que no estamos juntos. 2. Yo hago ejercicio dos veces por semana. 3. ¿Qué vas a hacer el domingo? 4. Estoy descansando porque estoy cansada. 5. Ella abre la puerta del carro.*

LECTURA I

Now you're ready to practice your reading skills! While indeed you've been "reading" the dialogues, the four LECTURA passages offer you the chance to practice reading as you would read a newspaper article or essay. First, read through each passage without referring to the accompanying vocabulary notes. Try to understand the main idea and the main points, guessing the meanings of any new words from the context or from their similarities to English. Don't worry if a passage seems long or if you don't know each word; you can go back and reread it, checking the vocabulary notes to learn the exact meaning of the new words and phrases. Now, let's begin!

LA VIDA DE PILAR ROJAS

Me llamo Pilar Rojas y tengo veintitrés años. Soy de Cuba y ahora estoy viviendo en Miami con mi familia: mis padres, mi hermanito,[1] mis hermanas, mi tía Sofía, y mis abuelos—los padres de mi madre. Mis tíos, sus padres y mis primos también viven en Miami en una casa muy cerca. Tengo unos parientes[2] en Nueva York[3] y voy a visitarlos[4] en diciembre.

Ahora yo trabajo en un almacén. Me gusta este trabajo porque estoy muy ocupada durante todo el día. Hay siempre mucha gente en el almacén y me gusta hablarle. Cuando no estoy trabajando, me gusta leer o ir a la playa[5] con unos amigos. Todo el mundo va a la playa en los fines de semana. Nadamos,[6] bebemos, comemos, bailamos,[7] jugamos al volibol[8]. . . ¡Maravilloso! Si no hace buen tiempo estoy en casa y leo, escucho unos discos compactos, escribo unas cartas,[9] o hablo con mi familia.

VOCABULARIO

1. *hermanito*	younger brother
2. *unos parientes*	some relatives
3. *Nueva York*	New York
4. *Voy a visitarlos.*	I'm going to visit them.
5. *la playa*	the beach
6. *nadamos (nadar)*	we swim (to swim)
7. *bailamos (bailar)*	we dance (to dance)
8. *jugamos al volibol*	we play volleyball
9. *unas cartas*	some letters

LECCION 11

COMIENDO EN LOS RESTAURANTES.   Eating at restaurants.

A. DIALOGO

El almuerzo en la Hacienda Maya de Antigua, Guatemala.

MESERA: **Buenas tardes, señor. ¿Almuerza Ud.?**

JUAN CARLOS: **Sí, señorita. ¿Puedo ver el menú? ¿Cuál es la especialidad de la casa?**

MESERA: **La especialidad de la casa es gallo en chicha con ensalada mixta y frijoles refritos. La sopa del día es puré de maíz.**

JUAN CARLOS: **Todo huele muy bien, pero no tengo mucha hambre. Me apetece la sopa.**

MESERA: **Sí, señor. Y ¿para beber? Hay vino blanco, vino tinto, cerveza, jugos de frutas y batidos.**

JUAN CARLOS: **Una botella de gaseosa. ¿Se puede fumar aquí? No veo un aviso . . .**

MESERA: **No, señor. Esta sección es de no fumar. Vuelvo en seguida.**

Pasa hora y media:

JUAN CARLOS: **Senorita, por favor, un café y la cuenta. La comida y el servicio son excelentes.**

Lunch at the Hacienda Maya restaurant in Antigua, Guatemala.

WAITRESS: Good afternoon, sir. Are you having lunch?

JUAN CARLOS: Yes, miss. Can I see the menu? What is the house specialty?

WAITRESS: The house specialty is chicken cooked in cider, with a tossed salad and refried beans. Today's soup is cream of corn.

JUAN CARLOS: Everything smells delicious, but I'm not too hungry. I'd like the soup.

WAITRESS: Yes, sir. And to drink? There is white wine, red wine, beer, fruit juices, and milkshakes.

JUAN CARLOS: A bottle of carbonated mineral water. Is smoking permitted here? I don't see a sign . . .

WAITRESS: No, sir. This is a non-smoking section. I'll be right back.

An hour and a half later:

JUAN CARLOS: Miss, an espresso and the bill, please. The food and the service are excellent.

B. GRAMATICA Y USOS

1. RADICAL CHANGING *O>UE* VERBS

Remember that an infinitive (for example, *almorzar,* "to eat lunch") is made up of two parts: the root or the radical *(almorz-)* and the infinitive ending *(-ar)*. There are a number of *-ar* and *-er* verbs in which the radical or root vowel changes when it is stressed. One of the patterns for this change is from *o* to *ue*.

PODER   TO BE ABLE TO

yo	*puedo*		nosotros, -as	*podemos*
tú	*puedes*		vosotros, -as	*podéis*
Ud., él, ella	*puede*		Uds., ellos, ellas	*pueden*

Notice that the stress falls on the radical syllable in all forms of the singular and in the third person plural. In this case, the stressed vowel *o* changes to *ue,* but the regular personal ending is added. When the stress is not on the radical syllable, then the *o* is maintained (first and second persons plural). Other verbs like *poder* include:

almorzar	to eat lunch
costar	to cost
dormir	to sleep
encontrar	to find, to meet
morir	to die
mostrar	to show

Él puede tomar una sopa.
    He can have soup.

Almorzamos al mediodía.
    We eat lunch at 12:00 p.m.

Encuentran lo que buscan.
    They find what they are looking for.

Cuesta mucho.
    It costs a lot.

Me muestra el menú.
    He's showing me the menu.

    Radical-changing *o>oe* verbs will be indicated in the vocabulary lists as follows: *poder (o>ue).*

2. THE IMPERSONAL *SE*

The impersonal pronoun *se* is used with the third person singular of the verb to request or state information. In English, the impersonal subject is "one/you/people/they."

No se fuma aquí.
    No smoking here. (One/People do not smoke here.)

Se dice que es verdad.
    People say that it is true.

Se puede hacerlo.
You can do it.

3. THE VERBS *VER* AND *OLER*

These verbs are irregular. Notice how the initial *o-* in *oler* changes to *hue-* when the stress falls on the radical syllable, like the *o>ue* verbs above:

VER	TO SEE	*OLER*	TO SMELL
yo	*veo*	*yo*	*huelo*
tú	*ves*	*tú*	*hueles*
Ud., él, ella	*ve*	*Ud., él, ella*	*huele*
nosotros, -as	*vemos*	*nosotros, -as*	*olemos*
vosotros, -as	*veis*	*vosotros, -as*	*oléis*
Uds., ellos, ellas	*ven*	*Uds., ellos, ellas*	*huelen*

No veo un aviso.
I don't see a sign.

No vemos un restaurante en esta calle.
We don't see a restaurant in this street.

Todo huele muy bien.
Everything smells very good.

Olemos algo delicioso.
We smell something delicious.

VOCABULARIO

el restaurante	restaurant
mesera	waitress
mesero	waiter
servicio	service
cuenta	bill
el/*la* cliente	customer

el menú	menu
almorzar *(o>ue)*	to eat lunch
tomar el almuerzo	to eat lunch
tomar el desayuno	to eat breakfast
cenar	to dine, to eat dinner
¿Puedo ver el menú?	Can I see the menu?
Todo huele bien.	Everything smells good.
tener hambre	to be hungry
tener sed	to be thirsty
tomar	to take, to drink, to eat
¿Qué toma?	What are you drinking?
tomar un trago	to have an alcoholic drink
plato	dish
plato del día	daily special
gallo, pollo	chicken
gallo en chicha	chicken cooked in cider
frijoles refritos	refried beans
ensalada mixta	tossed salad
sopa del día	soup of the day
puré de maíz	corn purée
especialidad de la casa	house specialty
bebidas	drinks
vino blanco	white wine
vino tinto	red wine
cerveza	beer
gaseosa	carbonated mineral water
jugos	juices
batidos	milkshakes
el café	coffee
aviso	sign
costar *(o>ue)*	to cost
dormir *(o>ue)*	to sleep
encontrar *(oue)*	to find, to meet
excelente	excellent
fumar	to smoke
morir *(o>ue)*	to die
mostrar *(o>ue)*	to show
oler	to smell

poder *(o>ue)*	to be able, can
volver *(o>ue)*	to return
Vuelvo en seguida.	I'll be right back.

EXAMEN

A. *Conteste la pregunta en una oración completa usando la pista.*

MODELO: *¿Te gusta este restaurante? (sí)*
    Sí, me gusta este restaurante.

1. *¿Se puede fumar aquí? (no)*
2. *¿Qué toma Ud. con el almuerzo? (vino blanco)*
3. *¿Dónde almuerza él? (en el restaurante)*
4. *¿Cómo es el servicio? (excelente)*
5. *¿Tienes mucha hambre? (sí)*

B. *Escriba una nueva oración usando el sujeto entre paréntesis.*

MODELO: *¿Qué ves? (Uds.)*
    ¿Qué ven Uds.?

1. *Volvemos en seguida. (La mesera)*
2. *Ése cuesta mucho. (Ésos)*
3. *¿A qué hora almorzamos? (Uds.)*
4. *Ellas ven el aviso. (Tú)*
5. *Huelo algo. (Nosotros)*

C. *Traduzca al español usando el se impersonal.* (Translate into Spanish using the impersonal *se.*)

MODELO: *They work hard here.*
    Aqui se trabaja mucho.

1. People sleep a lot.
2. You need to rest every day.
3. One eats well here.
4. They say that it is easy.
5. Can one see the menu?

D. *Use la forma correcta de los verbos ver y oler.*

1. *Yo no (ver) muy bien en la oscuridad.*
2. *El café (oler) rico.*
3. *Lo que ustedes (oler) son los frijoles refritos.*
4. *No (ver) bien el menú sin mis lentes.*
5. *Nosotros (ver) las novelas todos los días.*
6. *¡Tú y Javier (oler) mal!*
7. *¿(ver) lo que hiciste, Óscar?*

NOTAS CULTURALES

Breakfast *(el desayuno)* is usually eaten between 8:00 and 10:00 A.M. and is a light meal. Sometimes people have a light snack *(un antojo,* or *un bocadillo*—which also means "sandwich") between breakfast and lunch, at around 11:00 A.M. At home or in a restaurant lunch usually begins between 12:30 and 2:00 P.M. and can last for two hours; it is the heaviest meal of the day *(la comida)*. Dinner, *la cena,* a lighter meal, is eaten from 8:00 P.M. until late. Corn and corn flour products are food staples of Mexico, Central America and other Latin American countries and eaten at lunchtime and dinner.

RESPUESTAS

A. 1. *No se puede fumar aquí.* 2. *Tomo vino blanco con el almuerzo.* 3. *Él almuerza en el restaurante.* 4. *El servicio es excelente.* 5. *Sí, tengo mucha hambre.*

B. 1. *La mesera vuelve en seguida.* 2. *Ésos cuestan mucho.* 3. *¿A qué hora almuerzan?* 4. *Tú ves el aviso.* 5. *Nosotros olemos algo.*

C. 1. *Se duerme mucho.* 2. *Se necesita descansar todos los días.* 3. *Se come bien aquí.* 4. *Se dice que es fácil.* 5. *¿Se puede ver el menú?*

D. 1. *Yo no veo muy bien en la oscuridad.* 2. *El café huele rico.* 3. *Lo que ustedes huelen son los frijoles refritos.* 4. *No veo bien el menú sin mis lentes.* 5. *Nosotros vemos las novelas todos los días.* 6. *¡Tú y Javier huelen mal!* 7. *¿Ves lo que hiciste, Óscar?*

LECCION 12

POR TELEFONO.   Making a phone call.

A. DIALOGO

Por teléfono de Nueva York a Buenos Aires, Argentina.

JAVIER: **Sí, operadora, quiero hacer una llamada internacional persona a persona por cobrar a Buenos Aires, Argentina.**

OPERADORA: **¿Con quién quiere Ud. hablar?**

JAVIER: **Quiero hablar con mi esposa, la Señora Gil. El código de la ciudad es treinta y siete, y el teléfono es el tres, noventa y tres, sesenta y cinco, ochenta y siete.**

OPERADORA: **Muy bien, señor. Momentito. . . . Lo siento, señor. Pienso que la línea internacional está ocupada. Voy a intentar comunicar nuevamente. . . . El teléfono está sonando. . . . No atienden, señor.**

JAVIER: **Por favor, operadora, ¿se puede volver a llamar? A menudo no atienden inmediatamente.**

OPERADORA: **Bueno, senor. Está sonando ahora.**

Calling from New York to Buenos Aires, Argentina.

JAVIER: Yes, operator. I want to make a collect international call person to person to Buenos Aires, Argentina.

OPERATOR: With whom do you want to speak?

JAVIER: I want to speak to my wife, Mrs. Gil. The city code is 37 and the telephone number is 393-6587.

OPERATOR: Very well, sir. One moment. . . . I'm sorry, sir. I think that the international line is busy. I'll try to call once again. . . . The phone is ringing. . . . There is no answer, sir.

JAVIER: Please, operator, can you call again? Often they don't answer immediately.

OPERATOR: All right, sir. It's ringing now.

B. GRAMATICA Y USOS

1. RADICAL-CHANGING *E>IE* VERBS

Another group of radical-changing verbs are those that change *e* to *ie*.

PENSAR   TO THINK

yo	*pienso*	nosotros, -as	*pensamos*
tú	*piensas*	~~vosotros, -as~~	~~pensáis~~
Ud., él, ella	*piensa*	Uds., ellos, ellas	*piensan*

Note the use of pensar with these prepositions:

pensar en   ~think of~   to think of, about (someone, something)

pensar de   ~opinion~   to think of; to have an opinion of (someone, something)

¿En qué piensa Ud.?   ~3rd prsn S~
What are you thinking about?

Esto me da en que pensar.   ~infin. pensar~
This gives me something to think about.

Pienso en llamarle.
I'm thinking about calling him.   ~Pienso en cocinar el almuerzo.~

¿Qué piensa del libro?
What do you think of the book?

~formal Ud.~

These radical-changing verbs will be indicated in the vocabulary by "*(e>ie)*" following the infinitive.

Other verbs like *pensar* include:

atender	to answer (phone, door), to attend to
entender	to understand
perder	to lose
querer	to want
sentir	to feel, to regret

No atienden.
> They don't answer. No one is answering.

Entendemos el inglés.
> We understand English.

Quiero llamar a Marcos.
> I want to call Mark.

Ahora siento frío.
> I feel cold now.

Pierden siempre mi número de teléfono.
> They always lose my phone number.

2. ADVERBS

Many English adverbs are easily recognized by the ending "-ly." The Spanish adverbial ending is *-mente*. It is added to adjectives ending in a consonant; to the feminine form *(-a)* of adjectives in *o;* and to the final *e* of any adjective.

o ——> a mente

normal > normalmente	normally
nuevo > nuevamente	once again
rápido > rápidamente	rapidly
inmediato > inmediatamente	immediately
frecuente > frecuentemente	frequently

108

When two or more adverbs are used together, only the *final* one has the
-mente ending:

Ella trabaja diligente, rápida y eficientemente.
She works diligently, quickly, and efficiently.

Some common adverbs do not end in *-mente:*

hoy	today
mañana	tomorrow
a menudo	often
mucho[1]	much, a lot, hard, a great deal
aquí	here
allí	there (far away)
siempre	always
muy	very
después	after
antes	before
todavía	still

Pierden siempre mi número de teléfono.
They always lose my phone number.

A menudo no atienden inmediatamente.
Often they don't answer immediately.

Llamo después de comer.
I'll call after eating.

Está aquí.
It's here.

Están allí.
They are (over) there.

La línea está todavía ocupada.
The line is still busy.

---

[1] When used as an adverb, *mucho* is invariable: *Llueve mucho.* It's raining hard. *Ella llama mucho.* She calls a lot/a great deal.

3. OTHER QUESTION WORDS WITH *¿QUIÉN?*

Use *¿Con quién . . . ?* for "With whom?":

¿Con quién quiere Ud. hablar?
   With whom do you want to speak?

Use *¿A quién . . . ?* for "To whom?":

¿A quién vas a llamar?
   Whom are you going to call?

Use *¿Para quién?* for "For whom?":

¿Para quién es la llamada?
   For whom is the call?

Use *¿De quién?* for "Whose?" or "Of whom?":

¿De quién es el abrigo?
   Whose coat is it?

el/*la* operador*(a)*	operator
llamada por cobrar	collect call
llamada a larga distancia	long distance call
internacional	international
persona a persona	person to person
La línea está ocupada.	The line is busy.
¿Puede volver a llamar?	Can you call again?
¿Con quién quiere Ud. hablar?	With whom do you want to speak?
guía telefónica	telephone book
número equivocado	wrong number
Momentito.	Just a moment. One moment.
telefonear	to telephone
hacer una llamada	to make a call
marcar	to dial
tocar/sonar	to ring
atender *(e>ie)*	to answer (phone, door)
comunicar	to be talking on the phone
estar ocupado	to be busy
colgar *(o>ue)*	to hang up
¿Con quién hablo?	With whom am I speaking?
sentir *(e>ie)*	to feel, regret
Lo siento.	I'm sorry.
entender *(e>ie)*	to understand
pensar *(e>ie)*	to think, believe
pensar en	to think about (someone/something)
pensar de	to have an opinion of (someone/something)
querer *(e>ie)*	to wish, want
querer decir	to mean
volver *(o>ue)* *(+ a + infinitive)*	to do something again
nuevamente	once again
a menudo	often
inmediatamente	immediately

EXAMEN

A. *Conteste la pregunta en una oración completa usando la pista.*

MODELO: Qué hace ella? (atender el teléfono)
   Ella atiende el teléfono.

1. ¿Qué quiere hacer? (una llamada internacional)
2. ¿Qué número marcas? (el 662-3558)
3. ¿Qué pasa con la línea? (está ocupada)
4. ¿Cuál es el código de la ciudad? (el 155)
5. ¿Con quién quiere Ud. hablar? (con la señorita González)

B. *Responda con el verbo en la forma adecuada.* (Give the appropriate form of the verb.)

MODELO: Yo _____ el teléfono después de hablar. (colgar)/cuelgo

1. Yo lo _____. (sentir)
2. ¿En quién _____ tú? (pensar)
3. Ella _____ telefonearnos. (querer)
4. ¿Quiénes _____ el teléfono? (atender)
5. Jorge y yo lo _____ mucho (sentir).

C. *Traduzca al español.*

1. With whom do you want to speak?
2. We want to do the work immediately.
3. The operator says that it's an international call.
4. What does this mean?
5. The phone is still ringing.
6. I'm hanging up now.

D. *Convierta los adjetivos en adverbios.*

MODELO: (Normal) voy al supermercado los lunes.
   Normalmente voy al supermercado los lunes.

1. Quiero que vengas (inmediato).
2. Contesta el teléfono (rápido).

3. *Nosotros vamos al parque (frecuente).*
4. *Javier hace su trabajo (eficiente).*
5. *Consuelo y José (normal) vienen los domingos.*

NOTAS CULTURALES

While every Spanish-speaking country has a telephone system, reliability varies greatly from country to country and even from city to city.

Telephone numbers are usually given in groups of tens; when three numbers appear together, they are given with the first digit standing alone, as in the dialogue.

¿Aló? is used most often in Chile and Argentina to say "hello" on the phone. You might also use and hear the following:

Mexico:	*Bueno.*
Spain:	*Diga. Dígame.*
Argentina and Uruguay:	*Hola.*
Cuba and Puerto Rico:	*Oigo.*
Colombia:	*A ver.*

RESPUESTAS

A. 1. *Quiero hacer una llamada internacional.* 2. *Marco el seis sesenta y dos, treinta y cinco, cincuenta y ocho.* 3. *La línea está ocupada.* 4. *El código de la ciudad es el ciento cincuenta y cinco.* 5. *Quiero hablar con la señorita González.*

B. 1. *siento* 2. *piensas* 3. *quiere* 4. *atienden* 5. *sentimos.*

C. 1. *¿Con quién quiere Ud. hablar?* 2. *Queremos hacer el trabajo inmediatamente.* 3. *La operadora dice que es una llamada internacional.* 4. *¿Qué quiere decir esto?* 5. *El teléfono todavía está tocando/sonando.* 6. *Cuelgo ahora.*

D. 1. *Quiero que vengas inmediatamente.* 2. *Contesta el teléfono rapidamente.* 3. *Nosotros vamos al parque frecuentemente.* 4. *Javier hace su trabajo eficientemente.* 5. *Consuelo y José normalmente vienen los domingos.*

LECCION 13

EN LA JOYERÍA.   At the jewelry store.

A. DIALOGO

En la joyería Toledano de Toledo, España.

ELENA: **Buenos días, señor. ¿En qué puedo servirle?**

GERMAN: **Vengo a comprarle una pulsera a mi esposa para su cumpleaños.**

ELENA: **¿Desea una pulsera de oro, de plata o de diamantes?**

GERMAN: **No sé nada de joyas, pero conozco bien a mi esposa. A ella le gustan las joyas simples, no ostentosas. Esa pulsera de plata es muy preciosa. Me apetece mucho. ¿Cuánto piden Uds.?**

ELENA: **¿Sabe que tenemos una venta especial esta semana? Ofrecemos una rebaja de veinticinco por ciento sobre el precio de la etiqueta.**

GERMAN: **¡Qué bueno! La voy a llevar. ¿Puedo pagar con una tarjeta de crédito?**

ELENA: **¡Cómo no! Voy a envolverla.**

GERMAN: **Le agradezco mucho.**

At the Toledano jewelry shop in Toledo, Spain.

ELENA: Good morning, sir. How can I help you?

GERMAN: I've come to buy a bracelet for my wife for her birthday.

ELENA: Do you want a bracelet made of gold, silver, or diamonds?

GERMAN: I don't know anything about jewelry, but I know my wife well.

She likes simple, understated jewelry. That silver bracelet is very beautiful. It appeals to me very much. How much are you asking?

ELENA: Do you know that we're having a special sale this week? We're offering a 25% discount on the price tag.

GERMAN: How wonderful! I'll take it. Can I pay with a credit card?

ELENA: Of course. I'll wrap it.

GERMAN: I'm very grateful to you.

B. GRAMATICA Y USOS

1. RADICAL-CHANGING *E>I* VERBS

The final group of radical changing verbs are *-ir* verbs in which the radical *e* changes to *i* whenever the radical vowel is stressed.

PEDIR   TO ASK FOR

yo	*pido*	nosotros, -as	*pedimos*
tú	*pides*	vosotros, -as	*pedís*
Ud., él, ella	*pide*	Uds., ellos, ellas	*piden*

Other verbs like *pedir* include:

impedir	to prevent
repetir	to repeat
servir	to serve

Piden la pulsera.
They're asking for the bracelet.

El vendedor repite el precio.
The salesman repeats the price.

¿Para qué sirve esto?
What is this for?

The gerunds of these verbs also change from *e* to *i: pidendo, sirviendo, repitiendo.*

2. VERBS ENDING IN -*CER* AND -*CIR*

The only irregularity in verbs ending in -*cer* or -*cir* is in the first person of the present tense, which adds a *z* before the -*co* ending:

CONOCER   TO KNOW, TO BE ACQUAINTED WITH

yo	*conozco*	nosotros, -as	*conocemos*
tú	*conoces*	vosotros, -as	*conocéis*
Ud., él, ella	*conoce*	Uds., ellos, ellas	*conocen*

Other verbs like *conocer:*

agradecer	to be grateful, to thank
ofrecer	to offer
parecer	to seem

Conozco bien a mi esposa.
I know my wife well.

Le agradezco mucho.[1]
I'm very grateful/thankful to you.

Me ofrecen una rebaja.
They're offering me a discount.
Verbs ending in -*cir* have the same change in the first person, but maintain the regular -*ir* conjugation endings afterward:

---

[1] This phrase is interchangeable with the one seen in *Lección* 2: *Le estoy muy agradecido.* I'm very grateful to you.

yo	*produzco*	nosotros, -as	*producimos*
tú	*produces*	vosotros, -as	*producís*
Ud., él, ella	*produce*	Uds., ellos, ellas	*producen*

Another verb conjugated like *producir* is *traducir* (to translate).

Producen 200 pulseras al día.
They produce 200 bracelets per day.

Traduzco un libro al español.
I'm translating a book into Spanish.

3. THE USES OF *SABER* AND *CONOCER*

Both verbs mean "to know" in Spanish. However, each has specific uses. *Saber* means "to know" facts and "to know how to":

No sé nada de joyas.
I don't know anything about jewelry.

¿Sabes dónde vive Juan?
Do you know where Juan lives?

¿Saben conducir?
Do they know how to drive?

Conocer means "to be acquainted with," or "to meet" when referring to people. Sometimes it means to know things about which you can have an intimate knowledge (cities, countries, etc.). The personal *a* is almost always used with this verb.

Conozco bien a mi esposa.
I know my wife well.

Conocemos a Marisol y Rubén.
We know Marisol and Rubén.

Conocen todas las callecitas de la Plaza Mayor.
They know all the tiny streets of the Plaza Mayor.

VOCABULARIO

haciendo compras	shopping
¿En qué puedo servirle?	How can I help you?
Vengo a comprar . . .	I've come to buy
¿Puedo verlo?	May I see it?
¿Cuánto piden Uds.?	How much are you asking?
¡Qué bueno!	How wonderful!
Me apetece mucho.	It appeals to me a great deal.
precioso	handsome, precious; beautiful
bonito	beautiful
ostentoso	ostentatious
simple	simple
Lo voy a llevar.	I'll take it.
¿Puedo pagar con una tarjeta de crédito?	Can I pay with a credit card?
pagar en efectivo	to pay cash
Voy a envolverlo.	I'll wrap it.
rebaja	discount
rebaja de veinticinco por ciento	a 25% discount
etiqueta	price tag, sales tag
venta	sale
venta especial	special sale
conocer	to know, to be acquainted with, to meet
saber	to know, to know how to
ofrecer	to offer
agradecer	to be grateful to, to thank
apetecer	to appeal to
envolver *(o>ue)*	to wrap
impedir *(e>i)*	to prevent
pedir *(e>i)*	to request, ask for

repetir *(e>i)*	to repeat
servir *(e>i)*	to serve
producir	to produce
traducir	to translate
¡Cómo no!	Of course!

EXAMEN

A. *Escriba nuevamente la oración usando el nuevo sujeto en paréntesis.*
(Rewrite the sentence using the new subject in parenthesis.)

MODELO: Ofrezco la pulsera. (tú)
Tú ofreces la pulsera.

1. *Conocemos a Juan. (Yo)*
2. *Ofrecen una rebaja. (Nosotros)*
3. *Pedimos información. (Él)*
4. *¿Sirven café por la mañana? (Tú)*
5. *Ellas traducen libros al español. (Yo)*

B. *Traduzca la oración usando "saber" o "conocer."*

MODELO: She knows how to speak Spanish.
Sabe hablar español.

1. We know the address of the hotel.
2. I know Mary very well.
3. She is acquainted with your aunt and uncle.
4. Do you (familiar) know how to drive?
5. She knows how to translate it.

C. *Dé las expresiones en español.* (Give the expressions in Spanish.)

1. How wonderful!
2. I don't know anything.
3. Of course!
4. How can I help you, madam?
5. Can I pay with a credit card?

D. *Use el verbo correcto en las siguientes oraciones.*

1. *Yo (traducir) documentos para las Naciones Unidas.*
2. *Me (ofrecer) un precio bajo en la joyería porque mi hermano es el gerente.*
3. *Tú te (parecer) a tu mamá.*
4. *Elena siempre (decir) la verdad.*
5. *Javier y Estela (producir) películas de terror.*
6. *Mi esposa y yo (agradecer) su presencia en nuestra fiesta.*

NOTAS CULTURALES

One of the most glorious cities in Spain, Toledo, has always been a thriving center of culture. Located about 50 miles south of Madrid, it is the capital of the Castilla-La Mancha region. Christians, Arabs, and Jews lived here together harmoniously during medieval times. El Greco, the giant of Spanish Golden Age art, worked here, and today you can visit his home, which is a museum. Toledo is a Spanish national monument.

RESPUESTAS

A. 1. *conozco* 2. *ofrecemos* 3. *pide* 4. *sirves* 5. *traduzco.*

B. 1. *Sabemos la dirección del hotel.* 2. *Conozco muy bien a Maria.* 3. *Ella conoce a sus tíos.* 4. *¿Sabes conducir?* 5. *Ella sabe traducirlo.*

C. 1. *¡Qué bueno!* 2. *No sé nada.* 3. *¡Cómo no!* 4. *¿En qué puedo servirle, señora?* 5. *¿Puedo pagar con una tarjeta de crédito?*

D. 1. *Yo traduzco documentos para las Naciones Unidas.* 2. *Me ofrecen un precio bajo en la joyería porque mi hermano es el gerente.* 3. *Tú te pareces a tu mamá.* 4. *Elena siempre dice la verdad.* 5. *Javier y Estela producen películas de terror.* 6. *Mi esposa y yo agradecemos su presencia en nuestra fiesta.*

LECCION 14

EN LA FARMACIA.   At the pharmacy.

A. DIALOGO

En la Farmacia Huracán de Guadalajara, México.

GUADALUPE: **Buenos días. Tengo una receta de mi médico. La necesito lo más pronto posible.**

FARMACEUTICO: **Si Ud. me la deja ahora, se la lleno a Ud. en quince minutos. ¿Se va Ud. ahora, o busca otra cosa?**

GUADALUPE: **No, no me voy. Debo escoger varios otros productos. ¿Qué recomienda Ud. pare un resfriado?**

FARMACEUTICO: **Ud. puede elegir entre las marcas de jarabe para la tos o pastillas para la tos. Si el enfermo también tiene fiebre, usualmente escoge aspirina. Esos productos están en la sección diez.**

GUADALUPE: **Bien. Y mi hija necesita un antiácido.**

FARMACEUTICO: **Un buen antiácido protege el estómago. Están en la sección tres. ¿Necesita algo más?**

GUADALUPE: **Sí. ¿Dónde está el esmalte para las uñas?**

FARMACEUTICO: **Está en la sección de cosméticos a la entrada de la farmacia.**

At the Huracán Pharmacy in Guadalajara, Mexico.

GUADALUPE: Good morning. I have a prescription from my doctor. I need it as soon as possible.

PHARMACIST: If you leave it with me now, I'll fill it for you in fifteen minutes. Are you leaving now, or are you looking for something else?

GUADALUPE: No, I'm not leaving. I have to get other products. What do you recommend for a cold?

PHARMACIST: You can select from among the brands of cough syrup or cough drops. If the sick person also has fever, he/she usually chooses aspirin. Those products are in section ten.

GUADALUPE: Fine. And my daughter needs an antacid.

PHARMACIST: A good antacid protects the stomach. They're in section three. Do you need something else?

GUADALUPE: Yes. Where do you sell nail polish?

PHARMACIST: It's in the cosmetics section at the entrance to the pharmacy.

B. GRAMATICA Y USOS

1. DOUBLE OBJECT PRONOUNS

We have seen the use of individual direct and indirect object pronouns and their positioning in sentences. It is possible to use both kinds of object pronouns together in one sentence.

We give the money to the pharmacist.   We give it to him.

Whereas in English the word order is "direct object pronoun" + "indirect object pronoun" (She is giving it to me.), in Spanish it is the other way around:

"indirect object pronoun" + "direct object pronoun"
Ella me la deja ahora.

When you use the third person indirect object pronouns *(le, les)* in conjunction with a third person direct object pronoun, the indirect object pronoun changes to the form *se:*

Yo se la lleno a Ud. en quince minutes.
I'll fill it for you in fifteen minutes.

122

The *se* replaces the indirect object *le* and, like all indirect objects, is clarified by *a* ı the prepositional object pronoun.

While double object pronouns normally precede the conjugated verb as two separate words, they can also be attached to the end of the infinitive or to the end of the gerund, and then form one word with it.

Está dándonoslos. (or: *Nos los está dando.*)
   He's giving them to us.

Quieren dártelas. (or: *Te las quieren dar.*)
   They want to give them to you.

A written accent mark must be placed on the original point of stress in the infinitive or gerund: *dándonoslos, dártelas.*

2. VERBS ENDING IN *-GER* AND *-GIR*

Verbs which end in *-ger* and *-gir* change the *g* to *j* before the *-o* of *yo* the first-person singular. In addition, the *-gir* verbs have a radical change of *e* to *i:*

ESCOGER TO CHOOSE			*ELEGIR* TO SELECT	
yo	*escojo*		*yo*	*elijo*
tú	*escoges*		*tú*	*eliges*
Ud., él, ella	*escoge*		*Ud., él, ella*	*elige*
nosotros, -as	*escogemos*		*nosotros, -as*	*elegimos*
vosotros, -as	*escogéis*		*vosotros, -as*	*elegís*
Uds., ellos, ellas	*escogen*		*Uds., ellos, ellas*	*eligen*

Gerunds for *-gir* verbs with a radical *e* change *e* to *i: eligiendo.* Other verbs like *escoger:*

dirigir   to direct
proteger   to protect

Usualmente escoge aspirina.
   He usually chooses aspirin.

Un buen antiácido protege el estómago.
A good antacid protects the stomach.

Eligen buenos productos.
They select good products.

3. THE VERB *SALIR*

The verb *salir* (to leave, to go out) is irregular in the *yo* form:

SALIR   TO LEAVE

yo	salgo	nosotros, -as	salimos
tú	sales	vosotros, -as	salís
Ud., él, ella	sale	Uds., ellos, ellas	salen

Salimos de aquí rápidamente.
We're leaving here quickly.

Salen para Nueva York mañana.
They are leaving for New York tomorrow.

Salgo esta tarde.
I'm going out this afternoon.

VOCABULARIO

la farmacia	pharmacy
farmacéutico, -*a*	pharmacist
receta	prescription
recetar	to prescribe
el/*la* **médico**	doctor
llenar	to fill, to fill out
llenar una receta	to fill a prescription
resfriado	cold

la tos	cough
el jarabe para la tos	cough syrup
pastilla	pill, tablet
pastilla para la tos	cough drop
aspirina	aspirin
antiácido	antacid
los cosméticos	cosmetics
la uña	nail
el esmalte de uñas	nail polish
producto	product
marca	brand (name)
entregar	to give, deliver
recomendar *(e>ie)*	to recommend
salir	to leave
escoger	to choose
proteger	to protect
elegir *(e>i)*	to select, elect
cepillo *(de dientes)*	(tooth) brush
desodorante	deodorant
desinfectante	disinfectant
espejo	mirror
jabón	soap
peine	comb
vendas	bandages
contra	against
cosa	thing
entrada	entrance
salida	exit
usualmente	usually
varios, *-as*	several
lo más pronto posible	as soon as possible
¿Necesita algo más?	Do you need something else?

EXAMEN

A. *Conteste la pregunta en una oración completa usando la pista.*

MODELO: ¿Qué tiene? (una tos constante)
Tiene una tos constante.

1. *¿Cuándo sale Ud? (lo más pronto posible)*
2. *¿Qué escoge él? (un buen antiácido)*
3. *¿Qué toma ella para la fiebre? (aspirina)*
4. *¿Dónde están las pastillas para la tos? (a la entrada de la farmacia)*
5. *¿Qué te recomienda el médico? (un jarabe para la tos)*

B. *Añada los objectos en paréntesis a las oraciones.* (Add the object pronouns in parenthesis to the sentences.)

MODELO: Van a comprarlo. (nos)
Van a comprárnoslo.

1. *Yo lo entrego mañana. (te)*
2. *Ellas la venden a Juan. (se)*
3. *Quieren comprarla. (nos)*
4. *Van a entregar. (nos, lo)*
5. *Estamos recetando. (te, las)*

C. *Escriba en español.*

1. Say that you are choosing a cough drop.
2. Ask when your friend will deliver them (masc. pl.) to you (fam. sing).
3. Say that you are buying him an antacid to protect his stomach.
4. Ask when you the pharmacist can fill it (the prescription) for you.
5. Say that you don't know which brand to buy.

NOTAS CULTURALES

The Latin American pharmacist is permitted to give simple injections: such as allergy shots, flu shots—often not under the most hygienic of circumstances—and he/she acts as a doctor in prescribing medications. Another type of pharmacy in Latin America and the Caribbean is the *botánica,* where all sorts of herbs are sold to cure illnesses, and where one can obtain products related to popular spiritist religions, such as the Afro-Caribbean *santería.*

Because many Latin Americans do not have medical insurance and cannot afford regular visits to their doctor, they often self-medicate or see pharmacists as "preliminary" doctors. Pharmacists many times prescribe—legally or illegally—all sorts of medications and treatments. They may also give nutritional advice, physical therapy, and homeopathic treatments. You can find pharmacies on almost every block in the downtown section *(el centro)* of every city in Latin America.

RESPUESTAS

A. 1. *Salgo lo más pronto posible.* 2. *El escoge un buen antiácido.* 3. *Ella toma aspirina para la fiebre.* 4. *Las pastillas para la tos están a la entrada de la farmacia.* 5. *El médico me recomienda un jarabe para la tos.*

B. 1. *Yo te lo entrego mañana.* 2. *Ellas se la venden a Juan.* 3. *Quieren comprárnosla./Nos la quieren comprar.* 4. *Van a entregárnoslo/Nos lo van a entregar.* 5. *Estamos recetándotelas./Te las estamos recetando.*

C. 1. *Estoy escogiendo un jarabe para la tos./Escojo un jarabe para la tos.* 2. *¿Cuándo vas a entregármelos?* 3. *Estoy comprándole un antiácido para protegerle el estómago.* 4. *¿Cuándo puede llenármela el farmacéutico?* 5. *No sé qué marca comprar.*

LECCION 15

ACTIVIDADES DIARIAS.   Daily Activities.

A. DIALOGO

¡A levantarse! Son las cinco de la mañana en Fuenguadarrama, España.
Toca el despertador.

JULIO: **¡Ay, qué ruido!**

ANTONIA: **¿Qué dices? ¿Qué hora es?**

JULIO: **Son las cinco. Me levanto ahora y me baño.**

ANTONIA: **Pero, ¿por qué? ¿a esta hora temprana de la mañana?**

JULIO: **Comienza hoy el nuevo horario de trabajo. Voy a reunirme con el nuevo jefe a las siete y media; nos desayunamos juntos. Me pongo el traje azul.**

ANTONIA: **¿Y cómo se llama tu nuevo jefe?**

JULIO: **Se llama Diego Rodríguez-López. Vamos a vernos todos los martes a la misma hora.**

ANTONIA: **¡No lo puedo creer, a las siete y media! No te vas a acostumbrar a trabajar estas largas horas. Vas a enfermarte.**

JULIO: **¡Qué va, Antonia! Nosotros nos cuidamos mucho. Comemos bien, hacemos ejercicios. Tú lo sabes.**

ANTONIA: **Yo sí sé una cosa: que debes encontrarte otro puesto.**

Get up! Five o'clock in the morning in Fuenguadarrama, Spain.
The alarm clock rings.

JULIO: Oh, how noisy!

ANTONIA: What are you saying? What time is it?

JULIO: It's five o'clock. I'm getting up now and I'm bathing.

ANTONIA: But why, at this early hour of the morning?

JULIO: The new work schedule begins today. I'm going to meet with the new boss at seven thirty; we're having breakfast together. I'm putting on my blue suit.

ANTONIA: What's your new boss's name?

JULIO: His name is Diego Rodríguez-López. We're going to see each other every Tuesday at the same time.

ANTONIA: I can't believe it, at seven thirty! You won't get used to working these long hours. You'll get sick.

JULIO: Nonsense, Antonia! We take care of ourselves. We eat well and we exercise. You know that.

ANTONIA: I do know one thing: you should find another job.

B. GRAMATICA Y USOS

1. THE REFLEXIVE VERB

A reflexive verb shows that the subject of an action is also the object (recipient) of that same action. The action literally "reflects" back. This structure exists in English, but is used only for emphasis: "I did it to myself" ("myself" is a reflexive object pronoun). Reflexive verbs in Spanish are indicated by the reflexive pronoun *se* attached to the *-ar, -er,* or *-ir* infinitive, which distinguishes the reflexive form from the nonreflexive form of that same infinitive. Compare the verbs *levantar,* "to lift, raise," and *levantarse,* "to get up" ("to get oneself up"):

Él levanta los libros.
    He lifts the books.

Él se levanta temprano.
    He gets (himself) up early.

Many infinitives have both nonreflexive and reflexive forms with different meanings: for example: *lavar* (to wash) and *lavarse* (to wash oneself);

La madre lava al hijo.
The mother washes the child.

La madre se lava las manos.
The mother washes her hands.

In *Lección* 4 we saw the difference between *ganar* (to earn) and *ganarse* in the idiomatic expression *ganarse la vida* (to earn a living):

¡Ella gana mucho por año!
She earns a lot per year!

Es difícil ganarse la vida.
It's hard to earn a living.

2. THE REFLEXIVE OBJECT PRONOUNS

To conjugate the reflexive verb you must know the reflexive object pronouns. They are already familiar to you from your study of other types of object pronouns:

me	myself
te	yourself (familiar sg.)
se[1]	herself, itself, yourself (formal)
nos	ourselves
os	(familiar pl.)
se	themselves, yourselves (formal)

Vamos a bañarnos ahora.
We are going to bathe (ourselves) now.

¿Quieres ponerte un suéter?
Do you want to put on a sweater?

Reflexive object pronouns are positioned just like the direct and indirect object pronouns. In a sentence with other object pronouns the order is:
reflexive object + indirect object + direct object

[1] The word *se* serves as reflexive object pronoun for all third persons.

Ella se las pone todos los días.
She wears them every day.

Sometimes, reflexive object pronouns are used simply for emphasis:

Debes encontrarte otro puesto.
You should find (yourself) another job.

Me lo como todo.
I'm going to eat it all up (myself).

3. THE RECIPROCAL OBJECT PRONOUNS

A reciprocal verb expresses a mutual action or relationship; it requires a reciprocal pronoun. Thus in English:

> We love each other.
> They visit one another.

In Spanish, the reflexive pronouns *se* and *nos* can have the reciprocal meanings "each other" and "one another."

¿Cuándo se ven Uds.?
When do you see each other?

Nosotros nos vemos todos los martes.
We see one another every Tuesday.

For clarification, the expression *uno al otro* or una a la otra can be used.

Nosotros nos vemos uno al otro todos los martes.
We see one another every Tuesday.

4. THE VERBS *LLAMAR* AND *LLAMARSE*

The verb *llamar* means "to call":

Yo lo llamo por teléfono.
   I call him by telephone.

The verb *llamarse* means "to be called, to be named"

¿Cómo se llama Ud.?
   What is your name? (How do you call yourself?)

Me llamo Pedro.
   My name is Pedro. (I call myself Pedro.)

5. THE VERBS *PONER* AND *PONERSE*

The verb *poner* (to put, to place) is irregular:

PONER   TO PUT

yo	*pongo*	nosotros, -as	*ponemos*
tú	*pones*	vosotros, -as	*ponéis*
Ud., él, ella	*pone*	Uds., ellos, ellas	*ponen*

Pone el espejo en la bolsa.
   She's putting the mirror in the bag.

The reflexive form, *ponerse,* means "to put on (clothing)."

Me pongo el traje azul.
   I'm putting on the blue suit.

VOCABULARIO

actividades diarias	daily activities
el despertador	alarm clock
despertar *(e>ie)*	to awake (someone else)
despertarse *(e>ie)*	to awake (oneself)
levantar	to lift, raise
levantarse	to get up
lavar	to wash (someone else, something)
lavarse	to wash (oneself)
bañar	to bathe (someone else)
bañarse	to bathe (oneself)
cepillarse	to brush one's teeth
vestir *(e>i)*	to dress (someone else)
vestirse *(e>i)*	to dress (oneself)
peinarse	to comb one's hair
poner	to put, place
ponerse	to put on (clothing)
desayunarse	to eat breakfast
acostarse *(o>ue)*	to go to bed
llamar	to call
llamarse	to be named, to call oneself
¿Cómo se llama Ud.?	What is your name?
Me llamo . . .	My name is . . .
¡Qué va!	What nonsense!
Se llama . . .	His (her, your) name is
¡Qué ruido!	What a noise!/How noisy!
acostumbrarse a	to get used to
cuidar	to take care of (someone else)
cuidarse	to take care of oneself
reunirse	to meet, to get together
horario	schedule
sí	yes, indeed (emphatic)
Yo sí sé una cosa.	I do know one thing.

EXAMEN

A. *Conteste la pregunta que oye en una oración completa usando la pista.*

MODELO: *¿Qué se pone el sábado? (jeans)*
         Se pone jeans el sábado.

1. *¿Se levanta Ud. tarde por la mañana? (no, temprano)*
2. *¿A qué hora se desayuna? (8:30)*
3. *¿Se baña Ud. por la mañana o por la noche? (por la noche)*
4. *¿A qué hora se acuesta? (la medianoche)*
5. *¿Qué se pone Ud. para ir a trabajar? (un traje)*

B. *Cambie al verbo reflexivo y escriba de nuevo la oración.* (Use the reflexive verb and rewrite the sentence.)

MODELO: *Yo visto al niño.*
         Yo me visto.

1. *Yo baño al niño.*
2. *¿Por qué levantas temprano a su hijo?*
3. *Vamos a lavar los platos.*
4. *¿Cuándo van a despertar a su esposa?*
5. *Ella pone la blusa a su hermana.*

C. *Traduzca al español.*

1. What are your (pl.) names?
2. We're eating breakfast together at 8:00.
3. They know each other.
4. Why do you (familiar) get up early?
5. They can bathe the children tomorrow morning.

NOTAS CULTURALES

In Spain and Latin America, modern business practices have come into conflict with the traditional attitude towards work. There is a popular saying in Spanish:

¡Trabajo para vivir, no vivo para trabajar!
I work to live, I don't live to work!

And generally people seem to take this to heart, celebrating more holidays and taking more vacations than North Americans.

RESPUESTAS

A. 1. *No, me levanto temprano por la mañana.* 2. *Me desayuno a las ocho y media.* 3. *Me baño por la noche.* 4. *Me acuesto a la medianoche.* 5. *Me pongo un traje para ir a trabajar.*

B. 1. *Yo me baño.* 2. *¿Por qué te levantas temprano?* 3. *Vamos a lavarnos.* 4. *¿Cuándo van a despertarse?* 5. *Ella se pone la blusa.*

C. 1. *¿Cómo se llaman Uds.?* 2. *Nos desayunamos juntos a las ocho.* 3. *Ellos se cuidan uno del otro.* 4. *¿Por qué te levantas temprano?* 5. *Pueden bañar a los niños mañana por la mañana.*

TERCER REPASO

A. *Cambie la oración usando el se impersonal.* (Change the sentence, using the impersonal *se.)*

MODELO: Vivimos bien aquí.
Se vive bien aquí.

1. *Almorzamos a la una y media en España.*
2. *Muchas personas comen bien en los restaurantes venezolanos.*
3. *No fuman aquí.*
4. *Decimos que es excelente.*
5. *¿Podemos saber cuál es la especialidad de la casa?*

B. *Responda con las palabras entre paréntesis.*

MODELO: *¿Qué toma Ud.? (vino)*
      Tomo vino.

1. *¿A quién llamamos? (los tíos)*
2. *¿Cómo trabajan ellas? (diligentemente/eficientemente)*
3. *¿Piensas en tu familia? (siempre)*
4. *¿Cuándo están Uds. ocupados? (mañana)*
5. *¿Qué quieres tomar? (el desayuno)*

C. *Cambie la oración usando el verbo entre paréntesis.*

MODELO: *Protejo a los estudiantes. (elegir)*
      Elijo a los estudiantes.

1. *Le compro una pulsera a él. (pedir)*
2. *Su marido le prepara la comida. (servir)*
3. *¿Por qué estudias la lección? (repetir)*
4. *¿Qué te parece? (apetecer)*
5. *Yo le doy un anillo caro. (ofrecer)*

D. *Traduzca al español.*

1. She is delivering it (fem.) to them (masc.).
2. I'm selling them (masc.) to them (fem.).
3. Do you want to choose it (masc.) for her?
4. Can you do it (fem.) for me?
5. He is giving them (fem.) to us.

E. *Traduzca al español.*

1. She gets up every day at 6:30 a.m.
2. We bathe and dress.
3. He bathes and dresses the children.
4. She puts on her red dress.
5. They eat breakfast at work with our boss.
6. They take care of each other.
7. They don't want to get dressed.

F. Escriba las preguntas para estas respuestas usando la palabra quién. Siga el modelo.

MODELO: Teresa me lo dijo.
  ¿Quién te lo dijo?

1. Yo pagué $100,00.
2. Él es mi hermano.
3. Mi jefe es el Señor Enríquez.
4. Yo sé donde está el supermercado. Está a dos cuadras de aquí.
5. Yo no quiero comida china.
6. Lalo es de España.

RESPUESTAS

A. 1. Se almuerza a la una y media en España. 2. Se come bien en los restaurantes venezolanos. 3. No se fuma aquí. 4. Se dice que es excelente. 5. ¿Se puede saber cuál es la especialidad de la casa?

B. 1. Llamamos a los tíos. 2. Ellas trabajan diligente y eficientemente. 3. Siempre pienso en mi familia. 4. Estamos ocupados mañana. 5. Quiero tomar el desayuno.

C. 1. pido 2. sirve 3. repites 4. apetece 5. ofrezco.

D. 1. Ella está entregándosela a ellos./Ella se la está entregando a ellos. 2. Estoy vendiéndoselos a ellas./Se los estoy vendiendo a ellas. 3. ¿Quiere escogérselo a ella?/¿Se lo quiere escoger a ella? 4. ¿Puede hacérmela?/¿Me la puede hacer? 5. Él está dándonoslos./Él nos las está dando.

E. 1. Ella se levanta a las seis y media de la mañana todos los días. 2. Nosotros nos bañamos y nos vestimos. 3. Él baña y viste a los niños. 4. Ella se pone su vestido rojo. 5. Ellos se desayunan con nuestro jefe en el trabajo. 6. Ellos se cuidan el uno del otro. 7. Ellos no quieren vestirse.

F. 1. ¿Quién pagó cien dólares? 2. ¿Quién es él? 3. ¿Quién es tu jefe? 4. ¿Quién sabe donde está el supermercado? 5. ¿Quién quiere comida china? 6. ¿Quién es de España?

LECCION 16
EN EL AUTOBUS.   Traveling by bus.

A. DIALOGO

Rubén pide direcciones por teléfono para llegar a casa de Pancho en la Ciudad de Panamá, Panamá.

RUBEN: **Hola, Pancho. Acabo de llegar a la estación de autobuses. ¿Qué número tomo para llegar a tu casa?**

PANCHO: **Es mejor tomar el número ocho; lo consigues en el segundo piso. Si no está, puedes tomar el número once. Es más lento que el ocho.**

RUBEN: **Y ¿cuánto es el pasaje?**

PANCHO: **Ochenta balboas. El transporte en la ciudad es más caro que en el campo.**

RUBEN: **¿Lleva mucho tiempo el viaje?**

PANCHO: **No, menos de veinte minutos.**

RUBEN: **¿Dónde me bajo?**

PANCHO: **Bajas en la esquina de la calle Veinte y Avenida del Valle. La distingues por el Cine Oro.**

RUBEN: **¿Tengo que andar muchas cuadras hasta tu casa?**

PANCHO: **Al bajar, sigues derecho por la calle Veinte hasta el número 375.**

RUBEN: **Muy bien. Nos vemos en un rato.**

Ruben asks for directions by telephone to get to Pancho's house in Panama City, Panama.

RUBEN: Hi, Pancho. I have just arrived at the bus station. What bus do I take to your house?

PANCHO: It's better to take number eight; you get it on the second floor. If it isn't there, you can take number eleven. It's slower than number eight.

RUBEN: What's the fare?

PANCHO: Eighty balboas. Transportation in the city is more expensive than in the countryside.

RUBEN: Does the trip take long?

PANCHO: No, less than twenty minutes.

RUBEN: Where do I get off?

PANCHO: You get off at the corner of 20th Street and Valle Avenue. You'll recognize it by the Oro Theater.

RUBEN: Do I have to walk many blocks to your house?

PANCHO: When you get off, you go ahead on 20th Street to number 375.

RUBEN: Okay. We'll see each other shortly.

B. GRAMATICA Y USOS

1. COMPARATIVES

In English, there are two possible comparative forms for adjectives and adverbs: a synthetic form, "rich > richer," or a compound form, "beautiful > more beautiful; interesting > less interesting." In Spanish, the compound form is used, with the exception of a few irregular comparatives. There are three kinds of comparisons:

superiority: *más* + adjective, adverb or noun + *que*

El número once es más lento que el número ocho.
Number eleven is slower than number eight.

El ocho corre más rápidamente que el once.
   The eight runs faster than the eleven.

inferiority: *menos* + adjective, adverb or noun + *que*

En el campo hay menos autobuses que en la ciudad.
   In the countryside there are fewer buses than in the city.

equality: *tan* + adjective or adverb + *como:*

El número ocho es tan rápido como el once.
   Number eight is as fast as number eleven.

Note that the second part of a comparison of superiority or inferiority is introduced by *que.* Use the word *de* for "than" when a number follows:

El viaje es menos de veinte minutos.
   The trip is less than twenty minutes.

To make a comparison of equality for nouns, use the adjective:

tanto, -a, -os, -as (as much, as many) + noun + *como:*

Hay tantos autobuses en el campo como en la ciudad.
   There are as many buses in the country as in the city.

Tanto como is a set expression meaning "as much as":

Tenemos tanto como Ud.
   We have as much as you do.

Certain comparatives are irregular:

ADJECTIVE		COMPARATIVE	
bueno, -a	good	*mejor*	better
malo, -a	bad	*peor*	worse
mucho, -a	much, many	*más*	more
poco, -a	few	*menos*	fewer
grande	big	*más grande*	bigger
pequeño, -a	small	*menor*	younger

Es mejor tomar el número ocho.
   It's better to take number eight.

Ella es menor que nuestra hija.
   She is younger than our daughter.

2. VERBS ENDING IN *-GUIR*

Verbs ending in *-guir* drop the *u* in the *yo* form.

DISTINGUIR   TO DISTINGUISH

yo	distingo		nosotros, -as	distinguimos
tú	distingues		vosotros, -as	distinguís
Ud., él, ella	distingue		Uds., ellos, ellas	distinguen

La distingues por el Cine Oro.
   You'll recognize it (distinguish it) by the Oro Theater.

The verbs *seguir* (to follow) and *conseguir* (to get, obtain) also have this change; in addition, they are radical-changing *e>i* verbs.

SEGUIR   TO FOLLOW

yo	sigo		nosotros, -as	seguimos
tú	sigues		vosotros, -as	seguís
Ud., él, ella	sigue		Uds., ellos, ellas	siguen

Sigues una dieta alta en proteínas.
   You're following a high-protein diet.

Conseguimos información aquí.
   We'll get some information here.

Siguen un curso en la universidad.
   They are taking a course at the university.

Seguir can also mean to continue to do something when used with a gerund:

Seguimos estudiando español.
We continue to study (We're still studying) Spanish.

3. *ACABAR DE* + INFINITIVE

The verb *acabar* means "to finish." The expression *acabar de* means "to have just (done something)." In English this expression is followed by a past participle: "I have just arrived." In Spanish, the expression is followed by an infinitive: *Acabo de llegar.*

Acabamos de conseguirlo.
We have just obtained it.

Acaba de comer.
She just ate.

4. *AL* + INFINITIVE

Al + infinitive expresses the English concept of "on" + gerund.

Al bajar, sigues derecho.
When you get off (on getting off), you walk straight ahead.

VOCABULARIO

el transporte	transportation
llegar	to arrive
Acabo de llegar.	I have just arrived.
estación	station
el autobús/el bus	bus
estación de autobuses	bus station
piso	story, floor
tomar el autobús	to take the bus
subir	to go up
subir al autobús	to get on the bus

el pasaje	fare, ticket
bajar	to go down
bajar del autobús	to get off the bus
llevar	to take (time)
¿Cuánto tiempo lleva el viaje?	How long does the trip take?
direcciones	directions
seguir *(e>i)*	to follow
derecho	straight ahead
Sigues derecho.	You go straight ahead.
a la derecha	to the right
a la izquierda	to the left
esquina	corner
la calle	street
avenida	avenue
cuadra	block (street)
el cine	movie theater
acabar	to finish
acabar de (+ infinitive)	to have just (+ past participle)
campo	countryside
ciudad	city
conseguir *(e>i)*	to get, obtain
distinguir	to distinguish
pueblo	village, town
un rato	a short while
Nos vemos en un rato.	We'll see each other shortly.

EXAMEN

A. *Conteste la pregunta en una oración completa usando la pista.*

MODELO: ¿Cuánto es el pasaje? (veinte balboas)
El pasaje es veinte balboas.

1. *¿Dónde estás? (en la estación de autobuses)*
2. *¿Qué autobús debo tomar? (el número tres)*
3. *¿Dónde me bajo? (en la calle Valle)*

4. *Al bajar, ¿cómo voy a tu casa? (derecho)*

5. *¿Cuándo nos vemos? (un rato)*

B. *Llene el espacio en blanco con las palabras en paréntesis.* (Fill in the blank with the words in parenthesis.)

MODELO: Trabajamos _____ *ella.* (fewer hours than)/*menos horas que*

1. *El autobús número ocho es* _____ *el número once.* (faster than)
2. *El pasaje aquí es* _____ *en el campo.* (more expensive than)
3. *Aquí hay* _____ *en la ciudad.* (as many buses as)
4. *Rubén es* _____ *Pancho.* (older than)
5. *Tenemos que andar* _____ *Ud.* (fewer blocks than)

C. *Dé la forma correcta del verbo.*

MODELO: Yo _____ *a la derecha. (seguir)/sigo*

1. *Yo no* _____ *bien las calles. (distinguir)*
2. *Tú* _____ *derecho dos cuadras. (seguir)*
3. *¿Dónde* _____ *yo el autobús? (conseguir)*
4. *¿En qué calle nosotros nos* _____*? (bajar)*
5. *¿Quiénes* _____ *llegar? (acabar de)*

NOTAS CULTURALES

The majority of the population in Spain and Latin America travels by bus to and from work. While the most common word for "bus" is *autobús* or *bus,* in Puerto Rico people say *guagua,* in Argentina *colectivo,* in Mexico *camión* and in other countries words such as *ómnibus* and *microbús* are used. In some Latin American countries you can still find a *trolebús,* an electrified bus, and also a *tranvía,* an old-fashioned tram or streetcar.

RESPUESTAS

A. 1. *Estoy en la estación de autobuses.* 2. *Debes tomar el número tres.*
   3. *Bajas en la calle Valle.* 4. *Vas derecho.* 5. *Nos vemos en un rato.*
B. 1. *más rápido que* 2. *más caro que* 3. *tantos autobuses como* 4. *mayor que*
   5. *menos cuadras que*
C. 1. *distingo* 2. *sigues* 3. *consigo* 4. *se bajan* 5. *acaban de*

LECCION 17

EN EL TREN.   Traveling by train.

A. DIALOGO

En la estación ferroviaria, Pepe habla con el agente para comprar dos pasajes de Madrid a Roma.

PEPE: **Dígame, señorita ¿a qué hora parte el tren para Roma?**

AGENTE: **El que acaba de partir es el último de esta noche. Hay asientos para la partida de las dos y media de la mañana.**

PEPE: **¿Cuánto es el pasaje de ida y vuelta de primera clase?**

AGENTE: **Ochenta y cinco euros. El coche-cama cuesta noventa euros adicionales. Hay un transbordo en Barcelona.**

PEPE: **¿Y segunda clase?**

AGENTE: **Cuarenta y ocho euros.**

PEPE: **Bueno, déme dos pasajes de segunda. Mi esposa, con quien viajo, lleva este baúl. ¿Puedo traerlo conmigo a bordo?**

AGENTE: **No señor. Ud. puede caerse al subirlo al tren. Por favor, lléveselo al maletero, que se lo va a guardar a Ud. con el equipaje. ¡Buen viaje!**

PEPE: **Gracias. Por favor, ¿de qué andén sale el tren?**

AGENTE: **Lo anuncian una hora antes de la partida.**

At the Railroad Station, Pepe is talking to the agent about buying two tickets from Madrid to Rome.

PEPE: Please, miss, tell me at what time the train leaves for Rome.

AGENT: The one that just left is the last one tonight. There are seats for the 2:30 a.m. departure.

PEPE: How much is a first class round-trip ticket?

AGENT: Eighty-five euros. The sleeping car is 90 euros more. There is a transfer in Barcelona.

PEPE: And second class?

AGENT: Forty-eight euros.

PEPE: Okay, give me two second class tickets. My wife, with whom I'm traveling, is taking this trunk. Can I bring it on board with me?

AGENT: No sir. You might fall while lifting it on the train. Please take it to the porter, who will store it in the baggage car for you. Have a good trip!

PEPE: Thank you. Please, from which platform does the train leave?

AGENT: They announce it one hour prior to departure.

B. GRAMATICA Y USOS

1. POLITE COMMANDS

Using a command, we make requests or give orders to one person or to groups of people: Stop! Eat! These are direct commands. We can also soften a direct command by adding the word "please": "Please wait for me." In Spanish, there are similar forms of the command (which is also called the imperative). Commands can be made by using the expression *favor de* + infinitive:

Favor de responder a la pregunta.
Please answer the question.

Favor de decirme cuándo parte el tren.
Please tell me when the train is leaving.

This is an easy command form to use and it applies to either one person or groups of people.

Direct polite commands directed towards one person addressed as *Ud.*, or towards groups of people addressed as *Uds.*, are derived from the first person singular of the present tense of the verb.[1]

INFINITIVE	HABLAR TO SPEAK	COMER TO EAT	SALIR TO LEAVE	TRAER TO BRING
first person sg.	*hablo*	*como*	*salgo*	*traigo*
Ud. command	*hable*	*coma*	*salga*	*traiga*
Uds. command	*hablen*	*coman*	*salgan*	*traigan*

Hablen despacio.
Speak slowly.

Dígame la verdad.
Tell me the truth.

Dropping the first person singular ending *-o* of regular verbs, radical-changing verbs *(o>ue, e>ie, e>i)*, and many irregular verbs, forms the root of the command. The *-ar* verbs add *-e* for *Ud.* and *-en* for *Uds.*, while the *-er* and *-ir* verbs add *-a* for *Ud.* and *-an* for *Uds.*

Despiértese temprano.
Wake up early.

Piense en lo que hace.
Think about what you are doing.

Note the following spelling changes:[2]

        in *-car* verbs, *c>qu: busque, busquen*
        in *-gar* verbs, *g>gu: pague, paguen*
        in *-zar* verbs, *z>c: comience, comiencen*

---

[1] Familiar commands *(tú* and *vosotros)* will be discussed later.
[2] All these changes are necessary to maintain a hard sound.

Entregue las flores mañana.
   Deliver the flowers tomorrow.

Almuerce con la familia.
   Eat lunch with the family.

   Here are important irregular command forms:

	ESTAR TO BE	SER TO BE	IR TO GO	DAR TO GIVE	SABER TO KNOW
Ud.	*esté*	*sea*	*vaya*	*dé*	*sepa*
Uds.	*estén*	*sean*	*vayan*	*den*	*sepan*

No vayan por ahí.
   Don't go around there.

Déme dos pasajes.
   Give me two tickets.

   The object pronouns are attached to the affirmative forms of the
commands, but they precede the command in the negative:

Dígame.
   Tell me.

No me diga.
   You don't say. (Don't tell me.)

Lléveselo al maletero.
   Take it to the porter.

No se lo lleve al maletero.
   Don't take it to the porter.

   When the object pronouns are attached to the command, an accent
mark is added to the original point of stress:

¡Dígasela ahora mismo!
   Tell it to her right now!

2. RELATIVE PRONOUNS

A relative pronoun refers back to a previous noun, literally taking its place.
> The train that just left is the last one tonight.
> Take it to the porter, who will store it for you.

"That" refers back to the train; "who" refers back to the porter. In Spanish there are several relative pronouns. Use *que* (which, that, who) for both persons and things:

El tren que acaba de partir es el último de esta noche.
The train that just left is the last one tonight.

Lléveselo al portero que se lo va a guardar a Ud.
Take it to the porter, who will store it for you.

Use *quien, quienes* (whom) when the relative refers to people and is preceded by the prepositions *a, con, para, de:*

Mi esposa, con quien viajo, lleva este baúl.
My wife, with whom I'm traveling, is taking this trunk.

When the relative pronoun must specify one among several previous nouns, you can use a compound form made up of the definite article followed by either *que* or *cual(es)*. The definite article agrees in number and gender with the noun in question.

el la los las	+ *que/cual(es)*

Hay dos trenes. El que parte a la medianoche ya no tiene asientos.
There are two trains. The one that leaves at midnight no longer has seats available.

Ya no nos quedan esas maletas.
We no longer have those suitcases.

Acabamos de vender las que Ud. quiere.
We have just sold the ones you want.

3. THE VERBS *CAER* AND *TRAER*

The verbs *caer* (to fall) and *traer* (to bring, carry) are irregular in the first person singular and the gerund.

CAER TO FALL			*TRAER* TO BRING	
yo	caigo		yo	traigo
tú	caes		tú	traes
Ud., él, ella	cae		Ud., él, ella	trae
nosotros, -as	caemos		nosotros, -as	traemos
vosotros, -as	caéis		vosotros, -as	traéis
Uds., ellos, ellas	caen		Uds., ellos, ellas	traen

El libro siempre cae del estante.
The book is always falling from the shelf.

Traen los pasajes mañana.
They are bringing the tickets tomorrow.

The gerunds have a *y: cayendo, trayendo.*

Están trayendo las maletas.
They are bringing the suitcases.

VOCABULARIO

la estación ferroviaria	train station
el viaje	trip
hacer un viaje	to take a trip
¡Buen viaje!	Have a good trip.
el tren	train
el vagón	car (of a train)
el vagón restaurante	dining car

150

el coche-cama	sleeping car
partida	departure
partir	to leave
¿A qué hora parte el tren?	At what time does the train leave?
el andén	platform
¿De qué andén sale el tren?	From what platform does the train leave?
anunciar	to announce
pasaje de ida y vuelta	round trip ticket
¿Cuánto es el pasaje?	How much is the ticket?
primera clase	first class
segunda clase	second class
asiento	seat
transbordo	transfer
el equipaje	the baggage
el baúl	trunk
maleta	suitcase
traer	to bring
¿Puedo traerlo conmigo?	Can I bring it with me?
maletero	porter
subir	to lift (something) up
llevar	to carry, bring
guardar	to store, keep
a bordo	on board
que	that, who, whom
quien(es)	who, whom
el que/el cual	the one that, which, who
¡Dígame!	Tell me.
¡No me diga!	You don't say!/Don't tell me.

EXAMEN

A. *Conteste la pregunta en una oración completa usando la pista.*

MODELO: ¿Cuánto es el pasaje de primera clase? (Quince mil pesetas)
El pasaje de primara clase es quince mil pesetas.

1. ¿A qué hora sale el tren? (a la medianoche)
2. ¿Qué tipo de pasaje quiere? (de ida y vuelta)
3. ¿De qué andén sale el tren? (número seis)
4. ¿Qué hago con el baúl? (llevarlo al maletero) (use a command)
5. ¿Qué nos desea el agente? (un buen viaje)

B. *Dé la primera persona del presente y las formas Ud. y Uds. del imperativo para los siguientes infinitivos.* (Give the first person of the present tense and the *Ud.* and *Uds.* commands for the following verbs.)

MODELO: tocar/toco, toque, toquen

1. *salir*
2. *decir*
3. *traer*
4. *no ir*
5. *estar*
6. *no dar*
7. *saber*
8. *buscar*
9. *no pensar*
10. *comenzar*
11. *levantarse*
12. *no lavarse*

C. *Escriba en español.*

1. Tell the ticket agent that you want to buy a round trip ticket from Madrid to Rome.
2. Ask how much the first-class ticket in the sleeping car is.
3. Ask at what time the train leaves.
4. Say that you want to take a suitcase and a trunk on board with you.
5. Ask which platform the train leaves from.

NOTAS CULTURALES

Spanish trains are integrated into the European rail system and are quite comfortable. It's a nice way to see the countryside if you travel by day, and a comfortable way to go overnight in a *coche-cama* (sleeping car) for long distances. Discounts are available in accordance with the kilometers you travel, and if you are over 65, ask for a *tarjeta dorada* (gold card), which allows for reductions of 25–50 percent. It's a good idea to make reservations, which can be done at travel agencies or at the railway station.

Trains do not play an important role in the transportation system of most Latin American countries. Train travel can be uncomfortable and is generally spotty. However, train travel through Mexico, for example, does offer you economical fares and the chance to see interesting scenery. One of the most spectacular train rides you will ever experience is the *Tren Estrella* through Mexico's Copper Canyon. It is located southwest of El Paso, Texas, in the northern Mexican state of Chihuahua. Covering an area of 25,000 rugged square miles, Copper Canyon is four times larger than the Grand Canyon of Arizona. This remarkable area, also known as the Sierra de Tarahumara, after the native Tarahumaras who inhabit the canyons, is one of the last great wilderness areas in North America. The Tarahumara, who number about 50,000 and live in small settlements throughout the region, have been able to preserve their native culture better than any group in North America. A trip through this majestic region is a trip back in time. You might find the train ride slow and noisy; however, it is cheap—very cheap! The one-way fare is approximately $6.50 for general seating on the second-class train.

In Paraguay train lines are operated with steam locomotives that date to the 1800s. In Peru you can take the three-hour train to Machu Picchu from Cuzco. If you are willing to put up with a little discomfort, train travel through Latin America can be an exciting and adventurous way to explore a vast region.

RESPUESTAS

A. 1. *El tren sale a la medianoche.* 2. *Quiero un pasaje de ida y vuelta.* 3. *El tren parte del andén número seis.* 4. *Llévelo al maletero.* 5. *El agente nos desea un buen viaje.*

B. 1. *salgo, salga, salgan.* 2. *digo, diga, digan* 3. *traigo, traiga, traigan* 4. *no voy, no vaya, no vayan* 5. *estoy, esté, estén* 6. *no doy, no dé, no den* 7. *sé, sepa, sepan* 8. *busco, busque, busquen* 9. *no pienso, no piense, no piensen* 10. *comienzo, comience, comiencen* 11. *me levanto, levántese, levántense* 12. *no me lavo, no se lave, no se laven.*

C. 1. *Quiero comprar un pasaje de ida y vuelta de Madrid a Roma.* 2. *¿Cuánto es el pasaje de primera clase en el coche-cama?* 3. *¿A qué hora parte el tren?* 4. *Quiero llevar una maleta y un baúl a bordo conmigo.* 5. *¿De qué andén parte/sale el tren?*

LECCION 18

ALQUILANDO UN COCHE.   Renting a car.

A. DIALOGO

En la Agencia Autoalquila, Limitada, de Quito, Ecuador.

INES: **No entiendo nada, señor. Ud. dice que el coche más pequeño y más barato para alquilar por semana es este Ford.**

VICENTE: **Sí señora. ¿De qué se ríe Ud.?**

INES: **Pues, es carísimo. El precio del alquiler no incluye el costo de la gasolina, ni las cuotas por los kilómetros ni por los seguros de accidente y daño personal.**

VICENTE: **Es verdad, señora. No tenemos ningún coche más económico. Es un precio muy bueno y es la mejor oferta de esta agencia.**

INES: **¿Y cuánto cuesta el alquiler por día?**

VICENTE: **Son ochocientos sucres, que incluye el kilometraje y los seguros, pero excluye la gasolina. Ud. tiene que devolver el coche con el depósito lleno.**

INES: **¡No sé qué hacer! En realidad, no me queda remedio alguno. ¿Dónde firmo el contrato de arrendamiento?**

At the Autoalquila Agency, Inc., in Quito, Ecuador.

INES: I don't understand, sir. You say that the smallest and cheapest car to rent weekly is this Ford.

VICENTE: Yes, madam. What are you laughing about?

INES: Well, it's very expensive. The rental price doesn't include the cost of gasoline, nor the kilometer fee or the accident and personal injury insurance.

VICENTE: That's true, madam. We don't have any cheaper car. It's a very good price and it's this agency's best offer.

INES: And how much is the daily rental?

VICENTE: It's eight hundred sucres, which includes kilometers and insurance, but excludes gasoline. You have to bring the car back with the tank full.

INES: I don't know what to do! In reality, I have no choice whatsoever. Where do I sign the leasing contract?

B. GRAMATICA Y USOS

1. THE SUPERLATIVE

We have used the comparative to compare things, to show their relative value. With the superlative, no comparison is made; rather, one thing is said to show some extreme—good or bad—in its group. In English we use expressions such as "the most important person," "the least interesting book," "the fastest car," and "the best friend." In Spanish the patterns are as follows:

a. article + (noun) + *más* or *menos* + adjective + *(de)*

Es el coche más pequeño de la compañia.
It's the company's smallest car.

Son las menos caras.
They are the least expensive.

b. article + irregular comparative + noun + *(de)*

Es la mejor oferta que tenemos.
It is the best offer we have.

Son las peores del grupo.
They are the worst of the group.

The use of the noun is optional. Also, the *de* is necessary only when "in" or "of" is expressed.

The absolute superlative expresses the idea of "very." It is formed by using the adverb *muy* + adjective:

Es un precio muy bueno.
It's a very good price.

An alternative form of the absolute superlative is made by adding the suffix *-ísimo, -a, -os, -as* to an adjective minus its final vowel, or to an adjective ending in a consonant:

caro > carísimo
interesante > interesantísimo
cordial > cordialísimo

With adjectives whose final consonant before the vowel is *c,* the *c* changes to *qu:*

rico > riquísimo   rich > very rich

With adjectives whose final consonant before the vowel is *g,* the *g* changes to *gu:*

vago > vaguísimo   vague > very vague

Es una persona rarísima.
He's a very odd fellow.

Compraron unas blusas elegantísimas.
They bought some very elegant blouses.

2. AFFIRMATIVE AND NEGATIVE EXPRESSIONS

Certain common affirmative expressions have negative counterparts:

+

alguien	someone
algo	something

algún, alguno, -a	some
siempre	always
o . . . o	either . . . or

—

nadie	no one, nobody
nada	nothing
ningún, ninguno, -a	none, not any
nunca	never
ni . . . ni	neither . . . nor

The forms *algún* and *ningún* are used before masculine singular nouns. The plural forms of *ninguno* or *ninguna* are seldom used.

No tenemos ningún coche más barato.
　　We don't have any cheaper car.

Siempre tienen o un Ford o un Toyota.
　　They always have either a Ford or a Toyota.

3. DOUBLE NEGATION

While incorrect in English, double negation is perfectly correct and preferred in Spanish. Usually the word *no* immediately precedes the verb and another negative word follows the verb. (Don't forget that the Spanish word no is equivalent to both "no" and "not" in English.)

No, no hay nada más barato.
　　No, there isn't anything cheaper.

No tienen nunca ofertas.
　　They never have any special offers.

You can also begin the sentence with a negative noun, pronoun, or adverb and have single negation:

Nadie está aquí.
　　No one is here.

Nunca tienen ofertas.
They never have special offers.

To make a very emphatic negative, the affirmative word *alguno* can be used after the noun:

No me queda remedio alguno.
I have no choice whatsoever.

4. VERBS ENDING IN *-UIR*

All verbs ending in *-uir* (except for those ending in *-quir)* add a *y* before the inflection, except in the *nosotros, -as* and *vosotros, -as* forms.

INCLUIR TO INCLUDE

yo	*incluyo*	nosotros, -as	*incluimos*
tú	*incluyes*	vosotros, -as	*incluís*
Ud., él, ella	*incluye*	Uds., ellos, ellas	*incluyen*

Other verbs like *incluir* are:

concluir	to conclude	*excluir*	to exclude
construir	to construct	*instruir*	to instruct
destruir	to destroy		

El precio no incluye el costo de la gasolina.
The price does not include the cost of gasoline.

Destruyen este edificio.
They are destroying this building.

The gerunds are *incluyendo, excluyendo,* etc.

5. THE VERB *REÍRSE*

The verb *reír(se)* (to laugh) is irregular in the present tense:

REÍR   TO LAUGH

yo	*río*		nosotros, -as	*reímos*
tú	*ríes*		vosotros, -as	*ríes*
Ud., él, ella	*ríe*		Uds., ellos, ellas	*ríen*

¿De qué se ríe Ud?
What are you laughing about?

¿Por qué se ríen de él?
Why are they laughing at him?

Te ríes por nada.
The littlest thing makes you laugh. (You laugh over nothing.)

The gerund is *riéndose*.

VOCABULARIO

agencia	agency
coche	car
costar *(o>ue)*	to cost
alquilar	to rent
el alquiler	rental
¿Cuánto es el alquiler del coche por semana?	How much is the weekly car rental?
oferta	(special) offer
barato	cheap
caro	expensive
Es carísimo.	It's very expensive.
cuota	fee
kilómetro	kilometer
seguros	insurance
gasto	expense

159

depósito	(gas) tank
lleno	full
contrato	contract
arrendamiento	lease
firmar	to sign
¿Dónde firmo el contrato de arrendamiento?	Where do I sign the leasing contract?
alguien	someone
algo,	something
algún/alguno, *-a*	some
nadie	no one, nobody
nada	nothing
ningún/ninguno, *-a*	none, not any
concluir	to conclude
construir	to construct, build
destruir	to destroy
incluir	to include
excluir	to exclude
devolver *(o>ue)*	to return (something)
reírse *(de)*	to laugh (at, about)
entender *(e>ie)*	to understand
No entiendo nada.	I don't understand anything.
¡No sé qué hacer!	I don't know what to do!
en realidad	in reality, actually
No me queda otro remedio.	I have no other choice.

EXAMEN

A. *Escriba la oración usando la pista.*

MODELO: Él es rico. (riquísimo)
   El es riquísimo.

1. *El precio es barato. (el más barato)*
2. *El coche es caro. (carísimo)*
3. *El depósito está lleno. (llenísimo)*
4. *La agencia es buena. (la mejor de la ciudad)*

B. *Cambie al negativo.*

MODELO: *Véndame este coche.*
     No me venda este coche.

1. *Quiero algún coche caro.*
2. *Siempre pago la cuota por kilómetro.*
3. *¿Necesito devolver el coche también?*
4. *Déme o el Ford o el Toyota.*

C. *Escriba en español.*

1. Say that you want to rent a car.
2. Ask how much the daily and weekly rentals are.
3. Say that you need the cheapest car.
4. Ask how much the insurance costs.
5. Ask how much the charge is per kilometer.

NOTAS CULTURALES

It is always best to make arrangements with one of the major car rental agencies before departing. Most of the well-known agencies found in the U.S. also have offices in Spain and Latin America. You will also find local companies. Be sure to have adequate insurance coverage if you rent a car.

Roads in cities are rather good. In the countryside, however, there may be nothing more than a dirt or stone paved road for miles. Defensive driving is very important, because people have a more casual attitude towards the "rules of the road."

RESPUESTAS

A. 1. *Es el precio más barato.* 2. *El coche es carísimo.* 3. *El depósito está llenísimo.* 4. *La agencia es la mejor de la ciudad.*
B. 1. *No quiero ningún coche caro.* 2. *No pago nunca la cuota por kilómetro./Nunca pago la cuota por kilómetro.* 3. *¿No necesito devolver el coche tampoco?* 4. *No me dé ni el Ford ni el Toyota.*
C. 1. *Quiero alquilar un coche.* 2. *¿Cuánto es el alquiler por día y por semana?* 3. *Necesito el coche más barato.* 4. *¿Cuánto cuestan los seguros?* 5. *¿Cuánto es la cuota por kilómetro?*

LECCION 19

EN LA GASOLINERA.   At the gas station.

A. DIALOGO

En la gasolinera Super de Tijuana, Baja California.

JOSE: **Hola, Manuel. Voy a estacionar el automóvil aquí al lado de la bomba. Por favor, revise la batería. Estuve ayer en la ciudad cuando de repente se paró el motor.**

MANUEL: **De acuerdo, señor. Abrame el capó. . . . A la batería le falta agua.**

JOSE: **Muy bien. ¿Puede reviser el aceite y llenar el depósito con super?**

MANUEL: **Mire, señor. Esta llanta parece estar desinflada.**

JOSE: **Pero, ¡no es posible! La compré la semana pasada. Anoche estuvo bien. No sé qué pasó.**

MANUEL: **¿Tiene Ud. una llanta de repuesto?**

JOSE: **Ya no. La dejamos a nuestra cuñada. ¿Qué hacemos?**

MANUEL: **Voy a quitar la llanta y repararla ahora mismo.**

At the Super gasoline station in Tijuana, Baja California.

JOSE: Hi, Manuel. I'm going to park the car here near the pump. Please check the battery. I was in the city yesterday when the car stalled suddenly.

MANUEL: Okay, sir. Open the hood for me. . . . the battery needs water.

JOSE: Fine. Can you check the oil and fill the tank with super?

MANUEL: Look, sir. This tire seems to be flat.

JOSE: But, it isn't possible! I bought it last week. Last night it was fine. I don't know what happened.

MANUEL: Do you have a spare tire?

JOSE: Not anymore. We gave it to our sister-in-law. What do we do?

MANUEL: I'll take off the tire and repair it right now.

B. GRAMATICA Y USOS

1. THE CONCEPT OF THE PAST TENSES

Until now, we have only been using the present tense, speaking about present events or actions in the immediate future. We have also learned to talk about future events by using *ir* + *a* + infinitive. Now we will learn how to talk about past events. The concept of the past involves several tenses. The principal ones are the preterite and the imperfect, each with its distinctive uses.

The preterite is the simple past, describing a fact or an action that took place at one moment in the past and ended. Often, one of the following adverbs of time will appear in the sentence:

anoche	last night
ayer	yesterday
la semana pasada	last week
el año pasado	last year

La compré la semana pasada.
   I bought it last week.

Anoche estuvo bien.
   Last night it was okay.

2. THE PRETERITE OF REGULAR -*AR* VERBS

Remember that all infinitives are made up of two parts: the root and the infinitive ending. When we conjugated the verb in the present tense, we dropped off the infinitive ending and added personal inflections to the root which indicated both the tense and the person. The same procedure holds for the preterite; each inflection indicates the preterite tense and the person:

COMPRAR TO BUY

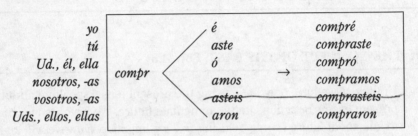

yo	é	compré
tú	aste	compraste
Ud., él, ella	ó	compró
nosotros, -as	amos	compramos
vosotros, -as	~~asteis~~	~~comprasteis~~
Uds., ellos, ellas	aron	compraron

There are accent marks on the first and third persons singular. For clarity, the third persons singular and plural must be used with their subject. The *nosotros, -as* form is the same in the present and preterite tenses; the context of the sentence (perhaps an adverb) will let you know which form you are dealing with.

There are two ways to translate the preterite into English:

Tú compraste el libro.
You bought the book. You did buy the book.

In English, the helping verb "did" shows that the main verb which follows is in the preterite tense.

Gustar and verbs like it are conjugated in the third persons singular and plural:

Nos gustaron los automóviles.
We liked the cars.

Le faltó agua a la batería.
The battery needed water.

Present tense radical-changing *-ar* verbs do not change in the preterite.

Pensé en él.
    I thought of him.

Costaron mucho.
    They (did) cost a lot.

Nosotros almorzamos a las dos.
    We ate lunch at 2:00.

3. THE IRREGULAR PRETERITE OF *ESTAR*

Estar is completely irregular in the preterite tense:

ESTAR   TO BE

yo	estuve	nosotros, -as	estuvimos
tú	estuviste	vosotros, -as	estuvisteis
Ud., él, ella	estuvo	Uds., ellos, ellas	estuvieron

Anoche estuvo bien.
    Last night it was fine.

Estuvieron aqui.
    They were here.

gasolinera	gas station
el automóvil	car
bomba	pump
batería	car battery
el motor	motor
el capó	hood
el aceite	oil
super	super gasoline
Llene el depósito.	Fill the tank.
llanta	tire.
quitar la llanta	to take off the tire
llanta de repuesto	spare tire
¿Tiene Ud. una llanta de repuesto?	Do you have a spare tire?
desinflado, -a	flat
estar desinflado	to be flat
estacionar	to park
revisar	to check
Revise la batería.	Check the battery.
Revise el aceite.	Check the oil.
reparar	to repair
pararse	to stop, to stall
El motor se paró.	The motor stalled.
anoche	last night
ayer	yesterday
el año pasado	last year
dejar	to leave, leave behind
¡No es posible!	It isn't possible.
Lo compré la semana pasada.	I bought it last week.
¿Qué hacemos?	What do we do?
ahora mismo	right now
de repente	suddenly
al lado de	next to

EXAMEN

A. *Escriba la oración usando la pista.*

MODELO: Anoche hablé con Juan. (Tú)
Anoche hablaste con Juan.

1. *Ayer estuvimos enfermos. (Yo)*
2. *¿Quiénes compraron el automóvil? (Tú)*
3. *El motor se paró de repente. (Ellos)*
4. *Quitaste la llanta. (Yo)*
5. *Llenaron el depósito ayer. (Ella)*

B. *Traduzca al español.*

1. Park the car next to the pump.
2. Check the oil.
3. Fill the tank with super gasoline.
4. Is the tire flat?
5. He took off the tire and fixed it.
6. Suddenly the car stopped.
7. I bought it last week.

NOTAS CULTURALES

Most Spaniards and Latin Americans have compact or mini-cars, because gasoline is much more expensive than in the United States. Don't be surpised to see American cars from the 1950s and 1960s still running, particularly in the rural areas. Although parts are no longer available, there are mechanics who are adept at making parts to fit these cars.

RESPUESTAS

A. 1. *Ayer yo estuve enfermo.* 2. *¿Tú compraste el automóvil?* 3. *Ellos se pararon de repente.* 4. *Quité la llanta.* 5. *Ella llenó el depósito ayer.*
B. 1. *Estacione el automóvil al lado de la bomba.* 2. *¡Revise el aceite!* 3. *Llene el depósito con super.* 4. *¿Está desinflada la llanta?* 5. *El quitó la llanta y la reparó.* 6. *De repente el automóvil se paró.* 7. *Lo compré la semana pasada.*

LECCION 20

ALQUILANDO UN APARTAMENTO.   Renting an apartment.

A. DIALOGO

Anita, corredora de inmuebles, ayuda a Ricardo a buscar un apartamento cerca de Bogotá, Colombia.

ANITA: ¿Qué tipo de apartamento busca Ud. ahora?

RICARDO: Debe tener varios dormitorios y baños, sala, comedor, cocina, y garaje. El apartamento ideal debe estar al lado del parque Independencia donde los niños pueden jugar.

ANITA: ¿Ya buscó Ud. tal apartamento?

RICARDO: Comencé a buscarlo en el periódico. Los alquileres son altísimos.

ANITA: ¿Cuánto paga Ud. por su apartamento actual?

RICARDO: Hasta el mes pasado, pagué ochocientos al mes. Pero, me tocó un aumento. Ahora pago novecientos treinta e incluye los gastos de gas, electricidad y garaje.

ANITA: ¿Cuándo tiene que mudarse?

RICARDO: Tengo que mudarme lo más pronto posible, u ocho días antes del fin del corriente mes.

Anita, a real estate agent, helps Ricardo to look for an apartment near Bogotá, Colombia.

ANITA: What type of apartment are you looking for now?

RICARDO: It must have several bedrooms and bathrooms, a living room, a dining room, a kitchen, and a garage. The ideal apartment is located near Independence Park where the children can play.

ANITA: Did you already look for such an apartment?

RICARDO: I began looking for it in the newspaper. The rents are very high.

ANITA: How much are you paying for your present apartment?

RICARDO: Until last month, I paid eight hundred monthly. But I got an increase. Now I'm paying nine hundred and thirty, and it includes gas, electricity, and garage expenses.

ANITA: When do you have to move?

RICARDO: I have to move as soon as possible, or eight days before the end of the current (month).

B. GRAMATICA Y USOS

1. IRREGULAR PRETERITES ENDING IN -CAR, -GAR, -ZAR

The first person singular of the preterite of these verbs has an irregular form.

a. Verbs ending in *-car* change *c* to *qu* before *e:*

TOCAR   TO PLAY

yo	toqué	nosotros, -as	tocamos
tú	tocaste	vosotros, -as	tocasteis
Ud., él, ella	tocó	Uds., ellos, ellas	tocaron

Toqué el piano anoche.
I played the piano last night.

Busqué el hotel.
I looked for the hotel.

b. Verbs ending in *-gar* change *g* to *gu* before *e:*

PAGAR TO PAY

yo	*pagué*	nosotros, -as	*pagamos*
tú	*pagaste*	vosotros, -as	*pagasteis*
Ud., él, ella	*pagó*	Uds., ellos, ellas	*pagaron*

Pagué ochocientos al mes.
   I paid eight hundred monthly.

Llegué a las tres.
   I arrived at 3:00.

c. Verbs ending in *-zar* change *z* to *c* before *e*.

COMENZAR TO BEGIN

yo	*comencé*	nosotros, -as	*comenzamos*
tú	*comenzaste*	vosotros, -as	*comenzasteis*
Ud., él, ella	*comenzó*	Uds., ellos, ellas	*comenzaron*

Comencé a buscarlo en el periódico.
   I began looking for it in the newspaper.

Almorcé con Elena.
   I ate lunch with Elena.

2. VERBS ENDING IN *-UAR* AND *-IAR*

Remember that *i* and *u* are weak vowels in Spanish and can be stressed only when they have an accent mark.

a. Verbs ending in *-uar* have an accent mark on the *u* in the present tense, except for the *nosotros, -as* and *vosotros, -as* forms.

CONTINUAR TO CONTINUE

yo	*continúo*	nosotros, -as	*continuamos*
tú	*continúas*	vosotros, -as	*continuáis*
Ud., él, ella	*continúa*	Uds., ellos, ellas	*continúan*

b. Verbs ending in *-iar* have an accent mark on the *i* in the present tense, except for the *nosotros, -as* and *vosotros, -as* forms.

ENVIAR   TO SEND

yo	*envío*	nosotros, -as	*enviamos*
tú	*envías*	vosotros, -as	*enviáis*
Ud., él, ella	*envía*	Uds., ellos, ellas	*envían*

Continúan leyéndolo.
They continue to read it.

Envía la carta a Juan.
She is sending the letter to Juan.

3. THE VERBS *TOCAR* AND *JUGAR*

a. *Tocar* means "to touch, to play" (an instrument), "to ring" (a telephone), "to knock" (on the door).

Juan toca la guitarra.
John plays the guitar.

Alguien toca a la puerta.
Someone's knocking on the door.

The expression *tocarle a uno* means "to be one's turn" or "to fall to someone":

Me tocó un aumento.
I got an increase. (It was my turn for an increase.)

b. *Jugar* means "to play" (a sport, a game). It is the only radical-changing *u>ue* verb in Spanish:

JUGAR   TO PLAY

yo	*juego*	nosotros, -as	*jugamos*
tú	*juegas*	vosotros, -as	*jugáis*
Ud., él, ella	*juega*	Uds., ellos, ellas	*juegan*

Juegan fútbol los domingos.
  They play soccer on Sundays.

4. SUBSTITUTION OF *E* FOR *Y* AND *U* FOR *O*

a. Before a word beginning in *i* or *hi, y* becomes *e:*

El alquiler es ochocientos e incluye gas, electricidad y garaje.
  The rent is eight hundred and includes gas, electricity, and garage.

b. Before a word beginning in *o* or *ho, o* becomes *u:*

Tengo que mudarme lo más pronto posible, u ocho días antes del fin del mes corriente.
  I have to move as soon as possible, or eight days before the end of the current month.

VOCABULARIO

buscar	to look for
apartamento/apartamiento/ departmento	apartment
buscar un apartamento en el periódico	to look for an apartment in the newspaper
¿Qué tipo de apartamento busca Ud.?	What kind of apartment are you looking for?
corredor, -a de inmuebles	real estate agent
barrio	neighborhood
dormitorio	bedroom
baño	bathroom
sala	living room
cocina	kitchen
el comedor	dining room
el garaje	garage
el alquiler/la renta	rent
aumento	increase
pagar al mes	to pay monthly

¿Cuánto paga Ud. al mes?	How much do you pay monthly?
Me tocó un aumento.	I got a raise.
gasto	expense
electricidad	electricity
gas	gas
mudarse	to move (one's residence)
Tengo que mudarme.	I have to move.
y/e	and
o/u	or
varios, -as	several
alto	high
actual	present
corriente	current (adj.)
lo más pronto posible	as soon as possible
jugar *(u>ue)*	to play (games)
tocar	to play (an instrument)
comenzar *(e>ie)*	to begin
continuar	to continue
enviar	to send

EXAMEN

A. *Conteste las preguntas usando el sujeto "yo".* (Answer the questions using the subject *yo*.)

MODELO: ¿Quién le pegó al niño?
         Yo le pegué al niño.

1. *¿Quién buscó un apartamento?*
2. *¿Quién le pagó el alquiler?*
3. *¿Quién jugó en el parque?*
4. *¿Quién comenzó a trabajar hoy?*
5. *¿Quién tocó el piano?*

B. *Escriba en español.*

1. woman or man
2. money and interest
3. sixty or eighty
4. gas and electricity
5. summer or fall

C. *Escriba en español.*

1. Say that you have to move before the end of the current month.
2. Say that you need a large apartment with several bedrooms.
3. Ask what the monthly rent is for an apartment with three bedrooms and garage.
4. Say that last month you paid eight hundred dollars (of) rent.
5. Ask if there is a park near the apartment.

NOTAS CULTURALES

While there is excellent housing in many cities throughout Latin America, the immediate outskirts of the cities may be made up of shantytowns. These have different names in different countries: *barrio bajo, villa miseria, barriada, rancho, limonada, pueblo joven*. The inhabitants of these areas are usually low paid civil servants, factory workers, or domestics.

RESPUESTAS

A. 1. *Yo busqué el apartamento.* 2. *Yo pagué el alquiler.* 3. *Yo jugué en el parque.* 4. *Yo comencé a trabajar hoy.* 5. *Yo toqué el piano.*

B. 1. *mujer u hombre* 2. *dinero e interés* 3. *sesenta u ochenta* 4. *gas y electricidad* 5. *verano u otoño*

C. 1. *Tengo que mudarme antes del fin del mes corriente.* 2. *Necesito un apartamento grande con varios dormitorios.* 3. *¿Cuánto es el alquiler al mes por un apartamento con tres dormitorios y garaje?* 4. *El mes pasado pagué ochocientos dólares de alquiler.* 5. *¿Hay un parque cerca del apartamento?*

CUARTO REPASO

A. *Escriba el comparativo opuesto.* (Write the opposite comparative.)

MODELO: Venden más coches que ellas.
         Venden menos coches que ellas.

1. *Juan es mayor que Jorge.*
2. *Lleva más tiempo que antes.*
3. *Consiguen menos pasajes que tú.*
4. *Estos coches son peores que los otros.*
5. *Se compra un automóvil más grande.*

B. *Dé el imperativo en lugar del infinitivo.* (Give the command in place of the infinitive.)

MODELO: comer (Ud.) mucho
        Coma mucho.

1. *partir (Uds.) a tiempo*
2. *traer (Ud.) el baúl*
3. *hacer (Uds.) un viaje a Roma*
4. *no anunciarlo (Uds.) a las dos*
5. *pagárselo (Ud.) ahora mismo*

C. *Escriba nuevamente en el negativo.* (Rewrite the sentence in the negative.)

MODELO: Tengo algo.
        No tengo nada. / Nada tengo.

1. *Tenemos un coche barato.*
2. *Alguien está pagando los seguros.*
3. *Yo siempre tengo mucho dinero también.*
4. *¿Quieres el rojo o el azul?*
5. *Algún día pienso comprarle algo.*

D. *Cambie los verbos al pretérito usando los adverbios en paréntesis.* (Change the verbs to the preterite using the adverb in parenthesis.)

MODELO: El compra un coche nuevo. (el año pasado).
  El compró un coche nuevo el año pasado.

1. *¿Dónde estás ahora? (anoche)*
2. *¿Compran muchos libros hoy? (ayer)*
3. *Este año viajamos al campo. (el año pasado)*
4. *La llanta está desinflada otra vez. (esta mañana)*
5. *¿Revisan Uds. el coche todos los días? (la semana pasada)*

E. *Cambie el verbo según la persona en paréntesis.* (Change the verb according to the person in parenthesis.)

MODELO: Jugamos fútbol anoche. (tú)
  Tú jugaste fútbol anoche.

1. *Ayer pagamos ochocientos dólares. (yo)*
2. *¿Entregaron el periódico a casa? (tú)*
3. *¿Tocó Ud. el piano anoche? (yo)*
4. *Llegaron tarde al pueblo. (yo)*
5. *¿A qué hora comenzaste a trabajar? (Uds.)*

F. *Traduzca al español.*

1. Go straight ahead.
2. He is the man who bought a round trip ticket to Rome.
3. Don't (you pl.) tell it to them (fem. pl.) now; tell (you pl.) it to them later.
4. We wanted to rent a very beautiful car for a very cheap rate.
5. He worked last year; this year I began to work.
6. Javier plays the piano.
7. I got an unlucky horse at the racetrack.
8. We liked the food.
9. Last night I went to bed early.
10. They are the most expensive.

RESPUESTAS

A. 1. *Juan es menor que Jorge.* 2. *Lleva menos tiempo que antes.* 3. *Consiguen más pasajes que tú.* 4. *Estos coches son mejores que los otros.* 5. *Se compra un automóvil más pequeño/menos grande.*

B. 1. *Partan Uds. a tiempo.* 2. *Traiga Ud. el baúl.* 3. *Hagan Uds. un viaje a Roma.* 4. *No lo anuncien Uds. a las dos.* 5. *Págueselo Ud. ahora mismo.*

C. 1. *No tenemos ningún coche barato.* 2. *Nadie está pagando los seguros.* 3. *Yo nunca tengo dinero tampoco.* 4. *¿No quieres ni el rojo ni el azul?* 5. *No pienso comprarle nada nunca./No pienso comprarle nada ningún día.*

D. 1. *¿Dónde estuviste anoche?* 2. *¿Compraron muchos libros ayer?* 3. *El año pasado viajamos al campo.* 4. *La llanta estuvo desinflada esta mañana.* 5. *¿Revisaron Uds. el coche la semana pasada?*

E. 1. *Ayer yo pagué ochocientos dólares.* 2. *¿Entregaste el periódico a casa?* 3. *¿Toqué el piano anoche?* 4. *Llegué tarde al pueblo.* 5. *¿A qué hora comenzaron a trabajar?*

F. 1. *Siga/Vaya derecho.* 2. *El es el hombre que compró un pasaje de ida y vuelta a Roma.* 3. *No se lo digan a ellos ahora; díganselo más tarde.* 4. *Deseamos alquilar un coche muy bonito (un coche bonitísimo) por una cuota muy barata (baratísima).* 5. *El trabajó el año pasado; este año yo comencé a trabajar.* 6. *Javier toca el piano.* 7. *Me tocó un caballo de mala suerte en el hipódromo.* 8. *Nos gustó la comida.* 9. *Anoche me acosté temprano.* 10. *Son los más caros.*

LECTURA II

EL TRABAJA EN UNA AGENCIA DE VIAJES[1]

Me llamo Raúl Martínez. Soy agente de viajes[1] y trabajo en una agencia de viajes de Santiago de Chile. La mayor parte del día, hablo por teléfono con mis clientes. Hago reservaciones pare excursiones nacionales e internacionales[2] y vendo pasajes[3] por barco, avión, trenes, etc. También les hago a mis clientes[4] las reservaciones en los hoteles y los conecto[5] con hermosas giras[6] y excursiones en grupos.

Si se trata de una gira local, los clientes reciben un folleto con información y también se les proporciona[7] una guía que les mostrará[8] los lugares más importantes, como por ejemplo[9] Santiago, capital del país. Hay giras de uno o dos días a Valparaíso y Viña del Mar, que son ciudades muy hermosas. Otras ciudades que se pueden conocer[10] son La Serena, Copiapo, Antofagasta, que quedan[11] al norte[12] del país. Al sur[12] están las ciudades de

Talca, Chillán, la región de los lagos,[13] la Patagonia, y muchos otros sitios preciosos. La Isla de Pascua, conocida también con el nombre de[14] "Isla de Robinson Crusoe," es bastante turística y ofrece mariscos deliciosos.

Muchos de mis clientes viajan por Europa.[15] Algunos viajes están cuidadosamente organizados[16] con actividades y comidas planeadas de antemano.[17] Otros prefieren[18] comprar los pasajes y hacerse su propio itinerario[19]. . . ¡cada uno con su gusto![20] ¡Buen viaje a todos![21]

VOCABULARIO

1. *Agente/agencia de viajes*	travel agent/agency
2. *excursiones nacionales e internacionales*	national and international tours *(e* is used instead of *y* when the following word begins with *i* or *hi)*
3. *pasajes*	passages, tickets
4. *les hago a mis clientes . . .*	I make for my clients . . .
5. *los conecto con*	I connect them (over) with; book them with
6. *gira*	outing, trip
7. *se les proporciona*	one provides them (with)
8. *una guía que les mostrará*	a guide who will show them
9. *por ejemplo*	for example
10. *se pueden conocer*	one/they can get to know
11. *quedan (quedar)*	are situated (also: to remain, to stay)
12. *norte/sur*	north/south
13. *la región de los lagos*	the lake region
14. *conocida también con el nombre de*	also known as/by the name of
15. *viajan por Europa*	(they) travel through Europe
16. *cuidadosamente organizados*	carefully organized
17. *planeadas de antemano*	planned beforehand
18. *otros prefieren*	others prefer
19. *hacerse su propio itinerario*	to make (themselves) their own itinerary
20. *¡Cada uno con su gusto!*	To each his/her own!
21. *¡Buen viaje a todos!*	Bon voyage to everyone!

LECCION 21

EN EL CONSULTORIO DEL MEDICO.   At the doctor's of fice.

A. DIALOGO

En la Clínica Placer de La Paz, Bolivia.

DOCTORA: **Por aquí, señor. Siéntese. ¿Qué tiene Ud.?**

SEÑOR ATLAS: **Cuando me levanté esta mañana, estuve enfermo. Tuve fuertes dolores de cabeza y de estómago. Fue muy desagradable. Fui al baño y tomé dos aspirinas.**

DOCTORA: **¿Pudo Ud. caminar sin sentir vértigo?**

SEÑOR ATLAS: **No, doctora. Tuve que apoyarme en los muebles. Comí unas tostadas y tomé té. Luego, volví a la cama y la llamé.**

DOCTORA: **¿Cómo se siente ahora? ¿Todavía continúan los dolores?**

SEÑOR ATLAS: **Poco a poco comenzaron a disminuir. Hace dos horas pude levantarme y me puse mucha ropa para venir aquí.**

DOCTORA: **¿Qué comió Ud. anoche?**

SEÑOR ATLAS: **Tuvimos una fiesta en casa. Hubo mucha comida y bebida. Nuestros invitados partieron muy tarde.**

DOCTORA: **Pues, señor Atlas, me parece que Ud. comió demasiado anoche. Hoy debe descansar y mañana Ud. va a estar perfectamente bien.**

At the Placer clinic in La Paz, Bolivia.

DOCTOR: This way, sir. Sit down. What's the matter with you?

SEÑOR ATLAS: When I got up this morning I was ill. I had a bad headache and stomach ache. It was very unpleasant. I went to the bathroom and took two aspirins.

DOCTOR: Were you able to walk without feeling dizzy?

SEÑOR ATLAS: No, doctor. I had to hold on to the furniture. I ate some toast and drank some tea. Then I went back to bed and called you.

DOCTOR: How do you feel now? Are the pains still continuing?

SEÑOR ATLAS: Little by little they began to diminish. Two hours ago I was able to get up and I put on lots of clothing to come here.

DOCTOR: What did you eat last night?

SEÑOR ATLAS: We had a party at home. There was lots of food and drink. Our guests left very late.

DOCTOR: Well, Mr. Atlas, it seems to me that you ate too much last night. Today you must rest and tomorrow you will be completely well.

B. GRAMATICA Y USOS

1. THE PRETERITE OF REGULAR -*ER* AND -*IR* VERBS

The endings for regular -*er* and -*ir* verbs are alike:

COMER TO EAT

yo		*í*	*comí*
tú		*iste*	*comiste*
Ud., él, ella	*com*	*ió*	*comió*
nosotros, -as		*imos*	*comimos*
vosotros, -as		*~~isteis~~*	*~~comisteis~~*
Uds., ellos, ellas		*ieron*	*comieron*

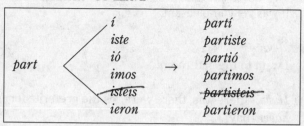

PARTIR TO LEAVE				
yo		*í*		*partí*
tú		*iste*		*partiste*
Ud., él, ella	*part*	*ió*	→	*partió*
nosotros, -as		*imos*		*partimos*
vosotros, -as		~~*isteis*~~		~~*partisteis*~~
Uds., ellos, ellas		*ieron*		*partieron*

2. IRREGULAR PRETERITES WITH *U*

Here is the *u* group of irregular preterite verbs that must be memorized.

PODER TO BE ABLE	ESTAR TO BE	TENER TO HAVE	PONER TO PUT	SABER TO KNOW	ANDAR TO WALK
pude	*estuve*	*tuve*	*puse*	*supe*	*anduve*
pudiste	*estuviste*	*tuviste*	*pusiste*	*supiste*	*anduviste*
pudo	*estuvo*	*tuve*	*puso*	*supo*	*anduvo*
pudimos	*estuvimos*	*tuvimos*	*pusimos*	*supimos*	*anduvimos*
pudisteis	*estuvisteis*	*tuvisteis*	*pusisteis*	*supisteis*	*anduvisteis*
pudieron	*estuvieron*	*tuvieron*	*pusieron*	*supieron*	*anduvieron*

Estuve enfermo ayer.
I was sick yesterday.

Nos pusimos mucha ropa.
We put on lots of clothing.

3. THE PRETERITE OF *IR, SER,* AND *HABER*

Ir and *ser* are the same in the preterite. The context will clarify the meaning.

IR TO GO AND SER TO BE			
yo	*fui*	nosotros, -as	*fuimos*
tú	*fuiste*	vosotros, -as	~~*fuisteis*~~
Ud., él, ella	*fue*	Uds., ellos, ellas	*fueron*

Fue muy desagradable.
   It was very unpleasant.

Fui al baño.
   I went to the bathroom.

   Hubo, "there was, there were," is the preterite form of the verb *haber* (hay).

Hubo mucha comida.
   There was lots of food.

4. *HACE* + PRETERITE

Hace + preterite expresses the concept of "ago":

Hace dos horas pude levantarme.
   Two hours ago I was able to get up.

VOCABULARIO

el médico/la médica	doctor
el doctor/la doctora	doctor
clínica	clinic, hospital
consultorio del médico	doctor's office
¡Siéntese!	Sit down. (formal)
¿Qué tiene Ud.?	What's the matter with you?
estar enfermo	to be sick
sentirse *(e>ie)*	to feel
¿Cómo se siente ahora?	How do you feel now?
fuerte	strong
débil	weak
perfectamente bien	completely well
cabeza	head
el dolor de cabeza	headache
estómago	stomach
el dolor de estómago	stomachache

vértigo/mareo	dizziness
sentir vértigo	to feel dizzy
Fue muy desagradable.	It was very unpleasant.
tomar una aspirina	to take an aspirin
apoyarse	to support oneself (physically)
caminar	to walk
Los dolores comenzaron a disminuir.	The pains began to diminish.
tostada	toast
el té	tea
cama	bed
fiesta	party
por aquí	this way
sin	without
poco a poco	little by little
al final	finally
hubo	there was, there were
demasiado	too much
todavía	still

EXAMEN

A. *Conteste la pregunta en una oración completa usando la pista.*

1. *¿Qué tiene? (dolor de cabeza)*
2. *¿Qué tomó Ud.? (dos aspirinas)*
3. *¿Comenzaron a disminuir los dolores? (poco a poco)*
4. *¿Cómo se siente ahora? (perfectamente bien)*
5. *¿Qué debo hacer? (descansar hoy)*

B. *Escriba la oración nuevamente en el pretérito.*

MODELO: *Se siente bien por la mañana.*
          Se sintió bien por la mañana.

1. *Cuando me levanto, me siento bien.*
2. *Tengo un dolor de estómago porque como demasiado.*
3. *Voy a ver al médico cuando estoy enfermo.*
4. *Ando un poco y siento vértigo.*
5. *Voy a las ocho y puedo sentarme en el tren.*

C. *Traduzca al español.*

1. What's the matter with you?
2. Sit down!
3. Do the pains still continue?
4. Do you feel strong or weak?
5. Yesterday I went to the doctor's office.

NOTAS CULTURALES

In Spain and a few Latin American countries, the term *doctor* or *doctora* is used as a polite form of address to any educated or professional person. It does not necessarily mean that they hold any advanced degree. A doctor of medicine is professionally called a *médico* and can be addressed as *doctor* or *doctora*.

You can obtain a list of English-speaking doctors whose training meets American standards from the International Association for Medical Assistance to Travelers in case you need medical attention while traveling throughout Spain or Latin America. You can contact them by writing to 417 Center St., Lewiston, NY 14092, or call them at (716) 754–4883. Their Web site is at www.sentex.net/~iamat/ci.html. If you travel with medication, have your doctor write out a prescription with the generic name of the drug in case you lose or misplace it.

RESPUESTAS

A. 1. *Tengo un dolor de cabeza.* 2. *Tomé dos aspirinas.* 3. *Sí, comenzaron a disminuir poco a poco.* 4. *Me siento perfectamente bien.* 5. *Debe descansar hoy.*

B. 1. *Cuando me levanté, me sentí bien.* 2. *Tuve un dolor de estómago porque comí demasiado.* 3. *Fui a ver al médico cuando estuve enfermo.* 4. *Anduve un poco y sentí vértigo.* 5. *Fui a las ocho y pude sentarme en el tren.*

C. 1. *¿Qué tiene Ud.?* 2. *¡Siéntese!* 3. *¿Todavía continúan los dolores?* 4. *¿Se siente fuerte o débil?* 5. *Ayer yo fui al consultorio del médico.*

LECCION 22

CON EL DENTISTA.   At the dentist's.

A. DIALOGO

¿Hay que arrancarme la muela?

AURORA: **Seguí sus consejos, doctor. Hice todo. Me cepillé los dientes tres veces al día y usé la seda dental. Fui a la farmacia y le pedí al farmacéutico un enjuague bucal contra el sarro.**

ARMANDO: **Muy bien. Y ¿por qué está aquí hoy?**

AURORA: **Anoche, las encías se me pusieron rojas, se hincharon y yo sentí un fuerte dolor en la quijada. No dormí nada.**

ARMANDO: **Voy a examinarle los dientes. Abra la boca. ¿Dónde le duele a Ud. más, aquí o aquí?**

AURORA: **Ahí mismo, en el primero.**

ARMANDO: **Me parece que murió la raíz. Para comprobarlo voy a sacarle una radiografía. Si es necesario, le hago un empaste de la raíz.**

AURORA: **¿Empaste de la raíz? ¿Puedo preguntarle algo, doctor? ¿Hay que arrancarme la muela?**

ARMANDO: **¡Claro que no! ¡No se ponga Ud. nerviosa! Sus dientes están en buenas condiciones. Tuvo pocas caries; las encías están sanas. Parece que cuida muy bien de los dientes.**

Do you have to pull out my tooth?

AURORA: I followed your advice, doctor. I did everything. I brushed my teeth three times a day and I used dental floss. I went to the pharmacy and asked the pharmacist for an anti-plaque mouthwash.

ARMANDO: Fine. And why are you here today?

AURORA: Last night my gums became red, swelled up, and I felt a severe pain in my jaw. I didn't sleep at all.

ARMANDO: I'll examine your teeth. Open your mouth. Where does it hurt more, here . . . or here?

AURORA: Right there, in the first one.

ARMANDO: I think that the root has died. To verify it, I'll take an x-ray. If necessary, I'll do a root canal.

AURORA: Root canal? Can I ask you something, doctor? Will you have to pull out the tooth?

ARMANDO: Of course not. Don't get nervous! Your teeth are in good shape. You had a few cavities; the gums are healthy. It seems that you take good care of your teeth.

B. GRAMATICA Y USOS

1. THE PRETERITE OF *HACER*

HACER TO DO

yo	hice	nosotros, -as	hicimos
tú	hiciste	vosotros, -as	hicisteis
Ud., él, ella	hizo	Uds., ellos, ellas	hicieron

Hice todo.
    I did everything.

¿Qué hiciste?
    What did you do?

Hicieron ejercicios.
    They did exercises.

2. RADICAL-CHANGING PRETERITES *E>I* AND *O>U*

There are *-ir* verbs that have a radical change only in the third persons singular and plural of the preterite. The inflections are totally regular.

	PEDIR (e>i) TO ASK FOR		dormir (o>u) TO SLEEP
yo	pedí	yo	dormí
tú	pediste	tú	dormiste
Ud., él, ella	pidió	Ud., él, ella	durmió
nosotros, -as	pedimos	nosotros, -as	dormimos
vosotros, -as	pedisteis	vosotros, -as	dormisteis
Uds, ellos, ellas	pidieron	Uds., ellos, ellas	durmieron

Le pidieron un enjuague bucal.
They asked him for a mouthwash.

Repitió la respuesta.
He repeated the answer.

No durmió para nada.
He didn't sleep at all.

Murió de pena.
She died of a broken heart.

Verbs with radical changes in the present and preterite will be indicated in the vocabulary as follows: *pedir (e>i) (e>i); dormir (o>ue) (o>u):* the information in the parenthesis refers to the present and preterite, respectively.

3. THE VERB *DOLER*

The verb *doler (o>ue)*, "to hurt" ("to be hurting"), is used like the verb *gustar:*

¿Dónde le duele a Ud. más?
Where does it hurt you more?

Me duele más el primer diente.

The first tooth hurts me more.

Me duelen las piernas.

My legs hurt me.

Doler does not have a radical change in the preterite:

Anoche le dolieron las encías.

Last night his gums hurt.

4. THE VERBS *PREGUNTAR* AND *PEDIR*

The verb *preguntar* means "to ask a question"; *pedir* means "to ask for, to request, to order."

¿Puedo preguntarle algo, doctor?

May I ask you something, doctor?

Le pedí al farmacéutico un enjuague bucal.

I asked the pharmacist for a mouthwash.

Pedimos bistec en el restaurante.

We order steak at the restaurant.

The indirect objects of these verbs are almost always people.

5. EXPRESSIONS FOR "TO BECOME"

The English verb "to become" has several equivalents in Spanish.

a. *Ponerse* and *volverse* are used to describe sudden changes in physical, emotional, or mental states:

No se ponga nervioso.

Don't become (get) nervous.

Se volvió loca después.
Later on, she went crazy.

b. *Hacerse* describes other sudden changes:

Ella se hizo rica al vender la casa.
She got rich by selling the house.

c. *Llegar a ser* is used to describe reaching a new status after long, hard work:

Llegó a ser presidente de la compañía después de veinticinco años de servicio a ella.
He became president of the company after twenty-five years of working there.

VOCABULARIO

dentista	dentist
la boca	mouth
¡Abra la boca!	Open your mouth!
muela	tooth
el diente	tooth
la seda dental	dental floss
sarro, placa	plaque
cepillo de dientes	toothbrush
pasta de dientes	toothpaste
la carie	cavity
la raíz	root
arrancar/sacar una muela	to pull out a tooth
cepillarse (los dientes)	to brush one's teeth
examinar	to examine
el empaste	filling
el empaste de la raíz	root canal
lengua	tongue
el enjuague bucal	mouthwash

el labio	lip
las encías	gums
quijada	jaw
radiografía	x-ray
sacar una radiografía	to take an x-ray
hincharse	to swell
estar sano, *-a*	to be healthy
seguir *(e>i)*	to follow
Seguí sus instrucciones.	I followed your instructions.
morir(se) *(o>ue) (o>u)*	to die
ponerse	to become
¡No se ponga nervioso!	Don't get nervous.
volverse	to become
hacerse	to become
llegar a ser	to become
hay que (+ infinitive)	it is necessary, one must
Hay que hacerlo.	It has to be done. One must do it.
tres veces al día	three times a day
ahí mismo	right there
¿Puedo preguntarle algo?	May I ask you something?

EXAMEN

A. *Conteste la pregunta en una oración completa usando la pista.*

1. *¿Dónde siente el dolor? (en la muela)*
2. *¿Qué pasó a las encias? (hincharse)*
3. *¿Cuántas veces al día se cepilla Ud.? (tres veces)*
4. *¿Qué vas a sacar? (una radiografía de los dientes)*

B. *Escoja el verbo correcto y dé la forma correcta del mismo.*

1. *Trabajó mucho; _____ presidente. (llegar a ser, ponerse)*
2. *De repente, ella _____ nerviosa. (ponerse, hacerse)*
3. *Ayer, él me _____ un favor. (pedir, preguntar)*
4. *Quiero _____ sobre su salud. (pedirle, preguntarle)*

C. *Escriba en una oración.*

1. Ask the dentist if you have any cavities.
2. Tell the dentist that you brush your teeth two or three times a day.
3. Ask the dentist if your gums are in good condition.
4. Tell the dentist that you get nervous when you have to visit him/her.

NOTAS CULTURALES

While there are private dentists' practices in both Spain and Latin America, the quality and conditions of treatment vary widely. Well-trained dentists are highly prized and very highly paid.

RESPUESTAS

A. 1. *Siento el dolor en la muela. 2. Las encías se hincharon. 3. Me cepillo tres veces al día. 4. Voy a sacar una radiografía de los dientes.*
B. 1. *llegó a ser* 2. *se puso* 3. *pidió* 4. *preguntarle*
C. 1. *¿Tengo algunas caries? 2. Yo me cepillo dos o tres veces al día. 3. ¿Están las encías en buenas condiciones? 4. Me pongo nervioso/a cuando tengo que visitarlo/la.*

LECCION 23
COMPRANDO UNA COMPUTADORA.   Buying a computer.

A. DIALOGO

En el campus de Southwestern College en Chula Vista, California.

OSCAR: ¿Cómo estás, Consuelo? ¿Qué llevas ahí?

CONSUELO: Conduje a Computer World esta mañana y compré una computadora. Voy a conectarme al Internet. Me muero por aprender a usar los navegadores, el correo electrónico, y crear una página personal.

OSCAR: ¡Oye, que bien! Necesitas conseguir un módem y un proveedor de servicio al Internet.

CONSUELO: Eso ya lo sé. Hazme un favor, Oscar. Ayúdame a instalar la computadora.

OSCAR: ¿Compraste todo lo necesario? Necesitas programas, discos, la pantalla, el ratón, y una buena impresora.

CONSUELO: Ya tengo todo, incluyendo a AOL (America Online) como proveedor de servicio y programas de Microsoft. ¡Estoy lista para navegar la red!

On campus at Southwestern College in Chula Vista, California.

OSCAR: How are you, Consuelo? What do you have there?

CONSUELO: I drove to Computer World this morning and I bought a computer. I am going to hook up to the Internet. I'm dying to learn how to use navigators, e-mail, and create a Web page.

OSCAR: Hey, that's great! You'll need to get a modem and an Internet service provider.

CONSUELO: I know that. Do me a favor, Oscar. Help me install my computer.

OSCAR: Did you buy all the necessary components? You need programs, disks, the monitor, the mouse, and a good printer.

CONSUELO: I have everything, including AOL as my service provider and Microsoft programs. I'm ready to surf the Web!

B. GRAMATICA Y USOS

In formal

1. AFFIRMATIVE FAMILIAR COMMANDS

tu

We have used the polite command *(Ud.)* for "you." The affirmative **tú** command comes from the third person of the present tense:

¡Habla!	Speak!
¡Come!	Eat!

The following verbs have irregular familiar commands:

decir: di	*hacer: haz*	*ir: ve*	*poner: pon*
salir: sal	*ser: sé*	*tener: ten*	*venir: ven*

Object pronouns and reflexive pronouns must be attached to these commands:

Hazlo.	Do it.
Dime.	Tell me.
Levántate.	Get up.

When you attach object pronouns, remember to write an accent mark on the original point of stress of the verb form:

Córtamelo.	Cut it for me.
Póntelo.	Put it on.

We shall see the negative familiar commands in a later lesson.

2. THE "LET'S" COMMAND: *VAMOS* + *A* + INFINITIVE

The first-person plural or "let's" command can be expressed by *vamos* + *a* + infinitive:

Vamos a comprarte una computadora. Let's buy you a computer.
Vamos a hacerle un favor. Let's do him a favor.

3. IRREGULAR PRETERITES WITH *J*

The following verbs have a *j* in their preterite forms:

	DECIR TO SAY	*TRAER* TO BRING	*TRADUCIR* TO TRANSLATE	*CONDUCIR* TO LEAD, DRIVE
yo	*dije*	*traje*	*traduje*	*conduje*
tú	*dijiste*	*trajiste*	*tradujiste*	*condujiste*
Ud., él, ella	*dijo*	*trajo*	*tradujo*	*condujo*
nosotros, -as	*dijimos*	*trajimos*	*tradujimos*	*condujimos*
vosotros, -as	*dijisteis*	*trajisteis*	*tradujisteis*	*condujisteis*
Uds., ellos, ellas	*dijeron*	*trajeron*	*tradujeron*	*condujeron*

No trajeron el ratón.
They didn't bring the mouse.

Conduje todo el día.
I drove all day long.

4. THE NEUTER *LO*

The neuter pronoun *lo* is used with the masculine singular form of adjectives to describe a general quality.

lo bueno   the good thing (about it), what's
                                                            good (about it)
lo peor   the worst thing, what's worse

Lo bueno de una computadora es que no hay que usar una maquina de escribir.

The good thing about a computer is that you don't have to use a typewriter.

VOCABULARIO

campus	campus
colegio	college
computadora, ordenador (Spain)	computer
conectar, instalar	hook up
muriendo	dying
navegador	navigators
correo electrónico	e-mail
crear	create
página Web	Web page
módem	modem
Internet	Internet
proveedor de servicio	service provider
componentes	components
programas	programs
discos	disks
pantalla	monitor
ratón	mouse
impresora	printer
programas	programs
navegar la red	surf the Web
archivo	file
formato	format
disco duro	hard drive
partes metales o plásticas de una computadora personal	hardware
teclado	keyboard

EXAMEN

A. *Conteste a la pregunta en una oración completa usando la pista.*

1. *De qué color quieres tu computadora? (azul)*
2. *Qué computadora usa Ud.? (iMac)*
3. *Dónde quieres el módem? (sobre el escritorio)*
4. *Qué impresora prefieres? (laser)*
5. *Qué tipo de pantalla quieres? (grande)*

B. *Relacione una palabra de la Columna A con una de la Columna B.*

COLUMNA A	COLUMNA B
1. *red*	a. disk
2. *pantalla*	b. hard drive
3. *ratón*	c. keyboard
4. *teclado*	d. monitor
5. *disco*	e. Web
6. *disco duro*	f. mouse

C. *Escriba una oración usando el imperativo formal.* (Write a sentence using the formal command.)

MODELO: Tell your salesman to put the computer in your car.
       Póngala en mi coche.

1. Tell Oscar to connect you to the Internet.
2. Tell him to do you a favor.
3. Tell him to pick up the printer.
4. Tell him to do it.
5. Tell him to go to Computer World with you.
6. Tell him to be nicer.
7. Tell him to come to your house.
8. Tell him to tell you the truth.

NOTAS CULTURALES

The Internet is a system of interconnected computer networks that enables machines to communicate directly. It was initially developed in 1973 as part of a project for the United States Department of Defense Advanced Research Projects Agency. The Internet began as a computer network that connected computers at several research labs and universities across the United States.

The World Wide Web is a collection of files, called Web sites or Web pages, with a specific address called a uniform resource locator (URL). Computer programs called browsers, such as Microsoft's Internet Explorer or Netscape's Navigator, use the URLs to find and display the Web site or Web page. There has been explosive growth in Internet development and the number of hosts, or any computer with a dedicated connection to the Internet, in Latin America. It should continue to grow in spite of factors such as limited phone lines, low penetration of personal computers, and low per capita income.

	Number of Hosts (1/1997)	Hosts per Million People	Percentage Growth of Hosts	Phone lines per 1,000 people
Argentina	12,688	370	905	78
Brazil	77,148	480	9,544	61
Chile	15,885	1,121	420	55
Colombia	9,054	250	703	52
Ecuador	590	54	80	30
Mexico	29,840	318	348	68
Peru	5,192	216	2,936	22
Venezuela	2,417	115	357	68
Rest of World	16,146,000	NA	332	NA

Source: Network Wizards at *http://www.nw.com/* and CIA Handbook

RESPUESTAS

A. 1. *La quiero azul.* 2. *Uso la computadora iMac.* 3. *Lo quiero sobre el escritorio.* 4. *Prefiero una impresora laser.* 5. *Quiero una pantalla grande.*

B. 1.—e. 2.—d. 3.—f. 4.—c. 5.—a. 6.—b.

C. 1. *Conéctame al Internet.* 2. *Hazme un favor.* 3. *Levanta la impresora.* 4. *Hazlo.* 5. *Ven a Computer World conmigo.* 6. *Sé mas bueno.* 7. *Ven a mi casa.* 8. *Dime la verdad.*

LECCION 24

EN LA TAQUILLA DEL TEATRO.   At the theater box office.

A. DIALOGO

En la taquilla del Teatro Liceo de Buenos Aires, Argentina.

VIRGINIA: **Vine a comprar dos entradas para *Fuenteovejuna* de Lope de Vega.**

TAQUILLERO: **No me quedan entradas para el estreno. Para mañana hay asientos en la galería y en las primeras filas de la platea—los más caros.**

VIRGINIA: **Me encanta tanto esta obra que estoy dispuesta a pagar lo que sea. Déme dos butacas de platea para mañana.**

TAQUILLERO: **Muy bien. ¿Leyó Ud. que la producción comenzó a representarse en Madrid y fue el mayor éxito de la temporada?**

VIRGINIA: **Sí. El público le dio muchos aplausos al protagonista. . . .**

TAQUILLERO: **Y los críticos le dieron un premio.**

VIRGINIA: **¡Qué maravilla! ¿A qué hora empieza?**

TAQUILLERO: **El telón va a subir a las ocho. Y hay dos entreactos. Aquí tiene las entradas: asientos veintiséis y veintiocho de la fila C. ¡Que se diviertan!**

At the Teatro Liceo box office in Buenos Aires, Argentina.

VIRGINIA: I came to buy two tickets for Lope de Vega's *Fuenteovejuna*.

BOX OFFICE AGENT: There are no tickets left for the opening. For tomorrow, there are balcony seats and seats in the first rows of the orchestra—the most expensive ones.

VIRGINIA: I like this play so much that I'm ready to pay whatever (the price). Give me two orchestra seats for tomorrow.

BOX OFFICE AGENT: Okay. Did you read that the production began playing in Madrid and that it was the greatest hit of the season?

VIRGINIA: Yes. The audience applauded the star a lot. . . .

BOX OFFICE AGENT: And the critics gave him a prize.

VIRGINIA: How marvelous! At what time does it begin?

BOX OFFICE AGENT: The curtain goes up at 8:00 o'clock. And there are two intermissions. Here are your tickets: seats 26 and 28 of row C. Enjoy yourselves!

B. GRAMATICA Y USOS

1. IRREGULAR PRETERITES WITH Y

The verbs *oír* (to hear), *caer* (to fall), and *leer* (to read) have irregular preterites with *y* in the third person forms:

	OÍR TO HEAR	*CAER(SE)* TO FALL	*LEER* TO READ
yo	*oí*	*caí*	*leí*
tú	*oíste*	*caíste*	*leíste*
Ud., él, ella	*oyó*	*cayó*	*leyó*
nosotros, -as	*oímos*	*caímos*	*leímos*
vosotros, -as	*oísteis*	*caísteis*	*leísteis*
Uds., ellos, ellas	*oyeron*	*cayeron*	*leyeron*

Other verbs like *oír* in the preterite:

creer   to believe
poseer   to possess, own

¿Leyó Ud. que la producción fue el mayor éxito de la temporada?
Did you read that the production was the greatest hit of the season?

El libro se cayó.
The book fell.

Leyeron mucho ayer.
They read a lot yesterday.

2. THE PRETERITE OF *QUERER, VENIR,* AND *DAR*

	QUERER TO WANT	*VENIR* TO COME	*DAR* TO GIVE
yo	*quise*	*vine*	*di*
tú	*quisiste*	*viniste*	*diste*
Ud., él, ella	*quiso*	*vino*	*dio*
nosotros, -as	*quisimos*	*vinimos*	*dimos*
vosotros, -as	*quisisteis*	*vinisteis*	*disteis*
Uds., ellos, ellas	*quisieron*	*vinieron*	*dieron*

Vine a comprar dos entradas.
I came to buy two tickets.

Le dieron un premio.
They gave him a prize.

No querer in the preterite means "to refuse":

Ella no quiso ir al teatro.
She refused to go to the theater.

3. VERB + PREPOSITION + INFINITIVE

Many conjugated verbs in Spanish are followed by a preposition before an infinitive. We have seen the use of *ir + a + *infinitive:

El telón va a subir a las ocho.   The curtain goes up at 8:00 o'clock.

Other verbs followed by *a* include:

venir a:	*Vine a comprar dos entradas.*
	I came to buy to tickets.
comenzar a:	*El protagonista comenzó a*
	representar en Madrid.
	The star began to play in Madrid.
empezar a:	*El elenco empieza a representar sus*
	papeles esta noche.
	The cast begins to play their roles
	tonight.
estar dispuesto a:	*Estoy dispuesta a pagar lo que sea.*
	I'm ready to pay whatever.
acostumbrarse a:	*Nunca te acostumbras a trabajar.*
	You'll never get used to working.

Other verbs are followed by *con* or *en*:

soñar con:	*Soñé tanto con ellos.*
	I dreamed so much about them.
insistir en:	*Insistí en venir ahora.*
	I insisted upon coming now.

4. ORDINAL NUMBERS

You already know the cardinal numbers—the numbers used in counting (one, two, three, etc.). The ordinal numbers (first, second, third, etc.) indicate position in a sequence. The numbers from "first" to "tenth" are adjectives, and are used frequently. For other ordinals substitute the cardinal number.

primer, primero, -*a*	first	**sexto,** -*a*	sixth
segundo, -*a*	second	**séptimo,** -*a*	seventh
tercer, tercero, -*a*	third	**octavo,** -*a*	eighth
cuarto, -*a*	fourth	**noveno,** -*a*	ninth
quinto, -*a*	fifth	**décimo,** -*a*	tenth

Primero and *tercero* drop the *o* before the masculine singular noun.

Nos quedan algunas en las primeras filas de la platea.
We have a few left in the first rows of the orchestra.

Es el tercer éxito de nuestra temporada.
It's our season's third hit.

Vive en el piso veinte.
He lives on the twentieth floor.

VOCABULARIO

taquilla/billetería	box office
entrada/billete/boleto	ticket
quedar	to remain, to have left over
No me quedan entradas.	I don't have any tickets left.
precio	price
estreno	opening (show); premiere
estrenarse	to open (a show); to premiere
encantarle a uno	to like
Me encanta esta pieza.	I like this play.
la representación	performance
representar un papel	to play a role
asiento	seat
platea	orchestra (in a theater)
butaca de platea	orchestra seat
galería	balcony
Déme dos entradas para la platea.	Give me two seats in the orchestra.
el actor	actor
la actriz	actress
el/*la* protagonista	star
público	audience
dar palmadas	to applaud, to clap
aplaudir	to applaud
crítico	critic
premio	prize
la producción	production
éxito	hit, success

El telón sube a las ocho.	The curtain goes up at eight.
fila	row
divertirse *(e>ie) (e>i)*	to enjoy oneself
¡Qué se diviertan!	Enjoy yourselves!
estar dispuesto a	to be ready to
soñar *(o>ue)* **con**	to dream about
insistir en	to insist upon
¡Qué maravilla!	How marvelous!

EXAMEN

A. *Conteste la pregunta en una oración completa usando la pista.*

1. *¿Dónde quieren sentarse? (en la platea)*
2. *¿Cuánto está Ud. dispuesto a pagar? (lo que sea)*
3. *¿Le gustan los actores? (encantarle a uno)*
4. *¿A qué hora sube el telón? (8:30)*
5. *¿Hay entreacto? (dos)*

B. *Dé la forma correcta del verbo en el pretérito.*

MODELO: José y Ana _____ tarde. (venir)/vinieron.

1. *Anoche Ud. _____ el periódico. (leer)*
2. *Ella _____ en el teatro. (caerse)*
3. *Nosotros no _____ ver la pieza. (querer)*
4. *Nadie _____ a visitarnos. (venir)*
5. *Nosotros _____ que el protagonista es hermoso. (oír)*
6. *¿Ud. le _____ las entradas a él? (dar)*

C. *Traduzca al español.*

1. I insisted upon seeing the play.
2. They sold all the balcony seats.
3. The cast is excellent.
4. The production was the season's hit.
5. The seats are in row C.

NOTAS CULTURALES

Spain has one of the world's most important theater traditions, including dramatists of Spain's Golden Age—such as Tirso de Molina and Calderón de la Barca. However, Lope Félix de Vega Carpio, better known as Lope de Vega, is usually considered the greatest Spanish playwright. His *comedias,* three-act plays in which comedy and tragedy are intertwined, usually involved historical subject matter. Representative of his "New Comedy," as Lope's popular, nonclassical drama came to be called, are three of his best-known plays, *El castigo sin venganza, El caballero de Olmedo,* and *Fuenteovenjuna.* Lope de Vega usually exalts the peasant's way of life, simple values, and lifestyle, while portraying the monarchy as the primary source of justice and social order. This great theater tradition was passed on to the Latin American colonies and continues to this day.

Theaters flourish throughout Latin America, but Buenos Aires is without doubt the capital, having some 45 theaters constantly presenting Argentine and foreign dramas as well as musicals.

RESPUESTAS

A. 1. *Queremos sentarnos en la platea.* 2. *Estoy dispuesto a pagar lo que sea.*
   3. *Me encantan los actores.* 4. *El telón sube a las ocho y media.* 5. *Si, hay dos entreactos.*
B. 1. *leyó* 2. *se cayó* 3. *quisimos* 4. *vino* 5. *oímos* 6. *dio*
C. 1. *Insistí en ver la obra.* 2. *Vendieron todos los asientos de la galeria./Se vendió todos los asientos de la galería.* 3. *El elenco es excelente.* 4. *La producción fue el éxito de la temporada.* 5. *Los asientos están en la fila C.*

LECCION 25

¡A REGATEAR! Bargaining.

A. DIALOGO

En el Rastro de Madrid, España.

DOÑA FLORINDA: **¿Cuánto cuesta esa cómoda cuya madera está bastante carcomida?**

DON VICENTE: **Es una antigüedad muy fina, señora. Lleva un precio de tres mil euros.**

DOÑA FLORINDA: **¡Dios mío! No vale tanto. Claro que nadie pagaba tal cantidad.**

DON VICENTE: **Llegaban ofertas, pero me gustaba tanto mirarla que no las aceptaba.**

DOÑA FLORINDA: **No tiene precio fijo. ¿A cuánto me lo deja Ud.?**

DON VICENTE: **Para Ud. se la dejo en la mitad del precio original: mil quinientos euros.**

DOÑA FLORINDA: **¡Menudo descuento! Como cliente antigua, Ud. tiene que ofrecérmela a un descuento de, por lo menos, setenta por ciento.**

DON VICENTE: **Bueno, señora. Ya sé que a Ud. le gusta regatear. Lléveselo al último precio de mil doscientos euros.**

At the Rastro in Madrid, Spain.

DOÑA FLORINDA: How much is that chest of drawers whose wood is so eaten through?

DON VICENTE: It's a very fine antique, madam. It has a price tag of 3,000 euros.

DOÑA FLORINDA: Good God! It's not worth that much. Of course nobody paid such a sum.

DON VICENTE: I got offers, but I liked looking at it so much that I didn't accept them.

DOÑA FLORINDA: It doesn't have a fixed price. For how much will you sell it to me?

DON VICENTE: I'll give it to you for half the original price: 1,500 euros.

DOÑA FLORINDA: What a discount! As an old customer, you have to sell it to me at a discount of at least seventy percent.

DON VICENTE: All right, madam. I know you like to bargain. Take it for my final price of 1,200 euros.

B. GRAMATICA Y USOS

1. THE CONCEPT OF THE IMPERFECT TENSE

You learned that the preterite tense relates an action looked upon as an event or fact that occurred once and ended. The imperfect is another past tense. It relates a continuous or habitual action, or describes the state of things over a period of time in the past. Very often, the imperfect is indicated by adverbial expressions of time describing these recurrent, continuous past actions or circumstances:

a menudo   *often*

siempre	always
todo el año pasado	all last year
toda la semana pasada	all last week
de joven	as a young person
de niño/a	as a child

a veces   *sometimes*

Todo el año pasado, llevaba un precio de medio millón de euros.
It had a price of 500,000 euros all last year.

Claro que nadie pagaba tal cantidad.
Of course nobody paid such a sum.

todos los días -

206

Siempre llevaba un precio fijo.
It always had a fixed price.

De joven, regateaba.
When I was young, I used to bargain.

2. THE IMPERFECT OF -*AR* VERBS

PAGAR   TO PAY

yo	aba	pagaba
tú	abas	pagabas
Ud., él, ella	aba	pagaba
nosotros, -as	ábamos →	pagábamos
vosotros, -as	abais	pagabais
Uds., ellos, ellas	aban	pagaban

pag

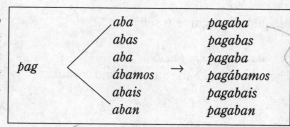

Nadie pagaba tal cantidad.   Nobody used to pay such a sum.
Nobody paid such a sum.
Nobody was paying such a sum.

Note that in English the helping verb "used to" often suggests the imperfect construction. Subject pronouns are frequently used with the first person singular and third persons singular and plural for clarity.

Yo hablaba por teléfono por la mañana.
I was talking on the phone in the morning.

Siempre pensaba en sus padres.
He was always thinking of his parents.

3. THE USES OF *TENER QUE, HAY QUE,* AND *DEBER*

These three expressions have been used in some of the dialogues we have studied. Generally all three mean "to have to, must, should." Use *tener que* to indicate strong need:

Tengo que venderlo ahora porque necesito el dinero.
I have to sell it now because I need the money.

Use *hay que* in an impersonal way:

Hay que regatear.
It is necessary/One has to bargain.

Use *deber* (to have to, must, should, ought to) to indicate personal obligation:

No debo venderla.
I shouldn't (ought not) sell it.

Deben tomar en cuenta la situación.
They should take the situation into account.

4. THE USE OF *CUYO*

Cuyo, -a, -os, -as is the adjective form of the possessive "whose." In Spanish, it agrees in number and gender with the thing possessed and *not* with the possessor.

¿Cuánto cuesta esa cómoda cuya madera está carcomida?
How much is that chest of drawers whose wood is eaten through?

La señora, a cuyos hijos le presenté, es amiga de su padre.
The lady whose children I introduced you to is a friend of your father's.

VOCABULARIO

regatear	to bargain
antigüedad	antique
precio fijo	fixed price
último precio	final price
precio máximo	top price
dejar a un precio	to sell at a price
etiqueta	(price) tag

pagar	to pay
cantidad	sum
dárselo a	to sell it for (a price)
oferta	offer
descuento	discount
mitad	half
la mitad del precio	half price
¡Menudo descuento!	What a discount! (meant ironically)
cuenta	account, bill
tomar en cuenta	to take into account
cliente	client
por ciento	percent
aumentar	to increase
bajar	to reduce
costar (o>ue)	to cost
¿Cuánto cuesta?	How much does it cost?
No vale tanto.	It's not worth that much.
Lléveselo.	Take it.
al por mayor	wholesale
al por menor	retail
¡Dios mío!	My God!
bastante	somewhat, sufficient
mirar	to look at
así	thus

EXAMEN

A. *Conteste la pregunta en una oración completa usando la pista.*

1. *¿Cuánto cuesta eso? (medio millón de pesetas)*
2. *¿Qué le gusta a ella? (regatear)*
3. *¿Cómo lo venden Uds.? (al por mayor)*
4. *¿Por qué no aceptaba él ofertas? (no desear venderlo)*
5. *¿A cuánto me lo deja Ud.? (un descuento de 50%)*

B. *Dé la forma correcta del verbo en paréntesis en el imperfecto.*

MODELO: El profesor _____ con el estudiante. (hablar)/hablaba

1. *Nosotros siempre _____ a la hora. (llegar)*
2. *El cliente _____ con el vendedor. (regatear)*
3. *Durante muchos años, los precios _____. (aumentar)*
4. *Yo _____ mucho porque me gustaba. (pagar)*
5. *¿Quiénes _____ la antigüedad? (mirar)*

C. *Escriba en español.*

1. Tell the salesman that the car is not worth that much.
2. Tell the saleswoman that you used to pay half the price for the dress.
3. Say that as a child you always used to take the bus to school.
4. Ask your friend if she used to visit her grandparents during weekends.
5. Say that you and your friend used to rent an apartment in the city.

NOTAS CULTURALES

In Spain, bargaining is still common, especially at markets like the outdoor bazaar in Madrid, *El Rastro.* In some places selling regional souvenirs in cities like Granada and Seville, you might ask for a discount.

Bargaining is far more common in Latin America. Salespeople are used to bargaining and know all the tricks. While vendors are usually prepared to lower their prices, be reasonable in your negotiations. In boutiques and department stores, the *etiqueta* indicates a *precio fijo,* although in boutiques there is a bit of leeway. If done properly, bargaining can be a lot of fun and a good way to practice your language skills!

RESPUESTAS

A. 1. *Eso cuesta medio millón de pesetas.* 2. *A ella le gusta regatear.*
   3. *Lo vendemos al por mayor.* 4. *Él no aceptaba ofertas porque no deseaba venderlo.* 5. *Se lo dejo a un descuento de cincuenta por ciento.*
B. 1. *llegábamos* 2. *regateaba* 3. *aumentaban* 4. *pagaba* 5. *miraban*
C. 1. *El coche no vale tanto.* 2. *Yo pagaba mitad del precio por el vestido.*
   3. *De niño/a, yo siempre tomaba el autobús a la escuela.* 4. *¿Visitabas a tus abuelos durante los fines de semana?* 5. *Nosotros/-as alquilábamos un departamento en la ciudad.*

QUINTO REPASO

A. *Cambie la oración al pretérito usando la pista.*

MODELO: *Siempre se pone triste. (anoche)*
Anoche se puso triste.

1. *Voy al médico. (ayer)*
2. *Tengo un dolor de cabeza. (anoche)*
3. *Comemos tres veces al día. (la semana pasada)*
4. *Nos ponemos abrigo porque hace frío. (esta mañana)*
5. *No saben nada. (el año pasado)*

B. *Rellene el espacio en blanco con la forma correcta del pretérito del verbo entre paréntesis.* (Fill in the blank with the correct preterite form of the verb in parenthesis.)

MODELO: *Ella la respuesta ayer. (saber)/supo*

1. *¿Quién _____ hasta la nueve? (dormir)*
2. *Ellas me _____ un favor. (pedir)*
3. *Me _____ las encías toda la noche. (doler)*
4. *Tú _____ furiosa. (ponerse)*
5. *Ellas _____ las bebidas. (traer)*

C. *Escriba los imperativos en las formas pedidas.* (Write the commands in the forms requested.)

MODELO: *Let's do it.*
Hagámoslo.

1. Tell it to him. (familiar)
2. Let's buy it. (formal)
3. Be good. (familiar)
4. Leave early. (familiar)
5. Let's rinse the clothing.

D. *Escriba la preposición "a," si es necesario.* (Write the preposition *a*, if need be.)

1. *Ellos comenzaron _____ cantar.*
2. *Quiso _____ venir.*
3. *Me acostumbré _____ levantarme tarde.*
4. *Vinieron _____ visitarnos.*
5. *Pudieron _____ venderla.*

E. *Cambie las oraciones al imperfecto.*

MODELO: *Visitamos a los tíos. Visitábamos a los tíos.*

1. *Entrego los resultados.*
2. *Hablaron con Juanito.*
3. *Compramos las antigüedades.*
4. *Siempre regatean.*
5. *Aumentamos el precio.*

F. *Traduzca al español.*

1. We went to the doctor's office two days ago.
2. Did the dentist ask you if your gums hurt a lot yesterday?
3. She brought them the best and she served it to them.
4. They insisted upon going to the theater and they fell in the snow.
5. As a young woman she wanted to live in the city.

RESPUESTAS

A. 1. *Ayer fui al médico.* 2. *Anoche tuve un dolor de cabeza.* 3. *La semana pasada comimos tres veces al día.* 4. *Esta mañana nos pusimos abrigo porque hizo frío.* 5. *El año pasado no supieron nada.*

B. 1. *durmió* 2. *pidieron* 3. *dolieron* 4. *te pusiste* 5. *trajeron*

C. 1. *Díselo a él.* 2. *Vamos a comprarlo.* 3. *Sé bueno.* 4. *Sal temprano.* 5. *Vamos a enjuagar la ropa.*

D. 1. *a* 2. - 3. *a* 4. *a* 5. -

E. 1. *Entregaba los resultados.* 2. *Hablaban con Juanito.* 3. *Comprábamos las antigüedades.* 4. *Siempre regateaban.* 5. *Aumentábamos el precio.*

F. 1. *Fuimos al consultorio del médico hace dos días.* 2. *¿Le preguntó el médico si le dolieron las encías ayer?* 3. *Ella les trajo lo mejor y se los sirvió.* 4. *Insistieron en ir al teatro y se cayeron en la nieve.* 5. *De joven deseaba vivir en la ciudad.*

LECCION 26

BUSCANDO UN TRABAJO.   Looking for a job.

A. DIALOGO

En la compañía Tela, San José, Costa Rica, Anita Benítez se presenta ante la señora Navarro, jefa del departamento de personal.

SEÑORA NAVARRO: **Dice en su vitae, señora Benítez, que Ud. estaba trabajando en la Compañía Celso. ¿Qué obligaciones tenía?**

ANITA: **Organizaba una campaña de ventas de computadores. Las ventas eran fenomenales. Hacía dos años que trabajaba en la compañía cuando me ofrecieron la dirección del mercadeo.**

SEÑORA NAVARRO: **Evidentemente, Ud. tuvo muchísimo éxito con la Celso. ¿Por qué dejó la posición?**

ANITA: **No había posibilidad de ascenso; mi jefe era joven y altamente competente.**

SEÑORA NAVARRO: **¿Y por qué quiere Ud. este trabajo?**

ANITA: **Este trabajo me ofrece nuevos desafíos.**

SEÑORA NAVARRO: **Muy bien, señora Benítez. Nuestro presidente leyó su solicitud y va a entrevistarla también.**

At the Tela company, San José, Costa Rica, Anita Benítez is being interviewed by Mrs. Navarro, Head of Personnel.

MRS. NAVARRO: It says in your resumé, Mrs. Benítez, that you worked for the Celso Company for several years. What were your responsibilities there?

ANITA: I was organizing a computer sales campaign. The sales were phenomenal. I had been working at the company for two years when they offered me the marketing manager position.

213

MRS. NAVARRO: Obviously, you have had a great deal of success at Celso. Why did you leave the job?

ANITA: There was no possibility for promotion; my boss was young and highly qualified.

MRS. NAVARRO: And why do you want this position?

ANITA: This position offers me new challenges.

MRS. NAVARRO: Very well, Mrs. Benítez. Our president read your application and will also interview you.

B. GRAMATICA Y USOS

1. THE IMPERFECT OF -*ER* AND -*IR* VERBS

Regular -*er* and -*ir* verbs have the same endings.

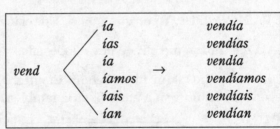

VENDER TO SELL

	vend			
yo		ía	→	vendía
tú		ías		vendías
Ud., él, ella		ía		vendía
nosotros, -as		íamos		vendíamos
vosotros, -as		íais		vendíais
Uds., ellos, ellas		ían		vendían

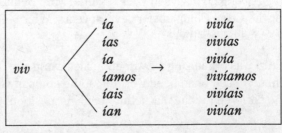

VIVIR TO LIVE

	viv			
yo		ía	→	vivía
tú		ías		vivías
Ud., él, ella		ía		vivía
nosotros, -as		íamos		vivíamos
vosotros, -as		íais		vivíais
Uds., ellos, ellas		ían		vivían

Vendía muchos computadores.
   You sold many computers.

Nos escribíamos muchas veces de jóvenes.
   We wrote to each other many times as children.

Comían aquí todo el año pasado.
   They ate here all last year.

Hacía buen tiempo.
   It was nice weather.

   The verb *haber* is regular in the imperfect: *había* (there was, there were)

Había una campaña de ventas.
   There was a sales campaign.

   Use the imperfect of *tener* to describe physical or emotional states in the past:

Teníamos mucha hambre pero no teníamos sueño.
   We were very hungry, but we were not sleepy.

Sentían mucho tu falta.
   They regretted your absence a great deal.

2. IRREGULAR IMPERFECTS OF *SER, IR,* AND *VER*

There are only three irregular verbs in the imperfect:

	SER TO BE	IR TO GO	VER TO SEE
yo	era	iba	veía
tú	eras	ibas	veías
Ud., él, ella	era	iba	veía
nosotros, -as	éramos	íbamos	veíamos
vosotros, -as	erais	íbais	veíais
Uds., ellos, ellas	eran	iban	veían

Iba a las reuniones todas las semanas.
    I used to go to the meetings weekly.

Era una entrevista interesante.
    It was an interesting interview.

De joven a menudo veía películas.
    He saw movies often as a child.

3. THE PAST PROGRESSIVE

To stress an action in progress in the past, use the imperfect of *estar* and the present participle/gerund:

Yo estaba trabajando allí durante varios años.
    I was working there for several years.

4. *HACIA* + TIME + *QUE* + IMPERFECT

To describe an action begun in the remote past and continuing into the more recent past, use this form:

> *Hacía* + time + *que* + imperfect

Hacía dos años que trabajaba en la compañía.
    I had been working at the company for two years.

Hacía seis semanas que buscábamos trabajo.
    We had been looking for jobs for six weeks.

5. THE PRETERITE AND IMPERFECT TOGETHER

To describe an action in the past, you can use either the preterite or the imperfect. The decision is based on how the action is looked at. Use the preterite for simple, past facts:

Llegué tarde esta mañana.
    I arrived late this morning.

El presidente me llamó por teléfono.
The president phoned me.

Trabajé allí cinco años y luego dejé el trabajo.
I worked there for five years and then I left the job.

Use the imperfect for descriptions of habitual actions or circumstances in the past:

Ganaba un buen salario.
I was earning a good salary.

Mi jefe era joven.
My boss was young.

De niña, vivía en el campo.
As a child, I lived in the countryside.

Cuando vivía en el Brasil, visitaba a los tíos todos los años.
When I was living in Brazil, I used to visit my aunt and uncle every year.

Use the imperfect to describe a continuing action in the past, during which another action occurred at one point. The other action will be in the preterite.

Trabajaba en la Companía Celso cuando lo conocí.
I was working for the Celso Company when I met him.

Ayer salí de la casa a las ocho y estaba lloviendo.
Yesterday I left the house at eight and it was raining.

VOCABULARIO

compañía	company
departamento	department
el personal	personnel
Departamento de Personal	Personnel Department
entrevista	interview

entrevistar a alguien	to interview someone
presentarse para una entrevista	to go for an interview
el vitae/el curriculum vitae/el historial de vida	résumé, curriculum vitae
la solicitud	application
la obligación	responsibility
el gerente/la gerenta	manager
las ventas	sales
campaña de ventas	sales campaign
el computador/la computadora/el ordenador *(Spain)*	computer
la informática	computer science
el programa de informática	computer program
mercadeo	marketing
la dirección	direction, management
la posición	job
los negocios	business
ofrecer	to offer
ofrecer una posición	to offer someone a job
dejar una posición	to leave a job
el ascenso	promotion
No había posibilidad de ascender.	There was no possibility for promotion.
desafío	challenge
ofrecer nuevos desafíos	to offer new challenges
altamente competente	highly qualified
¿Por qué quiere Ud. este trabajo?	Why do you want this job?
el presidente/la presidenta	the president
tener éxito	to be successful
campo	field (of interest, business, study)
sugerir *(e>ie), (e>i)* tácticas de venta	to suggest sales tactics
desarrollar un programa	to develop a program
fenomenal	phenomenal
anterior	previous

218

EXAMEN

A. *Conteste la pregunta en una oración completa usando la pista.*

1. *¿Qué obligaciones tenía en su posición? (gerente de ventas)*
2. *¿Qué campo le interesa más? (informática)*
3. *¿Qué le sugirió Ud. a la gerente? (tácticas de ventas)*
4. *¿Cuánto tiempo hacía que trabajaba en eso? (seis años)*
5. *¿Por qué quiere esta posición? (es un nuevo desafío)*

B. *Dé la primera persona (yo) del pretérito y la primera persona (yo) del imperfecto de los siguientes verbos.* (Give the preterite and imperfect of the following verbs in the first person singular.)

MODELO: saber / supe, sabía

1. *andar*
2. *buscar*
3. *pagar*
4. *dar*
5. *tener*
6. *ser*
7. *ver*
8. *caer*
9. *traducir*
10. *ir*

C. *Traduzca al español usando el imperfecto y el pretérito como sea necesario.* (Translate into Spanish, using the imperfect and preterite as necessary.)

1. I had a job interview last week.
2. They asked me why I left my previous job.
3. What programs were you developing at the company?
4. Were you highly qualified for the position?
5. What challenges did the job offer you?

D. *Relacione la columna A con la columna B.*

1. *entrevista*	a. company
2. *curriculum vitae*	b. interview
3. *mercadeo*	c. application
4. *computadora*	d. sales
5. *escritorio*	e. computer science
6. *jefe*	f. computer
7. *campaña de ventas*	g. marketing
8. *ventas*	h. boss
9. *solicitud*	I. sales campaign
10. *ascender*	j. resume
11. *informática*	k. go up; promotion
12. *compañía*	l. desk

NOTAS CULTURALES

The computer industry itself and all its related industries are thriving in the Spanish-speaking world. Hardware and software programs are made in Spanish in Spain and Latin America for their own markets. Much of the technical language, however, is in English: *¿Qué hardware le gusta más?*

RESPUESTAS

A. 1. *Yo era gerente de ventas.* 2. *Me interesa más la informática.* 3. *Le sugerí tácticas de ventas a la gerente.* 4. *Hacía seis años que trabajaba en eso.* 5. *Quiero esta posición porque es un nuevo desafío.*

B. 1. *anduve/andaba.* 2. *busqué/buscaba.* 3. *pagué/pagaba.* 4. *di/daba.* 5. *tuve/tenía.* 6. *fui/era.* 7. *vi/veía.* 8. *caí/caía.* 9. *traduje/traducía.* 10. *fui/iba.*

C. 1. *Tuve una entrevista de trabajo la semana pasada.* 2. *Me preguntaron por qué dejé mi trabajo anterior.* 3. *¿Qué programas desarrollaba Ud. en la compañía?* 4. *¿Era Ud. altamente competente para la posición?* 5. *¿Qué desafíos le ofrecía a Ud. el trabajo?*

D. 1. b; 2. j; 3. g; 4. f; 5. l; 6. h; 7. i; 8. d; 9. c; 10. k; 11. e; 12. a.

LECCION 27

EN EL CORREO.   At the post office.

A. DIALOGO

En el correo de Tegucigalpa, Honduras.

DIANA: **Quiero enviar este paquete por vía aérea a Miami.**

AGENTE: **¿Sabe Ud. cuánto pesa?**

DIANA: **No lo he pesado. ¡No he hecho nada más que trabajar hoy día!**

AGENTE: **Pesa tres kilos. ¿Quiere enviarlo certificado?**

DIANA: **¡Claro! Y asegurado, también.**

AGENTE: **Tiene que llenar estos formularios de certificación, seguro y aduana. ¿Algo más?**

DIANA: **Sí. Esta carta es para entrega inmediata. Y también necesito treinta estampillas locales para tarjetas postales. Cuando estuve aquí la semana pasada, Uds. no las tenían.**

AGENTE: **Las habíamos vendido todas y todavía no habían llegado las nuevas.**

DIANA: **Ay, por poco me olvido. Necesito un giro postal.**

AGENTE: **Lo consigue en la próxima ventanilla.**

At the post office in Tegucigalpa, Honduras.

DIANA: I want to send this package by air mail to Miami.

AGENT: Do you know how much it weighs?

DIANA: I haven't weighed it. I haven't done anything but work today!

AGENT: It weighs three kilos. Do you want to send it registered?

DIANA: Of course. And insured, also.

AGENT: You have to fill out these registration, insurance and customs forms. Anything else?

DIANA: Yes, this letter is for special delivery. And I also need thirty local postage stamps for postcards. When I was here last week, you didn't have them.

AGENT: We had sold all of them and the new ones hadn't arrived yet.

DIANA: Oh, I almost forgot. I need a money order.

AGENT: You get that at the next window.

B. GRAMATICA Y USOS

1. THE VERB *HABER*

We have already used the verb *haber* in the impersonal expressions *hay* (there is, there are), *hubo* and *había* (there was, there were).
The verb *haber* is a helping verb meaning "to have"; it is not a synonym of *tener,* and it is primarily used with the past participle (see below).
Here are the irregular forms of *haber* in the present and preterite tenses:

	PRESENT	PRETERITE
yo	*he*	*hube*
tú	*has*	*hubiste*
Ud., él, ella	*ha*	*hubo*
nosotros, -as	*hemos*	*hubimos*
vosotros, -as	*habéis*	*hubisteis*
Uds., ellos, ellas	*han*	*hubieron*

2. THE PAST PARTICIPLE

The past participle in English is the "-ed" or "-n" form of the verb: "asked, spoken, done." In Spanish, most past participles are formed as follows: for -ar verbs: drop the infinitive ending -ar and add -ado:

enviar/enviado	to send/sent
olvidar/olvidado	to forget/forgotten

For -er and -it verbs: drop the infinitive ending -er or -it and add -ido:

perder/perdido	to lose/lost
pedir/pedido	to ask for/asked for

There are many irregular forms:

abrir/abierto	to open/opened
cubrir/cubierto	to cover/covered
decir/dicho	to say/said
escribir/escrito	to write/written
hacer/hecho	to do/done
morir/muerto	to die/died
poner/puesto	to put/put, placed
ver/visto	to see/seen
volver/vuelto	to return/returned

The past participle can be used as an adjective. If so, it agrees with its noun:

la carta certificada	the registered letter
los paquetes asegurados	the insured packages

It is also used as part of the perfect tenses.

3. THE PERFECT TENSES: THE PRESENT AND PAST PERFECT TENSES

The present perfect tense expresses an action which was completed prior to the present:

I have spoken.
We have finished.

In Spanish, as in English, the invariable form of the past participle is used with the helping verb *haber* (to have) to form the perfect tenses. For the present perfect, use the present tense of *haber* and the past participle:

No lo he pesado.
I haven't weighed it.

Hemos perdido varios paquetes.
We have lost several packages.

Lo he visto pero no está aquí.
I've seen it but it isn't here.

The past perfect tense expresses an action which was completed prior to another action, stated or implied, in the past:

They had already left when we arrived.
I hadn't finished the course (when I went to Spain).

For the past perfect use the imperfect tense of *haber* and the past participle:

Habíamos vendido todas y todavía no habían llegado las nuevas.
We had sold all of them and the new ones hadn't arrived yet (last week when you were here).

4. *POR POCO* + PRESENT TENSE

To describe an action that almost occurred, use the expression *por poco* and the present tense:

Por poco me olvido.	I almost forgot.
Por poco se van.	They almost left.

VOCABULARIO

el correo	the postal system
ventanilla	(sales) window
el paquete	package
pesar	to weigh
carta	letter
tarjeta postal	postcard
cartero	mailman
giro	money order
giro postal	postal money order
estampilla/sello	stamp
certificar	to register
certificado	registered
certificación	registration
asegurar	to insure
asegurado	insured
seguro	insurance
aduana	Customs
formulario	form
llenar un formulario	to fill out a form
entrega	delivery
entrega inmediata	special delivery
enviar	to send, to mail
Quiero enviar una carta.	I want to mail a letter.
¿Cuántos sellos necesito para una tarjeta postal?	How many stamps do I need for a postcard?
por vía aérea	by air mail
por vía superficie	by surface mail
primera clase	first class

el buzón	mailbox
echar una carta al buzón	to mail (to throw into the mailbox) a letter
la casilla	post office box
olvidarse	to forget
¿Algo más?	Something else?
local	local
por poco	almost
todo	everything (n.), all (adj.)

EXAMEN

A. *Conteste la pregunta en una oración completa usando la pista.*

1. *¿Cómo quiere enviar el paquete? (asegurado)*
2. *¿Qué tengo que hacer? (llenar el formulario)*
3. *¿Qué más necesita Ud.? (estampillas y tarjetas postales)*
4. *¿Quién te lo entrega? (cartero)*
5. *¿Dónde están las cartas? (casilla)*

B. *Dé el participio pasado.*

MODELO: ver / visto

1. *entregar*
2. *hacer*
3. *enviar*
4. *certificar*
5. *partir*

C. *Traduzca al español.*

1. We had sent the package but they had not received it.
2. There were stamps at the post office yesterday.
3. We have done everything but we still haven't eaten.
4. I want to send this package by surface mail.
5. The mailman will deliver the special delivery letter this evening.

D. *Use la expresión "por poco" y el participio presente.*

MODELO: *No hago mi tarea.*
Por poco no hago mi tarea.

1. *Choco con un carro.*
2. *Compro una casa nueva.*
3. *Te envío un regalo por correo.*
4. *Echo la carta al buzón.*
5. *Pierdo los sellos.*

NOTAS CULTURALES

The postal systems in Spain and Latin America were once notorious for their inefficiency. In recent years, the situation has improved greatly in Spain, which is now part of the European Community. However, it has deteriorated in Latin America due to the economic problems faced by many countries, which allows them to devote only a very small part of their budget to modernize the system.

RESPUESTAS

A. 1. *Quiero enviar el paquete asegurado.* 2. *Tiene que llenar el formulario.*
   3. *Necesito estampillas y tarjetas postales.* 4. *El cartero me lo entrega.*
   5. *Las cartas están en la casilla.*
B. 1. *entregado* 2. *hecho* 3. *enviado* 4. *certificado* 5. *partido.*
C. 1. *Habíamos enviado el paquete pero no lo habían recibido.* 2. *Habían estampillas en el correo ayer.* 3. *Hemos hecho todo pero todavía no hemos comido.* 4. *Quiero enviar este paquete por vía superficie.* 5. *El cartero va a entregar la carta de entrega inmediata esta noche.*
D. 1. *Por poco choco con un carro.* 2. *Por poco compro una casa nueva.*
   3. *Por poco te envío un regalo por correo.* 4. *Por poco echo la carta al buzón.* 5. *Por poco pierdo los sellos.*

LECCION 28

EN LA PLAYA.   At the beach.

A. DIALOGO

En la Agencia Nacional de Turismo de Santo Domingo, República Dominicana.

TERESA: **Buenos días, señor. Este año pasaremos las vacaciones en un hotel que da a la playa. ¿Cuál sugiere Ud.?**

ESTEBAN: **Hay una playa excelente con una arena blanquita no muy lejos de aquí. Ofrecen buceo, barquitos como canoas, surfe, esquí acuático y pesca marina. Hay varias piscinas también.**

TERESA: **¿De veras? ¿Habrá una especial para los chiquitos? A nuestro Danielito le gusta mucho jugar en el agua. Todavía no sabe nadar.**

ESTEBAN: **Claro, esa piscina tiene varios instructores de natación y salvavidas. ¿Cuántos días permanecerán Uds. en la playa?**

TERESA: **Las vacaciones de mi esposo son cortitas, una semana, no más. Yo y Danielito nos quedaremos allí otra semana.**

ESTEBAN: **¡Buenas vacaciones!**

At the National Tourism Agency in Santo Domingo, Dominican Republic.

TERESA: Good morning, sir. This year we will spend our vacation at a hotel that is on the beach. Which one do you suggest?

ESTEBAN: There's an excellent beach with the whitest sand not very far from here. They offer scuba diving, little boats like canoes, surfing, water skiing and deep-sea fishing. There are also swimming pools.

TERESA: Really? I wonder if there's a special one for little children. Our little Danny likes to play in the water a lot. He still can't swim.

ESTEBAN: Of course, that pool has several swimming instructors and lifeguards. How many days will you spend at the beach?

TERESA: My husband's vacation is very short, one week, that's all. Little Danny and I will spend another week there.

ESTEBAN: Have a good vacation!

B. GRAMATICA Y USOS

1. THE CONCEPT OF THE FUTURE TENSE

You have already learned to talk about the future in two ways. The present tense may be used to indicate an immediate future event:

Hablo contigo mañana.   I'll talk to you tomorrow.

The expression *ir* + *a* + infinitive also expresses an immediate future event:

Voy a hablar contigo mañana.   I'm going to talk to you tomorrow.

But there is also a simple future tense.

2. THE FUTURE TENSE OF REGULAR VERBS

The future tense is made up of the whole infinitive plus an ending. All three conjugations have the same endings:

		PASAR TO SPEND	*SER* TO BE	*ABRIR* TO OPEN
yo	-é:	*pasaré*	*seré*	*abriré*
tú	ás:	*pasarás*	*serás*	*abrirás*
Ud., él, ella	-á:	*pasará*	*será*	*abrirá*
nosotros, -as	-emos:	*pasaremos*	*seremos*	*abriremos*
vosotros, -as	-éis:	*pasaréis*	*seréis*	*abriréis*
Uds., ellos, ellas	-án:	*pasarán*	*serán*	*abrirán*

229

Pasaremos las vacaciones en la playa.
   We will (shall) spend our vacation at the beach.

Nos quedaremos allí otra semana.
   We'll spend another week there.

3. THE PRESENT OF PROBABILITY

Use the future tense to state or ask if something is probable:

¿Habrá[1] allí varias piscinas?
   I wonder if there are several pools there?

Podré hacer mucho esquí acuático.
   I'll probably be able to do lots of water skiing.

4. DIMINUTIVES

The diminutive in Spanish normally indicates either small size or affection, and can be used for emphasis. With the proper intonation, it may also indicate disgust. The diminutive of nouns, adjectives and adverbs is formed as follows:

For words ending in *o* or *a,* drop the last vowel and add *-ito* or *-ita:*

ahora > ahorita	right now
corto > cortito	very short
vacaciones cortitas	a very short vacation

For words ending in *-co,* change the *c* to *qu* and add *-ito:*

blanco > blanquito	very white
barco > barquito	little boat

For words ending in *-go,* change *g* to *gu* and add *-ito:*

amigo > amiguito	a small friend

[1] The future of *haber* and other irregular verbs in the future tense will be covered in *Lección* 29.

For words ending in *-n, -l, -r, -e* or *-é*, add *-cito:*

grande > grandecito   big and cute
café > cafecito   a demitasse, espresso
mujer > mujercita   a small woman
hombre > hombrecito   a small man

Other possible diminutive suffixes are: *-illo* and *-ico*.[1]

VOCABULARIO

la playa	beach.
las vacaciones	vacation
estar de vacaciones	to be on vacation
el mar	sea
dar a la playa	to face the beach, to be on the beach
piscina	swimming pool
piscina calentada	heated pool
el agua	water
arena	sand
blanco	white
el parasol	beach umbrella
nadar	to swim
la natación	swimming
instructor, *-a*	instructor
el/*la* **salvavidas**	lifeguard
loción bronceadora	suntan lotion
diversiones acuáticas	water sports
surfe	surfing
hacer surfe	to go surfing
pesca	fishing
pesca marina	deep-sea fishing
el esquí acuático	water skiing
buceo	scuba diving
hacer buceo	to go scuba diving
barco	boat
barquito	a small boat

[1] Regional usage of diminutives varies greatly.

canoa	canoe
velero	sailboat
quedarse	to stay, to remain
permanecer	to remain
pasar	to spend (time)
fresco	cool
chiquito	little child (n.), very small (adj.)
¿De veras?	Really?
viajar	to travel
estar de viaje	to be on a trip, journey

EXAMEN

A. *Conteste la pregunta en una oración completa usando la pista.*

1. *¿Dónde pasarán las vacaciones? (la playa)*
2. *¿Cuánto tiempo estarán allí? (tiempito)*
3. *¿Qué diversión acuática le gustará más a él? (nadar)*
4. *¿Dónde se quedarán Uds.? (el hotel que da a la playa)*
5. *¿Qué serán ellos? (salvavidas)*

B. *Dé el diminutivo.*

MODELO: muchacho/muchachito

1. *rico*
2. *pobre*
3. *papel*
4. *chico*
5. *pregunta*

C. *Traduzca al español.*

1. We will go to the beach for (our) vacation.
2. Will you stay at a hotel with a heated pool?
3. I'll go swimming in the sea.
4. Do you suppose that there are lifeguards at the beach?
5. The sand is very white and the water is always very cool.

NOTAS CULTURALES

With some of the world's loveliest beaches, both Spaniards and Latin Americans, a large percentage of whom live near coastlines, are true beach fanatics. Many Latin American countries are in the tropics and the weather often allows for beach activities all year long.

Some of the most beautiful beaches in the world are located in Latin America. Beaches are one of the main reasons people visit countries like Mexico, Cuba, and Puerto Rico. However, with close to 20 million American visitors a year, Mexico has proven to be the number one destination for tourists north of the border. Mexico's Pacific Ocean is generally colder and rougher than the Caribbean, and the beaches are usually less pristine (many times due to offshore drilling). The Yucatán Peninsula—Cancún and surrounding areas—is well known for its clean beaches, clear waters, and great snorkeling. Deep-sea fishing is especially plentiful in the Sea of Cortés, between La Paz/Cabo San Lucas and Mazatlán/Puerto Vallarta, and you'll find great surfing all along the Baja California Peninsula and the state of Oaxaca.

RESPUESTAS

A. 1. *Pasaremos las vacaciones en la playa.* 2. *Estaremos allí un tiempito.* 3. *A él le gustará más nadar.* 4. *Nos quedaremos en el hotel que da a la playa.* 5. *Ellos serán salvavidas.*

B. 1. *riquito* 2. *pobrecito* 3. *papelcito* 4. *chiquito* 5. *preguntita*

C. 1. *Iremos a la playa para nuestras vacaciones.* 2. *¿Se quedará en un hotel con piscina calentada?* 3. *Iré a nadar en el mar.* 4. *¿Habrá salvavidas en la playa?* 5. *La arena es blanquita y el agua siempre es fresquita.*

LECCION 29

EN EL BANCO.   At the bank.

A. DIALOGO

En una sucursal del Banco Santanderino de Cartagena, Colombia.

PATRICIA: **Quiero abrir una cuenta corriente. ¿Qué servicios ofrece su banco?**

ROBERTO: **Ofrecemos cuentas de ahorros, certificados de depósito, préstamos y tarjetas de crédito. También, Ud. podrá depositar un cheque en uno de nuestros cajeros automáticos y tendrá acceso inmediato a su dinero.**

PATRICIA: **Muy bien. ¿Cuánto tendré que pagar por la chequera y por cheque cobrado?**

ROBERTO: **La chequera es gratuita y habrá cargos reducidos por cheque por seis meses.**

PATRICIA: **¿Y qué tasa de interés pagan Uds.?**

ROBERTO: **Por ahora el tres por ciento. Le diremos cuando cambia. Estará indicado en su estado de cuenta bancaria.**

PATRICIA: **¿Tienen Uds. representantes por todo el mundo?**

ROBERTO: **A decir verdad, señora, todavía no los tenemos. Pero, para el final del año, habremos hecho todos los trámites para establecerlos.**

At a branch of the Banco Santanderino in Cartagena, Colombia.

PATRICIA: I want to open a checking account. What services does your bank offer?

ROBERTO: We offer savings accounts, certificates of deposit, loans, and credit cards. Also, you will be able to deposit a check at one of our automatic teller machines and you will have immediate access to your money.

PATRICIA: Very well. How much will I have to pay for a checkbook and for each cashed check?

ROBERTO: The checkbook is free and there will be a reduced check charge for six months.

PATRICIA: And what interest rate do you pay?

ROBERTO: Right now three percent. We will tell you when it changes. It will be indicated on your bank statement.

PATRICIA: Do you have representatives throughout the world?

ROBERTO: To tell the truth, madam, we still don't have them. But by the end of the year, we will have carried out all the procedures to establish them.

B. GRAMATICA Y USOS

1. IRREGULAR VERBS IN THE FUTURE TENSE

While all future tense verbs have the same endings, there are changes in the roots of some of them.
Verbs which add -dr- to the root:

	TENER TO HAVE	*SALIR* TO LEAVE, TO GO OUT
yo	*tendré*	*saldré*
tú	*tendrás*	*saldrás*
Ud., él, ella	*tendrá*	*saldrá*
nosotros, -as	*tendremos*	*saldremos*
vosotros, -as	*tendréis*	*saldréis*
Uds., ellos, ellas	*tendrán*	*saldrán*

Other verbs like *tener* and *salir* in the future: *venir>vendré*

Tendrá acceso inmediato a su dinero.
You will have immediate access to your money.

Saldrán a las ocho.
They will go out at 8:00.

Vendrá el año próximo.
She'll come next year.

Verbs which add *-r-* to the root:

	HABER TO HAVE	*QUERER* TO WANT
yo	*habré*	*querré*
tú	*habrás*	*querrás*
Ud., él, ella	*habrá*	*querrá*
nosotros, -as	*habremos*	*querremos*
vosotros, -as	*habréis*	*querréis*
Uds., ellos, ellas	*habrán*	*querrán*

Remember that *habrá,* "there will be," is the future of *hay,* "there is," "there are":

Habrá cargos reducidos por cheque por seis meses.
There will be a reduced check charge for six months.

Other verbs like *haber* and *querer:*

caber>cabré
saber>sabré
poder>podré

Podrá depositar un cheque en uno de nuestros cajeros automáticos.
You'll be able to deposit checks at one of our automatic tellers.

Querré sacar dinero.
I will want to withdraw money.

236

Sabremos para el finul del año.
We'll know by the end of the year.

Decir and *hacer* make other changes in the future:

	DECIR TO SAY	HACER TO MAKE
yo	diré	haré
tú	dirás	harás
Ud., él, ella	dirá	hará
nosotros, -as	diremos	haremos
vosotros, -as	diréis	haréis
Uds., ellos, ellas	dirán	harán

Le diremos cuando cambia. We'll tell you when it changes.

Harán el depósito mañana. They will make the deposit
tomorrow.

2. THE FUTURE PERFECT TENSE

The future perfect expresses an action that will be completed by a specified time in the future. It is made up of the future of *haber* and the past participle:

Para el final del año, habremos hecho todos los trámites.
By the end of the year, we will have carried out all the procedures.

Habré depositado el cheque cuando él saque el dinero.
I will have deposited the check when he withdraws the money.

3. THE USES OF *POR*

The preposition **por** has various uses:

a. to tell time duration:

Habrá una carga reducida por seis meses.
There will be a reduced charge for six months.

Ganaremos mil pesetas por hora.
We will earn one thousand pesetas an hour.

b. to express "in exchange for":

¿Cuánto tendré que pagar por la chequera?
How much will I have to pay for the checkbook?

c. to express "through, along, throughout":

¿Tienen sucursales por toda la ciudad?
Do you have branches throughout the city?

d. to express "for the sake of" or "in place of":

¿Lo harás por mí?
Will you do it for me?

e. in common idiomatic expressions:

por ciento	percent
por favor	please
por eso	for that reason

VOCABULARIO

el banco	bank
la sucursal	branch
cuenta	account
cuenta de ahorros	savings account
cuenta corriente	checking account

Quiero abrir una cuenta corriente.	I want to open a checking account.
el cheque	check
chequera	checkbook
los cargos	charge
depositar un cheque	to deposit a check
hacer un depósito	to make a deposit
certificado de depósito	certificate of deposit
cobrar un cheque	to cash a check
papeleta	slip (deposit, etc.)
dinero	money
retirar/sacar dinero	to withdraw money
hacer un retiro	to make a withdrawal
cajero, -a	teller
cajero automático	automatic teller machine
tener acceso inmediato a su dinero	to have immediate access to one's money
préstamo	loan
tasa de interés	rate of interest
un cuarto por ciento	one-quarter percent
el billete	bill
moneda	coin
banquero, -a	banker
libreta de depósitos	bank passbook
el estado de cuenta bancario	bank statement
saldo	balance
crédito	credit
débito	debit
¿Qué servicios ofrece su banco?	What services does your bank offer?
los trámites	procedures
gratuito	free
por ahora	for now

EXAMEN

A. *Conteste la pregunta en una oración completa usando la pista.*

1. *¿Cuánto es la tasa de interés? (3%)*
2. *¿Dónde tienen Uds. cajero automático? (todas las sucursales)*
3. *¿Qué tipo de cuenta querrá Ud.? (cuenta corriente)*
4. *¿Qué servicios ofrecen? (préstamos y tarjetas de crédito)*
5. *¿Qué necesito para retirar dinero? (la libreta y la papeleta de retiros)*

B. *Relacione una palabra de la Columna A con su antónimo* (antonym) *de la Columna B.*

COLUMNA A

1. *retiro*
2. *débito*
3. *cobrar*
4. *billete*
5. *cheque*
6. *cajero*

COLUMNA B

a. *cajero automático*
b. *dinero*
c. *depósito*
d. *crédito*
e. *moneda*
f. *depositar*

C. *Dé la forma del verbo en el futuro.*

MODELO: él (venir)/vendrá

1. *ellos (tener)*
2. *¿quiénes? (venir)*
3. *ella (querer)*
4. *los niños (saber)*
5. *nadie (poder)*

D. *Traduzca al español.*

1. Will you be able to deposit the check in the savings account?
2. Will he do it for us?
3. There will be immediate access to your money.
4. Who will have made the withdrawal?
5. The banker will tell them the truth.

E. *Use la preposición "por" en las siguientes oraciones.*

MODELO: I went to Spain for three weeks.
Fui a España por tres semanas.

1. How much do you want for that red convertible?
2. You are doing it for her.
3. I earn one hundred dollars a day.
4. I went by your house yesterday.
5. I want to make a deposit, please.

NOTAS CULTURALES

In Spain and Latin America banking hours vary greatly from country to country. In general, banking hours are from 9:00 A.M. to 3:00 P.M. Monday through Friday, and Saturday mornings. There are also many half days and bank holidays, and banking procedures are different from those in the United States. From an American point of view, they perhaps seem more complicated.

RESPUESTAS

A. 1. *La tasa de interés es el tres por ciento.* 2. *Tenemos cajero automático en todas las sucursales.* 3. *Querré una cuenta corriente.* 4. *Ofrecemos préstamos y tarjetas de crédito.* 5. *Para retirar dinero, Ud. necesita la libreta y la papeleta de retiros.*

B. 1. c. 2. d. 3. f. 4. e. 5. b. 6. a.

C. 1. *tendrán* 2. *vendrán* 3. *querrá* 4. *sabrán* 5. *podrá*

D. 1. *¿Podrá Ud. depositar el cheque en la cuenta corriente?* 2. *¿Lo hará por nosotros?* 3. *Habrá acceso inmediato a su dinero.* 4. *¿Quién habrá hecho el retiro?* 5. *El banquero les dirá la verdad.*

E. 1. *¿Cuánto quiere por ese convertible rojo?* 2. *Lo estás haciendo por ella.* 3. *Yo gano cien dólares por día.* 4. *Pasé por tu casa ayer.* 5. *Quiero hacer un depósito, por favor.*

LECCION 30
EN LA AGENCIA DE CAMBIO.   At the currency exchange office.

A. DIALOGO

En la agencia de cambio Cero de Córdoba, Argentina.

RAMON: **Señorita, me gustaría cambiar unos cheques de viajero.**

DEBORA: **Sí, señor. Aceptamos varias divisas: dólares, libras, francos, y yenes.**

RAMON: **Tengo dólares norteamericanos. ¿A cuánto está el cambio hoy?**

DEBORA: **¿Para qué cantidad de dinero?**

RAMON: **Cambiaría mil dólares.**

DEBORA: **Para esa cantidad, el cambio está a ochenta el dólar.**

RAMON: **Y ¿cuánto cobran por la transacción?**

DEBORA: **Cobramos el uno por ciento del total. Para no pagar la tarifa, sería necesario cambiar por lo menos dos mil dólares.**

RAMON: **De acuerdo. Quisiera cambiar los mil dólares.**

DEBORA: **Por favor ¿podría poner la fecha de hoy y firmar los cheques? Necesito ver su pasaporte para fines oficiales.**

RAMON: **Habría cambiado más dinero, pero me quedo poco tiempo aquí.**

At the Zero exchange agency in Córdoba, Argentina.

RAMON: Miss, I would like to cash some traveler's checks.

DEBORA: Yes, sir. We accept several currencies: dollars, pounds, francs, and yen.

RAMON: I have U.S. dollars. What is the exchange rate today?

DEBORA: For what amount of money?

RAMON: I would change one thousand dollars.

DEBORA: For that sum, the exchange rate is 80 to the dollar.

RAMON: And, how much do you charge for the transaction?

DEBORA: We charge one percent of the total. In order not to pay the fee, it would be necessary to exchange at least two thousand dollars.

RAMON: Okay. I would like to exchange one thousand.

DEBORA: Please, would you date and sign the checks? I need to see your passport for official purposes.

RAMON: I would have changed more money, but I'm here a short time.

B. GRAMATICA Y USOS

1. THE PRESENT CONDITIONAL

The conditional tense tells what would happen if something else, stated or implied, were to happen.

> She wouldn't go (if she were invited).
> In that case, I would change more money.

To form the conditional, add the following endings to the complete infinitive. They are the same for all the conjugations.

		CAMBIAR TO EXCHANGE	SER TO BE	ABRIR TO OPEN
yo	-ía	cambiaría	sería	abriría
tú	-ías	cambiarías	serías	abrirías
Ud., él, ella	-ía	cambiaría	sería	abriría
nosotros, -as	-íamos	cambiaríamos	seríamos	abriríamos
vosotros, -as	-íais	cambiaríais	seríais	abriríais
Uds., ellos, ellas	-ían	cambiarían	serían	abrirían

Note that the verb *gustar* is regular in the conditional:

A Juan le gustaría cambiar unos cheques.
John would like to cash some checks.

Verbs with irregular future stems have the same irregularity in the conditional:

saber: sabría
tener: tendría
salir: saldría
poder: podría
hacer: haría
decir: diría
haber: habría
querer: querría

Habría, "there would be," is the conditional form of *hay* (there are).

En ese caso, habría muchas dificultades.
In that case, there would be many difficulties.

2. THE CONDITIONAL PERFECT

The conditional perfect expresses what would have happened if something else, stated or implied, had happened in the past. It is made up of the conditional of the verb *haber* and the past participle:

Habría cambiado los dos mil dólares, pero no los necesitaba.
I would have exchanged the two thousand dollars, but I didn't need them.

244

Habría endosado el cheque, pero la agencia de cambio no estaba abierta.
I would have endorsed the check but the currency exchange office
wasn't open.

3. THE PAST OF PROBABILITY

Use the conditional to talk about probable past events:

¿Ella estaría ocupada? I wonder if she was busy?
Llegarían tarde. They probably arrived late.

4. SOFTENED COMMANDS AND REQUESTS

There are several ways to give a command:

1. The direct command form:

¡Salga Ud. ahora! Get out now!
Ven a las cinco. Come (familiar) at five o'clock.

2. *Favor de* + infinitive:

Favor de sentarse. Please sit down.

A softened command or request makes a statement or demand seem
less abrupt. Several forms are used:

3. *Podría(n)* + infinitive

¿Podría Ud. cambiarme el dinero? Would you be able to change the
money for me?

4. *Quisiera* + infinitive

Quisiera cambiar estos cheques. I would like to cash these checks.

5. *(Me) gustaría* + infinitive

Me gustaría verte mañana. I would like to see you tomorrow.

5. THE USES OF *PARA*

The preposition *para* has various specific uses:

a. To express purpose ("in order to") with an infinitive:

Para no pagar la tarifa, debe cambiar dos mil dólares.
In order not to pay the fee, you must change two thousand dollars.

b. To indicate a specific future time:

Para el martes, entregaré el cheque.
I will deliver the check by Tuesday.

c. To indicate an intended recipient:

El cheque es para mí.
The check is for me.

d. To indicate a destination ("toward") or purpose:

Van para el parque.
They are going toward the park.

Necesito ver su pasaporte pare fines oficiales.
I need to see your passport for official purposes.

VOCABULARIO

cambio	change, exchange
el cheque de viajero	traveler's check
cambiar un cheque de viajero	to cash a traveler's check
poner la fecha	to date, to write the date
firmar un cheque	to sign a check
endosar	to endorse
divisa	(kind of) currency
el dólar	dollar
cambiar dólares a/en pesos	to change dollars into pesos
libra esterlina	pound sterling
franco	franc
el yen	yen
moneda	money, coin
centavos	cents
tasa de cambio	exchange rate
cantidad	quantity, amount
transacción	transaction
el total	total sum
tarifa	fee
cobrar	to charge (a price or fee)
el pasaporte	passport
mostrar *(o>ue)* su pasaporte	to show one's passport
¿A cuánto está el cambio hoy?	What is the exchange rate today?
Está a veinte el dólar.	It's at twenty to the dollar.
¿Podría Ud.? (+ infinitive)	Would you . . . ?
quisiera (+ infinitive)	I would like to . . .
gustaría (+ infinitive)	I would like to . . .
por lo menos	at least

EXAMEN

A. *Conteste la pregunta en una oración completa usando la pista.*

1. *¿A cuánto está el cambio hoy? (30 al dólar)*
2. *¿Qué divisa quiere cambiar? (libras esterlinas)*
3. *¿Qué debo hacer para cambiarlo? (poner la fecha y firmar el cheque)*
4. *¿Qué divisa querría Ud.? (euros)*
5. *¿Para cuándo necesita Ud. los cheques? (el martes)*

B. *Dé la forma del futuro seguido de la forma del condicional.* (Give the future form followed by the conditional.)

MODELO: ir (yo)   iré/iría

1. *venir (ellos)*
2. *saber (tú)*
3. *hacer (nosotros)*
4. *querer (¿quiénes?)*
5. *decir (yo)*
6. *poner (alguien)*
7. *tener (nadie)*

C. *Traduzca al español.*

1. They were probably sick.
2. We would have gone, but we did not have enough dollars.
3. What would you do in that situation?
4. What is the exchange rate for yen today?
5. She wants to change dollars for pesos.

NOTAS CULTURALES

Due to constant economic instabilities in many Latin American countries, their currencies are subject to extreme fluctuations. Repeated battles with double digit inflation have resulted in continuous devaluations. A great deal of currency is changed on the black or parallel market.

The Spanish currency is *el euro,* and Latin American currencies are as follows:

Monedas de América Latina Latin American currencies[1]

Argentina	*peso*	Honduras	*lempira*
Bolivia	*peso boliviano*	México	*peso mexicano*
Brasil	*cruzeiro*	Panamá	*balboa*
Chile	*peso*	Paraguay	*guaraní*
Colombia	*peso colombiano*	Perú	*sol*
Costa Rica	*colón*	Puerto Rico	*dólar estadounidense*
Cuba	*peso cubano*	República Dominicana	*peso dominicano*
Ecuador	*sucre*	Uruguay	*peso uruguayo*
El Salvador	*colón*	Venezuela	*bolívar*
Guatemala	*quetzal*		

RESPUESTAS

A. 1. *El cambio está a treinta al dólar.* 2. *Quiero cambiar libras esterlinas.*
3. *Debe poner la fecha y firmar el cheque.* 4. *Yo querría euros.*
5. *Necesito los cheques para el martes.*
B. 1. *vendrán/vendrían* 2. *sabrás/sabrías* 3. *haremos/haríamos*
4. *querrán/querrían* 5. *diré/diría* 6. *pondrá/pondría* 7. *tendrá/tendría.*
C. 1. *Estarían enfermos.* 2. *Habríamos ido, pero no tuvimos/teníamos*
suficientes dólares. 3. *¿Qué haría Ud. en esa situación?* 4. *¿A cuánto está el*
yen hoy? 5. *Ella quiere cambiar dólares en/a pesos.*

SEXTO REPASO

A. Cambie el verbo al imperfecto usando la palabra o expresión en
paréntesis. Escriba nuevamente la oración. (Change the verb to the
imperfect using the word or expression in parenthesis. Rewrite the
sentence.)

MODELO: *Vine tarde a la clase. (siempre)*
　　　　Siempre venía tarde a la clase.

---

[1] The currencies of the Latin American countries are all masculine nouns.

1. *Busqué trabajo.* (*Durante todo el año pasado*)
2. *Sugirió tácticas de mercadeo.* (*Frecuentemente*)
3. *Llenaron los formularios.* (*Siempre*)
4. *Tomamos vacaciones en México.* (*De joven*)
5. *Fuimos a la playa.* (*Todos los años*)

B. *Complete la oración con formas del verbo haber.* (Complete the sentence with forms of the verb *haber.*)

MODELO: ¿*Quién* _____ *por España?* (has traveled)/*ha viajado*

1. _____ *muchas personas en el correo.* (There are probably)
2. *Ella* _____ *el cheque.* (has deposited)
3. ¿*Quiénes no* _____ *las estampillas?* (had bought)
4. ¿*Adónde* _____ *los chiquitos?* (had gone)
5. *Ella* _____ *los cheques de viajero.* (would have changed)

C. *Responda en una oración completa usando la pista.*

1. ¿*Quién querrá ir?* (*nosotros*)
2. ¿*Qué dirás?* (*la verdad*)
3. ¿*Quién venderá el giro postal?* (*el agente*)
4. ¿*Cuándo harán Uds. el retiro?* (*mañana*)
5. ¿*Dónde se quedarán Uds.?* (*en el hotel*)

D. *Complete la oración con "por" o "para."* (Complete the sentence with *por* or *para.*)

MODELO: *Trabajo* _____ *vivir/para*

1. ¿*Cuánto ganarás* _____ *hora?*
2. *El café es* _____ *mi.*
3. *Pasearán* _____ *la playa.*
4. *Querré terminar* _____ *el lunes.*
5. *Vamos pedir un descuento de cincuenta* _____ *ciento.*

E. *Dé los imperativos pedidos.* (Give the commands requested.)

MODELO: Come early! (formal pl.)
        Vengan temprano.

1. Be happy! (familiar)
2. Put them (masc.) on them! (formal sg.)
3. Would you please write it down. (formal pl.)
4. Do it now! (familiar)
5. Don't forget to bring them. (formal sg.)

F. *Traduzca al español.*

1. How long had you been living in Madrid when she arrived?
2. I almost deposited the check in the savings account.
3. They're probably swimming at our favorite little beach.
4. I'll have to pass by the currency exchange office in order to buy pesetas for her.
5. I would like to buy two tickets for the opening.

RESPUESTAS

A. 1. *Durante todo el año pasado buscaba trabajo.* 2. *Frecuentemente sugería tácticas de mercadeo.* 3. *Siempre llenaban los formularios.* 4. *De joven tomábamos vacaciones en México.* 5. *Todos los años íbamos a la playa.*

B. 1. *Habrá* 2. *ha depositado* 3. *habían comprado* 4. *habían ido* 5. *habría cambiado*

C. 1. *Nosotros querremos ir.* 2. *Diré la verdad.* 3. *El agente venderá el giro postal.* 4. *Mañana haremos el retiro.* 5. *Nos quedaremos en el hotel.*

D. 1. *por* 2. *para* 3. *por* 4. *para* 5. *por*

E. 1. *¡Esté contento/feliz!/¡Sé feliz!* 2. *¡Póngaselos!* 3. *Podría usted escribirlo.* 4. *¡Hazlo ahora!* 5. *No se olvide de traerlos.*

F. 1. *¿Cuánto tiempo hacía que vivías en Madrid cuando ella llegó?* 2. *Por poco deposito el cheque en la cuenta de ahorros.* 3. *Estarán nadando en nuestra playita favorita.* 4. *Deberé pasar por la casa de cambio para comprar pesetas para ella.* 5. *Me gustaría/Quisiera comprar dos entradas para el estreno.*

las comidas mexicanas

Entre los platos típicos mexicanos hay muchos de origen hispano y otros de influencia azteca.[1] Los pilares[2] de la cocina[3] mexicana son el maíz, el arroz,[4] y las habichuelas,[5] acompañados de carne, puerco, cordero o pescado, dependiendo de la región.

La tortilla, que es un tipo de torta hecha de harina de maíz,[6] acompaña muchas comidas. Ella también es la base[7] de las enchiladas,[8] tostadas,[9] quesadillas,[10] y flautas.[11] Los mexicanos comen frijoles diariamente, en el desayuno o al final de una comida. Hay variedades[12] como las habichuelas[14] verdes y los frijoles negros. También hay más de veinte clases de ají picante[15] usadas en la preparación de estos platos típicos. Los mexicanos comen carne por lo menos una vez al día, y algunos platos incluyen tanto carne como aves.[16]

La cocina mexicana use ingredientes especiales y variadas salsas,[17] como el mole. El mole se trace de sabores diferentes: el maní,[18] la semilla de sésamo, chocolate, y chiles.[19] La preparación del mole es bastante complicada, y, por esta razón, sólo se sirve en ocasiones especiales como bautizos,[20] bodas, y cumpleaños. Muchos de los platos verdaderamente[21] mexicanos aprovechan productos y especias[22] locales; por eso, se necesita de un paladar[23] bastante aventurero.

La comida mexicana no le da mucha importancia a los vegetales y ensaladas, con excepción de los pimentones.[24] Los vegetales se usan con frecuencia en la preparación de sopas. Hay muchas deliciosas frutas tropicales, por ejemplo, la guayaba y el mango. Las bebidas de frutas, llamadas "licuados," son muy populares y están hechas con una inmensa variedad de frutas. La "horchata" es también muy notable: es una deliciosa y refrescante[25] bebida hecha de arroz. En México hay también muchas otras bebidas regionales, tanto alcohólicas como no-alcohólicas.

Esté listo para desear[26] "Buen apetito"[27] y "¡Salud!"[23]

1. *azteca* — Aztec
2. *los pilares* — the staples
3. *la cocina* — cuisine (also: kitchen)
4. *el arroz* — rice
5. *las habichuelas* — beans
6. *la tortilla, que es un panqueqe hecho de harina de maíz . . .* — the tortilla, which is a pancake made of corn flour . . .
7. *la base* — the basis
8. *enchilada* — rolled tortillas stuffed with chicken, meat, or cheese, topped with tomato sauce
9. *tostada* — tortilla with different fillings
10. *quesadilla* — tortilla folded in half and stuffed with cheese, tomato, sausage, beans, etc.
11. *flauta* — is like a tortilla sandwich, rolled and deep-fried
12. *variedades* — varieties
13. *frijoles* — kidney beans
14. *las habichuelas verdes* — green (string) beans
15. *ají picante* — spicy chili
16. *aves* — fowl
17. *salsa* — sauce
18. *el maní* — peanut
19. *la semilla de sésamo* — sesame seed
20. *bautizos, bodas y cumpleaños* — baptisms, weddings, and birthdays
21. *verdaderamente* — truly, really
22. *las especias* — spices
23. *un paladar bastante aventurero* — a rather adventurous palate
24. *los pimientos* — peppers
25. *refrescante* — refreshing
26. *Esté listo para desear* — Be ready to wish
27. *¡Buen apetito!* — Bon appetit!
28. *¡Salud!* — Cheers!

LECCION 31

EN LA COMISARIA.   At the police station.

A. DIALOGO

En la comisaría Ocho de Quito, Ecuador.

CATALINA: **Bueno, señor detective, el asalto se hizo rápida y eficazmente.**

DETECTIVE: **Cuéntemelo otra vez.**

CATALINA: **Fuimos asaltadas por dos personas con máscaras al salir del club.**

DETECTIVE: **¿Qué ropa llevaban los ladrones?**

CATALINA: **Ellos se vestían con pantalones y chaqueta negros.**

DETECTIVE: **¿Qué les dijeron?**

CATALINA: **Muy poco. ¡Manos arriba! Luego nos mostraron un revólver y un puñal.**

DETECTIVE: **¿Qué se les quitó?**

CATALINA: **Se nos quitaron las carteras y los relojes.**

DETECTIVE: **¿Intentaron Uds. escapar o gritar "¡Socorro!"?**

CATALINA: **No, señor. Fuimos tan asustadas por ellos que no pudimos reaccionar, sino que nos quedamos allí como congeladas en el mismo lugar.**

DETECTIVE: **¿Hubo testigos?**

CATALINA: **Nadie vio nada.**

DETECTIVE: **Tuvieron mala suerte, pero felizmente no se les ha hecho daño físico.**

At police station Eight in Quito, Ecuador.

CATALINA: Well, detective, the mugging was done rapidly and effectively.

DETECTIVE: Tell me once again.

CATALINA: We were attacked by two people in masks upon leaving the club.

DETECTIVE: What clothing were the thieves wearing?

CATALINA: They were dressed in black pants and jackets.

DETECTIVE: What did they say to you?

CATALINA: Very little. "Hands up!" Then they showed us a gun and a knife.

DETECTIVE: What was taken from you?

CATALINA: Our wallets and our watches were taken.

DETECTIVE: Did you try to escape or yell "Help!"?

CATALINA: No, sir. We were so frightened by them that we couldn't react; rather, we stood there as if frozen in place.

DETECTIVE: Were there witnesses?

CATALINA: No one saw anything.

DETECTIVE: You had bad luck, but fortunately, no physical harm was done to you.

B. GRAMATICA Y USOS

1. THE TRUE PASSIVE

There are two voices in language: active and passive. The active voice, which we normally use, describes the subject performing an action.

Los ladrones atacaron a los hombres.
The thieves attacked the men.

Ellos nos asustaron.
They frightened us.

In the passive voice, the subject receives the action:

Los hombres fueron atacados por los ladrones.
The men were attacked by the thieves.

Nosotras fuimos asustadas por ellos.
We were frightened by them.

The passive is formed with *ser* + past participle. In this usage, the past participle is an adjective and must agree with the subject in number and gender. The agent, the person performing the action, may or may not be mentioned. If mentioned, the agent is introduced by *por.* The passive can be used with any tense of the verb *ser:*

Las señoras habían sido asaltadas varias veces.
The women had been mugged several times.

Los ladrones serán prendidos por la policía.
The thieves will be arrested by the police.

In general, however, the active voice is preferred in Spanish.

2. THE PASSIVE *SE*

When the agent of the passive action is unknown or of no interest, the alternative passive *se* construction is used: *se* + the third person singular or plural form of the verb (depending on the number of the subject).

¿Qué se hizo?
What was done?

Se nos quitaron las carteras.
Our wallets were taken from us.

Similarly, in announcements or semi-official statements the passive *se* construction is used:

Aquí se habla español.
Spanish is spoken here.

Se prohibe fumar.
Smoking is prohibited.

3. *PERO* AND *SINO*

Pero means "but":

El asalto fue horrible, pero, por lo menos, no se les ha hecho daño.
The mugging was horrible, but at least no harm was done to you.

Sino means "but" or "but rather" and is used for purposes of direct contrast:

No pudimos reaccionar, sino nos quedamos como congeladas en el mismo lugar.
We couldn't react; rather, we were as if frozen in place.

VOCABULARIO

el/*la* **criminal**	criminal
asaltar	to mug, to rob
asalto	mugging
el/*la asaltante*	mugger
el ladrón, la ladrona	thief
robar	to rob

robo	robbery
¡Manos arriba!	Hands up!
el revólver	gun, revolver
el puñal	knife, dagger
quitar	to take (from someone)
¿Qué se les quitó?	What was taken from you?
atacar	to attack
hacer daño a	to harm
herir *(e>ie), (e>i)*	to wound
tirar	to shoot
matar	to kill
la víctima	victim
asustar	to frighten
reaccionar	to react
intentar escapar	to attempt escape
gritar	to yell
¡Ayuda!/¡Socorro!	Help!
testigo	witness
tener mala suerte	to be unlucky
la policía	police force
el policía	policeman
la mujer policía	policewoman
el/*la* detective	detective
prender	to arrest
preso, *-a*	prisoner
la cárcel	prison
¡Alto!	Stop!
¡Cuidado!	Careful! Watch out!
¡Déjeme en paz!	Leave me alone!
¡Dese prisa!	Hurry!
¡Deténga(n)lo!	Stop him!
¡Es una emergencia!	It's an emergency!
¡Policía!	Police!
mostrar *(o>ue)*	to show
felizmente	happily, fortunately
eficazmente	effectively

EXAMEN

A. *Conteste la pregunta en una oración completa usando la pista.*

1. *¿Qué les dijeron los ladrones? (¡Manos arriba!)*
2. *¿Cómo se sintieron? (asustados/as)*
3. *¿Qué se les quitó? (los relojes)*
4. *¿A quién llamaron? (la policía)*
5. *¿Qué daño les han hecho? (ningún)*

B. *Cambie a la voz pasiva.* (Change to the passive voice.)

MODELO: *Ellos nos sorprendieron.*
　　　　Fuimos sorprendidos por ellos.

1. *Los ladrones nos asaltaron en la calle.*
2. *Los asaltantes se vistieron de negro.*
3. *Nadie vio nada.*
4. *El detective va a prender a los criminales.*

C. *Traduzca al español.*

1. We were mugged but we weren't harmed.
2. They were frightened by the men with guns.
3. I was not attacked in the street but rather upon leaving the apartment.
4. Did you attempt to escape?
5. There weren't any witnesses.

D. *Use pero en las siguientes oraciones.*

MODELO: *Comí mucho anoche. Todavía tengo hambre.*
　　　　Comí mucho anoche, pero todavía tengo hambre.

1. *Practico el tenis todos los días. No sé jugar muy bien.*
2. *Me acosté temprano. No descansé mucho.*
3. *Estoy a dieta. No he bajado de peso.*
4. *Hablo español. Hablo más francés.*
5. *Mi casa es de dos recámaras. Necesito cuatro.*

NOTAS CULTURALES

Spain is a relatively safe country. Over the last twenty years, however, crime has increased substantially throughout Latin America for a number of reasons: the great disparity in income among the population; increased drug abuse throughout the world; the growth of cities surrounded by shanty-towns; internal political and socio-economic problems; and the lack of a reliable system of justice.

Despite Latin America's periods of apparent prosperity, poverty is still widespread. According to the World Resources Institute, the poorest 20 percent of the population receives a smaller share of the region's income here than in any other region, less than 4 percent. Land ownership is concentrated within a very small percentage of the population, and access to education is limited in most Latin American countries.

With the region's economic recession came declined social expenditures, urban pollution (fueled by the growing need for automobiles), and increased drug abuse and trafficking. Protests and conflicts became more common. What two decades ago was a climate of tolerance between rich and poor has broken down, and fear, overt hostility, and sometimes violence have taken its place. Colombia, Mexico, and a few other countries have seen a rise in kidnappings, murders, and related criminal violence. Many Latin Americans live in heavily guarded homes and apartment complexes in constant fear of organized gangs (many times headed by laid-off policemen) that prey on the wealthy. Be sure to research the situation in your country of destination.

RESPUESTAS

A. 1. *Nos dijeron "¡Manos arriba!"* 2. *Nos sentimos asustados/as.* 3. *Se nos quitaron los relojes.* 4. *Llamamos a la policía.* 5. *No nos han hecho ningún daño.*

B. 1. *Fuimos asaltados/as en la calle por los ladrones.* 2. *Los asaltantes fueron vestidos de negro.* 3. *Nada fue visto por nadie.* 4. *Los criminales serán prendidos por el detective.*

C. 1. *Fuimos asaltados/as pero no nos hicieron daño.* 2. *Fueron asustados/as por los hombres con revólveres.* 3. *No fui asaltado/a en la calle, sino al salir del departamento.* 4. *¿Intentó Ud. escapar?* 5. *No hubo testigos.*

D. 1. *Practico el tenis todos los días, pero no sé jugar muy bien.* 2. *Me acosté temprano, pero no descansé mucho.* 3. *Estoy a dieta, pero no he bajado de peso.* 4. *Hablo español, pero hablo más francés.* 6. *Mi casa es de dos recámaras, pero necesito cuatro.*

LECCION 32

MIRANDO LA TELEVISION.   Watching television.

A. DIALOGO

"¡Sábado gigante!," Miami, Florida.

PABLO: **Voy a poner la televisión. ¿Qué programa quieres que ponga?**

ELENA: **Según el programa del día, a esta hora sólo pasan novelas en las redes nacionales.**

PABLO: **Prefiero ver el noticiero del canal educativo, o tal vez una película en el cable, o un video en la video-grabadora.**

ELENA: **Como ya instalaste el disco, sintonicemos un programa por satélite.**

PABLO: **Pronto vendrán los niños. Pedirán que cambiemos el canal. Querrán mirar la "Plaza Sésamo," una comedia o unos dibujos animados.**

ELENA: **Tú sabes que no me gusta que ellos se sienten ante la pantalla por más de una hora al día.**

PABLO: **Como hoy es sábado, te aconsejo que no insistas en eso. Durante la semana, pides que te obedezcan y sí lo hacen.**

"¡Sábado gigante!," Miami, Florida.

PABLO: I'm going to turn on the television. What program do you want me to turn on?

ELENA: According to the daily listing, at this hour they're only showing soap operas on the national networks.

261

PABLO: I prefer to see the news on the educational channel, or perhaps a film on cable, or a video on the VCR.

ELENA: Since you already installed the satellite dish, let's tune in to a program by satellite.

PABLO: The kids will be here soon. They'll ask us to change the channel. They'll probably want to see Sesame Street, a comedy program or some cartoons.

ELENA: You know that I don't like them to sit in front of the screen for more than an hour a day.

PABLO: As today is Saturday, I advise you not to insist on it. During the week you ask them to obey you and they really do.

B. GRAMATICA Y USOS

1. THE CONCEPT OF THE SUBJUNCTIVE

Language has moods. Until now, you have studied tenses in the indicative mood, which is the mood of facts. In a very broad sense, the subjunctive mood might be called the "mood of doubt." What is in doubt is whether the action will indeed take place.

The subjunctive mood may be considered a form of the indirect command. With a command, you give an order to someone; whether or not the order will be carried out is in doubt—the person may or may not do what you wished, requested, demanded, or ordered. "Stop!" really means "I want you to stop." Whether or not the person will stop is uncertain. And therein lies the concept of the subjunctive mood.

2. THE PRESENT SUBJUNCTIVE OF REGULAR AND RADICAL-CHANGING VERBS

The forms of the present subjunctive are like the command forms. Remember that you get the command from the first person of the indicative by dropping the *o* and adding the opposite vowel: that is, for -*ar* verbs you add -*e;* for -*er* and -*ir* verbs you add *a.*

	MIRAR TO LOOK		PONER TO PUT		VIVIR TO LIVE	
yo		e		a		a
tú		es		as		as
Ud., él, ella	mir	e	pong	a	viv	a
nosotros, -as		emos		amos		amos
vosotros, -as		éis		áis		áis
Uds., ellos, ellas		en		an		an

Many irregular verbs, such as *poner, salir,* etc., have regular subjunctive forms using the first person singular of the present indicative mood:

ponga, salga, diga, haga, oiga, venga, etc.

In the first and second persons plural, *o>ue* and *e>ie* radical-changing verbs of the -*ar* and -*er* conjugations return to the original vowel of the infinitive:

	SENTAR TO SIT	QUERER TO WORK
yo	sient + e: siente	quier + a: quiera
tú	sient + es: sientes	quier + as: quieras
Ud., él, ella	sient + e: siente	quier + a: quiera
nosotros, -as	sent + emos: sentemos	quer + amos: queramos
vosotros, -as	sent + éis: sentéis	quer + áis: queráis
Uds., ellos, ellas	sient + en: sienten	quier + an: quieran

For *-ir* radical-changing verbs, the following vowel changes occur in the first and second persons plural:

e>*ie:* use *i*   o>*ue:* use *u*

	PREFERIR TO PREFER	MORIR TO DIE
yo	prefier + a: prefiera	muer + a: muera
tú	prefier + as: prefieras	muer + as: mueras
Ud., él, ella	prefier + a: prefiera	muer + a: muera
nosotros, -as	prefir + amos: prefiramos	mur + amos: muramos
vosotros, -as	prefir + áis: prefiráis	mur + áis: muráis
Uds., ellos, ellas	prefier + an: prefieran	muer + an: mueran

e>*i:* use *i*

PEDIR   TO ASK FOR

yo		a	pida
tú		as	pidas
Ud., él, ella	pid	a	pida
nosotros, -as		amos	→ pidamos
vosotros, -as		áis	pidáis
Uds., ellos, ellas		an	pidan

Also note that verbs ending in *-zar* change *c* to *z* in the subjunctive:

Sugiero que sintonices el canal ocho.
    I suggest you tune in to channel eight.

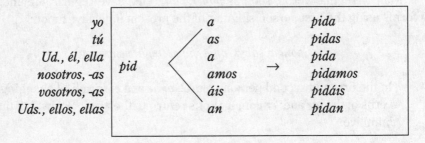

sintonizar

3. SUBJUNCTIVE CLAUSES EXPRESSING A REQUEST, DESIRE, OR DEMAND

In Spanish, a subjunctive form is used in a dependent clause[1] that follows verbs such as these:

querer	to wish, to want
desear	to wish, to want
pedir	to ask for, to request
insistir	to insist
recomendar	to recommend
sugerir	to suggest
preferir	to prefer

These and similar verbs are used to express a request, desire, or demand for an action by another person or group of people (who are the subject of the dependent clause):

Quiero que (tú) pongas la televisión.
I want you to turn on the television.

sentar

No me gusta que (ellos) se sienten ante la pantalla.
I don't like them to sit in front of the screen.

A sentence involving the subjunctive, such as these, is usually made up of a main clause and a dependent clause joined by the word *que,* "that":

(yo) Quiero + que + (tú) pongas la televisión.

Literally, "I want that you turn on the television" or "I want you to turn on the television."

---

[1] A dependent clause is one that depends on a main clause; it cannot stand alone.
main clause: dependent clause:
I suggest   that you turn off the TV.

¿Qué programa quieres que yo ponga?
　　What program do you want me to turn on?

Pedirán que cambiemos el canal.
　　They'll ask us to change the channel.

　　English does not use the subjunctive often; in these sentences it uses
　　the infinitive instead.
　　If there is no change in subject following the verb of desire, demand or
　　request, Spanish uses the infinitive, too.

Prefiero ver el noticiero.
　　I prefer to see the news.

VOCABULARIO

el televisor	television set
la tele, la televisión	television (programming)
poner la televisión	to turn on the television
apagar la televisión	to turn off the television
Quiero que pongas la televisión.	I want you to turn on the television.
encender *(e>ie)*	to turn on (lights, TV)
sintonizar	to tune in
mirar la televisión	to watch television
la pantalla	the screen
el programa	program
la red	network
(tele)novela	soap opera
pasar	to show
Esta noche pasa nuestra novela favorita.	Our favorite soap opera is on tonight.
noticiero	news broadcast
comedia	comedy
los dibujos animados	cartoons
película	film, movie
video/vídeo	video
video-grabadora	VCR

el canal	channel, station
el canal educativo	educational (public) television
cambiar el canal	to change channels
el cable	cable
discoantena	dish antenna
el satélite	satellite
por satélite	by satellite
nacional	national
instalar	to install
aconsejar	to advise
obedecer	to obey
insistir en (+ noun or infinitive)	to insist on
insistir en que	to insist that
según	according to

conseguir =
to get .
to obtain

EXAMEN

A. *Conteste la pregunta en una oración completa usando la pista.*

1. *¿Qué programa quieres que veamos? (una comedia)*
2. *¿Qué me sugieres? (cambiar el canal)*
3. *¿Qué pasan ahora en la tele? (el noticiero)*
4. *¿Qué no quieres que hagan los niños? (mirar la tele por muchas horas)*
5. *¿Qué me aconsejas? (instalar un disco)*

B. *Añada las palabras en paréntesis para hacer una oración del subjuntivo.*
(Add the words in parenthesis to make a sentence in the subjunctive.)

MODELO: Prefiero leer. (que tú)
       Prefiero que tú leas.

1. *Deseamos venderlo. (que ellas)*
2. *Insisto en salir ahora. (que él)*
3. *¿Prefieres encender la tele? (que yo)*
4. *Me gusta volver temprano. (que tú)*
5. *Queremos sentarnos aquí. (que Uds.)*

6. *Yo no quiero trabajar tanto. (que tú)*
7. *Insisto en ir contigo. (que ella)*
8. *Qué quieres comer? (que los niños)*
9. *Prefiero ver el canal 22. (que nosotros)*

C. *Escriba en una oración.*

1. Say that you want John to turn on the television.
2. Ask Elena which program she prefers to watch.
3. Tell Enrique that you do not recommend that he install a dish antenna.
4. Ask who insists on changing the channel.
5. Say that you do not want the family to tune in to the soap opera.

NOTAS CULTURALES

Latin American *telenovelas* (soap operas) are extremely popular among all classes and are produced primarily in Venezuela, Puerto Rico, Mexico, and Argentina. Yet, soap operas produced in the USA are also well known all over Latin America. They create a world of illusion for the poor people, who, for an hour or two a night, can participate in the lives and possessions of the wealthy middle class. Some of the most successful *telenovelas,* however, have been about the lives and customs of the poor.

RESPUESTAS

A. 1. *Quiero que veamos una comedia.* 2. *Te sugiero que cambies el canal.*
3. *Ahora pasan el noticiero.* 4. *No quiero que los niños miren la tele por muchas horas.* 5. *Te aconsejo que instales un disco.*
B. 1. *Deseamos que ellas lo vendan.* 2. *Insisto en que él salga ahora.*
3. *¿Prefieres que yo encienda la tele?* 4. *Me gusta que vuelvas temprano.*
5. *Queremos que Uds. se sienten aquí.* 6. *Yo no quiero que tú trabajes tanto.*
7. *Insisto que ella vaya contigo.* 8. *Qué quieres que los niños coman?*
9. *Prefiero que nosotros veamos el canal 22.*
C. 1. *Quiero que Juan ponga/encienda la tele.* 2. *Elena, ¿qué programa prefieres mirar?* 3. *No te recomiendo que instales un disco/una antena.*
4. *¿Quién insiste en cambiar el canal?* 5. *No deseo que la familia sintonice la novela.*

LECCION 33

EN EL CINE.   At the movies.

A. DIALOGO

En Juárez, México.

ARTURO: **Espero que podamos ir al cine esta noche.**

VERA: **Vamos a consultar la cartelera para ver que exhiben. Mira, amor mío, hay un festival de la obra de María Félix.**

ARTURO: **A ti te encantan las películas sentimentales. Pero, no te pongas a llorar, por favor. ¿A qué hora comienza la función?**

VERA: **A las ocho. ¡Vámonos!**

Más tarde en el Cine Estrella:

VERA: **¡Ay! ¡Qué muchedumbre!**

ARTURO: **Temo que el auditorio esté lleno. ¿Tomamos algo? ¿Rosetas de maíz, un refresco?**

VERA: **Claro. ¿Dónde nos sentamos?**

ARTURO: **Busquemos asientos cerca de la pantalla.**

VERA: **¡Qué pena que no lleves contigo los anteojos! No te aproximes mucho. Eh, bien, sentémonos aquí.**

ARTURO: **Ya comienza; es una película en blanco y negro.**

VERA: **¡Cállate! Vas a escuchar un diálogo apasionado.**

―――――――――――

In Juárez, México.

ARTURO: I hope we can go to the movies tonight.

VERA: Let's check the movie listings to see what's on. Look, darling, there's a María Félix film festival.

ARTURO: You like those romantic films. But please don't start crying. At what time does the show begin?

VERA: At eight o'clock. Let's go!

Later in the Estrella Theater:

VERA: Wow! What a crowd!

ARTURO: I'm afraid the theater may be full. Do you want to eat something? Popcorn, a soft drink?

VERA: Of course. Where shall we sit?

ARTURO: Let's find seats near the screen.

VERA: What a pity you don't take your glasses with you! Don't go too close. Let's sit here.

ARTURO: It's beginning now; it's a black and white film.

VERA: Be quiet! You're going to hear some passionate dialogue.

B. GRAMATICA Y USOS

1. IRREGULAR PRESENT SUBJUNCTIVE VERBS

While most present subjunctive forms come from the first person of the present indicative, the following verbs are totally irregular:

	ESTAR TO BE	SER TO BE	HABER TO HAVE	SABER TO KNOW	DAR TO GIVE	IR TO GO
yo	esté	sea	haya	sepa	dé	vaya
tú	estés	seas	hayas	sepas	des	vayas
Ud., él, ella	esté	sea	haya	sepa	dé	vaya

	ESTAR TO BE	SER TO BE	HABER TO HAVE	SABER TO KNOW	DAR TO GIVE	IR TO GO
nosotros, -as	estemos	seamos	hayamos	sepamos	demos	vayamos
vosotros, -as	estéis	seáis	hayáis	sepáis	deis	vayáis
Uds., ellos, ellas	estén	sean	hayan	sepan	den	vayan

Temo que el auditorio esté lleno.
I'm afraid the theater may be full.

¡Qué pena que no vayas!
What a pity that you aren't going!

Desean que les dé las entradas.
They want me to give them the tickets.

Prefiero que sean asientos atrás.
I'd prefer that they be seats in the back.

2. THE PRESENT SUBJUNCTIVE OF VERBS ENDING IN -CAR, -GAR, -ZAR

Verbs ending in *-car, -gar,* and *-zar* make the same spelling changes in the subjunctive as in the command forms:

	c>qu BUSCAR TO LOOK FOR	g>gu PAGAR TO PAY	z>c COMENZAR TO BEGIN
yo	busque	pague	comience
tú	busques	pagues	comiences
Ud, él, ella	busque	pague	comience
nosotros, -as	busquemos	paguemos	comencemos
vosotros, -as	busquéis	paguéis	comencéis
Uds., ellos, ellas	busquen	paguen	comiencen

Espero que la película comience ahora.
I hope the film is beginning now.

Me alegro que nos paguen las entradas.
I'm happy they're paying for the tickets.

3. SUBJUNCTIVE CLAUSES AFTER EXPRESSIONS OF EMOTION

When a verb of emotion is used in the main clause, the verb of the dependent clause is in the subjunctive. The following verbs require a subjunctive in the dependent clause:

alegrarse de	to be happy about
estar contento, -a/triste de	to be happy/sad about
lamentar	to regret
esperar	to hope
tener miedo de	to be afraid of
temer	to fear

¡Qué pena . . . !
 What a pity . . . !

Me alegro que haya tanta gente.
 I'm happy that there are so many people.

Temo que el auditoria esté lleno.
 I'm afraid the theater may be full.

¡Qué pena que no lleves contigo los anteojos!
 What a pity you don't take your glasses with you!

4. THE NEGATIVE FAMILIAR COMMAND AND THE "LET'S" COMMAND

a. The affirmative *tú* command comes from the third person singular of the present tense; there are a few exceptions. The negative *tú* command is the second person singular of the present subjunctive; there are no exceptions.

¡Mira! ¡No mires!   Look! Don't look!

The object pronouns are attached to the positive command, but precede the negative command:

272

| *Cállate.* | Be quiet. |
| *No te aproximes mucho.* | Don't go too close. |

b. We have used *vamos* + *a* + infinitive to form the "let's" command. This can also be expressed with the *nosotros, -as* form of the subjunctive verb. The only exception is *vamos,* "let's go"; in the negative form, the present subjunctive is used:

| *No vayamos.* | Let's not go. |

In the positive "let's" command, the final -*s* of the verb ending is dropped when the object pronoun *se* or *nos* is attached to it:

Vámonos.	Let's go.
Sentémonos aquí.	Let's sit here.
Vendámoselo.	Let's sell it to him.

The negative "let's" command requires the object pronoun before the verb:

| *No nos sentemos aquí.* | Let's not sit here. |

VOCABULARIO

el cine	movies, movie theater
el auditorio	auditorium
obra	work, opus
la película sentimental	the romantic film
cartelera	movie listings
consultar la cartelera	to check the movie listings
exhibir	to show
¿Qué exhiben esta noche?	What are they showing tonight?
tener en exhibición	to be showing
la función	showtime (play, film, etc.)
el festival de cine	film festival
la estrella	star
fila	row
asientos adelante	seats up front
asientos atrás	seats in the back

rosetas de maíz **(palomitas de maíz)**	popcorn
refresco	soft drink
en blanco y negro	in black and white
a colores	in color
diálogo	dialogue
el cineasta	moviemaker
el largometraje	feature (full-length) film
el cortometraje	short film
rodar una película	to film
los anteojos	eyeglasses
amor mío	darling
callarse	to be quiet!
¡Cállate!	Be quiet.
alegrarse de	to be happy about
estar triste	to be sad
esperar	to hope
temer	to fear
tener miedo de	to be afraid of
lamenter	to regret, lament
aproximarse a	to get close to

EXAMEN

A. *Conteste la pregunta en una oración completa usando la pista.*

1. *¿Qué esperas que ellas hagan? (llegar a la hora)*
2. *¿Qué temen ellos? (no hay asientos)*
3. *¿Qué me dices? (callarte)*
4. *¿Qué tipo de película es? (sentimental)*
5. *¿Qué lamentas? (la película es en blanco y negro)*

B. *Dé el imperativo familiar positivo y negativo de los siguientes verbos.* (Give the affirmative and negative familiar command of the following verbs.)

MODELO: venir / ven, no vengas

1. *dar*
2. *salir*
3. *hacer*
4. *poner*
5. *pagar*
6. *ser*

C. *Escriba en español.*

1. Say that you are happy that there are many people at the movies.
2. Ask Arturo if the theater is probably full.
3. Say that you want him and you to sit near the screen.
4. Say that your friend prefers that you and he not buy popcorn.
5. Tell your friend that you hope that the film is in color.

NOTAS CULTURALES

Spain, Mexico and Argentina have had high-quality film industries producing film classics by much admired directors. Talented Spanish-speaking actors and actresses have had successful careers in Hollywood since the silent film days. Films from the United States and other nations are extremely popular throughout the Spanish-speaking world.

RESPUESTAS

A. 1. *Espero que ellas lleguen a la hora.* 2. *Temen que no haya asientos.*
3. *Te digo que te calles.* 4. *Es una película sentimental.* 5. *Lamento que la película sea en blanco y negro.*
B. 1. *da/no des* 2. *sal/no salgas* 3. *haz/no hagas* 4. *pon/no pongas* 5. *paga/no pagues* 6. *sé/no seas.*
C. 1. *Me alegro que haya mucha gente en el cine.* 2. *Arturo ¿estará el auditoria lleno?* 3. *Quiero que nosotros nos sentemos cerca de la pantalla.*
4. *Mi amigo prefiere que no compremos rosetas de maíz.* 5. *Espero que la película sea a colores.*

LECCION 34
LOS DEPORTES. Sports.

A. DIALOGO

En un bar cerca del Estadio Bernabeu de Madrid, España.

EMILIO: **Dudo que haya otro deporte más exigente y emocionante que nuestro fútbol.**

CARMEN: **No creo que tú juegues otro deporte.**

EMILIO: **Quiero decir que para el espectador no hay otro que se compare con el fútbol.**

CARMEN: **Claro, los futbolistas se dedican al cultivo del cuerpo; son musculosos y delicados al mismo tiempo. No son como esos hombrones del fútbol norteamericano o los boxeadores.**

EMILIO: **Los deportistas tienen que mantenerse en forma. Son cuidadosos con lo que comen y no toman muchas bebidas alcohólicas.**

CARMEN: **¡Hombre! No todo es sacrificio. ¡Cómo a mí me gustaría pasar las horas de trabajo en un campo de fútbol, o en una cancha de tenis, o en una pista de atletismo!**

At a bar near the Bernabeu Stadium in Madrid, Spain.

EMILIO: I doubt that there's another sport more demanding and thrilling than our soccer.

CARMEN: I don't think you play another sport.

EMILIO: I mean that, for the spectator, no other one compares with soccer.

CARMEN: Of course soccer players are dedicated to the cult of their bodies; they are muscular and delicate at the same time. They aren't like those big men of North American football or boxers.

EMILIO: Athletes have to stay in shape. They are careful about what they eat, and they don't drink too much alcohol.

CARMEN: Well, it isn't all sacrifice. How I'd like to spend my working hours on a soccer field, or on a tennis court, or on a running track!

B. GRAMATICA Y USOS

1. SUBJUNCTIVE CLAUSES AFTER EXPRESSIONS OF DOUBT AND DENIAL

a. Expressions of doubt or denial take the subjunctive in a dependent clause. Verbs and other expressions followed by the subjunctive include:

dudar	to doubt
negar (i>ie)	to deny
tal vez/puede ser/quizás	perhaps

Dudo que haya otro deporte más exigente que nuestro fútbol.
I doubt that there's another sport more demanding than our soccer.

Niego que todo sea sacrificio.
I deny that it's all sacrifice.

Puede ser que él juegue al tenis contigo.
Perhaps he'll play tennis with you.

b. When you deny the existence of something or someone, you have a negative antecedent that requires the subjunctive. Expressions such as these take the subjunctive:

No hay nada que . . .	There is nothing that . . .
No hay nadie que . . .	There is no one who . . .
No hay ningún . . . que . . .	There is no . . . that/who . . .
No conocco a nadie que . . .	I know no one who . . .

c. The verb *creer* (to believe) is usually followed by the indicative.

Creo que todo está bien.
I think that everything is fine.

In a question or a negative sentence, however, *creer* is followed by the subjunctive:

No creo que juegues otro deporte.
I don't think you play another sport.

¿Crees que ellos vengan hoy?
Do you think they are coming today?

2. VERB + PREPOSITION + NOUN

You have learned that verbs take a preposition *(a, de, en)* when followed by an infinitive. There are also verbs which require a preposition when followed by a noun:

dedicarse a:

Se dedican al cultivo del cuerpo.
They are dedicated to the cult of their bodies.

compararse con:

No hay otro deporte que se compare con el fútbol.
There is no other sport comparable to soccer.

preocuparse por:

Ella se preocupa mucho por Juan.
She worries a great deal about John.

entrar en:

Vamos a entrar en esta casa.
We are entering this house.

salir de:

Salen de la clase a las ocho.
They leave class at 8 o'clock.

interesarse en:

Se interesan en los pobres.
They are interested in the poor.

3. AUGMENTATIVES

In Spanish, augmentative endings generally indicate large size, but can also indicate dislike. Most augmentatives are masculine words ending in *-ón;* when referring to females, however, use *-ona.*
To form the augmentative, drop the final vowel and add the ending:

la sala	room	> *el salón*	(large) reception room
la silla	chair	> *el sillón*	(big) easy chair
la cuchara	spoon	> *el cucharón*	ladle
el hombre	man	> *el hombrón*	big man
el soltero	bachelor	> *el solterón*	confirmed bachelor
la soltera	single woman	> *la solterona*	spinster, old maid

If the noun ends in a consonant, simply add the ending:

la mujer	woman	> *la mujerona*	big woman (pejorative)

VOCABULARIO

estadio	stadium
el deporte	sport
el/*la* **deportista**	athlete
el/*la* **atleta**	athlete
el fútbol	soccer
fútbol norteamericano	US football
el/*la* **futbolista**	soccer player
el tenis	tennis

jugar al tenis	to play tennis
el/*la* **tenista**	tennis player
boxeo	boxing
el/*la* **boxeador** *(a)*	boxer
el/*la* **espectador** *(a)*	spectator
músculo	muscle
musculoso	muscular
cultivo del cuerpo	cult of the body
campo	field (sports)
cancha	court (tennis)
pista	track (running)
mantenerse en forma	to keep in shape
el régimen	program, regimen; diet
dieta	diet
baloncesto	basketball
el béisbol	baseball
el golf	golf
esquiar	skiing
el tenis	tennis
bebida alcohólica	alcoholic drink
compararse con	to compare with, to be comparable to
cuidadoso	careful
dudar	to doubt
el bar	the bar
exigente	demanding
emocionante	thrilling
delicado	delicate
dedicarse a	to dedicate oneself to
interesarse en	to be interested in
negar *(e>ie)*	to deny
preocuparse por	to worry about
salir de	to leave (a place)
puede ser ⎫	
quizás ⎬	perhaps
tal vez ⎭	

EXAMEN

A. *Conteste la pregunta en una oración complete usando la pista.*

1. ¿A qué deporte se dedica Ud.? (tenis)
2. ¿Qué no crees? (ellos se mantienen en forma)
3. ¿Qué niegan? (hay deporte más exigente)
4. ¿Por quiénes se interesan? (los pobres)
5. ¿Qué dudas? (tú haces ejercicios)

B. *Cambie la oración usando la pista.*

MODELO: *Creo que vienen hoy. (No creer)*
   No creo que vengan hoy.

1. Hay muchas personas que hacen eso. (No hay nadie)
2. Creemos que son ricos. (Dudar)
3. Le gusta jugar al tenis. (Tal vez)
4. Piensa que lo hacen. (Negar)
5. Todo es muy interesante. (No hay nada)

C. *Escriba en una oración.*

1. Tell your friend you doubt that he can dedicate himself to a sport.
2. Ask your friend if she believes that soccer is the most thrilling sport.
3. Say you doubt that the athletes follow a special diet.
4. Say your friends deny that there'll be a crowd at the stadium.
5. Say you don't know anyone who is a better athlete than Jorge.

D. *Conteste las siguientes preguntas con la pista. Use el subjuntivo.*

1. ¿Hay muchas que están cerca de aquí? (No hay)
2. ¿Hay muchos que le ayudan a limpiar la casa? (No hay)
3. ¿Hay muchos libros que le interesan? (No hay)
4. ¿Conoce Ud. a alguien que es francés? (A nadie)
5. ¿Cree Ud. que encontraré el estadio? (No creo)

NOTAS CULTURALES

The most important sport in Spain and Latin America is soccer. Throughout the history of the game, Latin Americans have been among the leaders: Brazil and Argentina have won the World Cup (Brazil five times). Some soccer stadiums in Latin American capitals can seat more than 150,000 spectators. Many countries have weekly or daily newspapers totally dedicated to soccer. *Jai-alai,* similar to handball, but played with a long, curved basket, originated in the Basque region of Spain. It is very popular today in Spain and in Latin America.

RESPUESTAS

A. 1. *Me dedico al tenis.* 2. *No creo que ellos se mantengan en forma.*
   3. *Niegan que haya deporte más exigente.* 4. *Se interesan en los pobres.*
   5. *Dudo que hagas ejercicios.*
B. 1. *No hay nadie que haga eso.* 2. *Dudamos que sean ricos.* 3. *Tal vez le guste jugar al tenis.* 4. *Niega que lo hagan.* 5. *No hay nada que sea muy interesante.*
C. 1. *Dudo que tú puedas dedicarte a un deporte.* 2. *¿Crees tú que el fútbol sea el deporte más emocionante?* 3. *Dudo que los deportistas/atletas sigan una dieta especial.* 4. *Mis amigos niegan que haya una muchedumbre en el estadio.* 5. *No conozco a nadie que sea mejor atleta que Jorge.* 6. *No hay nada que esté cerca de aquí.* 7. *No hay nadie que me ayude a limpiar la casa.* 8. *No hay ningún libro que me interese.* 9. *No conozco a nadie que sea francés.* 10. *No creo que encuentres el estadio.*

LECCION 35
EN EL HOTEL.   At the hotel.

A. DIALOGO

En la recepción del hotel Cinco Estrellas de Acapulco, México.

GERENTE: **Tengo aquí su reservación, señor. Una habitación doble con baño particular y aire acondicionado.**

MIGUEL: **Es preferible que me den un cuarto que esté en un piso bajo.**

GERENTE: **La habitación 403 estará lista después de que la limpien. Aquí tiene la tarjeta-llave. ¿Por cuántos días se hospedará Ud. en nuestro hotel?**

MIGUEL: **Estaré aquí tres días. ¿Es posible que Uds. guarden el equipaje?**

GERENTE: **Claro. El botones se lo guardará aquí hasta que la habitación esté lista.**

MIGUEL: **Para mi reunión es necesario que yo busque una secretaria que sepa español y portugués.**

GERENTE: **Tenemos tal secretaria en este hotel.**

MIGUEL: **Muy bien. Dígame la extensión del servicio del cuarto.**

GERENTE: **Para comidas y bebidas, por favor, llame a la extensión 333.**

At the reception desk of the hotel Cinco Estrellas in Acapulco, Mexico.

MANAGER: I have your reservation here, sir. A double room with a private bath and air conditioning.

MIGUEL: It's preferable that you give me a room on a low floor.

MANAGER: Room 403 will be ready after they clean it. Here's the card-key. How many days will you be staying at our hotel?

MIGUEL: I'll be here for three days. Is it possible for you to hold my baggage?

MANAGER: Of course. The bellboy will keep it here until the room is ready.

MIGUEL: For my meeting, it's necessary that I find a secretary who knows Spanish and Portuguese.

MANAGER: We have such a secretary in this hotel.

MIGUEL: Very well. Tell me the extension for room service.

MANAGER: For food and drink, please call extension 333.

B. GRAMATICA Y USOS

1. THE SUBJUNCTIVE AFTER IMPERSONAL EXPRESSIONS

Impersonal expressions that indicate need, desire, request, demand, emotion, or doubt are followed by the subjunctive:

Es necesario que yo busque una secretaria.
It's necessary that I find a secretary.

Here are some additional impersonal expressions which are followed by the subjunctive:

es posible	it is possible
es imposible	it is impossible
es preferible	it is preferable

Impersonal expressions which express fact are followed by the indicative:

Es seguro que está ocupado.
It's certain that you are busy.

2. THE SUBJUNCTIVE AFTER CONJUNCTIONS OF TIME

The subjunctive follows conjunctions that indicate an indefinite future time:

La habitación estará lista después de que la limpien.
The room will be ready after they clean it.

Other conjunctions followed by the subjunctive include *mientras* (while) and *después que* (after).
If the event following the conjunction is in the past, then an indicative tense is used:

Llegué aquí después de que comenzó.
I arrived here after it began.

3. THE SUBJUNCTIVE WITH AN INDEFINITE ANTECEDENT

The subjunctive follows a relative pronoun referring to a person or thing not known for certain to exist.

Necesito una habitación que esté en un piso bajo.
I need a room on a low floor. (But such a room may not be available.)

Busco una secretaria que sepa español y portugués.
I'm looking for a secretary who knows Spanish and Portuguese.
(She may or may not exist or be available.)

If the relative pronoun refers to a person or thing known to exist, then the indicative is used:

Tenemos una secretaria que sabe español y portugués.
We have a secretary who knows Spanish and Portuguese.
(She definitely exists.)

285

VOCABULARIO

la recepción	lobby, reception desk
reservación	reservation
Tengo una reservación.	I have a reservation.
hacer una reservación	to make a reservation
hospedarse	to stay at a hotel
¿Por cuántos días se hospedará en el hotel?	How many days will you be staying at the hotel?
la habitación	room
Quisiera una habitación por una noche.	I'd like a room for one night.
habitación doble	double room
limpiar la habitación	to clean the room
estar listo	to be available
guardar el equipaje	to keep/hold the baggage
maleta	suitcase
el/la botones	bellboy/bellgirl
ducha	shower
baño	bath, bathroom
baño particular	private bath
servicio de cuarto	room service
el aire acondicionado	air conditioning
vista a la calle	a view facing the street
vista al mar	a view facing the ocean
una caja de valores	a safety-deposit box
la llave	key
la tarjeta-llave	card-key
la extensión	extension (telephone)
cuenta	bill
comidas y bebidas	food and drink
la capacidad	ability
mientras	while
hasta que	until
después de que	after
Es necesario.	It is necessary.
Es posible.	It is possible.
Es imposible.	It is impossible.

Es preferible.	It is preferable.
Es importante.	It is important.
Es mejor.	It is better.
Es seguro.	It is certain.

EXAMEN

A. *Conteste la pregunta en una oración completa usando la pista.*

1. *¿Qué tipo de habitación busca? (habitación doble)*
2. *¿Cuántas noches se hospedará Ud. en el hotel? (tres o cuatro)*
3. *¿Podré entrar en la habitación ahora? (cuando esté lista)*
4. *¿Hay una secretaria que hable portugués? (no, ninguna)*
5. *¿A quién pido comidas y bebidas? (servicio de cuarto)*

B. *Traduzca la oración al español.*

1. We need a manager who knows a lot about hotels.
2. It's important that the rooms be occupied all the time.
3. While she is here, we will be ready.
4. I know a man who can do it.
5. After the bellboy arnves, he will hold the baggage.

C. *Escriba una oración.*

1. Tell the manager that you have a reservation for a room with a private bath.
2. Ask the manager at what time the room will be ready.
3. Tell the bellboy to put the suitcases in your room.
4. Tell room service that you want them to prepare a small party.
5. Tell the manager that you need a secretary who speaks Spanish.

D. *Conteste las siguientes preguntas con la pista. Use el subjuntivo.*

1. *¿Vas a venir conmigo? (es posible)*
2. *¿Pagarás tus deudas este mes? (es imposible)*
3. *¿Tomo el autobús o el tren? (es preferible/el tren)*
4. *¿Qué tengo que requisitar? (es necesario/el formulario)*
5. *¿Van a terminar el proyecto hoy? (Sí, es posible)*

NOTAS CULTURALES

A wide variety of international and local hotels are found throughout the Spanish-speaking world. In Spain, and in some places in Latin America, you can take advantage of a *pensión*—a small hotel, often family owned and managed, offering simple accommodations, and, if you want, some meals. Not only are their rates lower than those of hotels, but they offer a bit of family atmosphere.

RESPUESTAS

A. 1. *Busco una habitación doble.* 2. *Me hospedaré en el hotel tres o cuatro noches.* 3. *Ud. podrá entrar en la habitación cuando esté lista.* 4. *No, no hay ninguna secretaria que hable portugués.* 5. *Ud. pide comidas y bebidas al servicio de cuarto.*

B. 1. *Necesitamos un gerente que sepa mucho de hoteles.* 2. *Es importante que los cuartos estén ocupados (que las habitaciones estén ocupadas) todo el tiempo.* 3. *Mientras ella esté aquí, estaremos listos.* 4. *Conozco a un hombre que puede hacerlo.* 5. *Después de que llegue el botones, guardará el equipaje.*

C. 1. *Tengo una reserva para una habitación con baño privado.* 2. *¿A qué hora estará lista la habitación?* 3. *Ponga las maletas en mi habitación.* 4. *Quiero que Uds. preparen una pequeña fiesta.* 5. *Necesito una secretaria que hable español.*

D. 1. *Es posible que vaya contigo.* 2. *Es imposible que pague mis deudas este mes.* 3. *Es preferible que tomes el tren en lugar del autobús.* 4. *Es necesario que requisites el formulario.* 5. *Sí, es posible que terminemos el proyecto hoy.*

SEPTIMO REPASO

A. *Cambie al pasivo.* (Change to the passive.)

MODELO: Los testigos vieron todo.
        Todo fue visto por los testigos.

1. *Vimos el programa.*
2. *Los ladrones asaltaron a las mujeres.*
3. *El cineasta rodó la película.*
4. *El deportista sigue un régimen.*
5. *El jefe hará el trabajo.*

B. *Complete la oración con la forma correcta del verbo en el subjuntivo.* (Complete the sentence with the correct form of the verb in the subjunctive.)

MODELO: Prefiero que tú _____ a la hora. (regresar)/regreses

1. *No quiero que tú _____. (venir)*
2. *Piden que nosotros _____ aquí a las cinco. (estar)*
3. *¿Te alegras que _____ tantas personas aquí? (haber)*
4. *¿Crees que ellos _____? (ir)*
5. *Prefieren que yo _____ temprano. (volver)*

C. *Dé el imperativo pedido.*

MODELO: Call room service (familiar sg.)
        Llama al servicio de cuarto.

1. Let's sit here. (two ways)
2. Don't come early. (familiar sg.)
3. Be good! (familiar sg.)
4. Let's keep in shape. (two ways)
5. Don't clean the room before noon. (familiar sg.)

D. *Complete la oración con el indicativo o subjuntivo, como sea necesario.* (Complete the sentence with the indicative or subjunctive, as necessary).

MODELO: Es seguro que _____ ocupado. (estar)/está

1. *Juegan para que nosotros _____ ganar. (poder)*
2. *Es evidente que ellas _____ razón. (tener)*
3. *Mientras nosotros _____ aquí, haremos el trabajo. (estar)*
4. *Comenzaron después que tú _____. (llegar)*
5. *Es imposible que el gerente _____ tanto. (saber)*

E. *Traduzca al español.*

1. Were there any witnesses?
2. In which hotel will you stay?
3. Soccer is a very demanding sport.
4. Let's turn on the television now.
5. I'm afraid that there are no seats in the movie theater.
6. They haven't harmed me, but they've taken my watch.
7. We want you to go to the movies with us.
8. The big man is a boxer.
9. There is no one who wants to do it.
10. It's important to tell John to come.

RESPUESTAS

A. 1. *El programa fue visto por nosotros.* 2. *Las mujeres fueron asaltadas por los ladrones.* 3. *La película fue rodada por el cineasta.* 4. *Un régimen es seguido por el deportista.* 5. *El trabajo será hecho por el jefe.*

B. 1. *vengas* 2. *estemos* 3. *haya* 4. *vayan* 5. *vuelva*

C. 1. *Sentémonos aquí./Vamos a sentarnos aquí.* 2. *No vengas temprano.* 3. *¡Sé bueno/a!* 4. *Mantengámonos en forma./Vamos a mantenernos en forma.* 5. *No limpies el cuarto/la habitación antes del mediodía.*

D. 1. *podamos* 2. *tienen* 3. *estemos* 4. *llegaste* 5. *sepa.*

E. 1. *¿Hubo testigos?* 2. *¿En qué hotel se hospedará Ud.?* 3. *El fútbol es un deporte muy exigente.* 4. *Pongamos la televisión ahora.* 5. *Temo que no haya asientos en el cine.* 6. *No me han hecho daño, pero me han quitado el reloj.* 7. *Queremos que vayas al cine con nosotros.* 8. *El hombrón es boxeador.* 9. *No hay nadie que quiera hacerlo.* 10. *Es importante decirle a Juan que venga.*

LECCION 36

LOS MEDIOS DE COMUNICACION. The media and communications.

A. DIALOGO

En San Juan, Puerto Rico.

HAROLDO: No quería que compraras el periódico de hoy.

GABRIELA: ¿Por qué? ¿Qué hubo?

HAROLDO: Los titulares de los periódicos traen noticias chocantes. La primera plana presenta noticias de desastres, robos, asesinatos, violaciones, guerras y sequías—nada más.

GABRIELA: Sería mejor que no hubiera tales noticias, pero ellas representan hechos reales.

HAROLDO: ¡Ojalá que aprendiéramos del pasado!

GABRIELA: Tal vez no debieras leer la primera plana ni los editoriales, para evitar las noticias chocantes.

HAROLDO: Poco me interesan las secciones de finanzas, deportes, reseñas de libros o clasificados.

GABRIELA: Podrías entretenerte con el crucigrama y las tiras cómicas o los chismes.

HAROLDO: Es mejor no comprar el periódico, no leerlo.

GABRIELA: La culpa no la tiene sólo la prensa. Los satélites y el fax permiten que hoy día sepamos todas las desgracias mundiales con mayor rapidez. Pero hay siempre algo interesante, ¡y estoy segura que habrá buenas noticias, también!

In San Juan, Puerto Rico.

HAROLDO: I didn't want you to buy the newspaper today.

GABRIELA: Why not? What happened?

HAROLDO: The newspaper headlines bring shocking news. The front page has news about disasters, robberies, murders, rapes, wars and droughts—nothing else.

GABRIELA: It would be better if there weren't any such news, but they are real events.

HAROLDO: If only we learned from the past!

GABRIELA: Maybe you shouldn't read the first page or the editorials in order to avoid the shocking news.

HAROLDO: The financial pages, sports, book reviews, and classified sections don't interest me much.

GABRIELA: You could entertain yourself with the crossword puzzle and the comic strips or the gossip column.

HAROLDO: It's better not to buy the paper, . . . not to read it.

GABRIELA: It's not only the fault of the press. Satellites and fax machines allow us to learn all the world's misfortunes with greater speed. But there's always something interesting, and I'm sure that there will be good news, too!

B. GRAMATICA Y USOS

1. FORMS OF THE IMPERFECT SUBJUNCTIVE

Form the root of the imperfect subjunctive of all verbs from the third person plural of the preterite. Drop the *-ron* and add the following endings:[1]

---

[1] In Spain, an alternative ending is used for the forms of the imperfect subjunctive. Drop the *-ron* ending and add the ending *-se:*

yo recomendase	*nosotros, -as recomendásemos*
tú recomendases	*vosotros, -as recomendaseis*
Ud., él, ella recomendase	*Uds., ellos, ellas recomendasen*

INFINITIVE: 3RD PERS. PRET. PL. IMP. SUBJ. ROOT		COMPRAR TO BUY COMPRARON COMPRA-	DEBER TO HAVE TO DEBIERON DEBIE-
yo	-ra	comprara	debiera
tú	-ras	compraras	debieras
Ud., él, ella	-ra	comprara	debiera
nosotros, -as	-ramos	compráramos	debiéramos
vosotros, -as	-rais	comprarais	debierais
Uds., ellos, ellas	-ran	compraran	debieran

INFINITIVE: 3RD PERS. PRET. PL. IMP. SUBJ. ROOT		HABER TO HAVE HUBIERON HUBIE-	DECIR TO SAY DIJERON DIJE-
yo	-ra	hubiera	dijera
tú	-ras	hubieras	dijeras
Ud., él, ella	-ra	hubiera	dijera
nosotros, -as	-ramos	hubiéramos	dijéramos
vosotros, -as	-rais	hubierais	dijerais
Uds., ellos, ellas	-ran	hubieran	dijeran

2. USES OF THE IMPERFECT SUBJUNCTIVE

The imperfect subjunctive is used in the same contexts as the present subjunctive: when the main clause expresses desire, doubt, etc.. The determining factor is the tense of the main verb, as described below.

Quería que no fuéramos.
He didn't want us to go.

Pidieron que tú vinieras a la hora.
They asked you to come on time.

Me alegré mucho que estuvieras presente.
I was very happy that you were present.

Había dudado que llegaran.
   I had doubted that they would arrive.

Era importante que termináramos.
   It was important for us to finish.

3. SEQUENCE OF TENSES WITH THE SUBJUNCTIVE

So far you have seen the forms and uses of the present subjunctive. The present subjunctive is used when the main verb expresses demand, desire, request, emotion, or doubt and is in one of the following tenses:

present tense:

No quiero que leas el periódico.
I don't want you to read the newspaper.

future tense:

No querré que vengas por la noche.
I won't want you to come in the evening.

present perfect tense:

Se ha hecho todo para que sepamos las noticias con mayor rapidez.
Everything has been done for us to learn the news with greater speed.

command:

Dígale que lea el periódico.
Tell him to read the newspaper.

The imperfect subjunctive is used when the main verb is in a past tense (preterite, imperfect, past perfect), or in the conditional tense:

imperfect:

No quería que compraras el periódico.
I didn't want you to buy the newspaper.

preterite:

Fue mejor que él escuchara la radio.
It was better for him to listen to the radio.

conditional:

Sería mejor que no hubiera tales noticias.
It would be better if there weren't any such news.

294

past perfect: *Ella había pedido que él dijera la*
                                                 verdad.
                                                 She had asked him to tell the truth.

Expressions such as *ojalá (que)* (if only, I wish that, I hope that) and *tal vez* can be followed by either the present or the imperfect subjunctive with the present or past meaning:

Tal vez aprenda la lección.
I hope he learns the lesson.

Ojalá (que) aprendiéramos del pasado.
If only we learned from the past!

4. THE SUBJUNCTIVE AFTER CERTAIN CONJUNCTIONS

The subjunctive is always used following these conjunctions:

para que	so that, in order that
sin que	without
con tal que	provided that
a menos que	unless
antes de que	before that

Se ha hecho todo para que sepamos las noticias con mayor rapidez.
Everything has been done for us to learn the news more quickly.

Te recomiendo la tele con tal que ignores el noticiero.
I recommend the television to you, provided that you ignore the news programs.

No compre más el periódico a menos que traiga solo buenas noticias.
Don't buy the newspaper anymore, unless it brings good news.

The word *aunque* (although, even though) is followed by the subjunctive when the speaker wishes to imply doubt:

No lo haré aunque ella insista.
    I won't do it although she may insist. (But maybe she won't.)

If no doubt is implied, the indicative is used:

Me gusta trabajar aunque me canso mucho.
    I like to work, although I get very tired.

VOCABULARIO

los medios	media
los medios de comunicación	means of communication, media
las noticias	news
prensa	press
periódico	newspaper
el titular	headline
primera plana	first page
la columna	column
los chismes	gossip
columna de chismes	gossip column
el editorial	editorial
artículo	article
el desastre	disaster
guerra	war
sequía	drought
asesinato	murder
violación	rape
tragedia	tragedy
las desgracias	misfortunes
sección	section
finanzas	finances, financial pages
los clasificados	classified ads
reseña	review (book, film, theater)
el crucigrama	crossword puzzle
las tires cómicas	comic strips
el/*la* radio	radio
el satélite	satellite
el fax	fax

mundial	worldwide
culpa	blame
ojalá *(que)*	if only..., I wish (that)..., I hope (that)...
la rapidez	rapidity
chocante	shocking
entretenerse	to entertain oneself, to have a good time
molestar	to bother
evitar	to avoid

EXAMEN

A. *Responda la pregunta en una oración completa usando la pista.*

MODELO: *¿Para qué quieres el periódico? (leer las finanzas)*
   Quiero el periódico para leer las finanzas.

1. *¿Qué noticias lleva la primera plana? (guerras y desastres)*
2. *¿Qué le era posible a Juan? (entretenerse con las tiras cómicas)*
3. *¿Para qué compraste el periódico? (tú podías leerlo)*
4. *¿Que te molestaba? (los titulares no eran interesantes)*
5. *¿Cómo llegan las noticias? (por satélite)*

B. *Escriba nuevamente la oración usando el verbo en paréntesis.*

MODELO: *Quiero que esté aquí. (Quería)*
   Queria que estuviera aquí.

1. *Busco un hombre que sepa hacerlo. (Buscaba)*
2. *Es importante que leamos las noticias. (Era)*
3. *Estamos tristes que no lo sepan. (Estábamos)*
4. *¿Dudas que puedan venir? (Dudabas)*
5. *Él no leyó el periódico. (Ojalá que)*
6. *No quiero que tú (ver) ese programa de televisión.*
7. *No querré que tú (cenar) conmigo el domingo.*

8. *(Tú/sentar) aquí, por favor.*
9. *Mamá, (comprarme) ese vestido, por favor.*
10. *Quiero que (limpiar) tu recámara.*

C. *Escriba en español.*

1. Say that you doubt that things will be better.
2. Ask your friend if it was necessary for him to buy the newspaper.
3. Say that you hoped that everyone would have a good time.
4. Tell your friend that you asked her to listen to the radio news about the drought.
5. Say that you recommended that we tell the truth.

NOTAS CULTURALES

Radio, television, newspapers, and magazines are extremely popular in the Spanish-speaking world. Cable and satellite television are available in large cities. Yet, as cable is very expensive, only members of higher income groups are able to afford it. Mexico has international Spanish networks offering high-quality news and entertainment programs. CNN is available all over Latin America and in Spain.

RESPUESTAS

A. 1. *La primera plana lleva noticias de guerras y desastres.* 2. *Era posible que Juan se entretuviera con las tiras cómicas.* 3. *Compré el periódico para que tú pudieras leerlo.* 4. *Me molestaba que los titulares no fueran interesantes.* 5. *Las noticias llegan por satélite.*
B. 1. *Buscaba un hombre que supiera hacerlo.* 2. *Era importante que leyéramos las noticias.* 3. *Estábamos tristes que no lo supieran.* 4. *¿Dudabas que pudieran venir?* 5. *Ojalá que él no lea el periódico.* 6. *No quiero que tú veas ese programa de televisión.* 7. *No querré que cenes conmigo el domingo.* 8. *Siéntate aquí, por favor.* 9. *Mamá, cómprame ese vestido, por favor.* 10. *Quiero que limpies tu recámara.*
C. 1. *Dudo que las cosas sean mejores.* 2. *¿Fue/Era necesario que compraras el periódico?* 3. *Esperaba que todo el mundo se entretuviera/se divirtiera.* 4. *Te pedí que escucharas las noticias del radio sobre la sequía.* 5. *Recomendé que dijéramos la verdad.*

LECCION 37

FERIADOS Y FESTIVALES.   Holidays and festivals

A. DIALOGO

Cerca de la calle Olvera de Los Angeles, California.

NORMA: ¡Qué rápido pasan los feriados del año! Parece como si ayer fuera el Año Nuevo y aquí estamos otra vez en la víspera de las Navidades!

RAUL: Si hubiera más fiestas durante el año, sin dude las celebraríamos.

NORMA: Hicimos mucho durante el año. En la Cuaresma, festejamos la quinceañera de la nieta. Durante la Semana Santa tomamos vacaciones.

RAUL: Después, el Día de los Trabajadores viajamos a Santa Bárbara. ¿No te acuerdas?

NORMA: Claro. Si pudiera, iría allá otra vez ahora.

RAUL: Y de nuevo estamos aquí, envolviendo regalos, escribiendo felicitaciones, y adornando la casa.

NORMA: Y preparando el lechón para una verdadera celebración Latina.

RAUL: ¿Es posible que hayamos olvidado algo?

NORMA: Sí, desearnos uno al otro ¡Feliz Navidad!

Near Olvera Street in Los Angeles, California.

NORMA: How quickly the year's holidays go by! It seems as if yesterday were New Year's and here we are again on Christmas Eve.

RAUL: If there were more holidays during the year, without a doubt we'd celebrate them.

NORMA: We did a lot this year. At Lent we celebrated our granddaughter's debut. During Easter Week we took our vacation.

RAUL: Afterwards, on Labor Day we visited Santa Barbara. Don't you remember?

NORMA: Of course. If I could, I'd go there again now.

RAUL: And here we are again wrapping presents, writing greeting cards, and decorating the house.

NORMA: And cooking the roast suckling pig for a real Latino celebration.

RAUL: Is it possible that we've forgotten anything?

NORMA: Yes—to wish each other Merry Christmas!

B. GRAMATICA Y USOS

1. CONTRARY-TO-FACT SENTENCES IN THE PRESENT

A contrary-to-fact sentence expresses an action that might have occurred but did not. In the present it is formed as follows:

si + imperfect subjunctive + conditional

Si hubiera más fiestas, sin duda las celebraríamos.
If there were more holidays, without a doubt we'd celebrate them. (But there aren't more.)

Si pudiera, iría allá otra vez.
If I could, I'd go there again. (But I can't.)

The sentence order can be reversed:

Iría allá otra vez, si pudiera.
I'd go there again, if I could.

2. THE EXPRESSION *COMO SI*

The expression *como si* (as if) is always followed by the imperfect subjunctive:

Parece como si ayer fuera el Año Nuevo.
It seems as if yesterday was (were) New Year's.

3. THE PRESENT PERFECT SUBJUNCTIVE

The present perfect subjunctive is made up of the present subjunctive of *haber* + past participle:

¿Es posible que hayamos olvidado algo?
Is it possible that we've forgotten anything?

When necessary, the present perfect subjunctive is used in a dependent clause following a verb in the present or future:

Es posible que no hayan hecho las preparaciones.
It's possible they haven't made the preparations.

VOCABULARIO

feriado	holiday (one day)
el festival	festival
¡Felices fiestas!	Happy holidays!
celebrar	to celebrate
la celebración	celebration
víspera	eve (before a holiday)
Año Nuevo	New Year's
las Navidades	Christmas
¡Feliz Navidad!	Merry Christmas!
adornar	to decorate
regalar	to give a gift
envolver regalos	to wrap gifts
felicitar	to greet, to congratulate
escribir felicitaciones	to write greeting cards

la Cuaresma	Lent
Pascuas/la Pascua Florida	Easter, Passover
Semana Santa	Easter week
domingo de Pascuas	Easter Sunday
los quince años	a girl's fifteenth birthday (party)
quinceañera	debutant party at fifteen years of age
festejar	to celebrate
el cumpleaños	birthday
festejar el cumpleaños	to celebrate one's birthday
Reyes	Epiphany
Día de los Trabajadores	Labor Day
Día de los Enamorados	Valentine's Day
Día de la Acción de Gracias	Thanksgiving Day
Día de la Raza	Columbus Day
Día de Todos los Santos	All Saints' Day
el santo	saint, saint's (birth)day
como si	as if
el lechón	roast suckling pig

EXAMEN

A. *Conteste la pregunta en una oración completa usando la pista.*

1. ¿Qué quieres que yo haga? *(envolver el regalo)*
2. ¿Qué no crees? *(ella ha celebrado su cumpleaños)*
3. ¿Si pudieras, adónde irías? *(a México)*
4. ¿Qué nos deseaban? *(pasamos felices fiestas)*
5. ¿Cómo vas a celebrar tu cumpleaños? *(comprarse un regalo)*

B. *Cambie la oración al tiempo pasado.*

MODELO: *Es imposible que llegan a tiempo.*
        Era imposible que llegaran a tiempo.

1. Quiero que vengan.
2. Esperamos que digas la verdad.
3. Tenemos miedo de que nadie nos visite.
4. Dudan que puedas llegar a tiempo.
5. Es seguro que está aquí.

C. *Escriba en español.*

1. Say that you wanted your friend to celebrate the holiday with your family.
2. Tell your friend that you feel as if you were a child with a new present.
3. Ask Raúl if he had the time, would he go to Santa Barbara again.
4. Ask your friend what she would do, if she had more money.
5. Say that Phillip would celebrate his birthday with his parents if they lived nearby.

D. *Conteste la pregunta usando el imperfecto del subjuntivo + el condicional.*

1. Si (haber) más tiempo, (ir) a todos los museos.
2. Si (tener) más dinero, te (comprar) el juguete.
3. Yo (comer) menos, si no (tener) tanta hambre.
4. Ella (trabajar) menos, si no (tener) tanto trabajo.
5. Nosotros (estudiar) hoy, si no (ser) tan perezosos.

NOTAS CULTURALES

Most Spaniards and Latin Americans have more religious and national holidays (half or full days off) than Americans. In addition, many people celebrate two birthdays: their own birthday and the day of their patron saint *(Santo Patrón)*, for whom they are named. Girls have their debutant party, *quinceañera,* when they reach their fifteenth birthday. Children receive most of their Christmas gifts on January 6, the day of the Epiphany. All family celebrations are important in the Spanish-speaking world.

There is a long, rich tradition of Hispanic presence in California. Part of that tradition is visible at the many remaining Spanish colonial missions originally founded to convert the Indians. The Mexican-Americans, or Chicanos, have long played an important role in California's agriculture. They have also developed a vibrant culture now widely recognized.

RESPUESTAS

A. 1. *Quiero que envuelvas el regalo.* 2. *No creo que ella haya celebrado su cumpleaños.* 3. *Si pudiera, iría a México.* 4. *Deseaban que pasáramos felices fiestas.* 5. *Voy a comprarme un regalo.*

B. 1. *Quería/Quise que vinieran.* 2. *Esperábamos/Esperamos que dijeras la verdad.* 3. *Teníamos/Tuvimos miedo de que nadie nos visitara.* 4. *Dudaban/Dudaron que pudieras llegar a tiempo.* 5. *Era/Fue seguro que estaba/estuvo aquí.*

C. 1. *Quería que tú celebraras el feriado con mi familia.* 2. *Me siento como si fuera un niño con un regalo nuevo.* 3. *Si tuvieras tiempo, ¿irías de nuevo a Santa Bárbara?* 4. *¿Qué harías si tuvieras más dinero?* 5. *Felipe celebraría su compleaños con sus padres si vivieran cerca.*

D. 1. *Si hubiera más tiempo, iría a todos los museos.* 2. *Si tuviera más dinero, te compraría el juguete.* 3. *Yo comería menos, si no tuviera tanta hambre.* 4. *Ella trabajaría menos, si no tuviera tanto trabajo.* 5. *Nosotros estudiaríamos hoy, si no fuéramos tan perezosos.*

LECCION 38

LA POLITICA Y LOS DERECHOS.   Politics and rights.

A. DIALOGO

En San Antonio, Texas.

ADRIANA: **¿Qué te parecen los resultados de las elecciones?**

GUSTAVO: **Si hubiera sabido que saldrían esos candidatos a alcalde, gobernador y representante, no habría votado.**

ADRIANA: **Bajo la ley, el voto es el derecho y la obligación de todo ciudadano.**

GUSTAVO: **Ya lo sé. Pero los candidatos que se presentan son cada vez más ineficaces.**

ADRIANA: **No habría salido así, si los votantes hubieran tomado más interés en las cuestiones que confronta nuestra sociedad: la economía, la situación de los niños, la contaminación del ambiente.**

GUSTAVO: **Es mucho pedirnos a todos nosotros para actualizarnos sobre todo. Si tú te hubieras postulado, habrías salido ganadora y habrías podido animar a la gente a levantar su voz y a actuar.**

In San Antonio, Texas

ADRIANA: What do you think of the election results?

GUSTAVO: If I had known that those candidates for mayor, governor and representative would win, I wouldn't have voted.

ADRIANA: Under the law, voting is the right and obligation of every citizen.

GUSTAVO: I know that. But the candidates that run for office are more and more ineffective

ADRIANA: It wouldn't have turned out like this, if the voters had taken more interest in the issues that confront our society: the economy, the situation of children, and environmental pollution.

GUSTAVO: It's a lot to ask of all of us to keep up-to-date about everything. If you had been a candidate, you'd have won and would have been able to get people to raise their voices and act.

B. GRAMATICA Y USOS

1. THE PAST PERFECT SUBJUNCTIVE

The past perfect subjunctive is made up of the imperfect subjunctive of *haber* + past participle.

GANAR   TO EARN

yo	*hubiera ganado*
tú	*hubieras ganado*
Ud., él, ella	*hubiera ganado*
nosotros, -as	*hubiéramos ganado*
vosotros, -as	*hubierais ganado*
Uds., ellos, ellas	*hubieran ganado*

It is used primarily in contrary-to-fact sentences in the past.

2. CONTRARY-TO-FACT SENTENCES IN THE PAST

To describe an action that could have happened in the past, but in fact did not, use the following structure:

si + past perfect subjunctive, + conditional perfect

Si hubiera sabido, no habría votado.
If I had known, I wouldn't have voted.

Si te hubieras postulado, habrías salido ganadora.
    If you had been a candidate, you'd have won.

The order of the clauses can be reversed:

Habrías salido ganadora, si te hubieras postulado.
    You'd have won, if you had been a candidate.

3. *PEDIR PARA* AS AN ALTERNATIVE TO THE SUBJUNCTIVE

While the subjunctive forms are quite collequial in Spanish, you can avoid the subjunctive with the verb *pedir.*
    With *pedir que,* a new clause is created and the subjunctive must be used.

Es mucho pedirnos a todos nosotros que (nosotros) nos actualicemos sobre todo.
    It's a lot to ask all of us to keep up-to-date about everything.

But with *pedir para,* an infinitive follows the preposition and no subjunctive is necessary.

Es mucho pedirnos a todos nosotros para actualizarnos sobre todo.
    It's a lot to ask of all of us to keep up-to-date about everything.

4. THE EXPRESSION *CADA VEZ MAS/MENOS*

The expression *cada vez más* or *menos* is used with adverbs and adjectives to express "more and more" and "less and less":

Los candidatos son cada vez más ineficaces.
    The candidates are more and more ineffective.

Las lecciones son cada vez menos difíciles.
    The lessons are less and less difficult.

política	policy
político, -a	politician
derecho	right (n.)
los resultados	results
elección	election
candidato	candidate
postularse/presentarse	to become a candidate
votar	to vote
votar por un candidato	to vote for a candidate
el/la votante	voter
voto	voting, vote
el alcalde/la alcaldesa	mayor
el gobernador, -a	governor
el senador, -a	senator
el representante	congressman
el presidente/la presidente	president
el dictador, -a	dictator
dictadura	dictatorship
democracia	democracy
el ganador, -a	winner
ganar	to win
salir ganador, -a	to win
perder (e>ie)	to lose
la ley	law
obligación	obligation
ciudadano	citizen
cuestión	issue
contaminación del ambiente	environmental pollution
ineficaz	ineffective
actualizarse sobre las cuestiones	to be (keep) up-to-date on the issues
animar	to inspire, to arouse, to excite
levantar la voz	to raise one's voice
actuar	to act
tomar interés en	to take an interest in
bajo	under, beneath

EXAMEN

A. *Conteste la pregunta en una oración completa usando la pista.*

1. *¿Qué cuestión le anima a Ud.? (la contaminación del ambiente)*
2. *¿Cómo son los candidatos? (cada vez menos interesantes)*
3. *Si hubieras sabido la verdad, ¿qué habrías hecho en esa situación? (no haber votado)*
4. *¿Qué cosa es difícil? (actualizarme sobre todo)*
5. *¿Qué nos pide? (para votar por el candidato eficaz)*

B. *Complete la oración con el subjunctivo, el indicativo, o el infinitivo del verbo entre paréntesis.* (Complete the sentence using the subjunctive, indicative, or infinitive of the verb in parenthesis.)

1. *Me pidió que _____ por él. (votar)*
2. *No creyó que ella _____ sobre la cuestión. (levantar la voz)*
3. *Preferí que tú _____. (actuar)*
4. *Te piden que _____ su situación. (tomar interés por)*
5. *Los políticos desean que nosotros _____ sobre todas las cuestiones. (actualizarse)*

C. *Escriba en español.*

1. Say that if you had had time, you would have voted in the election.
2. Tell your friend that under the law, she has the right and obligation to vote.
3. Ask your friend if you would have won the election, if you had been a candidate.
4. Say that politicians are more and more ineffective.
5. Tell your friend that you would have kept up-to-date on the issues, if you had had time to read the newspapers.

D. *Escriba la pregunta para las siguientes respuestas.*

MODELO: Quiero que llegues a las tres en punto.
¿A qué hora quieres que llegue?

1. *Voy a festejar mi luna de miel en Madrid.*
2. *Si tuviera dinero, lo compraría.*
3. *Quería que no fuéramos.*
4. *Me pidieron que yo fuera con ellos.*
5. *No quería que tomaras tanto.*
6. *Busco un vestido negro.*
7. *Si pudiera, trabajaría menos.*

NOTAS CULTURALES

A period of dictatorships in Latin America has hopefully come to an end. Most nations are on the path to full democracy, though it is somewhat bumpy. True democracy will appear when social injustices are finally corrected, which, at the present moment, is more of a desire than a plausible goal. Nonetheless, some progress has been made.

RESPUESTAS

A. 1. *Me anima la cuestión de la contaminación del ambiente.* 2. *Los candidatos son cada vez menos interesantes.* 3. *Si hubiera sabido la verdad, no habría votado en esa situación.* 4. *Es difícil actualizarme sobre todo.* 5. *Nos pide para votar por el candidato eficaz.*

B. 1. *votara* 2. *levantara la voz* 3. *actuaras* 4. *tomes interés en* 5. *nos actualicemos.*

C. 1. *Si hubiera tenido el tiempo, habría votado en la elección.* 2. *Bajo la ley, tienes el derecho y la obligación de votar.* 3. *¿Habría yo ganado la elección si me hubiera postulado?* 4. *Los políticos son cada vez más ineficaces.* 5. *Yo me habría actualizado sobre las cuestiones, si hubiera tenido tiempo para leer los periódicos.*

D. 1. *¿Dónde vas a festejar tu luna de miel?* 2. *¿Lo comprarías, si tuvieras dinero?* 3. *¿Qué querías?* 4. *¿Qué te pidieron (ellos)?* 5. *¿Qué quería?* 6. *¿Qué buscas?* 7. *¿Si pudieras, trabajarías menos?*

LECCION 39

A. DIALOGO

En casa de los Orbe de Oviedo, España.

DOÑA PILAR: **Tu papá y yo estamos totalmente agotados después de la fiesta. Te pedimos que vayas a hacernos unos recados.**

ANTONIO: **¡Vale, mamá! El descansar os hará bien.**

DOÑA PILAR: **Primero, vete a la tintorería . . . eh . . . ¿cómo se llama?**

ANTONIO: **Pues . . . Cristal, creo yo.**

DOÑA PILAR: **Sí, claro. Recoge allí mi vestido. Quise que el tintorero me sacara la mancha de chocolate de la manga izquierda. Míralo bien, por favor.**

ANTONIO: **Pues . . . no sé . . . sacar una mancha de chocolate no es fácil. Ojalá que lo haya conseguido.**

DOÑA PILAR: **Después, hijo, pasa por la sastrería y dile al sastre que arregle la cintura de estos pantalones, y deja estas camisas en la lavandería con tal que puedan tenerlas listas para mañana.**

ANTONIO: **De acuerdo. No os preocupéis; ¡tumbaos un rato!**

At the Orbes' home in Oviedo, Spain.

DOÑA PILAR: Your father and I are totally exhausted after the party. We're asking you to run some errands for us.

ANTONIO: Okay, Mother. Resting will do you good.

DOÑA PILAR: First, go to the dry cleaner's . . . uh . . . what's its name?

311

ANTONIO: Well . . . I think it's Cristal.

DOÑA PILAR: Yes, of course. Pick up my dress there. I wanted the dry cleaner to take out the chocolate stain on the left sleeve. Look at it carefully, please.

ANTONIO: Well . . . I don't know . . . taking out a chocolate stain isn't easy. I hope that he's managed to do it.

DOÑA PILAR: Afterwards, dear son, go by the tailor's shop and tell the tailor to fix the waist on these pants, and leave these shirts at the laundry, provided that they can have them ready by tomorrow.

ANTONIO: Okay. Don't worry; take a nap!

B. GRAMATICA Y USOS

1. REVIEW OF THE USES OF THE SUBJUNCTIVE

a. The subjunctive is used following verbs, impersonal expressions, and other expressions of need, desire, request, emotion, doubt, and denial:

Te pedimos que voyas a hacernos unos recados.
We're asking you to run some errands for us.

Quise que el tintorero me sacara la mancha.
I wanted the dry cleaner to take out the stain.

Ojulá que lo haya conseguido.
I hope that he's managed to do it.

b. The subjunctive is used following antecedents that express doubt or denial about the existence of a person or thing:

¿Existe una tintorería que pueda sacar la mancha?
Is there a dry cleaner who can take out the stain?

Buscamos una lavandería que pueda hacerlo para hoy.
We're looking for a laundry that can do it for today.

c. The subjunctive is used following certain conjunctions, including those of indefinite future time and purpose:

Déjalas con tal que puedan tenerlas listas para mañana.
Leave them provided that they can have them ready by tomorrow.

Lavarán la ropa cuando tengan tiempo.
They'll wash the clothing when they have time.

2. THE *VOSOTROS* COMMANDS

a. The *vosotros* commands are principally used in Spain. The affirmative command for all verbs is made by dropping the final *r* of the infinitive and adding *d:*

hablar>hablad	speak	*ser>sed*	be
comer>comed	eat	*salir>salid*	go out

b. For reflexive verbs, the *d* is dropped when the reflexive object pronoun *os* is added:

tumbar>tumbad	*tumbarse>tumbaos*	lie down
dormir>dormid	*dormirse>dormíos*	go to sleep
lavar>lavad	*lavarse>lavaos*	wash yourselves

Note the written accent required on the *i* to break up the diphthong: *dormíos.* Only the verb *irse* is irregular in the affirmative: *idos.*

c. The negative *vosotros* command comes from the second person plural of the subjunctive. There are no irregular forms.

¡No gritéis!	Don't yell!
No os preocupéis.	Don't worry.

3. PAUSE WORDS

Several words and expressions are used in Spanish for pausing to think while speaking:

... *eh* ...
... *¿eh?* ...
... *pues* ...
... *sabe(s)* ...
... *o sea* ...

Vete a la tintorería ... eh ... ¿cómo se llama?
Go to the dry cleaner's ... uh ... what's its name?

4. THE INFINITIVE USED AS A NOUN

The infinitive can be used as a noun in Spanish. It may or may not be preceded by the masculine definite article.

El descansar os hará bien.
Resting will do you good.

Sacar una mancha de chocolate no es fácil.
Taking out a chocolate stain isn't easy.

VOCABULARIO

recados domésticos	househould errands
hacer un recado	to run an errand
tintorería	dry cleaner's
tintorero, -*a*	dry cleaner
lavar en seco	to dry clean
teñir	to dye (clothing)
mancha	stain
sacar una mancha	to take out a stain
sastrería	tailor's shop
el sastre	tailor
la modista	seamstress, dressmaker
coser	to sew
traje (*vestido*) **a medida**	a made-to-order suit (dress)
manga (*del vestido*)	(dress) sleeve

314

arreglar la cintura	to fix the waist
poner *(reemplazar)* **un botón**	to put on (replace) a button
lavandería	laundry
lavado	washing, laundry
lavandero, -a	launderer
lavar	to launder, wash
planchar	to iron, to press (clothes)
lavado y planchado	washing and ironing
encoger	to shrink (material)
zapatería	shoe repair shop
zapatero	shoemaker
el tacón	heel (shoe)
planta	sole (foot)
agotar	to exhaust, to wear out
agotarse	to exhaust oneself, to wear oneself out
tumbarse	to lie down
¡Tumbaos!	Lie down!
preocuparse	to worry
¡No os preocupéis!	Don't worry!
Vale.	Okay.
pasar por	to pass by
dejar	to drop off
recoger	to pick up
el descansar	rest
. . . eh . . .	. . . uh . . .
. . . pues . . .	. . . well . . .
. . . sabe(s) . . .	. . . you know . . .

EXAMEN

A. *Conteste la pregunta en una oración completa usando la pista.*

1. *¿Qué quieres que yo te haga? (unos recados)*
2. *¿Podrá sacar la mancha el tintorero? (Ojalá que)*
3. *¿Qué nos hará bien? (el descansar)*
4. *¿Qué esperabas? (vosotros os tumbastais un rato)*
5. *¿Qué buscaréis? (un sastre que sabe arreglar los pantalones)*

B. *Dé el imperativo pedido en "vosotros."* (Give the imperative requested using *vosotros.)*

MODELO: Don't come late.
      No vengáis tarde.

1. Sit down.
2. Dress yourselves.
3. Don't get up early.
4. Put on the shirts.
5. Don't wear yourself out.

C. *Escriba en una oración.*

1. Say that you want Antonia to run some errands for you.
2. Tell the dry cleaner to take out the stain of the blouse.
3. Tell Juanito that working too much will exhaust him.
4. Say that you must stop by the dry cleaner's, the tailor's shop and the shoe repair shop.

NOTAS CULTURALES

In Spain, local "mom-and-pop" shops are still common for all sorts of household needs; quite often the maid runs the errands. In Latin America people tend to repair all sorts of items from clothing to cars over and over again rather than replace them, because new things are expensive. It is not uncommon to see vintage toasters still toasting or North American cars from the 1950s and 1960s still running on the roads, owing to the ingenuity of repairmen.

RESPUESTAS

A. 1. *Quiero que me hagas unos recados.* 2. *Ojalá que el tintorero pueda sacar la mancha.* 3. *El descansar os hará bien.* 4. *Esperaba que vosotros os tumbarais un rato.* 5. *Buscaremos un sastre que sepa arreglar los pantalones.*
B. 1. *Sentaos.* 2. *Vestíos.* 3. *No os levantéis temprano.* 4. *Poneos las camisas.* 5. *No os agotéis.*
C. 1. *Quiero que Antonia me haga unos recados.* 2. *Saque la mancha de la blusa.* 3. *Juanito, el trabajar demasiado te agotará.* 4. *Tengo que pasar por la tintorería, la sastrería, y la zapatería.*

LECCION 40

EN EL AEROPUERTO.   At the airport.

A. DIALOGO

En un mostrador del aeropuerto Maiquetía de Caracas, Venezuela.

FRANCISCA: **Con permiso, señor, aquí tiene nuestros pasajes, pasaportes y visas.**

ERNESTO: **Perdóneme, señora. Este pasaporte no es suyo. Es de una niña.**

FRANCISCA: **¿No es mío? ¡Caray! Disculpe; sí que me he equivocado. La hija nuestra no viaja con nosotros. Momentito. Pues . . . es éste mismo.**

ERNESTO: **El vuelo está atrasado. Saldrá de la Puerta 23 a las ocho y media. ¿Desean Uds. facturar maletas?**

FRANCISCA: **La mía no, pero la suya sí.**

ERNESTO: **Aquí está el recibo. Sigan Uds. a la derecha. Pasen por la seguridad, y luego tendrán que hacer una declaración en la Aduana.**

FRANCISCA: **Queremos escoger asientos en la sección de no fumar.**

ERNESTO: **En la puerta de embarque misma habrá un agente que les asignará asientos. ¡Buen viaje!**

At a ticket counter at Maiquetía Airport in Caracas, Venezuela.

FRANCISCA: Pardon me, sir, here are our tickets, passports, and visas.

ERNESTO: Excuse me, madam. This passport isn't yours. It belongs to a young girl.

FRANCISCA: It isn't mine? Darn! I'm sorry; I have indeed made a mistake. Our daughter isn't traveling with us. One moment. Well, this is the one.

ERNESTO: The flight is delayed. It will leave from gate 23 at 8:30. Do you want to check luggage?

FRANCISCA: Mine no, but his yes.

ERNESTO: Here is the receipt. Go to the right. Pass through security and then you will have to make a Customs declaration.

FRANCISCA: We want to choose seats in the no-smoking section.

ERNESTO: Right at the departure gate there'll be an agent who will assign you seats. Have a good trip!

B. GRAMATICA Y USOS

1. THE LONG POSSESSIVES

You already know the short forms of the possessive adjectives (lesson 8). There are also long forms that are used with the definite article.

	SINGULAR	PLURAL
my (mine)	*(el) mío, (la) mía*	*(los) míos, (las) mías*
your(s) (familiar)	*(el) tuyo, (la) tuya*	*(los) tuyos, (las) tuyas*
his, her(s), your(s)	*(el) suyo, (la) suya*	*(los) suyos, (las) suyas*
our(s)	*(el) nuestro, (la) nuestra*	*(los) nuestros, (las) nuestras*
your(s) (familiar)	*(el) vuestro, (la) vuestra*	*(los) vuestros, (las) vuestras*
their(s)	*(el) suyo, la suya*	*(los) suyos, (las) suyas*

These long forms are used for emphasis and thus less frequently than the short forms. They follow the noun, agreeing with it in number and gender.

La hija nuestra no viaja con nosotros.
Our daughter isn't traveling with us.

More commonly, they serve as pronouns with the definite article, referring to an antecedent:

¿Desean Uds. facturar maletas?
Do you want to check luggage?

La mía no, pero la suya sí.
Mine no, but his yes.

After the verb *ser*, the definite article is not used:

Este pasaporte no es suyo.
This passport isn't yours.

¿No es mío?
It isn't mine?

2. THE EMPHATIC *SI* AND *MISMO*

a. *Sí (que)* is used as an emphatic adverb often meaning "indeed."

Sí (que) me he equivocado.
I have indeed made a mistake.

¿Fue Ud. que lo ha hecho?—Sí que fui yo.
Was it you who did it?—Indeed it was me.

b. *Mismo, -a, -os, -as* can be used to emphasize "-self," sometimes with a reflexive verb. It has various translations.

Se fue él mismo.
He himself went.

En la puerta de embarque misma habrá un agente.
There'll be an agent right at the departure gate.

c. Other emphatic expressions include:

ahora mismo	right now
claro que sí	of course

3. *PROPIO*

Propio can have three different meanings depending on its usage. It can have the meaning of "-self":

¡Habló con el propio piloto!
She spoke to the pilot himself!

Notice the usage in these terms:

amor propio   self respect

It can mean "suitable for" or "characteristic of":

Eso es un juego propio de niños.
It's a game suitable for children.

Eso sería lo propio.
That would fit the case / be appropriate.

Propio can also mean "one's own," "one's very own":

Son sus propias palabras.
They're his own words.

El niño tiene su propio pasaporte.
The boy has his own passport.

4. INTERJECTIONS

There are many popular expressions of disbelief, disgust, dismay, or anger throughout the Spanish-speaking world. While many are regional, some are universal:

¡Caray!   Darn! (for anger)
¡Caramba!   Good heavens! (for astonishment)

When someone sneezes, say:

¡Salud!   Bless you!
¡Jesús, María y José!

320

el aeropuerto	the airport
el mostrador	(ticket) counter
el pasaje	ticket
el pasaporte	passport
visa	visa
visa de turista	tourist visa
visa de negociante	business visa
vuelo	flight
atrasar	to delay
El vuelo está atrasado.	The flight is delayed.
puerta de embarque *(llegada)*	departure/arrival gate
maleta	suitcase
facturar	to check
recibo	receipt
seguridad	security
Aduana	Customs
llenar la declaración de la Aduana	to fill out the Customs declaration
Estoy de vacaciones.	I'm here on vacation.
Estoy aquí en viaje de negocios.	I'm here on a business trip.
No tengo nada para declarer.	I have nothing to declare.
¿Tengo que pagar derechos? (impuestos)	Do I have to pay duty?
asiento	seat
asiento al pasillo	aisle seat
asiento a la ventanilla	window seat
escoger asientos	to choose seats
asignar asientos	to assign seats
la sección de no fumar	non-smoking section
(Con) Permiso.	Pardon me. Excuse me.
Con permiso, señor, aquí tiene nuestros pasajes.	Pardon me sir, here are our tickets.
Permiso, ¿puedo pasar?	Pardon me, may I pass through?
Disculpe*(n)*.	
Dispense*(n)*.	Excuse me. I'm sorry.
Perdón. Perdóne*(n)*me.	

Disculpe, sí que me he equivocado.	I'm sorry, I have indeed made a mistake.
Dispense, no pensaba molestarle.	Pardon me, I didn't mean to bother you.
sí	indeed
ahora mismo	right now
claro que sí	of course
¡Caramba!	Damn!
¡Caray!	Good heavens! Damn!
equivocarse	to make a mistake

EXAMEN

A. *Conteste la pregunta en una oración completa usando la pista.*

1. *¿De quién es este pasaje? (suyo)*
2. *¿Qué necesito tener para el viaje? (el pasaporte y la visa)*
3. *¿Dónde pasamos por la seguridad? (a la izquierda)*
4. *¿Qué no cree el agente? (el vuelo sale atrasado)*
5. *¿Dónde escogemos asientos? (la puerta de embarque misma)*

B. *Traduzca usando los posesivos.*

1. Is this your passport or is it hers?
2. They have his tickets, yours and ours.
3. I'll fill out my Customs declaration and his.
4. Excuse me, may I have his passport and yours?
5. Darn! Their flight left and mine is delayed.

C. *Escriba la oración en español.*

1. Tell your friend that you have your tickets and hers.
2. Ask the agent if they assign seats at the counter or right at the gate.
3. Tell the agent that you do indeed want a window seat.
4. Ask the agent's pardon and say that you have made a mistake.
5. Say that you want to check your suitcases and his.

NOTAS CULTURALES

Spain and almost every Latin American country have their own international airline; Iberia, Viasa, Aerolíneas Argentinas, Lan Chile, Aeroperú, and others are among the major carriers. Overall, national airline travel is rather expensive, even for short distances. Spaniards tend to travel on trains, while Latin Americans favor buses, both of which are substantially cheaper.

RESPUESTAS

A. 1. *Este pasaje es suyo.* 2. *Ud. necesita el pasaporte y la visa.* 3. *Uds. pasan por la seguridad a la izquierda.* 4. *El agente no cree que el vuelo salga atrasado.* 5. *Escogen asientos en la puerta de embarque misma.*

B. 1. *¿Es éste su pasaporte o es suyo?* 2. *Tienen sus pasajes, los suyos y los nuestros.* 3. *Llenaré mi declaración de Aduana y la suya.* 4. *Permiso, ¿puedo tener su pasaporte y el suyo?* 5. *¡Caray! Salió su vuelo y el mío está atrasado.*

C. 1. *Tengo mi pasaje y el suyo.* 2. *¿Asignan asientos en el mostrador o en la puerta de embarque misma?* 3. *Sí quiero un asiento a la ventanilla.* 4. *Perdón/Perdóneme/Disculpe/Dispense, me he equivocado.* 5. *Quiero facturar mis maletas y las suyas (la suya).*

OCTAVO REPASO

A. *Dé la forma correcta del verbo en el subjuntivo.*

1. *Yo no quería que tú _____ estas noticias. (leer)*
2. *Ellos irían también si _____. (poder)*
3. *Tendrían miedo de que te _____. (perder)*
4. *Negaba que los políticos _____ tan ineficaces. (ser)*
5. *¿No les habéis dicho que ellos _____ los trajes? (recoger)*

B. *¿Subjuntivo o no?*

1. *Era como si nosotros _____ ricos. (ser)*
2. *Invitaron a todos para que nosotros _____ el cumpleaños. (festejar)*
3. *Llegaron temprano al aeropuerto para que tú no _____ el vuelo.
   (perder)*
4. *Pagaste impuestos para que la ciudad _____ limpias las calles.
   (mantener)*
5. *Hicimos todo antes de que ellos _____. (venir).*
6. *Si (ser) más inteligente, no te (haber) pasado algo tan horrible.*
7. *Estudiamos mucho para que (poder) aprobar el examen.*
8. *Quise que tu (venir) conmigo.*
9. *Te acompañaré al teatro cuando (tener) tiempo.*

C. *Dé los imperativos en "vosotros."*

1. Get up!
2. Don't entertain them!
3. Decorate the house!
4. Don't get dressed too late!
5. Keep up-to-date about (sobre) style!
6. Clean the apartment!
7. Do what I say!
8. Sit down!
9. Be nice!
10. Forget it!

D. *Traduzca al español.*

1. If you (familiar) read the newspaper, you would know the gossip.
2. It was impossible for us to wrap all the gifts.
3. She asked me to take an interest in the problem. (two ways)
4. I hope that he has obtained it.
5. Arriving on time is more and more difficult.
6. Check your baggage and go to the departure gate. (Use *vosotros*.)
7. If you (polite pl.) had picked up my dress from the dry cleaner's, I
   would have gone to the party.
8. Is it possible that New Year's has arrived once again?
9. I was looking for a tailor who could fix my suit.
10. It was necessary for us to leave that day.

RESPUESTAS

A. 1. *leyeras* 2. *pudieran* 3. *perdieras* 4. *fueran* 5. *recojan*

B. 1. *fuéramos* 2. *festejáramos* 3. *perdieras* 4. *mantuviera* 5. *vinieron* 6. *Si fueras más inteligente, no te habría pasado algo tan horrible.*
7. *Estudiamos mucho para que podamos aprobar el examen.* 8. *Quise que tu vinieras conmigo.* 9. *Te acompañaré al teatro cuando tenga tiempo.*

C. 1. *¡Levantaos!* 2. *¡No los entretengáis!* 3. *¡Adornad la casa!* 4. *No os vistáis demasiado tarde.* 5. *¡Actualizaos sobre la moda!* 6. *¡Limpia el apartamento!* 7. *¡Haz lo que te digo!* 8. *¡Siéntate!* 9. *¡Se bueno!*
10. *¡Olvídalo!*

D. 1. *Si leyeras el periódico, sabrías los chismes.* 2. *Fue/Era imposible que envolviéramos todos los regalos.* 3. *Ella me pidió que tomara interés en el problema./Ella me pidió para tomar interés en el problema.*
4. *Espero/Ojalá que lo haya conseguido.* 5. *(El) Llegar a la hora es cada vez más difícil.* 6. *Facturad vuestro equipaje e idos a la puerta de embarque.*
7. *Si Uds. hubieran recogido mi vestido de la tintorería, habría podido ir a la fiesta.* 8. *¿Es posible que haya llegado el Año Nuevo otra vez?* 9. *Buscaba un sastre que pudiera arreglar mi traje.* 10. *Era necesario que nosotros partiéramos aquel día.*

LECTURA IV

el festival de san fermin

La ciudad de Pamplona, situada[1] en el norte de España, es famosa por la corrida de toros[2] durante el Festival de San Fermín, patrón de dicha ciudad.[3] Ernest Hemingway dio a conocer[4] esta particular fiesta en su novela "El sol también sale."

El Festival de San Fermín comienza exactamente a la medianoche del 7 de julio. A esa hora, los habitantes se reúnen[5] en la plaza central, en medio de fuegos artificiales,[6] para celebrar esta tradición. A las siete de la mañana se lanza un cohete[7] y luego se sueltan[8] seis toros, que corren libremente por las angostas callejuelas[9] que conducen[10] a la Plaza de Toros.

Tanto españoles[11] como extranjeros vienen a presenciar este suceso.[12] Corren delante de los toros, llevando los tradicionales pañuelos blancos y rojos alrededor del cuello[13] y periódicos enrollados con los cuales golpean a los toros[14] con el fin de animarlos.[15] Algunos participantes sueñan con llegar[16] a ser toreros[17] pero todos arriesgan[18] su vida con gusto al participar en esta hazaña.[19] Si todo sale bien y nadie resulta herido de seriedad,[20] los toros llegan a la Plaza de Toros en dos minutos y medio y allí todos participan en una corrida de toros.

Más adelante, españoles y turistas toman parte en diferentes concursos[21] y bailan "La jota," la danza local. También se realizan desfiles[22] y conciertos y otras diversiones.[23] De nuevo, a la medianoche, comienzan[24] los fuegos artificiales.

La mayor parte del dinero recaudado[25] en el festival se dedica a mantener el hogar de ancianos[26] de la ciudad.

VOCABULARIO

1.	*situada*	situated
2.	*la corrida de toros*	bullfight
3.	*patrón de dicha ciudad*	patron saint of the said/stated city
4.	*dio a conocer (dar a conocer)*	made known
5.	*los habitantes se reúnen*	the inhabitants gather/population gathers
6.	*fuegos artificiales*	fireworks
7.	*se lanza un cohete*	a skyrocket is launched (passive *se)*
8.	*se sueltan (soltar)*	are let loose (passive *se)*
9.	*angostas callejuelas*	narrow alleyways
10.	*conducen (conducir)*	to lead (also, to drive)
11.	*tanto los españoles como los extranjeros*	Spaniards and foreigners alike
12.	*presenciar este suceso*	to be present at, to witness this event
13.	*alrededor del cuello*	around their necks
14.	*con los cuales golpean a los toros*	with which they swat the bulls
15.	*con el fin de animarlos*	for the purpose of encouraging/animating them
16.	*sueñan con llegar a ser*	dream of becoming
17.	*toreros*	bullfighters
18.	*arriesgan (arriesgar)*	risk

19.	*hazaña*	feat
20.	*herido de seriedad*	seriously wounded
21.	*concursos*	competitions, contests
22.	*desfiles*	parades
23.	*diversiones*	amusements
24.	*comienzan (comenzar)*	to begin, commence
25.	*recaudado (recaudar)*	collected
26.	*el hogar de ancianos*	senior citizens' home

¡FELICITACIONES!

Now that you have completed the course, you'll be able to use this manual as a reference book for grammar and expressions. The appendixes that follow provide even more information for additional study. We also recommend that you review the material, looking carefully at sections that seemed difficult. Both sets of recordings will be of further use as you study and review at home, in your car, or while jogging . . . keep up the good work!

APPENDIXES

A. GLOSSARY OF NATIONS, NATIONALITIES, LANGUAGES, AND GEOGRAPHIES

Names of languages are usually the same as the masculine form of the nationality, e.g., *francés: Julian habla francés*. The language of Spanish-speaking countries is called *español* or *castellano*.

ESPAÑOL–INGLÉS

NACIÓN	NATION	NACIONALIDAD	NATIONALITY
África del Sur	South Africa	**surafricano (-a)**	South African
Alemania	Germany	**alemán (-a)**	German
América del Norte	North America	**norteamericano (-a)**	North American
América del Sur	South American	**suramericano (-a)**	South American
Argentina	Argentina	**argentino (-a)**	Argentine
Australia	Australia	**australiano (-a)**	Australian
Bolivia	Bolivia	**boliviano (-a)**	Bolivian
el Brasil	Brazil	**brasileño (-a)/ brasilero (-a)**	Brazilian
Canadá	Canada	**canadiense**	Canadian
Chile	Chile	**chileno (-a)**	Chilean
la China	China	**chino (-a)**	Chinese
Colombia	Colombia	**colombiano (-a)**	Colombian
Comunidad de Estados Independientes	Commonwealth of Independent States		
Costa Rica	Costa Rica	**costarricense**	Costa Rican
Cuba	Cuba	**cubano (-a)**	Cuban
Dinamarca	Denmark	**danés (-nesa)**	Danish/Dane
Ecuador	Ecuador	**ecuatoriano (-a)**	Ecuadoran
Egipto	Egypt	**egipcio (-a)**	Egyptian
El Salvador	El Salvador	**salvadoreno (-a)**	Salvadoran
España	Spain	**español (-a)**	Spanish/Spaniard
los Estados Unidos	United States	**estadounidense [norteameri-eano (-a)]**	U.S. American

Finlandia	Finland	**finlandés (-desa)**	Finnish/Finn, Finnlander
Francia	France	**francés (-cesa)**	French
Gran Bretaña	Great Britain	**británico (-a)**	British
Grecia	Greece	**griego (-a)**	Greek
Guatemala	Guatemala	**guatemalteco (-a)**	Guatemalan
Holanda	Holland	**holandés (-desa)**	Dutch/Hollander
Honduras	Honduras	**hondureño (-a)**	Honduran
Inglaterra	England	**inglés (-glesa)**	English
Irlanda	Ireland	**irlandés (-desa)**	Irish
Islandia	Iceland	**islandés (-desa)**	Icelandic/Icelander
Israel	Israel	**israelí**	Israeli
Italia	Italy	**italiano (-a)**	Italian
el Japón	Japan	**japonés (-nesa)**	Japanese
Marruecos	Morocco	**marroquí**	Moroccan
México	Mexico	**mexicano (-a)**	Mexican
Nicaragua	Nicaragua	**nicaragüense**	Nicaraguan
Noruega	Norway	**noruego (-a)**	Norwegian
Panamá	Panama	**panameño (-a)**	Panamanian
Paraguay	Paraguay	**paraguayo (-a)**	Paraguayan
el Perú	Peru	**peruano (-a)**	Peruvian
Polonia	Poland	**polaco (-a)**	Polish/Pole
Portugal	Portugal	**portugués (-guesa)**	Portuguese
Puerto Rico	Puerto Rico	**puertorriqueño (-a)**	Puerto Rican
la República Dominicana	Dominican Republic	**dominicano (-a)**	Dominican
Rusia	Russia	**ruso (-a)**	Russian
Suecia	Sweden	**sueco (-a)**	Swedish/Swede
Suiza	Switzerland	**suizo (-a)**	Swiss
Turquía	Turkey	**turco (-a)**	Turkish/Turk
el Uruguay	Uruguay	**uruguayo (-a)**	Uruguayan
Venezuela	Venezuela	**venezolano (-a)**	Venezuelan

Continente	Continent
Océano	Ocean
África	Africa
Norteamérica	North America
Sudamérica	South America
Australia	Australia
Antártida	Antarctica
Asia	Asia
Europa	Europe
Atlántico	Atlantic
Pacífico	Pacific
Indíco	Indian

Nation	Nación	Nationality	Nacionalidad
Argentina	Argentina	Argentine	argentino (-a)
Australia	Australia	Australian	australiano (-a)
Bolivia	Bolivia	Bolivian	boliviano (-a)
Brazil	el Brasil	Brazilian	brasileño (-a), brasilero (-a)
Canada	Canadá	Canadian	canadiense
Chile	Chile	Chilean	chileno (-a)
China	la China	Chinese	chino (-a)
Colombia	Colombia	Colombian	colombiano (-a)
Commonwealth of Independent States	Comunidad de Estados Independientes		
Costa Rica	Costa Rica	Costa Rican	costarricense
Cuba	Cuba	Cuban	cubano (-a)
Denmark	Dinamarca	Danish/Dane	danés (-nesa)
Dominican Republic	la República Dominicana	Dominican	dominicano (-a)
Ecuador	Ecuador	Ecuadoran	ecuatoriano (-a)
Egypt	Egipto	Egyptian	egipcio (-a)
El Salvador	El Salvador	Salvadoran	salvadoreño (-a)
England	Inglaterra	English	inglés (-glesa)
Finland	Finlandia	Finnish/Finn, Finnlander	finlandés (-desa)
France	Francia	French	francés (-cesa)
Germany	Alemania	German	alemán (-a)
Great Britain	Gran Bretana	British	británico (-a)
Greece	Grecia	Greek	griego (-a)
Guatemala	Guatemala	Guatemalan	guatemalteco (-a)
Holland	Holanda	Dutch/Hollander	holandés (-desa)
Honduras	Honduras	Honduran	hondureño (-a)
Iceland	Islandia	Icelandic/ Icelander	islandés (-desa)
Ireland	Irlanda	Irish	irlandés (-desa)
Israel	Israel	Israeli	israelí [Hebrew hebreo (a)]
Italy	Italia	Italian	italiano (-a)
Japan	el Japón	Japanese	japonés (-nesa)
Mexico	México	Mexican	mexicano (-a)
Morocco	Marruecos	Moroccan	marroquí
Nicaragua	Nicaragua	Nicaraguan	nicaragüense
North America	América del Norte	North American	norteamericano (-a)
Norway	Noruega	Norwegian	noruego (-a)
Panama	Panamá	Panamanian	panameño (-a)

Paraguay	Paraguay	**Paraguayan**	paraguayo (-a)
Peru	el Perú	**Peruvian**	peruano (-a)
Poland	Polonia	**Polish/Pole**	polaco (-a)
Portugal	Portugal	**Portuguese**	portugués (-guesa)
Puerto Rico	Puerto Rico	**Puerto Rican**	puertorriqueño (-a)
Russia	Rusia	**Russian**	ruso (-a)
South Africa	África del Sur	**South African**	surafricano (-a)
South America	América del Sur	**South American**	suramericano (-a)
Spain	España	**Spanish/ Spaniard**	español (a)
Sweden	Suecia	**Swedish/Swede**	sueco (a)
Switzerland	Suiza	**Swiss**	suizo (-a)
Turkey	Turquía	**Turkish/Turk**	turco (-a)
United States	los Estados Unidos	**U.S. (American)**	estadounidense [norteamericano (-a)]
Uruguay	el Uruguay	**Uruguayan**	uruguayo (-a)
Venezuela	Venezuela	**Venezuelan**	venezolano (-a)

Continent	Continente
Ocean	Océano
Africa	África
North America	Norteamérica
South America	Sudamérica
Asia	Asia
Australia	Australia
Antarctica	Antártida
Europe	Europa
Atlantic	Atlántico
Pacific	Pacífico
Indian	Indíco

B. VERB CHARTS

1. THE FORMS OF THE REGULAR VERBS

INDICATIVE

INFINITIVE	PRES. & PAST PARTICIPLES	PRESENT INDICATIVE	IMPERFECT	PRETERITE	FUTURE	CONDITIONAL
I. -ar ending hablar to speak	hablando hablado	hablo hablas habla hablamos habláis hablan	hablaba hablabas hablaba hablábamos hablabais hablaban	hablé hablaste habló hablamos hablasteis hablaron	hablaré hablarás hablará hablaremos hablaréis hablarán	hablaría hablarías hablaría hablaríamos hablaríais hablarían
II. -er ending comer to eat	comiendo comido	como comes come comemos coméis comen	comía comías comía comíamos comíais comían	comí comiste comió comimos comisteis comieron	comeré comerás comerá comeremos comeréis comerán	comería comerías comería comeríamos comeríais comerían
III. -ir ending vivir to live	viviendo vivido	vivo vives vive vivimos vivís viven	vivía vivías vivía vivíamos vivíais vivían	viví viviste vivió vivimos vivisteis vivieron	viviré vivirás vivirá viviremos viviréis vivirán	viviría vivirías viviría viviríamos viviríais vivirían

PRESENT PERFECT	PAST PERFECT	PRETERITE PERFECT
he has ha hablado hemos habéis han	había habías había hablado habíamos habíais habían	hube hubiste hubo hablado hubimos hubisteis hubieron
he has ha comido hemos habéis han	había habías había comido habíamos habíais habían	hube hubiste hubo comido hubimos hubisteis hubieron
he has ha vivido hemos habéis han	había habías había vivido habíamos habíais habían	hube hubiste hubo vivido hubimos hubisteis hubieron

SUBJUNCTIVE

	FUTURE PERFECT	CONDITIONAL PERFECT	PRESENT	IMPERFECT (-r-)	IMPERFECT (-s-)	PRESENT PERFECT	PAST PERFECT (-r-)	PAST PERFECT (-s-)	IMPERATIVE
I.	habré	habría	hable	hablara	hablase	haya	hubiera	hubiese	
	habrás	habrías	hables	hablaras	hablases	hayas	hubieras	hubieses	¡Habla (tú)!
	habrá hablado	habría hablado	hable	hablara	hablase	haya hablado	hubiera hablado	hubiese hablado	¡Hable (Ud.)!
	habremos	habríamos	hablemos	habláramos	hablásemos	hayamos	hubiéramos	hubiésemos	¡Hablemos (nosotros)!
	habréis	habríais	habléis	hablarais	hablaseis	hayáis	hubierais	hubieseis	¡Hablad (vosotros)!
	habrán	habrían	hablen	hablaran	hablasen	hayan	hubieran	hubiesen	¡Hablen (Uds.)!
II.	habré	habría	coma	comiera	comiese	haya	hubiera	hubiese	
	habrás	habrías	comas	comieras	comieses	hayas	hubieras	hubieses	¡Come (tú)!
	habrá comido	habría comido	coma	comiera	comiese	haya comido	hubiera comido	hubiese comido	¡Coma (Ud.)!
	habremos	habríamos	comamos	comiéramos	comiésemos	hayamos	hubiéramos	hubiésemos	¡Comamos (nosotros)!
	habréis	habríais	comáis	comierais	comieseis	hayáis	hubierais	hubieseis	¡Comed (vosotros)!
	habrán	habrían	coman	comieran	comiesen	hayan	hubieran	hubiesen	¡Coman (Uds.)!
III.	habré	habría	viva	viviera	viviese	haya	hubiera	hubiese	
	habrás	habrías	vivas	vivieras	vivieses	hayas	hubieras	hubieses	¡Vive (tú)!
	habrá vivido	habría vivido	viva	viviera	viviese	haya vivido	hubiera vivido	hubiese vivido	¡Viva (Ud.)!
	habremos	habríamos	vivamos	viviéramos	viviésemos	hayamos	hubiéramos	hubiésemos	¡Vivamos (nosotros)!
	habréis	habríais	viváis	vivierais	vivieseis	hayáis	hubierais	hubieseis	¡Vivid (vosotros)!
	habrán	habrían	vivan	vivieran	viviesen	hayan	hubieran	hubiesen	¡Vivan (Uds.)!

2. RADICAL-CHANGING VERBS

o>ue

INFINITIVE*	PRESENT INDICATIVE	PRESENT SUBJUNCTIVE	IMPERATIVE	SIMILARLY CONJUGATED VERBS		
contar(ue) to count	*cuento* *cuentas* *cuenta* *contamos* *contáis* *cuentan*	*cuente* *cuentes* *cuente* *contemos* *contéis* *cuenten*	*cuenta* *contad*	*acordar* *acordarse* *acostarse* *almorzar* *apostar* *aprobar*	*avergonzar* *avergonzarse* *colgar* *costar* *encontrar* *jugar (u to ue)*	*probar* *recordar* *recordarse* *sonar* *soñar*
volver(ue) to return	*vuelvo* *vuelves* *vuelve* *volvemos* *volvéis* *vuelven*	*vuelva* *vuelvas* *vuelva* *volvamos* *volváis* *vuelvan*	*vuelve* *volved*	*devolver* *doler* *dolerse* *llover* *morder* *mover*	*oler* *soler*	

o>ue/u

INFINITIVE*	PRESENT INDICATIVE	PRETERITE INDICATIVE	PRESENT SUBJUNCTIVE	IMPERATIVE	SIMILARLY CONJUGATED VERBS
dormir(ue) to sleep	*duermo* *duermes* *duerme* *dormimos* *dormís* *duermen*	*dormí* *dormiste* *durmió* *dormimos* *dormisteis* *durmieron*	*duerma* *duermas* *duerma* *durmamos* *durmáis* *duerman*	*duerme* *dormid*	*morir* (past parti.: *muerto*)

* In all the other tenses, these verbs are conjugated like all other regular verbs.

e>ie

INFINITIVE*	PRESENT INDICATIVE	PRESENT SUBJUNCTIVE	IMPERATIVE	SIMILARLY CONJUGATED VERBS	
pensar (ie) to think	pienso piensas piensa pensamos pensáis piensan	piense pienses piense pensemos penséis piensen	piensa pensad	acertar apretar calentar cerrar confesar despertar	empezar encerrar gobernar plegar quebrar sentarse temblar tentar
perder (ie) to lose	pierdo pierdes pierde perdemos perdéis pierden	pierda pierdas pierda perdamos perdáis pierdan	pierde perded	ascender atender defender descender encender entender	extender tender

e>ie/i

INFINITIVE*	PRESENT INDICATIVE	PRETERITE INDICATIVE	PRESENT SUBJUNCTIVE	IMPERATIVE	SIMILARLY CONJUGATED VERBS	
sentir (ie) to feel	siento sientes siente sentimos sentís sienten	sentí sentiste sintió sentimos sentisteis sintieron	sienta sientas sienta sintamos sintáis sientan	siente sentid	advertir arrepentirse consentir convertir diferir divertir	herir mentir preferir presentir referir sugerir

e>i

INFINITIVE*	PRESENT INDICATIVE	PRETERITE INDICATIVE	PRESENT SUBJUNCTIVE	IMPERATIVE	SIMILARLY CONJUGATED VERBS	
pedir to ask	pido pides pide pedimos pedís piden	pedí pediste pidió pedimos pedisteis pidieron	pida pidas pida pidamos pidáis pidan	pide pedid	competir conseguir corregir despedir despedirse elegir	expedir reír repetir seguir servir vestir

* In all the other tenses, these verbs are conjugated like all other regular verbs.

3. SPELLING-CHANGE VERBS

ENDING	MODEL	PRETERITE INDICATIVE	PRESENT SUBJUNCTIVE	SIMILARLY CONJUGATED VERBS			
-car	*buscar* to look for	*busqué* *buscaste* *buscó* *buscamos* *buscasteis* *buscaron*	*busque* *busques* *busque* *busquemos* *busquéis* *busquen*	*acercar* *educar* *explicar* *fabricar* *indicar* *pecar* *sacar*	to place near to educate to explain to manufacture to indicate to sin to take out	*sacrificar* *secar* *significar* *tocar* *verificar*	to sacrifice to dry to signify, mean to touch, play (music) to verify
-gar	*pagar* to pay	*pagué* *pagaste* *pagó* *pagamos* *pagasteis* *pagaron*	*pague* *pagues* *pague* *paguemos* *paguéis* *paguen*	*ahogar* *apagar* *arriesgar* *cargar* *castigar* *congregar* *entregar*	to drown to extinguish to risk to load to punish to congregate to deliver	*investigar* *juzgar* *llegar* *obligar* *otorgar* *pegar* *tragar*	to investigate to judge to arrive to compel to grant to hit to swallow
-zar	*gozar* to enjoy	*gocé* *gozaste* *gozó* *gozamos* *gozasteis* *gozaron*	*goce* *goces* *goce* *gocemos* *gocéis* *gocen*	*abrazar* *alcanzar* *cruzar* *enlazar*	to embrace to reach to cross to join	*organizar* *rechazar* *rezar* *utitizar*	to organize to reject to pray to utilize
-guar	*averiguar* to ascertain	*averigüé* *averiguaste* *averiguó* *averiguamos* *averiguasteis* *averiguaron*	*averigüe* *averigües* *averigüe* *averigüemos* *averigüéis* *averigüen*	*aguar* *atestiguar*	to water, dilute to attest		

ENDING	MODEL	PRESENT INDICATIVE	PRESENT SUBJUNCTIVE	SIMILARLY CONJUGATED VERBS			
-ger	coger to catch	cojo coges coge cogemos cogéis cogen	coja cojas coja cojamos cojáis cojan	acoger escoger	to welcome to choose, select	proteger recoger	to protect to gather
-gir	dirigir to direct	dirijo diriges dirige dirigimos dirigís dirigen	dirija dirijas dirija dirijamos dirijáis dirijan	afligir erigir exigir	to afflict to erect to demand	rugir surgir	to roar to come forth
-guir	distinguir to distinguish	distingo distingues distingue distinguimos distinguís distinguen	distinga distingas distinga distingamos distingáis distingan	conseguir extinguir	to get, obtain to extinguish	perseguir seguir	to persecute to follow
-cer	conocer to know	conozco conoces conoce conocemos conocéis conocen	conozca conozcas conozca conozcamos conozcáis conozcan	aborrecer acaecer acontecer agradecer amanecer anochecer aparecer carecer compadecer complacer crecer desaparecer desobedecer desvanecer	to hate to happen to happen to be grateful to dawn to grow dark to appear to lack to pity to please to grow to disappear to disobey to vanish	embellecer envejecer fallecer favorecer merecer nacer obedecer ofrecer oscurecer padecer parecer permanecer pertenecer placer reconocer	to embellish to grow old to die to favor to merit to be born to obey to offer to grow dark to suffer to seem to last to belong to to please to recognize

(continued)

ENDING	MODEL	PRESENT INDICATIVE	PRESENT SUBJUNCTIVE	SIMILARLY CONJUGATED VERBS		
-cir	lucir to shine	luzco luces luce lucimos lucís lucen	luzca luzcas luzca luzcamos luzcáis luzcan	conducir traducir	to drive to translate	
-iar	enviar to send	envío envías envía enviamos enviáis envían	envíe envíes envíe enviemos enviéis envíen	confiar criar desafiar desconfiar fiar guiar	to trust to bring up to challenge to distrust to give credit to guide	
-uar	continuar to continue	continúo continúas continúa continuamos continuáis continúan	continúe continúes continúe continuemos continuéis continúen	actuar efectuar evaluar perpetuar	to act to carry out to evaluate to perpetuate	

ENDING	MODEL	PRESENT INDICATIVE	PRETERITE INDICATIVE	SIMILARLY CONJUGATED VERBS		
-uir (except -guir and -quir)	construir to build	construyo construyes construye construimos construís construyen	construí construiste construyó construimos construisteis construyeron	atribuir constituir contribuir destituir destruir distribuir excluir huir influir instruir reconstruir restituir substituir	to attribute to constitute to contribute to deprive to destroy to distribute to exclude to flee to influence to instruct to rebuild to restore to substitute	

4. THE FORMS OF THE IRREGULAR VERBS*

INFINITIVE, PRESENT AND PAST PARTICIPLES	PRESENT INDICATIVE	PRESENT SUBJUNCTIVE	IMPERFECT	PRETERITE	FUTURE	CONDITIONAL	IMPERATIVE
andar to walk *andando* *andado*	*ando* *andas* *anda* *andamos* *andáis* *andan*	*ande* *andes* *ande* *andemos* *andéis* *anden*	*andaba* *andabas* *andaba* *andábamos* *andabais* *andaban*	*anduve* *anduviste* *anduvo* *anduvimos* *anduvisteis* *anduvieron*	*andaré* *andarás* *andará* *andaremos* *andaréis* *andarán*	*andaría* *andarías* *andaría* *andaríamos* *andarías* *andarían*	*anda* *andad*
caber to fit, to be contained in *cabiendo* *cabido*	*quepo* *cabes* *cabe* *cabemos* *cabéis* *caben*	*quepa* *quepas* *quepa* *quepamos* *quepáis* *quepan*	*cabía* *cabías* *cabía* *cabíamos* *cabíais* *cabían*	*cupe* *cupiste* *cupo* *cupimos* *cupisteis* *cupieron*	*cabré* *cabrás* *cabrá* *cabremos* *cabréis* *cabrán*	*cabría* *cabrías* *cabría* *cabríamos* *cabríais* *cabrían*	*cabe* *cabed*
caer to fall *cayendo* *caído*	*caigo* *caes* *cae* *caemos* *caéis* *caen*	*caiga* *caigas* *caiga* *caigamos* *caigáis* *caigan*	*caía* *caías* *caía* *caíamos* *caíais* *caían*	*caí* *caíste* *cayó* *caímos* *caísteis* *cayeron*	*caeré* *caerás* *caerá* *caeremos* *caeréis* *caerán*	*caería* *caerías* *caería* *caeríamos* *caeríais* *caerían*	*cae* *caed*
conducir to lead, to drive *conduciendo* *conducido*	*conduzco* *conduces* *conduce* *conducimos* *conducís* *conducen*	*conduzca* *conduzcas* *conduzca* *conduzcamos* *conduzcáis* *conduzcan*	*conducía* *conducías* *conducía* *conducíamos* *conducíais* *conducían*	*conduje* *condujiste* *condujo* *condujimos* *condujisteis* *condujeron*	*conduciré* *conducirás* *conducirá* *conduciremos* *conduciréis* *conducirán*	*conduciría* *conducirías* *conduciría* *conduciríamos* *conduciríais* *conducirían*	*conduce* *conducid*

(continued)

INFINITIVE, PRESENT AND PAST PARTICIPLES	PRESENT INDICATIVE	PRESENT SUBJUNCTIVE	IMPERFECT	PRETERITE	FUTURE	CONDITIONAL	IMPERATIVE
dar to give	doy	dé	daba	di	daré	daría	
dando	das	des	dabas	diste	darás	darías	da
dado	da	dé	daba	dio	dará	daría	dad
	damos	demos	dábamos	dimos	daremos	daríamos	
	dais	deis	dabais	disteis	daréis	daríais	
	dan	den	daban	dieron	darán	darían	
decir	digo	diga	decía	dije	diré	diría	
to say,	dices	digas	decías	dijiste	dirás	dirías	di
to tell	dice	diga	decía	dijo	dirá	diría	decid
diciendo	decimos	digamos	decíamos	dijimos	diremos	diríamos	
dicho	decís	digáis	decíais	dijisteis	diréis	diríais	
	dicen	digan	decían	dijeron	dirán	dirían	
estar to be	estoy	esté	estaba	estuve	estaré	estaría	
estando	estás	estés	estabas	estuviste	estarás	estarías	está
estado	está	esté	estaba	estuvo	estará	estaría	estad
	estamos	estemos	estábamos	estuvimos	estaremos	estaríamos	
	estáis	estéis	estabais	estuvisteis	estaréis	estaríais	
	están	estén	estaban	estuvieron	estarán	estarían	
haber to have (auxiliary)	he	haya	había	hube	habré	habría	
habiendo	has	hayas	habías	hubiste	habrás	habrías	
habido	ha	haya	había	hubo	habrá	habría	
	hemos	hayamos	habíamos	hubimos	habremos	habríamos	
	habéis	hayáis	habíais	hubisteis	habréis	habríais	
	han	hayan	habían	hubieron	habrán	habrían	

* To form compound tenses, use the appropriate form of *haber* together with the past participle of the irregular verb.

(continued)

INFINITIVE, PRESENT AND PAST PARTICIPLES	PRESENT INDICATIVE	PRESENT SUBJUNCTIVE	IMPERFECT	PRETERITE	FUTURE	CONDITIONAL	IMPERATIVE
hacer to do to make haciendo hecho	hago haces hace hacemos hacéis hacen	haga hagas haga hagamos hagáis hagan	hacía hacías hacía hacíamos hacíais hacían	hice hiciste hizo hicimos hicisteis hicieron	haré harás hará haremos haréis harán	haría harías haría haríamos haríais harían	haz haced
ir to go yendo ido	voy vas va vamos vais van	vaya vayas vaya vayamos vayáis vayan	iba ibas iba íbamos ibais iban	fui fuiste fue fuimos fuisteis fueron	iré irás irá iremos iréis irán	iría irías iría iríamos iríais irían	ve id
oír to hear oyendo oído	oigo oyes oye oímos oís oyen	oiga oigas oiga oigamos oigáis oigan	oía oías oía oíamos oíais oían	oí oíste oyó oímos oísteis oyeron	oiré oirás oirá oiremos oiréis oirán	oiría oirías oiría oiríamos oiríais oirían	oye oíd
poder to be able, can pudiendo podido	puedo puedes puede podemos podéis pueden	pueda puedas pueda podamos podáis puedan	podía podías podía podíamos podíais podían	pude pudiste pudo pudimos pudisteis pudieron	podré podrás podrá podremos podréis podrán	podría podrías podría podríamos podríais podrían	puede poded
poner to put to place poniendo puesto	pongo pones pone ponemos ponéis ponen	ponga pongas ponga pongamos pongáis pongan	ponía ponías ponía poníamos poníais ponían	puse pusiste puso pusimos pusisteis pusieron	pondré pondrás pondrá pondremos pondréis pondrán	pondría pondrías pondría pondríamos pondríais pondrían	pon poned

341

(continued)

INFINITIVE, PRESENT AND PAST PARTICIPLES	PRESENT INDICATIVE	PRESENT SUBJUNCTIVE	IMPERFECT	PRETERITE	FUTURE	CONDITIONAL	IMPERATIVE
querer to want to love queriendo querido	quiero quieres quiere queremos queréis quieren	quiera quieras quiera queramos queráis quieran	quería querías quería queríamos queríais querían	quise quisiste quiso quisimos quisisteis quisieron	querré querrás querrá querremos querréis querrán	querría querrías querría querríamos querríais querrían	quiere quered
reír to laugh riendo reído	río ríes ríe reímos reís ríen	ría rías ría ríamos riáis rían	reía reías reía reíamos reíais reían	reí reíste rió reímos reísteis rieron	reiré reirás reirá reiremos reiréis reirán	reiría reirías reiría reiríamos reiríais reirían	ríe reíd
saber to know sabiendo sabido	sé sabes sabe sabemos sabéis saben	sepa sepas sepa sepamos sepáis sepan	sabía sabías sabía sabíamos sabíais sabían	supe supiste supo supimos supisteis supieron	sabré sabrás sabrá sabremos sabréis sabrán	sabría sabrías sabría sabríamos sabríais sabrían	sabe sabed
salir to go out, to leave saliendo salido	salgo sales sale salimos salís salen	salga salgas salga salgamos salgáis salgan	salía salías salía salíamos salíais salían	salí saliste salió salimos salisteis salieron	saldré saldrás saldrá saldremos saldréis saldrán	saldría saldrías saldría saldríamos saldríais saldrían	sal salid
ser to be siendo sido	soy eres es somos sois son	sea seas sea seamos seáis sean	era eras era éramos erais eran	same as preterite of ir:	seré serás será seremos seréis serán	sería serías sería seríamos seríais serían	sé sed

(continued)

INFINITIVE, PRESENT AND PAST PARTICIPLES	PRESENT INDICATIVE	PRESENT SUBJUNCTIVE	IMPERFECT	PRETERITE	FUTURE	CONDITIONAL	IMPERATIVE
tener to have *teniendo* *tenido*	tengo tienes tiene tenemos tenéis tienen	tenga tengas tenga tengamos tengáis tengan	tenía tenías tenía teníamos teníais tenían	tuve tuviste tuvo tuvimos tuvisteis tuvieron	tendré tendrás tendrá tendremos tendréis tendrán	tendría tendrías tendría tendríamos tendríais tendrían	ten tened
traer to bring *trayendo* *traído*	traigo traes trae traemos traéis traen	traiga traigas traiga traigamos traigáis traigan	traía traías traía traíamos traíais traían	traje trajiste trajo trajimos trajisteis trajeron	traeré traerás traerá traeremos traeréis traerán	traería traerías traería traeríamos traeríais traerían	trae traed
valer to be worth *valiendo* *valido*	valgo vales vale valemos valéis valen	valga valgas valga valgamos valgáis valgan	valía valías valía valíamos valíais valían	valí valiste valió valimos valisteis valieron	valdré valdrás valdrá valdremos valdréis valdrán	valdría valdrías valdría valdríamos valdríais valdrían	val valed
venir to come *viniendo* *venido*	vengo vienes viene venimos venís vienen	venga vengas venga vengamos vengáis vengan	venía venías venía veníamos veníais venían	vine viniste vino vinimos vinisteis vinieron	vendré vendrás vendrá vendremos vendréis vendrán	vendría vendrías vendría vendríamos vendríais vendrían	ven venid
ver to see *viendo* *visto*	veo ves ve vemos veis ven	vea veas vea veamos veáis vean	veía veías veía veíamos veíais veían	vi viste vio vimos visteis vieron	veré verás verá veremos veréis verán	vería verías vería veríamos veríais verían	ve ved

343

C. LETTER WRITING

1. FORMAL INVITATIONS AND RESPONSES

INVITATIONS

marzo de 1993

Jorge Fernández y Sra.—Tienen el gusto de participar a Ud. y familia el próximo enlace matrimonial de su hija Carmen con el Sr. Juan García, y los invitan a la Ceremonia que se verificará en la Iglesia de Nuestra Señora de la Merced, el día 6 de los corrientes, a las 6 de la tarde. A continuación tendrá lugar una recepción en la casa de los padres de la novia en honor de los contrayentes.

March 1993

Mr. and Mrs. George Fernandez take pleasure in announcing the wedding of their daughter Carmen to Mr. Juan García, and invite you to the ceremony that will take place at the Church of Nuestra Señora de la Merced, on the 6th of this month at 6 P.M. There will be a reception for the newlyweds afterwards at the residence of the bride's parents.

Los señores Suárez ofrecen sus respetos a los señores García y les ruegan que les honren viniendo a comer con ellos el lunes próximo, a las ocho.

Mr. and Mrs. Suárez present their respects to Mr. and Mrs. García and would be honored to have their company at dinner next Monday at 8 o'clock.

Los señores Suárez y Navarro saludan afectuosamente a los señores Del Vayo y les ruegan que les honren asistiendo a la recepción que darán en honor de su hija María, el domingo 19 de marzo, a las nueve de la noche.

Mr. and Mrs. Suárez y Navarro cordially greet Mr. and Mrs. Del Vayo and request the honor of their presence at the party given in honor of their daughter María, on Sunday evening, March 19, at nine o'clock.

Los señores Del Vayo les agradecen infinito la invitación que se han dignado hacerles y tendrán el honor de asistir a la recepción del domingo 19 de marzo.

Thank you for your kind invitation. We shall be honored to attend the reception on March 19th.

Los señores García tendrán el honor de acudir al convite de los señores Suárez y entretanto les saludan cordialmente.

Mr. and Mrs. García will be honored to have dinner with Mr. and Mrs. Suárez. With kindest regards.

Los señores García ruegan a los señores Suárez se sirvan recibir las gracias por su amable invitación y la expresión de su sentimiento al no poder aceptarla por hallarse comprometidos con anterioridad.

Mr. and Mrs. García thank Mr. and Mrs. Suárez for their kind invitation and regret that they are unable to come owing to a previous engagement.

2. THANK-YOU NOTE

5 de marzo de 2000

Querida Anita,

La presente es con el fin de saludarte y darte las gracias por el precioso florero que me has enviado de regalo. Lo he colocado encima del piano y no te imaginas el lindo efecto que hace.

Espero verte pasado mañana en la fiesta que da Carmen, la cual parece que va a ser muy animada.

Deseo que estés bien en compañía de los tuyos. Nosotros sin novedad. Te saluda cariñosamente, tu amiga.

Laura

March 5, 2000

Dear Anita,

This is just to say hello and also to let you know that I received the beautiful vase you sent me as a gift. I've put it on the piano and you can't imagine the beautiful effect.

I hope to see you at Carmen's party tomorrow. I think it's going to be a very lively affair.

I hope your family is well. Everyone here is fine.

Your friend,
Laura

3. BUSINESS LETTERS

Aranjo & Cía.
Paseo de Gracia, 125
Barcelona—España

2 de abril de 2000

González e hijos
Madrid—España

Muy señores nuestros:

Nos es grato presentarles al portador de la presente, Sr. Carlos de la Fuente, nuestro viajante, quien se propone visitar las principales ciudades de esa región. No necesitamos decirles que cualquier atención que le dispensen la consideraremos como un favor personal. Anticipándoles las gracias, nos es grato reiterarnos de Uds. coma siempre,

Sinceramente,

Aranjo & Cía.

Presidente.

Aranjo & Co., Inc.
125 Paseo de Gracia
Barcelona—Spain

April 2, 2000

Gonzalez & Sons
Madrid
Spain

Gentlemen:

We have the pleasure of introducing to you the bearer of this letter, Mr. Carlos de la Fuente, one of our salesmen, who is visiting the principal cities of your region. Needless to say, we shall greatly appreciate any courtesy you extend to him. ("It is needless to say to you that we shall consider any courtesy you extend him as a personal favor.") Thanking you in advance, we remain

Very truly yours,
Aranjo & Co., Inc.

_____

President

Pananá

3 de marzo de 2000

Sr. Julián Pérez
Apartado 22
Buenos Aires
Argentina

Muy Señor mío:

   Sírvase encontrar adjunto un cheque de $5 por un año de subscripción a la revista de su digna dirección.

                    Atentamente,

María Pérez de Pereira
Apartado 98
Panamá, Panamá

                    P.O. Box 98
                    Panama, Republic of Panama

                    March 3rd, 2000

Mr. Julián Pérez
P.O. Box 22
Buenos Aires
Argentina

Dear Sir:

   Enclosed please find a check for $5.00 for a year's subscription to your magazine.

                    Very truly yours,
                    Mrs. Maria Pereira

Mi querido Pepe:

Me ha sido sumamente grato recibir tu última carta. Ante todo déjame darte la gran noticia. Pues he decidido por fin hacer un viaje a Madrid, donde pienso pasar todo el mes de mayo.

Isabel se viene conmigo. A ella la encanta la idea de conoceros.

Los negocios marchan bien por ahora y confío que continuará la buena racha. El otro día estuve con Antonio y me preguntó por ti.

Procura mandar a reservarnos una habitación en el Nacional, que te lo agradeceré mucho.

Escríbeme pronto. Dale mis recuerdos a Elena y recibe un abrazo de tu amigo,

Juan

Dear Pepe,

I was very happy to get your last letter. First of all, let me give you the big news. I have finally decided to make a trip to Madrid, where I expect to spend all of May.

Isabel is coming with me. She is extremely happy to be able to meet the two of you at last.

Business is good now and I hope it will stay that way ("that the good wind will continue"). I saw Anthony the other day and he asked me about you.

I'd appreciate your trying to reserve a room for us in the "National."

Write soon. Give my regards to Helen.

Yours,
John

5. FORMS OF SALUTATIONS AND COMPLIMENTARY CLOSINGS

1. SALUTATIONS:

FORMAL

Señor:	Sir:
Señora:	Madam:
Señorita:	Miss:
Muy señor mío:	Dear Sir:
Muy señores míos:	Gentlemen:
Estimado señor:	Dear Sir:
De mi consideración:	Dear Sir:
Muy distinguido señor:	Dear Sir:
Muy señor nuestro:	Dear Sir:
Muy señores nuestros:	Gentlemen:
Señor profesor:	My dear Professor:
Excelentísimo señor:	Dear Sir: ("Your Excellency:")
Estimado amigo:	Dear Friend:
Querido amigo:	Dear Friend:

INFORMAL

Don Antonio (Aguilera),	My dear Mr. Aguilera,
Doña María (de Suárez),	My dear Mrs. Suárez,
Señorita Laura (Suárez),	My dear Miss Suárez,
Antonio,	Anthony,
Querida Laura,	Dear Laura:
Mi querida Laura,	My dear Laura:
Amada mía,	My beloved,
Querida mía,	My dear, My beloved,

350

2. COMPLIMENTARY CLOSINGS:

"Muy atentamente" is equivalent to our "Very sincerely yours."

Cariñosamente.	Affectionately yours,
Atentamente.	Sincerely yours,
Sinceramente.	Sincerely yours,
Afectuosamente.	Affectionately yours,
Quien mucho le aprecia.	Affectionately,
De quien te estima.	Affectionately,
De su amigo que le quiere.	Affectionately,
De tu querida hija.	Your loving daughter,
Besos y abrazos.	
De todo corazón.	With love,
De quien te adora.	

3. FORM OF THE LETTER:

FORMAL

Estimado Señor:
or *Muy señor mío:*
(Dear Sir:)

_____

_____
_____

                                 Sinceramente,
                                 (Sincerely yours,)

Querido Juan:
(Dear John,)

_____

_____

_____

Cariñosamente,
(Affectionately,)

4. COMMON FORMULAS:

Beginning a letter—

1. *Me es grato acusar recibo de su atenta del 8 del corriente. Tengo el agrado de . . .*
   This is to acknowledge receipt of your letter of the 8th of this month. I am glad to . . .
2. *Obra en mi poder su apreciable carta de fecha 10 de marzo . . .*
   I have received your letter of March 10th.
3. *En contestación a su atenta carta de ayer . . .*
   In answer to your letter of yesterday . . .
4. *De conformidad con su grata del . . .*
   In accordance with your letter of . . .
5. *Con referencia a su anuncio en "La Nación" de hoy . . .*
   In reference to your ad in today's issue of The Nation, . . .
6. *Por la presente me dirijo a Ud. para . . .*
   This letter is to . . .
7. *Nos es grato anunciarle que . . .*
   We are pleased to announce that . . .
8. *Me es grato recomendar a Ud. al Sr. . . .*
   I take pleasure in recommending to you Mr. . . .
9. *La presente tiene por objeto confirmarle nuestra conversación telefónica de esta mañana . . .*
   This is to confirm our telephone conversation of this morning . . .

Ending a letter—

1. *Anticipándole las gracias, saludo a Ud. atentamente,*
   Thanking you in advance, I am

                                    Sincerely yours,

2. *Anticipándoles las más expresivas gracias, quedamos de Uds.*
                                    Sinceramente,
   Thanking you in advance, we are

                                    Sincerely yours,

3. *Quedamos de Ud. atentos y SS.*
   We remain

                                    Sincerely yours,

4. *En espera de sus gratas noticias, me repito de Ud.*
   Sinceramente,
   Hoping to hear from you, I am

                                    Sincerely yours,

5. *Esperando su grata y pronta contestación, quedo,*
                                    Sinceramente,
   Hoping to hear from you at your earliest convenience, I am
                                    Sincerely yours,

The following are often used when beginning a business correspondence:

6. *Aprovecho esta ocasión para ofrecerme.*
   . . . I am taking advantage of this opportunity to introduce myself.

   Aprovechamos esta ocasión para suscribirnos.
   . . . We are taking this opportunity to introduce ourselves.

Félix Valbueña y Cía
Calle de Zurbarán, 6
Madrid

Señor Don
Ricardo Fitó,
Apartado 5042
Barcelona

M. Navarro-Suárez
San Martín, 820
Buenos Aires

Señores
M. Suárez y Coello,
Paseo de la Castellana, 84
Madrid, España

Señorita
Laura Navarro
Gran Vía de Germanías, 63
Valencia

Antonio de Suárez
Calle del Sol, 2
Chamartín
Madrid

GLOSSARY

Abbreviations

adjective	*adj.*	masculine	*m.*
adverb	*adv.*	noun	*n.*
article	*art.*	object	*obj.*
definite	*def.*	plural	*pl.*
direct	*dir.*	preposition	*prep.*
familiar	*fam.*	pronoun	*pron.*
feminine	*f.*	possessive	*poss.*
formal	*fml.*	singular	*sg.*
literal	*lit.*	subjective	*subj.*

ESPAÑOL-INGLÉS

A

a *to, at, in, on, by, for*
  a bordo *on board*
  a casa *(to) home*
  a causa de *on account of; because of*
  a menudo *often*
  a pesar de *in spite of*
  a pie *on foot*
  a tiempo *on time*
  a veces *at times*
  al aire libre *in the open air; outdoors*
  al fin *finally; at last*
  al (+ infinitive) *on (upon) (+ gerund)*
  Al llegar . . . *Upon arriving . . .*
el abogado, -a *lawyer*
el abrigo *overcoat; shelter*
  abril *April*
  abrir *to open*
  ¡Abra la boca! *Open your mouth!*
  abuchear *to boo*
el abuelo, -a *grandfather, grandmother*
  acabar *to finish*
  acabar de *to have just (done something)*
  Acabo de llegar. *I have just arrived.*

el aceite *oil*
  aceptar *to accept*
  aconsejar *to advise*
  acostarse *to go to bed*
  acostumbrarse a *to get used to,*
    accustom
la actividad *activity*
  actividades diarias *daily activities*
el actor/la actriz *actor/actress*
  actualizar *to update, modernize*
  actualizarse sobre las cuestiones *to*
    keep up-to-date on issues
  actuar *to act*
  adiós *good-bye*
  adornar *to decorate*
  adquirir *to acquire*
la Aduana *Customs*
  llenar la declaración de la Aduana
    to fill out the Customs
    declaration
  No tengo nada para declarar. *I have*
    nothing to declare.
  ¿Tengo que pagar
    derechos/impuestos? *Do I have to*
    pay duty?

355

el aeropuerto *airport*
    en el aeropuerto *at the airport*
afeitarse *to shave*
    hoja de afeitar *shaving blade*
    navaja de afeitar *shaving razor*
la agencia *agency*
    la agencia de cambio *currency exchange office*
    la agencia de viajes *travel agency*
el/la agente *agent*
agosto *August*
agotar *to exhaust, to wear out*
agotarse *to exhaust oneself, wear oneself out*
agradecer *to be grateful to, thank*
el agua *water*
el agujero *hole*
ahí *there*
ahora *now*
    ahora mismo *right now*
el aire *air, wind; aspect, look*
    aire acondicionado *air conditioning*
el alcalde/la alcadesa *mayor*
alegrarse *to be happy*
    alegrarse de *to be happy about*
algo *something*
    ¿Algo más? *Something else?*
el algodón *cotton*
alguien *someone*
algún, alguno, -a *some, any*
el almacén *department store; warehouse*
almorzar *to eat lunch*
el almuerzo *lunch*
alquilar *to rent*
    alquilar un coche *to rent a car*
el alquiler *rent; rental; lease*
la altitud *altitude*
alto, -a *high, tall; loud*
    alta calidad *first-rate; high quality*
    ¡Alto! *Stop!*
los (alto)parlantes *loudspeakers*
allí *there (far away)*
    Están allí. *They are (over) there.*
amarillo, -a *yellow*
el amigo, -a *friend*
amor *love*
    amor mío *my darling*
anaranjado, -a *orange (color)*
el andén *platform*
animar *to inspire, arouse, excite*
anoche *last night*
el antiácido *antacid*
los anteojos *eyeglasses*
anterior *previous*

antes *before*
la antigüedad *antiquity; antique*
    tienda de antigüedades *antique shop*
antipático, -a *unpleasant*
anunciar *to announce*
    anuncios clasificados *classified ads*
el año *year*
    Año Nuevo *New Year*
    el año pasado *last year*
    ¡Feliz Año Nuevo! *Happy New Year!*
    por año *yearly, annually*
    todo el año *all year long*
apagar *to turn off*
    apagar la televisión *to turn off the TV*
el aparato *appliance; equipment*
    aparato de discos compactos *CD player*
    los aparatos electro-domésticos *household appliances*
    los aparatos electrónicos *electronic equipment*
el apartamento/apartamiento *apartment*
el apartado *P.O. Box*
el aparto-hotel *apartment hotel*
el apellido *last name, family name*
apetecer *to appeal to*
aplaudir *to applaud, clap*
apoyarse *to support oneself (physically)*
aprender *to learn*
aproximarse a *to get close to*
aquel, aquella, aquellos, aquellas *that, those (far away) (adj.)*
aquél, aquélla, aquéllos, aquéllas *that one, those ones (far away) (pron.)*
aquello *that thing, idea, concept (pron.)*
aquí *here*
    Está aquí. *It's here.*
la arena *sand*
arrancar *to uproot, pull out; to start up the car*
    arrancar una muela *to pull out a tooth*
el arranque *car ignition*
arreglar *to fix*
    arreglar las uñas *to do one's nails*
el arrendamiento *lease*
arriba *on top, above*
    la calle arriba *up the street*
arribar *to arrive; to reach*
    ¡Manos arriba! *Hands up!*
el arroz *rice*
el artículo *article*
el/la asaltante *mugger*

asaltar *to mug, to rob*
el asalto *mugging*
ascender *to promote*
el ascenso *promotion*
asegurado *insured*
asegurar *to insure*
el asesinato *murder*
así *thus*
el asiento *seat*
   asiento a la ventanilla *window seat*
   asiento adelante *front seat*
   asiento al pasillo *aisle seat*
   asiento atrás *back seat*
   asignar *to assign*
   asignar asientos *to assign seats*
la aspirina *aspirin*
   asustar *to frighten*
   atacar *to attack*
   atar *to tie, to tie up*
la atención *attention*
   prestar atención *to pay attention*
   atender *to answer (phone, door), to attend to*
el/la atleta *athlete*
   atrasar *to delay*
el atún *tuna*
el auditorio *auditorium*
   aumentar *to increase*
el aumento *increase, growth, raise*
la aurora *dawn, daybreak*
el auto(móvil) *automobile, car*
el autobús *bus*
   la estación de autobuses *bus station*
el autocar *bus (in Spain)*
   automático *automatic*
   autorizar *to authorize*
el avance *advancement, promotion*
   No había posibilidad de avance. *There was no possibility for advancement.*
el ave *(f.) bird, fowl*
la avenida *avenue*
el aviso *sign*
   ayer *yesterday*
   ayer por la tarde *yesterday afternoon*
   ayudar *to help*
   ¡Ayuda! *Help!*
   azul *blue*

B

el bacalao *codfish*
bailar *to dance*
bajar *to get off; to go down*

   bajar del autobús *to get off the bus*
   bajar de peso *to lose weight*
   bajo *under, beneath; short*
el baloncesto *basketball*
el banco *bank*
   en el banco *at the bank*
   ¿Qué servicios ofrece su banco? *What services does your bank offer?*
el banquero, -a *banker*
el bañador *bathing suit*
   bañar *to bathe (someone)*
   bañarse *to bathe (oneself)*
el baño *bath; bathroom; bathtub*
   baño particular *private bath*
el bar *bar*
   barato, -a *cheap*
la barba *beard*
la barbería *barbershop*
el barbero *barber*
el barco *boat*
el barquito *a small boat*
el barrio *neighborhood*
   bastante *enough, somewhat, sufficient, rather, fairly*
la batería *car battery*
el batido *milkshake*
el baúl *trunk, chest*
   beber *to drink*
la bebida *drink*
   bebida alcohólica *alcoholic drink*
el béisbol *baseball*
   bien *well, right; properly; very; easily; fully; gladly; willingly; about*
   perfectamente bien *completely well*
   ¡Bienvenido! *Welcome!*
el bigote *moustache*
el billete *ticket*
   billete de ida y vuelta *round-trip ticket*
la billetería *box office*
   blanco, -a *white*
   en blanco y negro *in black and white*
la blusa *blouse*
la boca *mouth*
   ¡Abra la boca! *Open your mouth!*
el bocadillo *snack; sandwich*
la boda *wedding*
el boleto *ticket*
la bolsa *bag, purse*
la bomba *pump*
   bonito, -a *pretty, beautiful, graceful*
la botánica *pharmacy (herbs)*
el/la botones *bellhop*
el boxeador, -a *boxer*
el boxeo *boxing*

el brazo *arm*
la broma *joke, jest*
  bromear *to joke, to have fun*
  broncearse *to sunbathe*
el buceo *scuba diving*
  hacer buceo *to go scuba diving*
  bueno, -a *good; Okay.*
    Buenos días. *Good morning.*
    Buenas noches. *Good evening. Good night.*
    Buenas tardes. *Good afternoon.*
la bujía *spark plug*
el bus *bus*
  buscar *to look for*
    buscando un departamento *looking for an apartment*
    buscando un trabajo *looking for a job*
    buscar un departamento en el periódico *to look for an apartment in the newspaper*
    ¿Qué tipo de departamento busca Ud.? *What kind of apartment are you looking for?*
el buzón *mailbox*
  echar al buzón *to mail*

C

el cabello *hair*
la cabeza *head*
  el dolor de cabeza *headache*
el cable *cable*
  cada *each*
el café *coffee; café*
la caja *box, case; coffin; chest*
  caja de valores *safety-deposit box*
el cajero *teller*
  cajero automático *automatic teller machine*
la cajita *small box*
los calcetines *socks*
la calidad *quality; condition, capacity*
  caliente *warm, hot*
  calor *hot*
  callarse *to be quiet*
    ¡Cállate! *Be quiet.*
la calle *street*
la cama *bed*
la cámara *camera*
los camarones *shrimp*
  cambiar *to cash; to change*
    cambiar un cheque de viajero *to cash a traveler's check*

cambiar dólares a/en pesos *to change dollars into pesos*
  cambiar el canal *to change channels*
el cambio *change, exchange*
  la agencia de cambio *currency exchange office*
  el cambio de marchas *gear shift*
caminar *to walk*
la camisa *shirt, chemise*
el campo *countryside; (sports) field; area (of interest); background*
la caña de azúcar *sugar cane*
el canal *channel, station*
  el canal educativo *educational (public) television*
  cambiar el canal *to change channels*
la canción *song*
la cancha *(tennis) court*
el candidato *candidate*
la canoa *canoe*
la cantidad *sum; quantity, amount*
la capacidad *ability; capacity*
el capó *hood (car)*
el capricho *whim; fancy*
  ¡Caramba! *Good heavens! Darn!*
  ¡Caray! *Darn!*
el carbohidrato *carbohydrate*
la cárcel *prison*
el cargo *charge*
la carie *cavity (tooth)*
la carne *meat, flesh*
  la carne de res *beef*
la carnicería *butcher's shop*
  caro, -a *expensive*
    Es carísimo. *It's very expensive.*
el carrito *shopping cart*
el carro *cart; car, automobile*
la carretera *road*
  servicio de carretera *road service*
la carta *letter; card*
  la carta-llave *card-key*
  cartas de referencia *letters of recommendation*
la cartelera *movie listings*
  consultar la cartelera *to check the movie listings*
el cartero, -a *mailman*
la casa *house; home*
  la casa de cambio *currency exchange office*
  Jorge está en casa. *Jorge is at home.*
  Julia va a casa. *Julia goes home.*
  Paso el día en casa de Jorge. *I'm spending the day at Jorge's house.*

la casilla *post office box*
la caspa *dandruff*
cartorce *fourteen*
la cebolla *onion*
la celebración *celebration*
celebrar *to celebrate*
la cena *supper, dinner*
cenar *to dine, to eat dinner*
el centavo *cent*
centígrado, -a *centigrade, Celsius*
el centro *center; middle; core; club, social circle*
el centro de turismo *tourist office*
centros comerciales *shopping centers*
cepillarse *to brush one's teeth*
el cepillo *brush*
cepillo de dientes *toothbrush*
cerca (de) *near, nearby*
cero *zero*
la certificación *registration*
certificado, -a *registered (mail)*
certificar *to register*
la cerveza *beer*
cien(to) *one hundred*
ciento un, uno, -a *one hundred and one*
cierto, -a *certain; certainly*
el cigarrillo *cigarette*
el cigarro *cigar; cigarette (Mexican)*
cinco *five*
cincuenta *fifty*
cincuenta mil *fifty thousand*
el cine *movie, movie theater*
en el cine *at the movies*
el/la cineasta *moviemaker*
la cinta *cassette tape*
la cintura *waist*
el cintúron *belt*
la cita *appointment, date*
hacer una cita *to make an appointment*
la ciudad *city*
el ciudadano *citizen*
claro *clear*
¡Claro! *Of course! Obviously!*
claro que sí *of course*
más claro *clearest*
la clase *class; kind, type*
primera clase *first class*
segunda clase *second class*
los clasificados *classified ads*
el/la cliente *customer*
la clínica *clinic, hospital*

cobrar *to collect, receive; to gain, acquire; to charge (a price or fee)*
cobrar un cheque *to cash a check*
la cocina *kitchen*
cocinar *to cook*
el coche *car*
el coche-cama *sleeping car (train)*
el cognado *cognate*
colgar *to hang up*
colocar *to put, place*
el color *color; tendency, policy; aspect; pretext*
a colores *in color*
la columna *column*
columna de chismes *gossip column*
la comedia *comedy*
el comedor *dining room*
comenzar *to begin, commence*
comer *to eat*
las cómicas *comics*
tiras cómicas *comic strips*
la comida *food; meal*
comidas y bebidas *food and drinks*
¿cómo? *what? how?*
¿Cómo está Ud.? *How are you?*
¡Cómo no! *Of course!*
como si *as if*
la compañía *company*
compararse con *to compare with, be comparable to*
competente *competent; able, capable*
altamente competente *highly qualified*
complemento directo *direct object pronoun*
comprar *to buy, shop*
Lo compré la semana pasada. *I bought it last week.*
comprender *to understand*
el computador/la computadora *computer*
común *usual*
la comunicación *communication*
comunicar *to be talking on the phone*
con *with*
con frecuencia *frequently, often*
con mucho gusto *gladly; with great pleasure*
conmigo *with me*
contigo *with you*
consigo *with him, her, you, them*
concluir *to conclude*
el conductor, -a *driver*
la confusión *confusion, perplexity*
el congelador *freezer*

conocer *to know, be acquainted with, meet*

conseguir *to get, obtain*

la **consonante** *consonant*

construir *to construct, build; to construe*

consultar *to check, to consult*
   consultar la cartelera *to check the movie listings*

el **consultorio** *information bureau; consulting-room*
   consultorio del médico *doctor's office*

la **contaminación** *pollution*
   contaminación del ambiente *environmental pollution*

contento, -a *happy*

continuar *to continue*

contra *against*

el **contrato** *contract*

la **copia** *copy*

la **corbata** *tie, necktie*

el **cordero** *lamb*

el **corredor (-a) de inmuebles** *real estate agent*

el **correo** *post office*
   en el correo *at the post office*

correr *to run*

el **correr** *jogging*

la **corrida de toros** *bullfight*
   plaza de toros *bullring*

cortar *to cut*
   cortar un poco *to trim*

el **corte** *haircut*

el **cortometraje** *short film*

la **cosa** *thing*

coser *to sew*

el **cosmético** *cosmetic, make-up*

el **costado** *side*

costar *to cost*
   ¿Cuánto cuesta? *How much does it dcost?*

el **crédito** *credit*

creer *to believe*
   No creo. *I don't think so. (I don't believe so.)*

el **crimen** *crime*

el/la **criminal** *criminal*

el **crítico** *critic*

el **crucigrama** *crossword puzzle*

la **cuadra** *block (street)*

cual *the one that, which, who*

¿cuál? *what? which one?*

cuanto *as much as, as many as*
   Compre cuantas naranjas encuentre.
   Buy as many oranges as you can find.

cuanto más . . . tanto más
   the more . . . the more . . .

¿cuánto? *how much? how many?*
   ¿Cuánto es el pasaje? *How much is the ticket?*

cuarenta *forty*

la **Cuaresma** *Lent*

cuarto *fourth, quarter*

el **cuarto** *room*

cuatro *four*

cuatrocientos, -as *four hundred*

el **cuello** *neck; collar*

la **cuenta** *bill, account; score (game)*
   cuenta de ahorros *savings account*
   cuenta corriente *checking account*
   el estado de cuenta bancario *bank statement*

el **cuero** *leather*

el **cuerpo** *body*

el **cuidado** *care, attention*
   ¡Cuidado! *Careful! Watch out!*

cuidadoso *careful*

cuidar *to take care of (someone)*

cuidarse *to take care of oneself*

la **culpa** *blame*

el **cultivo** *culture; cultivation; crop*
   cultivo de cuerpo *cult of the body*

el **cumpleaños** *birthday*
   Feliz cumpleaños. *Happy birthday.*
   festejar el cumpleaños *to celebrate one's birthday*
   quinceañera *girl's fifteenth birthday party*

el **cuñado, -a** *brother-in-law, sister-in-law*

la **cuota** *fee*

el **curriculum vitae** *résumé*

CH

el **champú** *shampoo*

la **chaqueta** *jacket, coat*

el **chayote** *cheyote*

el **cheque** *check*
   el cheque de viajero *traveler's check*

la **chequera** *checkbook*

el **chico, -a** *boy, girl*

la **china** *orange (Puerto Rico)*

chiquito, -a *very small*

el **chiquito, la chiquita** *little child*

la **chirimoya** *cherimoya*

los **chismes** *gossip*
    columna de chismes *gossip column*
chocante *shocking*
el **chorizo** *sausage*
la **chuleta** *cutlet, chop*
    chuleta de puerco *pork chop*
    chuleta de cordero *lamb chop*

D

dar *to give; to deal (cards); to show (a movie)*
    dar a la calle, el jardín *to face the street, the garden*
    dar a luz *to give birth*
    dar bien con *to go well with, to get along with*
    dar con alguien/algo *to meet, to come upon*
    dar de comer *to feed*
    dar la mano a alguien *to shake hands with someone*
    dar las gracias a *to thank*
    dar los buenos días *to say good morning, to greet*
    dar palmadas *to applaud, clap*
    dar recuerdos/memorias *to give one's regards*
    dar un paseo *to take a walk or a ride*
    darse cuenta *to realize*
    darse la mano *to shake hands with each other*
    darse prisa *to hurry*
    dárselo a *to sell it for (a price)*
    ¡Dése prisa! *Hurry up!*
de *of; from; for; by; on*
    ¿De dónde es Ud.? *Where are you from?*
    de esta manera/modo *in this way*
    De nada. *You're welcome.*
    de nuevo *again*
    de pronto/repente *suddenly*
    de vez en cuando *from time to time*
    la casa de mi amigo *my friend's house*
    una taza de café *a cup of coffee*
deber *to need to, must, ought to; to owe*
    Debemos irnos. *We have to go.*
    No me debe nada. *You don't owe me anything.*
débil *weak*
el **débito** *debit*
décimo, -a *tenth*

decir *to say; to tell; to call, name*
    ¡Diga! ¿Quién habla? *Hello. Who's speaking?*
    ¡Dígame! *Tell me.*
    el decir *speech; saying*
    es decir *that is to say*
    ¡No me diga! *You don't say! Don't tell me!*
    Se lo diré. *I'll tell him/her.*
dedicarse a *to dedicate oneself to*
el **dedo** *finger; toe*
dejar *to leave; to drop off; to sell, yield*
    dejar a un precio *to sell at a price*
    dejar una posición *to leave a job*
    ¡Déjeme en paz! *Leave me alone!*
delante de *in front of*
delicado, -a *delicate*
demasiado *too much*
la **democracia** *democracy*
el/la **dentista** *dentist*
el **departamento** *apartment*
el **deporte** *sport*
el/la **deportista** *athlete*
depositar *to deposit*
    depositar un cheque *to deposit a check*
el **depósito** *(gas) tank; deposit*
    certificado de depósito *certificate of deposit*
    libreta de depósitos *bank passbook*
derecho, -a *right; straight; right-hand*
    a la derecha *to the right*
    Sigues derecho. *You walk straight ahead.*
el **derecho** *law, justice; claim, title; right*
    derechos de aduana *customs duties*
el **desafío** *challenge*
    ofrecer nuevos desafíos *to offer new challenges*
desagradable *unpleasant, disagreeable*
desarrollar *to develop*
    desarrollar un programa *to develop a program*
el **desastre** *disaster*
desayunarse *to eat breakfast*
el **desayuno** *breakfast*
descansar *to rest*
el **descanso** *rest*
el **descuento** *discount*
    ¡Menudo descuento! *What a discount! (ironic)*
desear *to want, desire, wish*
el **deseo** *desire, wish*
el **desfile** *parade*

la **desgracia** *misfortune*
el **desinfectante** *disinfectant*
desinflado, -a *flat (tire, etc.)*
el **desodorante** *deodorant*
despegar *to take off (plane)*
el **despegue** *take-off (plane)*
el **despertador** *alarm clock*
despertar *to awake (someone)*
despertarse *to awake (oneself)*
después *after*
después de que *after*
destruir *to destroy*
el/la **detective** *detective*
detener *to stop, detain; to arrest*
¡Deténganlo! *Stop him!*
detrás de *behind*
devolver *to return (something)*
el **día** *day*
los días laborables *workdays*
el **diálogo** *dialog*
el **dibujo** *drawing*
los dibujos animados *cartoons*
diciembre *December*
el **dictador, -a** *dictator*
la **dictadura** *dictatorship*
diecinueve *nineteen*
dieciocho *eighteen*
dieciséis *sixteen*
diecisiete *seventeen*
el **diente** *tooth*
cepillo de dientes *toothbrush*
pasta de dientes *toothpaste*
la **dieta** *diet*
seguir una dieta *to follow a diet*
diez *ten*
diferente *different*
difícil *difficult*
Diga. *Hello (on the phone, only).*
el **dinero** *money*
¡Dios mío! *My God!*
diptongos *diphthongs*
la **dirección** *address; direction, management*
dirigir *to direct*
el **disco** *record; dish antenna*
aparato de discos compactos *CD player*
el disco compacto *compact disc (CD)*
Disculpe(n). *Excuse me. I'm sorry.*
Disculpe, sí que me he equivocado. *I'm sorry. I have indeed made a mistake.*
disminuirse *to lessen, diminish*

Los dolores comenzaron a disminuir. *The pains began to diminish.*
Dispense(n). *Excuse me. I'm sorry.*
Dispense, no pensaba molestarle. *Pardon me, I didn't mean to bother you.*
distinguir *to distinguish*
la **diversión** *diversion, amusement, entertainment*
diversiones acuáticas *water sports*
divertirse *to enjoy oneself*
¡Que se diviertan! *Enjoy yourselves!*
la **divisa** *currency*
el **doblaje** *dubbling*
doblar *to dub*
doce *twelve*
el **doctor, -a** *doctor*
el **dólar** *dollar*
el **dolor** *ache, pain; sorrow*
dolor agudo/constante *sharp/constant pain*
el dolor de cabeza *headache*
el dolor de estómago *stomachache*
tener dolores *to have pains*
doméstico *household*
el **domingo** *Sunday*
Don/Doña *title of respect (m./f.)*
¿dónde? *where?*
¿A dónde vas? *Where are you going?*
¿De dónde es usted? *Where are you from?*
dormir *to sleep*
el **dormitorio** *bedroom*
dos *two*
los dos *both*
doscientos, -as *two hundred*
la **ducha** *shower*
la **duda** *doubt*
dudar *to doubt*
durante *during*

E

echar *to mail*
echar una carta al buzón *to mail a letter*
el **editorial** *editorial (newspaper)*
efectivo, -a *effective, certain, actual*
el **efectivo** *money, cash*
eficazmente *effectively*
...eh... *...uh...*

el ejemplo *example*
   por ejemplo *for example*
el ejercicio *exercise*
   hacer ejercicios *to exercise*
el *the (def. art.)*
él *he*
la elección *election*
la electricidad *electricity*
elegir *to select, elect*
ella *she*
ellos, ellas *they*
el embrague *clutch*
la emergencia *emergency*
   ¡Es una emergencia! *It's an*
    emergency!
la emisión *broadcast*
emitir *to broadcast*
emocionante *thrilling*
el empaste *filling*
   el empaste de la raíz *root canal*
empezar *to begin*
el empleado, -a *employee*
en *in, on*
   en blanco y negro *in black and white*
   en casa de *at the home of*
   en cuanto a *as for, as regards*
   en julio *in July*
   en lugar de *instead of, in place of*
   en medio de *in the middle of*
   en punto *sharp, on the dot*
   en realidad *in reality, actually*
   en seguida *at once, immediately*
   en verano *in summer*
enamorarse de *to fall in love with*
encantador, -a *charming*
encantar *to love*
   encantarle a uno *to like*
   Me encanta esta pieza. *I like this play.*
encender *to turn on (lights, TV)*
las encías *gums (mouth)*
encoger *to shrink (material)*
encontrar *to find, meet*
endosar *to endorse*
enfadarse *to get angry*
enfermo, -a *sick, ill, diseased*
el enfermo, -a *patient; invalid*
enfrente de *in front of; opposite*
enjuagar *to rinse*
el enjuague bucal *mouthwash*
el enlace *linking (pronunciation)*
la ensalada *salad*
   ensalada mixta *tossed salad*
entender *to understand*

No entiendo nada. *I don't understand*
   anything.
la entrada *entrance; ticket*
   Deme dos entradas para la platea.
    Give me two tickets in the orchestra.
entrar (en) *to enter*
entre *between*
la entrega *delivery*
   entrega inmediata *special delivery*
   entrega nocturna *overnight delivery*
entregar *to give, deliver*
entretener *to entertain*
entretenerse *to entertain oneself, have*
   a good time
el entretenimiento *amusement*
la entrevista *interview*
entrevistar *to interview*
entrevistarle a alguien *to interview*
   someone
enviar *to send, mail*
   Quiero enviar una carta. *I want to*
    mail a letter.
   por vía aérea/superficie *by*
    air/surface mail
envolver *to wrap*
   envolver regalos *to wrap presents*
el equipaje *baggage*
   facturar el equipaje *to check baggage*
el equipo *equipment*
   equipo de música/sonido
    music/sound equipment
   equipo de video *video equipment*
   equipo estereofónico *stereo equipment*
equivocarse *to be mistaken*
escalera *staircase*
   bajar/subir la escalera *to go down/up*
    the stairs
escapar *to escape*
   intentar escapar *to attempt escape*
la escena *scene*
escoger *to choose*
   escoger asientos *to choose seats*
escribir *to write*
   escribir felicitaciones *to write greeting*
    cards
escuchar *to listen*
ese, esa, esos, esas *that, those (adj.)*
ése, ésa, ésos, ésas *that one, those*
   (ones) (pron.)
el esmalte *enamel*
eso *that thing, idea, concept (pron.)*
especial *special*
la especialidad *specialty*

especialidad de la casa *house specialty*

las especias *spices*

el espectador, -a *spectator*

el espejo *mirror*

esperar *to hope*

el esposo/la esposa *husband/wife*

el esquí acuático *water skiing*

esquiar *to ski*

la esquina *corner*

en la esquina *on the corner*

la estación *season*

estacionar *to park*

el estadio *stadium*

la estampilla *stamp*

estar *to be*

¿Es usted de . . . ? *Are you from . . . ?*

Está bien. *It's all right./Okay.*

Están cansados. *They are tired.*

estar de pie *to be standing*

estar desinflado *to be flat*

estar dispuesto, -a *to be ready to*

estar enfermo, -a *to be sick*

estar listo, -a *to be available, to be ready*

estar ocupado, -a *to be busy*

estar para/a punto de *to be about to*

estar por *to be in favor of*

estar sano, -a *to be healthy*

estar seguro, -a *to be sure*

estar triste *to be sad*

Estoy bien. *I am well.*

este, esta, estos, estas *this, these (adj.)*

esta noche *tonight*

éste, ésta, éstos, éstas *this one, these (ones) (pron.)*

el estereofónico *stereo; stereophonic*

equipo estereofónico *stereo equipment*

esto *this thing, idea, concept (pron.)*

el estómago *stomach*

el/la estrella *star (performer); (f.) star (sky)*

estrenarse *to open (a show)*

el estreno *opening (show)*

el/la estudiante *student*

estudiar *to study*

la estufa *stove*

la etiqueta *price tag, sales tag*

evitar *to avoid*

el examen *quiz, test*

examinar *to examine*

excelente *excellent*

excluir *to exclude*

la exhibición *exhibition, showing*

exhibir *to show*

¿Qué exhiben esta noche? *What are they showing tonight?*

el éxito *hit, success*

expresión *expression*

expresión de cortesía *polite expression*

extensión *extension (telephone, etc.)*

extra *extra*

el extranjero, -a *foreigner*

F

la fábrica *factory*

fácil *easy*

fácilmente *easily*

facturar *to check*

facturar el equipaje *to check baggage*

la falda *skirt*

faltar *to lack*

faltarle a uno *to need, to be lacking*

Me falta el tiempo para descansar. *I need time to rest.*

la familia *family*

el farmacéutico, -a *pharmacist*

la farmacia *pharmacy*

la fatiga *fatigue, weariness*

fatigar *to tire; to annoy*

favorito, -a *favorite*

el fax *facsimile, fax*

febrero *February*

la fecha *date*

poner la fecha *to date, write the date*

la felicitación *greeting*

escribir felicitaciones *to write greeting cards*

felicitar *to greet, congratulate*

feliz *happy*

¡Felices fiestas! *Happy holidays!*

¡Feliz Navidad! *Merry Christmas!*

felizmente *happily, fortunately*

fenomenal *phenomenal*

feo, -a *ugly*

el feriado *holiday*

Día de la Acción de Gracias *Thanksgiving Day*

Día de la Raza *Columbus Day*

Día de los Enamorados *Valentine's Day*

Día de los Trabajadores *Labor Day*

el Año Nuevo *New Year*

el Pascuas *Easter*

la Cuaresma *Lent*

la Nochebuena *Christmas Eve*

la Nochevieja *New Year's Eve*

las Navidades *Christmas*

los Reyes *Epiphany*
Víspera de Todos los Santos
Halloween
festejar *to celebrate*
festejar el cumpleaños *to celebrate one's birthday*
el festival *festival*
el festival de cine *film festival*
la fiebre *fever; excitement*
tener fiebre *to have fever*
la fiesta *party*
la fila *row*
el film *movie*
la filosofía *philosophy*
el fin *end*
el fin de semana *weekend*
el final *end, final*
al final *finally, at last*
las finanzas *finances, financial pages (newspaper)*
firmar *to sign*
¿Dónde firmo el contrato de arrendamiento? *Where do I sign the leasing contract?*
firmar un cheque *to sign a check*
el formulario *form*
llenar un formulario *to fill out a form*
el franco *franc*
frecuente *frequent*
frecuentemente *frequently*
los frenos *brakes*
la fresa *strawberry*
fresco, -a *fresh, cool*
los frijoles *kidney beans*
frijoles negros *black beans*
frío, -a *cold*
la fruta *fruit*
la frutería *fruit store*
el fuego *fire*
los fuegos artificiales *fireworks*
fuerte *strong*
fumar *to smoke*
sección de no fumar *non-smoking section*
la función *show (play, film, etc.)*
el fútbol *soccer*
fútbol norteamericano *U.S. football*
el/la futbolista *soccer player*

G

la gala *gala affair*
la galería *balcony*
el ganador, -a *winner*

salir ganador *to win*
ganar *to earn, win*
ganarse la vida *to earn a living*
el garaje *garage*
la garantía *guarantee*
la garganta *throat*
el gas *gas*
la gaseosa *carbonated mineral water*
la gasolina *gasoline*
la super *super gasoline*
la gasolinera *gas station*
el gasto *expense*
general *general (adj.), usual*
el general *general*
la gente *people, crowd*
el/la gerente *manager*
gigante *gigantic*
el gigante *giant*
la gira *outing, trip*
el giro *money order*
giro postal *postal money order*
el gobernador, -a *governor*
el golf *golf*
gordo, -a *fat, stout*
el gordo *first prize in lottery (Spain)*
gozar *to enjoy, to possess*
Goza de buena salud. *She enjoys good health.*
la grabadora *recorder*
grabadora para cintas *tape recorder*
video-grabadora *video recorder; VCR*
Gracias. *Thank you.*
las gradas *bleachers, tiers of seats (stadium)*
la gramática *grammar*
gramática y usos *grammar and usages*
gran, grande *great (before noun); big (after noun)*
grasoso, -a *greasy*
gratuito, -a *free*
gris *gray*
gritar *to yell*
la guanábana *bread fruit*
guapo, -a *good-looking, attractive*
guardar *to store, keep; to guard, take care of*
la guayaba *guava*
la guerra *war*
la guía telefónica *telephone book*
el guineo *sweet banana*
gustar *to like, be pleasing to*
Como Ud. guste. *As you please.*
¿Le gusta a Ud. . . . ? *Do you like . . . ?*
Me gusta. *I like (it, him, her, you).*

Me gusta mucho este modelo. *I like this model a lot.*
(Me) gustaría (+ infinitive) *I would like to . . .*
No me gustan. *I don't like them.*
el gusto *taste; pleasure, liking*
estar a gusto *to feel at home, comfortable*
¡Mucho gusto (en conocerle)! *It's a pleasure to meet you.*

H

haber (see also hay, below) *to have; to be, exist*
haber de (+ infinitive) *to be (supposed) to*
Han de llegar el sábado. *They are to arrive on Saturday.*
había *there was, there were*
las habichuelas *beans*
la habitación *room*
habitación doble *double room*
Quisiera una habitación por una noche. *I'd like a room for one night.*
hablar *to talk, speak*
hacer *to make, do; to be (cold, warm, etc.)*
Hace buen/mal tiempo. *It's good/bad weather.*
Hace calor/frío. *It's warm/cold.*
Hace + time expression + preterite *ago*
hacer compras *to shop*
hacer daño a *to harm*
hacer el favor de (+ infinitive) *please (+ command)*
hacer falta *to lack*
hacer la maleta *to pack one's suitcase*
hacer las uñas *to do one's nails*
hacer un viaje *to take a trip*
hacer una llamada *to make a call*
hacer una pregunta *to ask a question*
hacer una reserva *to make a reservation*
¿Qué tiempo hace? *What's the weather like?*
hacerse *to become*
hasta *until*
Hasta luego. *See you later.*
Hasta mañana. *See you tomorrow.*
hasta que *until*
hay *there is, there are*

hay que (+ infinitive) *it is necessary; one must.*
Hay que hacerlo. *It has to be done. One must do it.*
hay (+ noun + *que* + infinitive) *there is/are (+ noun + verb)*
Hay trabajo que hacer. *There is work to do.*
No hay de qué. *You're welcome.*
el helado *ice cream*
helar *to freeze*
herir *to wound*
el hermanito *younger brother*
el hermano, -a *brother, sister*
el hijo, -a *son, daughter*
los hijos *children*
hincharse *to swell*
la hinchazón *swelling*
hispano, -a *hispanic*
el historial de vida *résumé*
¡Hola! *Hello!*
el hombre *man*
el hombro *shoulder*
la hora *clock time*
¿Qué hora es? *What time is it?*
el horario *schedule*
el horno *oven*
hospedarse *to stay at a hotel*
¿Por cuántos días se hospedará en el hotel? *How many days will you be staying at the hotel?*
el hotel *hotel*
en el hotel *at the hotel*
hoy *today*
hoy día *nowadays*
la humedad *humidity, moisture*
húmedo, -a *humid*

I

la idea *idea*
Es una buena idea. *It's a good idea.*
impedir *to prevent*
el impermeable *raincoat*
importante *important*
Es importante. *It is important.*
importar *to import*
imposible *impossible*
Es imposible. *It is impossible.*
los impresos *printed matter*
incluir *to include*
indicar *to indicate*
ineficaz *ineffective*

la **información** *information; inquiry*
la **informática** *computer science*
    programa de informática *computer program*
inmediatamente *immediately*
inmediato, -a *immediate*
insistir *to insist*
    insistir en *to insist upon*
    insistir en que *to insist that*
instalar *to install*
la **instrucción** *instruction*
el **instructor, -a** *instructor*
inteligente *intelligent*
intentar *to attempt*
el **interés** *interest*
    tasa de interés *rate of interest*
interesar *to interest*
interesarse en *to be interested in*
internacional *international*
el **invierno** *winter*
la **invitación** *invitation*
invitar *to invite*
ir *to go*
el **izquierdo, -a** *left, left hand/side*
    a la izquierda *to the left*

J

el **jabón** *soap; cake of soap*
el **jamón** *ham*
el **jarabe** *syrup*
el **jardín** *garden*
el **jeans** *jeans*
el **jefe/la jefa** *boss*
el **jogging** *jogging*
joven *young*
el/la **joven** *youngster*
    los jóvenes *young people*
el **jueves** *Thursday*
    jugar a *to play*
      jugar al tenis *to play tennis*
      jugar al volibol *to play volleyball*
el **jugo** *juice*
julio *July*
junio *June*
junto, -a *together*
jurar *to swear, take oath*

K

el **kilómetro** *kilometer*

L

la *her, you (fml.); it (f.); the (def. art.)*
el **labio** *lip*
el **lado** *side*
    al lado de *next to*
el **ladrón/la ladrona** *thief*
lamentar *to regret, lament*
la **lana** *wool*
largo, -a *long*
el **largo metraje** *feature-length film*
las *them (people and things); you (fml. pl. and f.); the (pl. def. art.)*
latino/latina *U.S. citizen or resident of Hispanic background*
el **lavado** *washing, laundry*
la **lavandería** *laundry*
el **lavandero, -a** *launderer*
el **lavaplatos** *dishwasher*
lavar *to wash*
    lavar a seco *to dry clean*
    lavado y planchado *washing and ironing*
lavarse *to wash oneself*
le *to/for him, her, you (fml. ind. obj. pron.)*
la **lección** *lesson*
la **lechería** *dairy store*
el **lechón** *roast suckling pig*
la **lechuga** *lettuce*
leer *to read*
la **legumbre** *vegetable*
lejos (de) *far away (from)*
la **lengua** *tongue; language*
les *to/for them (m. f. pl.); to/for you (fml. pl. ind. obj. pron.)*
levantar *to lift, raise*
    levantar la voz *to raise one's voice*
levantarse *to get oneself up*
la **ley** *law; legal standard of quality, weight or measure*
la **libra esterlina** *pound sterling*
el **libro** *book*
el **límite** *limit, boundary*
el **limpiaparabrisas** *windshield wiper*
limpiar *to clean*
    limpiar la habitación *to clean the room*
la **limpieza de los dientes** *cleaning (teeth)*
la **lista** *list*
listo, -a *ready*
    estar listo *to be ready*
lo *him, you (fml.); it (m. dir. obj. pron.)*
    lo importante *the important thing*

local *local*

la loción *lotion*

    loción bronceadora *suntan lotion*

los *them (people and things, m. pl. and m. + f. pl.); you (fml. pl. dir. obj. pron.)*

lucir *to shine*

    ¡Cómo vas a lucir! *How beautiful you'll look!*

el luchador *fighter, wrestler*

la luna *moon*

el lunes *Monday*

la luz *light; daylight*

LL

la llamada *call; marginal note*

    llamada de larga distancia *long distance call*

    llamada de persona a persona *person to person call*

    llamada por cobrar *collect call*

llamar *to call*

llamarse *to be called, to be named*

    ¿Cómo se llama Ud.? *What is your name?*

    Me llamo . . . *My name is . . .*

    Se llama . . . *His (her, your) name is . . .*

la llanta *tire*

    ¿Tiene Ud. una llanta de repuesto? *Do you have a spare tire?*

la llave *key*

    la carta-llave *card-key*

llegar *to arrive; to come; to reach, succeed*

    llegar a ser *to become*

    puerta de llegada/salida *arrival/departure gate*

llenar *to fill, fill out*

    llenar un formulario *to fill out a form*

    llenar una receta *to fill a prescription*

    Llene el depósito. *Fill the gas tank.*

llevar *to carry, bring; to take (time); to wear (clothing)*

    ¿Cuánto tiempo lleva el viaje? *How long does the trip take?*

    Lléveselo. *Take it.*

llorar *to cry, lament*

llover *to rain*

    Llueve./Está lloviendo. *It's raining.*

M

la madre *mother*

el madrugador, -a *early-riser*

el maíz *corn*

    rosetas de maíz *popcorn*

mal, malo, -a *bad*

la maleta *suitcase*

el maletero *porter*

la mancha *stain*

    sacar una mancha *to take out a stain*

manera *manner*

    de manera que *so that, so as to*

el mango *mango; handle*

el maní *peanut*

la manicura *manicure*

la mano *hand*

mantener *to maintain, support; to hold, keep*

    mantenerse en forma *to keep in shape*

la manzana *apple*

mañana *tomorrow*

    pasado mañana *the day after tomorrow*

la mañana *morning*

    de la mañana *in the morning; a.m.*

    mañana por la mañana *tomorrow morning*

el mapa *map*

el maquillaje *make-up*

la máquina *machine (in general)*

    la máquina filmadora *video recorder (lit., filming machine)*

    la máquina de lavar y secar *washer/dryer*

el mar *sea*

maravilloso, -a *marvelous, wonderful*

la marca *brand name*

marcar *to dial*

el mareo *dizziness; motion-, sea-, air-, travel-sickness*

los mariscos *seafood*

marrón *brown*

el martes *Tuesday*

marzo *March*

más *more; most; over; besides; plus*

    más grande *bigger*

    más pequeño *smaller*

matar *to kill*

el matador *primary bullfighter; the one who kills the bull*

mayo *May*

mayor *older*

al por mayor *wholesale*
la mayor parte de *most of, the majority of*
me *me; to me; myself*
la medianoche *midnight*
las medias *stockings*
el/la médico *doctor*
   en el consultorio del médico *at the doctor's office*
medio, -a *half*
el mediodía *noon*
los medios *means*
   los medios de comunicación *means of communication, media*
mejor *better; rather*
   Es mejor. *It is better.*
menor *younger*
   al por menor *retail*
menos *fewer; minor*
   por lo menos *at least*
-mente *adverbial ending "-ly"*
el menú *menu*
el mercadeo *marketing*
el mercado *market*
   mercado negro *black market*
   mercado paralelo *parallel market*
el mes *month*
la mesa *table*
el mesero, -a *waiter, waitress*
mi, mis *my (poss. adj.)*
mí *me (prep. obj. pron.)*
mientras *while*
el miércoles *Wednesday*
mil *thousand*
millón *one million*
mirar *to look at, watch*
   mirando la televisión *watching television*
mismo, -a *same*
   ahí mismo *right there*
la mitad *half*
   la mitad del precio *half price*
la moda *fashion, style*
el/la modelo *model*
moderno *modern*
la modista *seamstress, dressmaker*
molestar *to bother*
Momentito. *Just a moment. One moment.*
la moneda *money, coin*
moreno, -a *brunette*
morir(se) *to die*
el mostrador *ticket counter*

mostrar *to show*
   mostrar su pasaporte *to show one's passport*
el motor *motor, engine*
mucho, -a *much, many, a great deal; hard*
mudarse *to move (one's residence)*
   Tengo que mudarme. *I have to move.*
la muela *tooth*
la mujer *woman*
la multa *penalty, fine*
mundial *worldwide*
el mundo *world*
el músculo *muscle*
musculoso *muscular*
la música *music*
muy *very*

N

la nación *nation*
nacional *national*
la nacionalidad *nationality*
nada *nothing*
   De nada. *You're welcome. It's nothing.*
   nada más *nothing else, nothing more*
nadar *to swim*
nadie *no one, nobody*
la naranja *orange*
la nariz *nose*
la natación *swimming*
la naturaleza *nature*
las Navidades *Christmas*
   ¡Feliz Navidad! *Merry Christmas!*
Nochebuena *Christmas Eve*
la neblina *mist, light fog*
necesario, -a *necessary*
   Es necesario. *It is necessary.*
necesitar *to need*
   Necesito información. *I need (a piece of/some) information.*
negar *to deny*
los negocios *business*
negro, -a *black*
   en blanco y negro *in black and white*
nervioso, -a *nervous*
nevar *to snow*
   Nieva. *It's snowing.*
el nieto/la nieta *grandchild*
el nilón *nylon*
ningún, ninguno, ninguna *none, not any*

no *no, not*
la noche *evening, p.m.*
    de/por la noche *in the evening, p.m.*
la Nochebuena *Christmas Eve*
la Nochevieja *New Year's Eve*
el nombre *name; noun*
    Mi nombre es . . . *My name is . . .*
    nombre de pila *given name*
el nopal *small cactus*
    normal *normal*
    normalmente *normally*
    nos *us; to us; ourselves (obj. pron.)*
    nosotros, nosotras *we; us (subj. and
        prep. obj. pron.)*
    notas culturales *cultural notes*
las noticias *news*
el noticiero *news broadcast*
la (tele)novela *soap opera*
    Esta noche pasa nuestra telenovela
        favorita. *Our favorite soap opera is
        on tonight.*
    noveno, -a *ninth*
    noventa *ninety*
    noviembre *November*
el novio, -a *boyfriend, groom, girlfriend,
        bride*
    nuevamente *once again*
    nueve *nine*
    Nueva York *New York*
    nuevo, -a *new*
el número *number*
    número equivocado *wrong number*

O

    obedecer *to obey*
la obligación *responsibility; obligation*
la obra *work, labor; play, opus (theater);
        building; repairs (house); deed,
        action*
la obturación *filling (tooth)*
    ochenta *eighty*
    ocho *eight*
    ochocientos, -as *eight hundred*
    octavo, -a *eighth*
    octubre *October*
    ocupado, -a *busy*
    ocuparse *to busy oneself*
        ocuparse de *to busy oneself with, to be
            concerned with*
la oferta *(special) offer*
    hacer una oferta *to make an offer*

¡Hágame una oferta! *Make me an
    offer!*
la oficina *office*
    ofrecer *to offer*
    ofrecerle una posición *to offer
        someone a job*
    ojalá (que) *if only . . . ; I wish, hope
        (that) . . .*
el ojo *eye; attention, care; keyhole*
    ¡Olé! *Bravo!*
    oler *to smell*
    olvidarse *to forget*
    once *eleven*
el operador, -a *operator*
el operario, -a *factory worker*
    opinar *to give an opinion*
el ordenador *computer (Spain)*
la oreja *(outer) ear*
    os *you; to you (fam. pl.); yourselves
        (reflexive, obj. pron.)*
    ostentoso *ostentatious*
el otoño *autumn*
    otro, -a, -os, -as *other(s)*
    otras expresiones *other expressions*
    otra vez *again*

P

el padre *father*
    pagar *to pay*
    pagar con efectivo *to pay cash*
    pagar al mes *to pay monthly*
    ¿Cuánto paga Ud. al mes? *How much
        do you pay monthly?*
el pago *payment*
    pagos mensuales *monthly payments*
el país *country*
la panadería *bakery*
los pantalones *pants*
la pantalla *screen*
el pañuelo *handkerchief*
el papel *paper; role, part*
la papa *potato*
la papeleta *slip (deposit, etc.)*
el paquete *package*
el par *pair*
    un par de zapatos *a pair of shoes*
    para *for, toward, in order to*
el parabrisas *windshield*
el/los paraguas *umbrella*
    pararse *to stop; to stall*
    El motor se paró. *The motor stalled.*

el **parasol** *beach umbrella*
parecer *to seem*
el **parentesco** *family relationship*
el **pariente/la parienta** *relative, family
member*
participar *to participate; to share (in)*
la **partida** *departure*
partir *to leave*
¿A qué hora parte el tren? *At what
time does the train leave?*
el **pasaje** *fare; ticket*
pasaje de ida y vuelta *round-trip ticket*
el **pasajero, -a** *traveler, passenger*
el **pasaporte** *passport*
pasar *to spend (time); to show*
pasar novelas (películas) *to show soap
operas (films)*
pasar por *to pass by*
el **Pascuas/La Pascua Florida** *Easter,
Passover*
domingo de Pascuas *Easter Sunday*
Semana Santa *Easter week*
la **pastilla** *pill, tablet*
la **patata** *potato (Spain)*
el **pato** *duck*
el **pecho** *chest; bosom*
pedir *to request, ask for*
pedir direcciones *to ask for directions*
pedir un préstamo *to ask for a loan*
pegar *to hit; to stick*
el **peinado** *hairdo*
peinarse *to comb one's hair*
el **peine** *comb*
la **película** *film, movie*
película sentimental *romantic film*
pelirrojo, -a *red hair color*
el **pelirrojo** *redhead*
el **pelo** *hair*
pelo teñido *dyed hair*
la **peluca** *wig*
la **peluquería** *hairdresser's shop*
el **peluquero, -a** *hairdresser*
pensar *to think, believe*
pensar en *to think of/about; to direct
one's thoughts to*
pensar de *to think of; to have an
opinion of*
peor *worse*
pequeño, -a *small*
perder *to lose*
Perdón./Perdóneme. *Excuse me; I'm
sorry (when you have caused some
harm, confusion or disappointment).*

perfectamente *perfectly; fine, excellent*
el **periódico** *newspaper*
permanecer *to remain*
la **permanente** *permanent (hair style)*
Permiso./Con Permiso. *Excuse me;
pardon me (to attract attention or
ask permission).*
permitir *to permit, let, allow*
pero *but*
la **persona** *person*
el **personal** *personnel*
Departamento de Personal *Personnel
Department*
pesar *to weigh*
la **pesca** *fishing*
la pesca marina *deep-sea fishing*
el **pescado** *fish (caught)*
el **pez** *fish (live)*
el **piano** *piano*
la **picazón** *itching*
el **pie** *foot, leg; footing, basis*
la **piel** *skin*
la **pierna** *leg*
la **pieza** *piece; play; room*
el **pijama** *pajamas*
los **pimentones** *peppers*
la **piña** *pineapple*
la **piscina** *swimming pool*
piscina calentada *heated pool*
el **piso** *floor (building), storey*
la **pista** *(running) track; clue*
el **plan** *plan*
la **plana** *page*
primera plana *first page*
planchar *to iron, press (clothes)*
la **planta** *sole (foot)*
el **plátano** *plantain*
la **platea** *orchestra (in a theater)*
butaca de platea *orchestra seat*
el **plato** *dish*
plato del día *daily special*
la **playa** *beach*
en la playa *at the beach*
dar a la playa *to face/be on the beach*
la **plaza** *plaza; square*
plaza de toros *bullring*
poco, -a *few*
poco a poco *a little by little*
por poco *almost*
poder *to be able, can*
¿Podría Ud. (+ infinitive) *Would
you . . . ?*
puede ser *perhaps*

el **policía** *policeman*
    la mujer policía *policewoman*
    ¡Policía! *Police!*
la **policía** *police force*
el **poliéster** *polyester*
la **política** *politics, policy*
el **político, -a** *politician*
el **pollo** *chicken*
  poner *to put, place*
    poner la fecha *to date, to write the date*
    poner la mesa *to set the table*
    poner la televisión *to turn on the TV*
    poner un botón *to put on a button*
    Quiero que pongas la mesa. *I want you to set the table.*
  ponerse *to put on (clothing); to become*
    ¡No se ponga nervioso! *Don't get nervous.*
  por *by, through, for*
    al por mayor *wholesale*
    al por menor *retail*
    por aquí *this way*
    por ciento *percent*
    por ejemplo *for example*
    por favor *please*
    por fin *finally, at last*
    por la mañana/tarde/noche *in the morning/afternoon/evening*
    por lo general *generally*
    por lo menos *at least*
    por poco *almost*
    por supuesto *of course*
    por todas partes *everywhere*
    por vía aérea *by air mail*
    por vía superficie *by surface mail*
    un cuarto por ciento *one-quarter percent*
  ¿por qué? *why?*
porque *because*
portátil *portable*
posible *possible*
    Es posible. *It is possible.*
    ¡No es posible! *It isn't possible.*
postularse *to become a candidate*
el **precio** *price*
    precio fijo *fixed price*
    la mitad del precio *half price*
    precio máximo *top price*
    último precio *final price*
precioso, -a *handsome, precious; beautiful*
preferible *preferable*
    Es preferible. *It is preferable.*

preguntar *to ask, inquire*
    ¿Puedo preguntarle algo? *May I ask you something?*
el **premio** *prize*
  prender *to seize; to pin; to arrest, capture*
la **prensa** *press*
  preocuparse (por/de) *to worry (about)*
    ¡No os preocupéis! *Don't worry!*
  presentar *to present, to introduce, to show*
    Le presento a Juan. *I'd like you to meet Juan.*
  presentarse *to put in an appearance, to show up; to present oneself*
el **presidente/la presidenta** *president*
el **preso** *prisoner*
el **préstamo** *loan*
  prestar *to lend*
    prestar atención *to pay attention*
la **primavera** *spring*
primer, primero, -a *first*
el **primo, -a** *cousin*
el **problema** *problem*
la **procesadora de palabras** *wordprocessor*
la **producción** *production*
  producir *to produce*
el **producto** *product*
el **programa** *program*
    desarrollar un programa *to develop a program*
  prometer *to promise*
  pronto *prompt; quick*
    lo más pronto posible *as soon as possible*
la **pronunciación** *pronunciation*
propio, -a *own, self; fit, suitable*
el/la **protagonista** *star (performer)*
  proteger *to protect*
la **proteína** *protein*
la **publicación** *publication*
el **público** *audience*
el **pueblo** *village, town; people, nation*
el **puerco** *pork*
la **puerta** *gate*
    puerta de embarque *departure gate*
    puerta de llegada *arrival gate*
    . . . **pues** . . . *well, well then*
el **puñal** *knife, dagger*
el **puntaje** *score (game)*
la **puntuación** *score (game)*

Q

que *that, which, who, whom; than*
¿qué? *what? how?*
  ¡Qué bueno! *How wonderful!*
  ¿Qué hacemos? *What do we do?*
  ¿Qué hay de nuevo? *What's new?*
  ¿Qué pasa? *What's going on?*
  ¡Qué ruido! *What a noise!*
  ¿Qué tal? *How's it going? How are
    things?*
  ¡Qué va! *What nonsense!*
quedar(se) *to remain; to have left; to fit;
  to be*
  No me quedan entradas. *I don't have
    any tickets left.*
  ¿Cuántos dólares le quedan? *How
    many dollars does he (do you) have
    left?*
  Le queda un dólar. *He has one dollar
    left.*
  Quédese sentado. *Remain seated.*
  Este traje le queda bien. *This suit fits
    you well.*
  Esto queda entre los dos. *This is just
    between the two of us.*
querer *to wish, want, desire; to like; to
  love*
  querer a *to love*
  Quiero a mis padres. *I love my
    parents.*
  querer decir *to mean*
  Quisiera + infinitive *I would like to ...*
querido, -a *beloved, dear*
quien, -es *who, whom*
  ¿Con quién ...? *With whom ...?*
  ¿A quién ...? *To whom ....?*
  ¿Para quién ...? *For whom ...?*
  ¿De quién ...? *Whose ...? Of whom ...?*
quieto, -a *quiet, still*
la quijada *jaw*
el quilómetro *kilometer*
quince *fifteen*
quinceañera *girl's fifteenth birthday
  party*
quinientos, -as *five hundred*
quinto, -a *fifth*
quitar *to take (from someone)*
  quitar la llanta *to take off the tire*
  ¿Qué se les quitó? *What was taken
    from you?*
  quitarse (+ article of clothing) *to take
    off* (+ article of clothing)
quizás *perhaps*

R

el/la radio *radio*
  el radio-cassette (para cintas)
    radio/cassette player
la radiografía *X ray*
  sacar una radiografía *to take an x-ray*
la raíz *root*
rápidamente *rapidly*
rápido, -a *rapid*
el rato *a short while*
  Nos vemos en un rato. *We'll see each
    other shortly.*
la raya *part (hair)*
la razón *reason; right (see* tener)
reaccionar *to react*
la realidad *reality; truth*
realizar *to accomplish, perform, realize*
la rebaja *discount*
  rebaja de veinticinco por ciento *a 25%
    discount*
el recado *errand*
  recados domésticos *household
    errands*
la recepción *lobby, reception desk*
el/la recepcionista *receptionist*
la receta *prescription*
recetar *to prescribe*
recibir *to receive, accept*
el recibo *receipt*
recoger *to pick up*
recomendar *to recommend*
la red *network*
reemplazar *to replace*
  reemplazar un botón *to replace a
    button*
el refresco *soft drink, refreshment*
el refrigerador *refrigerator*
regalar *to give a gift*
el regalo *gift, present*
  envolver regalos *to wrap gifts*
regatear *to bargain*
el régimen *program, regimen; diet*
reírse *to laugh*
  reírse de *to laugh at, laugh about*
el reloj *watch, clock*
el remedio *remedy; cure; help*
  No me queda otro remedio. *I have no
    other choice.*
la renta *rent*
renunciar una cuota *to waive a fee*
reparar *to repair*
el reparto *cast (theater)*
repaso *review*

repente: de repente *suddenly*
repetir *to repeat*
  Repita eso, por favor. *Please repeat that.*
la representación *performance*
el/la representante *representative, congressperson*
  representar *to represent; to express; to perform*
  representar un papel *to play a role*
el repuesto *spare part, extra*
la reseña *review (book, film, theater)*
la reserva *reservation*
  hacer una reserva *to make a reservation*
  Tengo una reserva. *I have a reservation.*
la reservación *reservation*
el resfriado *cold (illness)*
la respuesta *answer*
el restaurante *restaurant*
los resultados *results*
el resumen *résumé*
  retirar *to withdraw; to pull back; to conceal*
  retirar dinero *to withdraw money*
el retiro *withdrawal*
  hacer un retiro *to make a withdrawal*
  reunirse *to meet, get together*
  revisar *to check; to review*
  Revise la batería. *Check the battery.*
  Revise el aceite. *Check the oil.*
el revólver *gun, revolver*
los Reyes *Epiphany*
  rico, -a *rich*
el riesgo *risk*
el río *river*
el rizo *curl*
  robar *to rob*
el robo *robbery*
el rock *rock music*
  rodar *to film*
  rojo, -a *red*
la ropa *clothing*
la rosa *rose*
  roseta: rosetas de maíz *popcorn*
  rubio, -a *blond*
el ruido *noise*

S

el sábado *Saturday*
  saber *to know, know how to*

...sabe(s) ......*you know*...
sacar *to draw; to take out, pull out*
  sacar dinero *to withdraw money*
  sacar una mancha *to take out a stain*
  sacar una muela *to pull out a tooth*
  sacar una radiografía *to take an x-ray*
la sala *living room*
el salario *salary*
el saldo *balance*
la salida *exit*
  salir *to leave, go out*
  ¿De qué andén sale el tren? *From what platform does the train leave?*
  salir bien/mal *to come out well/poorly*
  salir de *to leave (a place); to go out of*
  salir ganador, -a *to win*
el salmón *salmon*
el salón *salon*
  el salón de belleza *beauty parlor*
la salsa *sauce*
la salud *health*
  ¡Salud! *Cheers!*
los saludos *greetings*
el/la salvavidas *lifeguard*
la santería *Afro-Caribbean spiritist religions*
el santo *saint, saint's (birth)day*
  Día de Todos los Santos *All Saint's Day*
el sastre *tailor*
la sastrería *tailor's shop*
el satélite *satellite*
  por satélite *by satellite*
  se *to him, her, it, you; oneself, himself, herself, itself; impersonal one, you, they (used to form passive obj. pron.)*
el secador *dryer*
  secar *to dry*
la sección *section*
  sección de no fumar *nonsmoking section*
la seda *silk*
  seguir *to follow; to pursue; to continue*
  Seguí sus instrucciones. *I followed your instructions.*
  según *according to*
  segundo, -a *second*
  seguramente *surely*
la seguridad *security*
  seguro, -a *sure*
el seguro *insurance; safety*
  Es seguro. *It is certain.*
  seguro social *social security*
  seis *six*

el sello *stamp*
la semana *week*
   el fin de semana *weekend*
   la semana pasada *last week*
   Semana Santa *Easter week*
el senador, -a *senator*
   sentar *to sit*
   ¡Siéntese! *Sit down! (fml.)*
   ¡Siéntate! *Sit down! (fam.)*
   sentir *to feel; to regret*
   Lo siento. *I'm sorry.*
   sentir vértigo *to feel dizzy*
el sentir *feeling, opinion*
   sentirse *to feel*
la señal *signal*
el señor *Mister, sir, gentleman*
la señora *Mrs., madam, Ms.*
la señorita *Miss, Ms.*
   septiembre *September*
   séptimo, -a *seventh*
la sequía *drought*
   ser *to be*
   Fue muy desagradable. *It was very unpleasant.*
   ser de *to be from*
   Soy de . . . *I am from . . .*
el servicio *service*
   servicio de carretera *road service*
   servicio de cuarto *room service*
   servir *to serve; to do a favor; to be for*
   ¿En qué puedo servirle? *How can I help you?*
   ¿Para qué sirve esta máquina? *What's this machine for?*
   No sirve para nada. *It's no good./It's good for nothing.*
   servirse de *to use, to make use of*
   sesenta *sixty*
   setenta *seventy*
   sexto, -a *sixth*
   si *if*
   sí *yes, indeed (emphatic)*
   Yo sí sé una cosa. *I do know one thing.*
   siempre *always; ever*
   siete *seven*
   similar *similar*
   simpático, -a *pleasant*
   simple *simple*
   sin *without*
   sin duda *without doubt*
   sintonizar *to tune in*
el sobrino, -a *nephew, niece*
   ¡Socorro! *Help!*
la soda *soda*

   el refresco *soft drink*
el sol *sun*
la solicitud *application*
la sombra *shade*
el sombrero *hat*
   sonar *to ring*
   soñar *to dream*
   soñar con *to dream about*
la sopa *soup*
   sopa del día *soup of the day*
   subir *to go up; to lift (something) up*
   subir a *to get on (the bus, train, etc.)*
la sucursal *branch (agency)*
el sueldo *salary*
la suerte *luck*
   Buena suerte. *Good luck.*
el suéter *sweater*
   sufrir *to suffer*
   sugerir *to suggest*
   sugerir tácticas de venta *to suggest sales tactics*
la super *super gasoline*
el supermercado *supermarket*
el surfe *surfing*
   hacer surfe *to go surfing*

T

el tacón *heel (shoe)*
la táctica *tactic*
   tal vez *maybe, perhaps*
   también *too, also*
   tan *so, so much; as, as much*
la taquilla *box office*
   la taquilla del teatro *theater box office*
   tarde *late*
   más tarde *later*
la tarde *afternoon*
   por/de la tarde *in the afternoon, p.m.*
la tarifa *fee*
la tarjeta postal *postcard*
   ¿Cuántos sellos necesito para una tarjeta postal? *How many stamps do I need for a postcard?*
la tasa *rate, price; appraisement, measure*
   tasa de cambio *exchange rate*
el taxi *taxi, cab*
el taxímetro *meter (of a taxi)*
la taza *cup (of coffee)*
   te *you; to you (fam.); yourself (fam. obj. pron.)*
el teatro *theater, playhouse*
la tela *cloth, material*

telefonear *to telephone*
el teléfono *telephone*
    por teléfono *by phone*
    la guía telefónica *telephone book*
la tele(visión) *television*
el televisor *television set*
    televisor de/a color *color TV set*
el telón *curtain (theater)*
    El telón sube a las ocho. *The curtain goes up at eight.*
temer *to fear*
temprano *early*
tener *to have, possess; to hold; to take; to be (hungry, warm, etc.)*
    tener acceso a *to have access*
    tener . . . años *to be . . . years old*
    tener calor/frío *to be warm/cold*
    tener cuidado *to be careful*
    tener en exhibición *to be showing*
    tener éxito *to be successful*
    tener ganas de *to feel like (doing something)*
    tener hambre/sed *to be hungry/thirsty*
    tener la bondad de + infinitive *please + infinitive*
    tener lugar *to take place*
    tener (mala) suerte *to be (un)lucky*
    tener miedo de *to be afraid of*
    tener planes *to have plans*
    tener prisa *to be in a hurry*
    tener que *to have to*
    tener sueño *to be sleepy*
    (no) tener razón *to be right (wrong)*
    tener tiempo *to have time*
    tener una cita *to have an appointment, date*
    ¿Qué tiene Ud.? *What's the matter with you?*
el tenis *tennis*
    jugar al tenis *to play tennis*
    la cancha de tenis *tennis court*
el/la tenista *tennis player*
  teñir *to bleach; to dye; to tint; to darken*
  tercer, tercero, -a *third*
  terrible *terrible*
el testigo *witness*
  ti *you (fam. prep. obj. pron.)*
el tiempo *weather*
la tienda *store*
las tijeras *scissors*
  tilde *accent mark, at, over the n (ñ)*
el tinte *color (of a dye)*
la tintorería *dry cleaner's*

el tintorero, -a *dry cleaner*
el tío, -a *uncle, aunt*
    los tíos *aunts and uncles*
tirar *to shoot*
el titular *headline*
la toalla *towel*
el tocadiscos *record player*
tocar *to touch; to play (an instrument); to ring; to concern, to interest*
    ¿A quién le toca? *Whose turn is it?*
    Me tocó un aumento. *I got a raise.*
    ¡No tocar! *Don't touch!*
    Toca el piano. *She plays the piano.*
    tocarle a uno *to be one's turn*
todavía *yet; still*
todavía no *not yet*
todo, -a, -os, -as *all, every*
todo el mundo *everybody*
el todo *everything*
tomar *to take; to eat; to drink*
    tomar a bien/mal *to take it well, the right way/the wrong way*
    tomar a broma *to take as a joke*
    tomar el almuerzo *to have lunch*
    tomar el autobús *to take the bus*
    tomar el desayuno *to have breakfast*
    tomar el pelo *to make fun of, to tease*
    tomar en cuenta *to take into account*
    tomar interés en *to take an interest in*
    tomar parte en *to take part in*
    tomar un trago *to have a(n alcoholic) drink*
el tomate *tomato*
el torero *bullfighter*
la tormenta *storm*
el toro *bull*
la tortilla *corn flour pancake (Mexico, Central America); omelette (Spain)*
la tos *cough*
    el jarabe para la tos *cough syrup*
    la pastilla para la tos *cough drop*
la tostada *(a piece of) toast*
  trabajar *to work*
el trabajo *work, job*
    buscando un trabajo *looking for a job*
    ¿Por qué quiere Ud. este trabajo? *Why do you want this job?*
  traducir *to translate*
  traer *to bring*
    ¿Puedo traerlo conmigo? *Can I bring it with me?*
la tragedia *tragedy*
el trago *drink (alcoholic)*

el traje *suit; costume*
    traje a medida *a made-to-order suit (dress)*
el trámite *procedure*
la transacción *transaction*
el transbordo *transfer*
el transporte *transportation*
tratar(se) *to treat; to deal; to try; to discuss*
    ¿De qué se trata? *What's it all about?*
    tratar de *to try to*
trece *thirteen*
treinta *thirty*
treinta y dos *thirty-two*
treinta y uno *thirty-one*
el tren *train*
    la estación ferroviaria/de trenes *train station*
tres *three*
    tres veces al día *three times a day*
triste *sad*
trocar *to exchange*
tú *you* (sg. fam. subj. pron.)
tumbarse *to lie down*

U

un, uno, -a *one*
la uña *nail*
    el esmalte de uñas *nail polish*
usar *to use, be accustomed to; to wear*
usted (Ud., Vd.) *you (sg. fml.)*
ustedes (Uds., Vds.) *you (pl. fml. and fam. in Latin America; fml. in Spain)*
usual *usual*
usualmente *usually*
las uvas *grapes*

V

las vacaciones *vacation*
    estar de vacaciones *to be on vacation*
    Estoy aquí de vacaciones. *I'm here on vacation.*
el vagón *car (of a train)*
    el vagón-restaurante *dining car*
    Vale. *Okay. (Spain)*
valer *to be worth*
    No vale tanto. *It's not worth that much.*

el valor *value, worth, merit*
varios, -as *several*
la vecindad *neighborhood*
veinte *twenty*
veinticinco *twenty-five*
veinticuatro *twenty-four*
veintidós *twenty-two*
veintinueve *twenty-nine*
veintiocho *twenty-eight*
veintiséis *twenty-six*
veintisiete *twenty-seven*
veintitrés *twenty-three*
veintiuno *twenty-one*
el velero *sailboat*
la venda *bandage*
vendar *to bandage, dress (a wound)*
el vendedor, -a *salesperson*
vender *to sell*
venir *to come*
la venta *sale*
    venta especial *special sale*
    campaña de ventas *sales campaign*
    tácticas de venta *sales tactics*
la ventanilla *(sales) window*
ver *to see*
verano *summer*
veras: ¿De veras? *Really?*
la verdad *correct, right*
    ¿No es verdad? *Isn't it true? Right?*
    ¿Verdad? *Is that so?*
verde *green*
la verdura *vegetable, greens*
el vértigo *dizziness, vertigo*
    sentir vértigo *to feel dizzy*
el vestido *dress*
vez *time; turn*
    a la vez *at the same time; while*
    a veces *at times; occasionally*
    algunas/unas veces *sometimes*
    de vez en cuando *from time to time*
    muchas veces *many times*
    otra vez *again*
    tal vez *perhaps*
    una vez, dos veces *once, twice*
viajar *to travel*
el viaje *trip*
    ¡Buen viaje! *Have a good trip!*
    estar de viaje *to be on a trip, journey*
    Estoy aquí en viaje de negocios. *I'm here on a business trip.*
    hacer un viaje *to take a trip*
el/la víctima *victim*
el video/vídeo *video*

equipo de video *video equipment*
la **video-grabadora** *VCR, video recorder*
el **viento** *wind*
   Hace viento. *It's windy.*
el **viernes** *Friday*
el **vino** *wine*
   vino blanco *white wine*
   vino tinto *red wine*
la **violación** *rape*
la **visa** *visa*
   visa de turista *tourist visa*
   visa de negociante *business visa*
la **visita** *visit, call*
 visitar *to visit*
la **víspera** *eve (before a holiday)*
   Víspera de Todos Los Santos
    Halloween
la **vista** *view*
   vista a la calle *a view facing the street*
   vista al mar *a view facing the ocean*
 vivir *to live*
el **vocabulario** *vocabulary*
el **volibol** *volleyball*
 volver *to return*
   volver a + infinitive *to do something
    again*
   Vuelvo en seguida. *I'll be right back.*
 volverse *to become*

vosotros/vosotras *you (pl. sub. pron.,
   Spain)*
el/la **votante** *voter*
 votar *to vote*
   votar por/en un candidato *to vote for
    a candidate*
el **voto** *voting, vote*
el **vuelo** *flight*
   El vuelo está atrasado. *The flight is
    delayed.*

Y

 y *and*
 ya *already; now; finally*
   ya no *no longer*
 yo *I*
la **yoga** *yoga*
   una clase de yoga *a yoga class*
la **yuca** *manioc*

Z

la **zapatería** *shoe repair shop*
el **zapatero** *shoemaker*
el **zapato** *shoe*
la **zona** *zone, area; belt*

ENGLISH-SPANISH

A

able (to be) *poder*
accept (to) *aceptar*
accomplish (to) *realizar*
according to *según*
account *la cuenta*
   checking account *cuenta corriente*
   savings account *cuenta de ahorros*
   bank statement *el estado de cuenta
    bancario*
accustom (to) *acostumbrarse a*
ache *el dolor*
acquire (to) *adquirir*
act (to) *actuar*
activity *la actividad*
actor *el actor*
actress *la actriz*
actual *real, verdadero*
address *la dirección*

advancement *el avance*
advise (to) *aconsejar*
after *después*
afternoon *la tarde*
   in the afternoon, P.M. *por/de la tarde*
again *de nuevo, otra vez, nuevamente*
against *contra*
agency *la agencia*
agent *el/la agente*
aid (to) *ayudar, prestar*
air *el aire*
   air conditioning *aire acondicionado*
   air sickness *el mareo*
airport *el aeropuerto*
aisle *el pasillo*
all *todo, -a, -os, -as*
allow (to) *permitir*
almost *casi; por poco*
already *ya*
also *también*

altitude *la altitud*
always *siempre*
amount *la cantidad*
amusement *la diversión*
and *y, e*
angry (to get) *enfadarse*
announce (to) *anunciar*
annoy (to) *molestar*
answer *la respuesta*
answer (to) *atender (door, phone);
    responder*
antacid *el antiácido*
antique *la antigüedad*
  antique shop *tienda de antigüedades*
any *algún, alguno, alguna*
apartment *el apartamento/apartamiento,
    el departamento*
appeal to (to) *apetecer*
appearance (to make an) *presentarse*
applaud (to) *aplaudir*
apple *la manzana*
appliance *el aparato eléctrico*
  household appliances *aparatos
    electrodomésticos*
application *la solicitud*
appointment *la cita*
April *abril*
area *la zona; el área*
arm *el brazo*
arouse (to) *animar*
arrest (to) *detener, prender*
arrival *la llegada*
  arrival gate *puerta de llegada*
arrive (to) *llegar, arribar*
article *el artículo*
as many as *tanto (-a, -os, -as) . . . como*
as much as *tan . . . como*
ask (to) *preguntar*
ask for (to) *pedir*
aspirin *la aspirina*
assign (to) *asignar*
at *a*
  at times *a veces*
athlete *el/la atleta, el/la deportista*
attack (to) *atacar*
attempt (to) *intentar*
attend to (to) *atender*
attention *la atención, el cuidado*
  to pay attention *prestar atención*
attractive *guapo, -a*
audience *el público*
auditorium *el auditorio*
August *agosto*
aunt *la tía*

automatic *automático, -a*
automobile *el auto, el coche, el carro*
autumn *el otoño*
avenue *la avenida*
avoid (to) *evitar*
awake (to) *despertar*
  to wake up *despertarse*

B

back *atrás; la espalda (body)*
bad *mal, malo, -a*
bag *la bolsa*
baggage *el equipaje*
bakery *la panadería*
balance *el saldo (bank account)*
balcony *la galería*
banana *el guineo; la banana*
bandage *la venda*
bandage (to) *vendar*
bank *el banco*
banker *el banquero, la banquera*
bar *el bar*
barber *el barbero, el peluquero, -a*
barbershop *la barbería, la peluquería*
baseball *el béisbol*
basketball *el baloncesto, el basquetbol*
bath *el baño*
bathe (to) *bañar*
bathing suit *el bañador*
bathroom *el baño*
be (to) *estar; hacer; quedar(se); ser; tener*
  I am well. *Estoy bien.*
  It's warm/cold. *Hace calor/frío.*
  They are to arrive Saturday. *Han de
    llegar el sábado.*
  to be right *tener razón*
beach *la playa*
beans *las habichuelas*
beard *la barba*
beautiful *bonito, -a; precioso, -a; guapo, -a*
because *porque*
become (to) *hacerse, llegar a ser, ponerse,
    volverse*
bed *la cama*
bedroom *el dormitorio*
beef *la carne de res*
beer *la cerveza*
before *antes*
begin (to) *comenzar*
behind *detrás de*
believe (to) *creer, pensar*
bellhop *el/la botones*

beloved *querido, -a*
belt *el cinturón; la zona (área)*
beneath *bajo, -a*
besides *más, además de*
better *mejor*
between *entre*
big *grande*
   bigger *más grande*
bill *la cuenta*
bird *el ave; el pájaro*
birthday *el cumpleaños*
   Happy birthday. *Feliz cumpleaños.*
   girl's fifteenth birthday party *quinceañera*
black *negro, -a*
blame *la culpa*
bleach (to) *teñir; blanquear*
bleachers (stadium) *las gradas*
block (street) *la cuadra, la manzana*
   (Spain)
blond *rubio, -a*
blouse *la blusa*
blue *azul*
boat *el barco*
body *el cuerpo*
boo (to) *abuchear*
book *el libro*
bosom *el pecho*
boss *el jefe/la jefa*
bother (to) *molestar*
boundary *el límite*
box *la caja*
   safety-deposit box *caja de valores*
boxer *el boxeador, -a*
boxing *el boxeo*
box office *la billetería, la taquilla*
boy *el chico*
boyfriend *el novio*
branch *la sucursal*
brand name *la marca*
Bravo! *¡Olé!*
bread fruit *la guanábana*
breakfast *el desayuno*
   to eat breakfast *desayunarse; tomar el*
     desayuno
bride *la novia*
bring (to) *llevar; traer*
broadcast *la emisión*
broadcast (to) *emitir*
brother *el hermano*
   younger brother *el hermanito*
brother-in-law *el cuñado*
brown *marrón*
brunette *moreno, -a*

brush *el cepillo*
building *el edificio, la obra*
bullfight *la corrida de toros*
   bullring *plaza de toros*
bullfighter *matador, torero*
bus *el autobús; bus*
   bus station *la estación de autobuses*
business *los negocios*
busy *ocupado, -a*
busy oneself (to) *ocuparse*
but *pero*
butcher's shop *la carnicería*
buy (to) *comprar*
by *por*

C

cab *el taxi*
cable *el cable*
cactus *el cacto*
   small cactus *el nopal*
call *la llamada; la visita (visit)*
   collect call *llamada por cobrar*
   long distance call *llamada de larga*
     distancia
   person to person call *persona a persona*
call (to) *llamar*
camera *la cámara*
can (to be able) *poder*
candidate *el candidato*
   to become a candidate *postularse*
canoe *la canoa*
capacity *la capacidad*
capture (to) *prender*
car *el coche, el automóvil, el auto*
   car battery *la batería*
   dining car *el vagón restaurante*
   sleeping car *el coche-cama*
   train car *el vagón*
carbohydrate *el carbohidrato*
carbonated mineral water *la gaseosa*
care *el cuidado, el ojo*
   careful *cuidadoso*
carry (to) *llevar*
cart *el carro*
   shopping cart *el carrito*
cartoons *los dibujos animados*
case *la caja*
cash *el efectivo*
cash (to) *cambiar*
   to cash a traveler's check *cambiar un*
     cheque de viajero

cassette *el cassette*
  cassette player *la cinta*
  cassette recorder *grabadora para cintas*
cast (theater) *el reparto*
cavity *la carie*
celebrate (to) *celebrar, festejar*
celebration *la celebración*
cent *el centavo*
center *el centro*
  shopping centers *centros comerciales*
centigrade (Celsius) *centígrado, -a*
certain *cierto, -a*
challenge *el desafío*
change, exchange *el cambio*
  currency exchange office *la agencia de*
    cambio, la casa de cambio
change (to) *cambiar*
  to change channels *cambiar el canal*
  to change dollars into pesos *cambiar*
    dólares a/en pesos
channel *el canal*
charge *el cargo*
charming *encantador, -a*
cheap *barato, -a*
check *el cheque*
  to cash a check *cobrar un cheque*
  traveler's check *el cheque de viajero*
  check book *la chequera*
check (to) *consultar, facturar, revisar*
Cheers! *¡Salud!*
chemise *la camisa*
cherimoya *la chirimoya*
chest *el baúl, la caja; el pecho (body)*
cheyote *el chayote*
chicken *el pollo*
children *los hijos*
choose (to) *escoger*
chop *la chuleta*
Christmas *las Navidades*
  Merry Christmas! *¡Feliz Navidad!*
  Christmas Eve *la Nochebuena*
cigar *el cigarro*
cigarette *el cigarrillo*
citizen *el ciudadano*
city *la ciudad*
claim *el derecho*
clap (to) *aplaudir*
class *la clase*
  first class *primera clase*
classified *los clasificados*
clean (to) *limpiar*
clear *claro, -a*
clinic *la clínica*

clock *el reloj*
close to (to get) *aproximarse a*
cloth *la tela*
clothing *la ropa*
club *el centro, el club*
coat *la chaqueta*
codfish *el bacalao*
coffee *el café*
coffin *el cajón, el ataúd*
cognate *el cognado*
coin *la moneda*
cold *el frío (weather); el resfriado (illness)*
collar *el cuello*
collect (to) *cobrar*
color *el color; el tinte (dye)*
Columbus Day *Día de la Raza*
column *la columna*
comb *el peine*
  comb one's hair (to) *peinarse*
come (to) *llegar, venir*
comedy *la comedia*
comics *las cómicas*
  comic strips *tiras cómicas*
communication *la comunicación*
compact disc, CD *el disco compacto*
  compact disc player *aparato de discos*
    compactos
company *la compañía*
compare with (to) *compararse con*
competent *competente*
computer *el computador/la computadora,*
  el ordenador (Spain)
  computer science *la informática*
  computer program *programa de*
    informática
conceal (to) *esconder, retirar*
concern (to) *tocar*
conclude (to) *concluir*
condition *la calidad*
confusion *la confusión*
congratulate (to) *felicitar*
congressperson *el/la representante*
construe (to) *construir*
continue (to) *continuar, seguir*
contract *el contrato*
cook (to) *cocinar*
cool *fresco, -a*
copy *la copia*
corn *el maíz*
  corn flour pancake *la tortilla*
corner *la esquina*
  on the corner *en la esquina*
correct *la verdad*

cosmetic *el cosmético*
cost (to) *costar, valer*
costume *el traje*
cotton *el algodón*
cough *la tos*
  cough syrup *el jarabe para la tos*
  cough drop *la pastilla para la tos*
country *el país*
countryside *el campo*
course *el lado, el curso, el clase*
cousin *el primo, -a*
credit *el crédito*
crime *el crimen*
criminal *el/la criminal*
critic *el crítico, -a*
crossword puzzle *el crucigrama*
crowd *la gente*
cry (to) *llorar*
culture *el culto; la cultura*
  cultural notes *notas culturales*
cup *la taza*
cure *el remedio*
curl *el rizo*
currency *la divisa*
  currency exchange office *la agencia de cambio*
curtain *el telón (theater)*
customer *el/la cliente*
Customs *la Aduana*
  to fill out the Customs Declaration *llenar la declaración de la Aduana*
cut (to) *cortar*
cutlet *la chuleta*

D

dagger *el puñal*
dairy store *la lechería*
dance (to) *bailar*
dandruff *la caspa*
Darn! *¡Caramba! ¡Caray!*
date *la cita; la fecha*
  to date, write the date *poner la fecha*
daughter *la hija*
dawn, daybreak *la aurora*
day *el día*
daylight *la luz*
deal (to) *dar, tratar*
dear *querido, -a*
December *diciembre*
decorate (to) *adornar*
dedicate oneself to (to) *dedicarse a*
delay (to) *atrasar*

delicate *delicado, -a*
deliver (to) *entregar*
delivery *la entrega*
  overnight delivery *entrega nocturna*
democracy *la democracia*
dentist *el/la dentista*
deny (to) *negar*
deodorant *el desodorante*
department store *el almacén*
departure *la partida*
  departure gate *puerta de embarque*
deposit *el depósito*
  certificate of deposit *certificado de depósito*
deposit (to) *depositar*
desire *el deseo*
desire (to) *querer*
destroy (to) *destruir*
detain (to) *detener*
detective *el/la detective*
develop (to) *desarrollar*
dial (to) *marcar*
dialog *el diálogo*
dictator *el dictador, -a*
dictatorship *la dictadura*
die (to) *morir(se)*
diet *la dieta, el régimen*
different *diferente*
difficult *difícil*
diminish (to) *disminuirse*
dine (to) *cenar*
dining room *el comedor*
dinner *la cena*
diphthongs *diptongos*
direct (to) *dirigir*
direction *la dirección, el lado*
disagreeable *desagradable*
disaster *el desastre*
discount *el descuento, la rebaja*
discuss (to) *tratar*
diseased *enfermo, -a*
dish *el plato*
dishwasher *el lavaplatos*
disinfectant *el desinfectante*
distinguish (to) *distinguir*
diversion *la diversión*
dizziness *el mareo, el vértigo*
  to feel dizzy *sentir vértigo*
do (to) *hacer*
doctor *el doctor, la doctora, el/la médico*
  doctor's office *consultorio del médico*
dollar *el dólar*
doubt *la duda*
  without doubt *sin duda*

doubt (to) *dudar*
draw (to) *sacar*
dream (to) *soñar*
dress *el vestido*
dressmaker *la modista*
drink *la bebida*
  alcoholic drink *bebida alcohólica, el trago*
  soft drink *el refresco*
drink (to) *beber, tomar*
drought *la sequía*
dry (to) *secar*
dry clean (to) *lavar a seco*
dry cleaner *el tintorero, -a*
dry cleaner's *la tintorería*
dryer *el secador*
dub (to) *doblar*
dubbing *el doblaje*
duck *el pato*
during *durante*

E

ear *la oreja*
early *temprano*
early-riser *madrugador, -a*
earn (to) *ganar*
easily *fácilmente*
Easter *el Pascuas*
  Easter Sunday *el domingo de Pascuas*
  Easter week *Semana Santa*
easy *fácil*
eat (to) *comer, tomar*
  to eat breakfast *desayunarse*
  to eat lunch *almorzar*
editorial *el editorial*
effective *efectivo*
effectively *eficazmente*
eight *ocho*
eighteen *dieciocho*
  eight hundred *ochocientos, -as*
eighth *octavo*
eighty *ochenta*
elect (to) *elegir*
election *la elección*
electricity *la electricidad*
eleven *once*
emergency *la emergencia*
employee *el empleado, -a*
enamel *el esmalte*
end *el final*
endorse (to) *endosar*
engine *el motor*

enjoy (to) *gozar*
enjoy oneself (to) *divertirse*
enough *bastante*
enter (to) *entrar (en)*
entertain (to) *entretener*
entertainment *la diversión*
entrance *la entrada*
Epiphany *los Reyes*
equipment *el aparato, el equipo*
  electronic equipment *los aparatos electrónicos*
  video equipment *equipo de video*
  music/sound equipment *equipo de música/sonido*
  stereo equipment *equipo estereofónico*
errand *el recado*
escape (to) *escapar*
eve *la víspera*
evening, p.m. *la noche*
ever *siempre*
every *todo, -a, -os, -as*
everybody *todo el mundo*
everything *todo*
examine (to) *examinar*
example: for example *por ejemplo*
excellent *excelente*
exchange *el cambio*
  currency exchange office *la agencia de cambio, la casa de cambio*
excite (to) *animar*
excitement *la fiebre*
exclude (to) *excluir*
exercise *el ejercicio*
exercise (to) *hacer ejercicios*
exhaust (to) *agotar*
  to exhaust oneself *agotarse*
exhibition *la exhibición*
exist (to) *existir; haber*
exit *la salida*
expense *el gasto*
expensive *caro, -a*
express (to) *representar*
expression *la expresión*
extension *la extensión*
extra *extra; el repuesto (spare part)*
eye *el ojo*
eyeglasses *los anteojos*

F

facsimile, fax machine *el fax*
factory *la fábrica*
  factory worker *operario, -a*

family *la familia*
  family relationship *el parentesco*
  family member *el pariente/la parienta*
fare *el pasaje*
fashion *la moda*
fat *gordo, -a*
fatigue *la fatiga*
father *el padre*
favor *el favor*
favorite *favorito*
fear (to) *temer*
February *febrero*
fee *la cuota, la tarifa*
feed (to) *dar de comer*
feel (to) *sentirse*
feeling *el sentir, el sentimiento*
festival *el festival*
fever *la fiebre*
few *poco, -a, -os, -as*
  fewer *menos*
fifteen *quince*
fifth *quinto, -a*
fifty *cincuenta*
fifty thousand *cincuenta mil*
fighter *el luchador*
fill (to) *llenar*
filling *el empaste*
film *la película*
film (to) *rodar*
final *el final*
finally *al final, ya*
finances *las finanzas*
find (to) *encontrar*
fine *perfectamente*
finger *el dedo*
finish (to) *acabar*
fireworks *los fuegos artificiales*
first *primer, primero, -a*
fish *el pescado (caught)*
fishing *la pesca*
  deep-sea fishing *la pesca marina*
fit *propio, -a*
fit (to) *quedarse, caber*
five *cinco*
  five hundred *quinientos, -as*
fix (to) *arreglar*
flat *desinflado, -a*
flight *el vuelo*
floor *el piso*
fog *la niebla*
  light fog *la neblina*
follow (to) *seguir*
food *la comida*

food and drinks *comidas y bebidas*
foot *el pie*
football *fútbol norteamericano*
for *para, por*
foreigner *el extranjero, la extranjera*
forget (to) *olvidarse*
form *el formulario*
fortunately *felizmente*
forty *cuarenta*
four *cuatro*
  four hundred *cuatrocientos, -as*
fourteen *catorce*
fourth *cuarto, -a*
fowl *el ave*
franc *el franco*
free *gratuito, -a*
freeze (to) *helar*
freezer *el congelador*
frequent *frecuente*
frequently *frecuentemente*
fresh *fresco, -a*
Friday *el viernes*
friend *el amigo, -a*
frighten (to) *asustar*
from *de*
  Where are you from? *¿De dónde es Ud.?*
    ¿De dónde eres tú? (fam.)
fruit *la fruta*
  fruit store *la frutería*

G

gain (to) *ganar*
gala *la gala*
garage *el garaje*
garden *el jardín*
gas *el gas*
gasoline *la gasolina,*
  gas station *la gasolinera*
  gas tank *el depósito*
  super gasoline *la super gasolina*
gate *la puerta*
  arrival gate *puerta de llegada*
  departure gate *puerta de embarque*
general *general (adj.); el general (n.)*
  generally *por lo general*
gentlemen *el señor*
get on (to) *subir a*
get used to (to) *acostumbrarse a*
giant *el gigante*
gift *el regalo*
gigantic *gigante*

girl *la chica, la muchacha*
girlfriend *la novia*
give (to) *dar, entregar*
  to give birth *dar a luz*
  to give a gift *regalar*
go (to) *ir; irse*
  go out (to) *salir*
  go up (to) *subir*
golf *el golf*
good *bueno, -a*
Good-bye. *Adiós.*
gossip *los chismes*
  gossip column *columna de chismes*
governor *el gobernador, la gobernadora*
graceful *bonito, -a; gracioso,-a; elegante*
grammar *la gramática*
  grammar and usage *gramática y usos*
grandchild *el nieto, -a*
grandparent *el abuelo, -a*
grateful to (to be) *agradecer*
gray *gris*
greasy *grasoso, -a*
great *gran(de)*
green *verde*
greens (vegetables) *las verduras*
greet (to) *dar los buenos días; felicitar*
greeting *la felicitación, el saludo; saludar*
groom *el novio*
growth *el aumento*
guarantee *la garantía*
guard (to) *guardar*
guava *la guayaba*
gums (mouth) *las encías*
gun *el revólver*

H

hair *el cabello, el pelo*
  red head; red hair color *pelirrojo, -a*
  bleached hair *pelo teñido, blanqueado*
haircut *el corte*
hairdo *el peinado*
hairdresser *el peluquero, la peluquera*
hairdresser's shop *la peluquería*
half *medio, -a*
Halloween *Víspera de Todos los Santos*
ham *el jamón*
hand *la mano*
handkerchief *el pañuelo*
handle *el mango*
handsome *bonito, hermoso, guapo*
hang up (to) *colgar*

happily *felizmente*
happy *contento, -a; feliz*
happy (to be) *alegrarse*
harm (to) *hacer daño a*
hat *el sombrero*
have (to) *tener, haber*
he *él*
head *la cabeza*
headache *el dolor de la cabeza*
headline *el titular*
health *la salud*
heel *el tacón*
Hello! *¡Hola!*
Help! *¡Socorro!*
help *la ayuda*
help (to) *ayudar*
her *la (object)*
here *aquí*
high *alto, -a*
  first-rate *alta calidad*
hispanic *hispano, -a*
hold (to) *tener*
hole *el agujero*
holiday *el feriado*
  Happy holidays! *¡Felices fiestas!*
home *la casa*
hood *el capó*
hope (to) *esperar*
hospital *la clínica*
hot *caliente*
hotel *el hotel*
house *la casa*
how? *¿cómo? ¿qué?*
how much? how many? *¿cuánto, -a, -os, -as?*
however *sin embargo*
humid *húmedo*
humidity *la humedad*
hundred *cien(to)*
  one hundred and one *ciento uno*
hurry (to) *darse prisa*
husband *el esposo*

I

I *yo*
ice cream *el helado*
idea *la idea*
if *si*
ill *enfermo, -a*
immediate *inmediato, -a*
immediately *en seguida, inmediatamente*

import (to) *importar*
important *importante*
impossible *imposible*
impulse *el impulso*
in *a, en*
  in black and white *en blanco y negro*
  in spite of *a pesar de*
  in the open air; outdoors *al aire libre*
include (to) *incluir*
increase *el aumento*
increase (to) *aumentar*
indeed *sí*
ineffective *ineficaz*
information *la información*
inquire (to) *preguntar*
insist (to) *insistir*
inspire (to) *animar*
install (to) *instalar*
instruction *la instrucción*
instructor *el instructor, -a*
insurance *el seguro*
  social security *seguro social*
insure (to) *asegurar*
insured *asegurado*
intelligent *inteligente*
interest *el interés*
interest (to) *interesar*
  to be interested *interesarse*
international *internacional*
interview *la entrevista*
interview (to) *entrevistar*
introduce (to) *presentar*
invalid *el enfermo, -a*
invitation *la invitación*
invite (to) *invitar*
iron (to) *planchar*
it *(obj. pron.) lo (m.); la (f.)*

J

jacket *la chaqueta*
jeans *el jeans*
job *el trabajo*
jogging *el correr, el jogging*
joke *la broma*
joke (to) *bromear*
juice *el jugo*
July *julio*
June *junio*
justice *la justicia*

K

keep (to) *guardar, mantener*
  to keep in shape *mantenerse en forma*
key *la llave*
keyhole *el ojo*
kidney beans *los frijoles*
kill (to) *matar*
kilometer *el kilómetro, el quilómetro*
kind *la clase; el tipo*
kitchen *la cocina*
knife *el cuchillo*
know (to) *conocer, saber*

L

labor *la obra*
Labor Day *Día de los Trabajadores*
lack (to) *faltar, hacer falta*
  to be lacking *faltarle a uno*
lamb *el cordero*
lament (to) *lamentar, sentir*
language *la lengua*
late *tarde*
  later *más tarde*
laugh (to) *reírse*
  to laugh at/about *reírse de*
launderer *el lavandero, -a*
laundry *el lavado; la lavandería (place)*
law *el derecho, la ley*
lawyer *el abogado, -a*
learn (to) *aprender*
lease *el arrendamiento*
leave (to) *dejar, partir, salir*
left *izquierdo, -a*
  to the left *a la izquierda*
leg *la pierna*
lend (to) *prestar*
Lent *la Cuaresma*
lessen (to) *disminuir*
lesson *la lección*
let (to) *permitir, dejar*
letter *la carta*
  letters of recommendation *cartas de referencia*
lettuce *la lechuga*
lie down (to) *tumbarse*
lifeguard *el/la salvavidas*
lift (to) *levantar*
light *la luz*
like (to) *gustar, encantarle a uno, querer*
liking *el gusto*

limit *el límite*
lip *el labio*
listen (to) *escuchar*
live (to) *vivir*
living room *la sala*
loan *el préstamo*
   to ask for a loan *pedir un préstamo*
lobby *la recepción*
local *local*
long *largo, -a*
look for (to) *buscar*
lose (to) *perder*
lotion *la loción*
   suntan lotion *loción bronceadora*
love *el amor*
   amor mío *my darling*
love (to) *encantar, querer, amar*
   to fall in love with *enamorarse de*
luck *la suerte*
   Good luck! *¡Buena suerte!*
lunch *el almuerzo*

M

machine *la máquina*
mail (to) *enviar*
   by air mail *por vía aérea*
   by surface mail *por vía superficie*
   to mail a letter *echar una carta al buzón*
mailbox *el buzón*
mailman *el cartero, -a*
maintain (to) *mantener*
majority *la mayoría*
make (to) *hacer*
make-up *el cosmético*
man *el hombre*
management *la dirección*
manager *el/la gerente*
manicure *la manicura*
manioc *la yuca*
manner *manera*
many *mucho, -a*
map *el mapa*
March *marzo*
market *el mercado*
   black market *mercado negro*
marketing *el mercadeo*
marvelous *maravilloso, -a*
material (fabric) *la tela*
May *mayo*
maybe *tal vez*
mayor *el alcalde/la alcaldesa*

me *me; mí (prep. obj. pron.)*
meal *la comida*
mean *el medio*
mean (to) *querer decir*
measure *la ley (standard)*
meat *la carne*
media *los medios de comunicación*
meet (to) *encontrar, reunirse*
menu *el menú*
merit *el valor*
meter *el metro*
middle *el centro*
midnight *la medianoche*
milkshake *el batido*
million *millón*
mind *la mente*
minor *menor*
mirror *el espejo*
misfortune *la desgracia*
Miss *la señorita*
mist *la neblina*
mistaken (to be) *equivocarse*
Mister *el señor*
model *el/la modelo*
modern *moderno, -a*
modernize (to) *actualizar*
moisture *la humedad*
moment *momento*
   Just a moment. One moment.
    Momentito.
Monday *el lunes*
money *el dinero, el efectivo, la moneda*
money order *el giro*
month *el mes*
moon *la luna*
more *más*
morning *la mañana*
most of *la mayor parte de*
mother *la madre*
motor *el motor*
moustache *el bigote*
mouth *la boca*
mouthwash *el enjuague bucal*
move (to) *mudarse*
movie *el cine, el film, la película*
   movie listings *la cartelera*
   movie theater *el cine*
moviemaker *el/la cineasta*
Mrs., madam *la señora*
much *mucho, -a*
mug (to) *asaltar*
mugger *el/la asaltante*
mugging *el asalto*

murder *el asesinato*
muscle *el músculo*
muscular *musculoso, -a*
music *la música*
  rock music *el rock*
my *mi, mis (poss. adj.)*
myself *me*

N

name *el nombre*
  given name *nombre de pila*
named (to be) *llamarse*
  My name is . . . *Me llamo . . .*
nation *la nación, el pueblo*
national *nacional*
nationality *la nacionalidad*
nature *la naturaleza*
near, nearby *cerca (de)*
necessary *necesario, -a*
neck *el cuello*
necktie *la corbata*
need (to) *necesitar*
neighborhood *el barrio*
nephew *el sobrino*
nervous *nervioso, -a*
network *la red*
new *nuevo, -a*
  New Year *Año Nuevo*
news *las noticias*
  news broadcast *el noticiero*
newspaper *el periódico*
New York *Nueva York*
niece *la sobrina*
night *la noche*
  last night *anoche*
nine *nueve*
nineteen *diecinueve*
ninety *noventa*
ninth *noveno, -a*
no *no*
nobody *nadie*
noise *el ruido*
none *ningún, ninguno, ninguna*
noon *el mediodía*
normal *normal*
normally *normalmente*
nose *la nariz*
not *no*
nothing *nada*
  You're welcome. *De nada.*
noun *el nombre*

November *noviembre*
now *ahora, ya*
  right now *ahora mismo*
  no longer *ya no*
number *el número*

O

obey (to) *obedecer*
obligation *la obligación*
obtain (to) *conseguir*
October *octubre*
of *de*
  a cup of coffee *una taza de café*
  of course *claro*
offer *la oferta*
  to make an offer *hacer una oferta*
offer (to) *ofrecer*
office *la oficina; el despacho (Spain)*
often *a menudo*
oil *el aceite*
okay *bueno, -a*
old *viejo, -a*
  older *mayor*
on *a, en*
  on, upon; Upon arriving . . . *al +
    infinitive; Al llegar . . .*
  on account of; because of *a causa de*
  on board *a bordo*
  on foot *a pie*
  on the dot, sharp *en punto*
  on time *a tiempo*
once *una vez*
onion *la cebolla*
open (to) *abrir; estrenarse*
opening (show) *el estreno*
operator *el operador, -a*
opinion *el sentir*
  to give an opinion *opinar*
opposite *en frente de*
orange *la china (Puerto Rico), la naranja*
orchestra *la platea*
  orchestra seat *la butaca de platea*
ostentatious *ostentoso, -a*
other, another *otro, -a, -os, -as*
ourselves *nos*
outdoors *al aire libre*
oven *el horno*
overcoat *el abrigo*
owe (to) *deber*
own *propio, -a*

P

package *el paquete*
page *la página*
  first page *la primera plana*
pain *el dolor*
pair *el par*
pajamas *el pijama*
pants *los pantalones*
paper *el papel*
parade *el desfile*
park (to) *estacionar*
part *el papel, la raya (hair)*
participate (to) *participar*
party *la fiesta*
Passover *La Pascua Florida*
passport *el pasaporte*
patient *el enfermo, -a*
pay (to) *pagar*
payment *el pago*
  monthly payments *pagos mensuales*
peanut *el maní*
penalty *la multa*
people *la gente, el pueblo*
peppers *los pimentones*
percent *por ciento*
perfectly *perfectamente*
perform (to) *realizar, representar*
  to perform a role *representar un papel*
performance *la representación*
perhaps *puede ser, quizás, tal vez*
permanent *la permanente*
permit (to) *permitir*
person *la persona*
personnel *el personal*
  Personnel Department *Departamento de Personal*
pharmacist *el farmacéutico, -a*
pharmacy *la botánica (herbs); la farmacia*
phenomenal *fenomenal*
philosophy *la filosofía*
piano *el piano*
pick up (to) *recoger*
pill *la pastilla*
pin (to) *prender*
pineapple *la piña*
place (to) *poner*
plan *el plan*
plantain *el plátano*
platform *el andén*
play *la pieza*
play (to) *jugar a (game), tocar (musical instrument)*

playhouse *el teatro*
plaza *la plaza*
pleasant *simpático, -a*
please *por favor*
pleasure *el gusto*
plus *más*
police force *la policía*
policeman *el policía*
policewoman *la mujer policía*
policy *la política*
politician *el político, -a*
politics *la política*
pollution *la contaminación*
pool (swimming) *la piscina*
popcorn *las rosetas de maíz*
pork *el puerco*
  roast suckling pig *el lechón*
portable *portátil*
porter *el maletero*
possess (to) *tener*
possible *posible*
postal system *el correo*
  at the post office *en el correo*
  post office box *la casilla de correo*
postcard *la tarjeta postal*
potato *la patata (Spain), la papa*
pound sterling *la libra esterlina*
precious *precioso, -a*
preferable *preferible*
prescribe (to) *recetar*
presciption *la receta*
present *el regalo*
present (to) *presentar*
present oneself (to) *presentarse*
president *el presidente, la presidenta*
press (newspaper) *la prensa*
press clothes (to) *planchar*
pretty *bonito, -a*
prevent (to) *impedir*
previous *anterior*
price *el precio*
  price tag *la etiqueta*
printed matter *los impresos*
prison *la cárcel*
prisoner *el preso, -a*
prize *el premio*
problem *el problema*
procedure *el trámite*
produce (to) *producir*
product *el producto*
production *la producción*
program *el programa, el régimen*
promise (to) *prometer*

promote (to) *ascender; promover*
promotion *el avance, el ascenso*
prompt *pronto, listo*
  as soon as possible *lo más pronto posible*
pronunciation *la pronunciación*
protect (to) *proteger*
protein *la proteína*
publication *la publicación*
pull out (to) *arrancar*
pump *la bomba*
purse *la bolsa*
pursue (to) *seguir*
put (to) *poner*
put on (to) *ponerse*

Q

quality *la calidad*
quantity *la cantidad*
quarter *cuarto, -a*
quick *pronto, rápidamente*
quiet *quieto, -a*
quiet (to be) *callarse*
quiz *el examen*

R

radio *la radio*
  radio/cassette player *el radio-cassette*
    (para cintas)
rain (to) *llover*
  It's raining. *Llueve. Está lloviendo.*
raincoat *el impermeable; la gabardina*
    (Spain)
raise *el aumento*
raise (to) *levantar*
rape *la violación*
rapid *rápido, -a*
rapidly *rápidamente*
rate *la tasa*
  exchange rate *tasa de cambio*
rather *más bien, sino; bastante*
reach (to) *llegar*
react (to) *reaccionar*
read (to) *leer*
ready *listo, -a*
real estate *los inmuebles*
  real estate agent *el corredor (-a) de*
    inmuebles
reality *la realidad*
realize (to) *darse cuenta*

reason *la razón*
receipt *el recibo*
receive (to) *recibir*
reception desk *la recepción*
receptionist *el/la recepcionista*
recommend (to) *recomendar*
record player *el tocadiscos*
recorder *la grabadora*
red *rojo, -a*
redhead *el pelirrojo*
reduce (to) *bajar; reducir*
refreshment *el refresco*
refrigerator *el refrigerador; la nevera*
    (Spain)
regimen *el régimen*
register (to) *certificar*
registration *la certificación*
regret (to) *lamentar, sentir*
  I'm sorry. *Lo siento.*
relationship: family relationship *el*
    parentesco
relative *el pariente/la parienta*
remain (to) *permanecer, quedar(se)*
rent *el alquiler, la renta*
rent (to) *alquilar*
repair (to) *reparar*
repeat (to) *repetir*
replace (to) *reemplazar*
represent (to) *representar*
request (to) *pedir*
reservation *la reserva, la reservación*
responsibility *la obligación*
rest *el descanso*
rest (to) *descansar*
restaurant *el restaurante, restaurán,*
    restorán
results *los resultados*
résumé *el resumen, el curriculum vitae, el*
    historial de vida
retail *al por menor*
return (to) *devolver, volver*
review *la reseña (book, film, theater);*
    repaso
revolver *el revólver*
rice *el arroz*
rich *rico, -a*
right *la derecha; ¡Bien!*
  right there *ahí mismo*
  to be right *tener razón*
  to the right *a la derecha*
ring (to) *sonar; tocar*
rinse (to) *enjuagar*
risk *el riesgo*

river *el río*
rob (to) *asaltar, robar*
robbery *el robo*
rock music *el rock*
role *el papel*
　to perform a role *representar un papel*
room *el cuarto, la habitación*
　room service *el servicio de cuarto*
root *la raíz*
　root canal *el empaste de la raíz*
rose *la rosa*
row *la fila*
run (to) *correr*

S

sad *triste*
safety *la seguridad*
sailboat *el velero*
saint *el santo*
　All Saint's Day *Día de Todos los Santos*
salad *la ensalada*
salary *el salario, el sueldo*
sale *la venta*
　retail *al por menor*
　sales tag *la etiqueta*
　special sale *venta especial*
　wholesale *al por mayor*
salesperson *el vendedor, -a*
salmon *el salmón*
salon *el salón*
　beauty parlor *el salón de belleza*
sand *la arena*
sandwich *el bocadillo*
satellite *el satélite*
　by satellite *por satélite*
Saturday *el sábado*
sauce *la salsa*
sausage *el chorizo*
say (to) *decir*
scene *la escena*
schedule *el horario*
scissors *las tijeras*
score (game) *la cuenta, el puntaje, la puntuación*
screen *la pantalla*
scuba diving *el buceo*
sea *el mar*
seafood *los mariscos*
seamstress *la modista*
seasickness *el mareo*
season *la estación*

seat *el asiento*
second *segundo, -a*
section *la sección*
security *la seguridad*
see (to) *ver*
seem (to) *parecer*
seize (to) *prender*
select (to) *elegir, escoger*
self *propio, -a*
sell (to) *vender, dejar a un precio*
senator *el senador, -a*
send (to) *enviar*
September *septiembre*
serve (to) *servir*
service *el servicio*
seven *siete*
seventeen *diecisiete*
seventh *séptimo, -a*
seventy *setenta*
several *varios, -as*
sew (to) *coser*
shade *la sombra*
shampoo *el champú*
shape *la forma*
　to keep in shape *mantenerse en forma*
shape (to) *formar*
share (to) *participar; compartir*
sharp *en punto (on the dot); agudo, -a (point, pain)*
shave (to) *afeitarse*
shaving blade *hoja de afeitar*
shaving razor *navaja de afeitar*
she *ella*
shelter *el abrigo*
shine (to) *lucir*
shirt *la camisa*
shocking *chocante*
shoe *el zapato*
　shoe repair shop *la zapatería*
shoemaker *el zapatero*
shoot (to) *tirar*
shop (to) *comprar, hacer compras*
　shopping centers *centros comerciales*
short while (a) *un rato*
shoulder *el hombro*
show (to) *exhibir, mostrar, pasar (film), presentar*
show up (to) *presentarse*
shower *la ducha*
showtime (play, film, etc.) *sesión*
shrimp *los camarones*
sick *enfermo, -a*
side *el lado, el costado*

next to *al lado de*
sign *el aviso*
sign (to) *firmar*
silk *la seda*
similar *similar*
simple *simple*
sir *el señor*
sister *la hermana*
sister-in-law *la cuñada*
sit down (to) *sentarse*
six *seis*
sixteen *dieciséis*
sixth *sexto*
sixty *sesenta*
skiing *el esquiar*
  water skiing *esquí acuático*
skin *la piel*
skirt *la falda*
sleep (to) *dormirse*
  to go to sleep *acostarse*
slip (deposit, etc.) *la papeleta*
small *pequeño, -a*
  smaller *más pequeño*
smell (to) *oler*
smoke (to) *fumar*
  non-smoking section *sección de no fumar*
snack *el bocadillo; las tapas, la merienda (Spain)*
snow (to) *nevar*
  It's snowing. *Nieva. Está nevando.*
snow *la nieve*
so *tan*
  so much, many *tantos, -as*
soap *el jabón*
soap opera *la (tele)novela*
soccer *el fútbol*
  soccer player *el/la futbolista*
socks *los calcetines*
soda *la soda, el refresco*
sole (foot) *la planta*
some *algún, alguno, -a*
someone *alguien*
something *algo*
  Something else? *¿Algo más?*
sometimes *algunas/unas veces, a veces*
somewhat *bastante*
son *el hijo*
song *la canción*
sorrow *el dolor*
soup *la sopa*
space *el espacio*
spare *el repuesto*
speak (to) *hablar*

speakers *los (alto)parlantes*
special *especial*
specialty *la especialidad*
spectator *el espectador, -a*
spend time (to) *pasar*
  to pass by *pasar por*
spices *las especias*
sport *el deporte*
  water sports *diversiones acuáticas*
spring *la primavera*
square (plaza) *la plaza, zocolo (Mexico)*
stadium *el estadio*
stain *la mancha*
  to take out a stain *sacar una mancha*
staircase *escalera*
  to go down/up *bajar/subir*
stall (to) *pararse*
stamp *la estampilla, el sello*
star (performer) *el/la estrella, el/la protagonista*
stereo *el estereofónico*
  stereo equipment *equipo estereofónico*
still *quieto, -a; todavía (adv.)*
stockings *las medias*
stomach *el estómago*
  stomachache *el dolor de estómago*
Stop! *¡Alto!*
stop (to) *detener, pararse*
store *la tienda*
store (to) *guardar*
storey *el piso*
storm *la tormenta*
stout *gordo*
stove *la estufa*
straight *derecho*
  You walk straight ahead. *Sigues derecho.*
strawberry *la fresa*
street *la calle*
strong *fuerte*
student *el/la estudiante*
study (to) *estudiar*
style *la moda*
succeed (to) *triunfar; tener éxito*
success *el éxito*
sudden *repentino, -a*
  suddenly *de pronto, de repente*
suffer (to) *sufrir*
suggest (to) *sugerir*
suit *el traje*
suitable *propio, -a*
suitcase *la maleta*
sum *la cantidad*
summer *el verano*

sun *el sol*
   to be sunny *hacer sol*
sunbathe (to) *broncearse*
Sunday *el domingo*
supermarket *el supermercado*
supper *la cena*
sure *seguro, -a*
   surely *seguramente*
surfing *el surfe*
   to go surfing *hacer surfe*
surname, last name *el apellido*
swear (to) *jurar*
sweater *el suéter*
sweet banana *el guineo*
swell (to) *hincharse*
swim (to) *nadar*
swimming *la natación*
syrup *el jarabe*

T

table *la mesa*
tablet *la pastilla*
tailor *el sastre*
   tailor's shop *la sastrería*
take (to) *tomar, llevar, quitar*
take care (to) *cuidar*
   to take care of oneself *cuidarse*
take-off *el despegue (plane)*
take off (to) *despegar*
talk (to) *hablar*
tall *alto, -a*
taste *el gusto*
taxi *el taxi*
telephone *el teléfono*
   by phone *por teléfono*
   telephone book *la guía telefónica*
telephone (to) *telefonear*
television *la tele(visión); el televisor (TV set)*
   color TV set *televisor de color/a colores*
teller *el cajero, -a*
   automatic teller *cajero automático*
ten *diez*
tennis *el tenis*
   tennis court *la cancha*
   to play tennis *jugar al tenis*
tennis player *el/la tenista*
terrible *terrible*
test *el examen*
than *que*
thank (to) *agradecer, dar las gracias a*

Thank you. *Gracias.*
Thanksgiving Day *Día de la Acción de Gracias*
that; that one *ese, esa; aquel, aquella (adj.); ése, ésa; aquél, aquélla (pron.)*
theater *el teatro*
them *los (dir. obj.); les*
there *ahí; allí (far away)*
   there is, there are *hay*
these *estos, estas (adj.); éstos, éstas (pron.)*
they *ellos, ellas*
thief *el ladrón/la ladrona*
thing *la cosa*
think (to) *pensar*
third *tercer, tercero, -a*
thirteen *trece*
thirty *treinta*
this *este, esta (adj.); éste, ésta (pron.)*
those *esos, esas; aquellos, aquellas (adj.); ésos, ésas; aquéllos, aquéllas (pron.)*
thousand (one) *mil*
three *tres*
thrilling *emocionante*
through *por*
Thursday *el jueves*
thus *así*
ticket *el boleto, la entrada, el pasaje, el billete*
   ticket counter *el mostrador*
   round-trip ticket *pasaje de ida y vuelta*
tie *corbata*
tie (to) *atar*
time *la hora, la vez*
tire *la llanta*
tire (to) *fatigar, cansar*
to *a*
toast *la tostada (bread); el brindis (salute)*
today *hoy*
toe *el dedo del pie*
together *junto, -a*
   to get together *reunirse*
tomato *el tomate*
tomorrow *la mañana*
   the day after tomorrow *pasado mañana*
tongue *la lengua*
tonight *esta noche*
tooth *el diente, la muela*
   to brush one's teeth *cepillarse; lavarse los dientes (Spain)*
   toothbrush *cepillo de dientes*
   toothpaste *pasta de dientes, dentífrico*
touch (to) *tocar*
tourism *el turismo*

tourist office *el centro de turismo*
tourist *el/la turista*
toward *para, hacia*
towel *la toalla*
town *el pueblo*
track (running) *la pista*
tragedy *la tragedia*
train *el tren*
train station *la estación ferroviaria/de trenes*
transaction *la transacción*
transfer *el transbordo*
translate (to) *traducir*
transportation *el transporte*
travel (to) *viajar*
travel agency *la agencia de viajes*
travel sickness *el mareo*
treat (to) *tratar*
trim (to) *cortar un poco*
trip *el viaje*
trunk *el baúl*
truth *la verdad, la realidad*
try (to) *tratar*
Tuesday *el martes*
tuna *el atún*
tune in (to) *sintonizar*
turn (chance) *la vez*
turn off (to) *apagar*
turn on (to) *encender*
twelve *doce*
twenty *veinte*
twice *dos veces*
two *dos*
the two of them, both *los dos, ambos*
two hundred *doscientos, -as*
type *la clase, el tipo*

U

ugly *feo, -a*
umbrella *el/los paraguas*
beach umbrella *el parasol*
uncle *el tío*
under *bajo, debajo de*
understand (to) *comprender, entender*
unpleasant *desagradable, antipático, -a*
until *hasta*
update (to) *actualizar*
uproot (to) *arrancar*
us *nos; nosotros, nosotras (obj. pron.)*
usual *común, general*

V

Valentine's Day *Día de los Enamorados*
value *el valor*
vegetable *la legumbre, la verdura*
vertigo *el vértigo*
very *muy, bien*
victim *el/la víctima*
video *el video/vídeo*
video equipment *equipo de video*
video recorder, VCR *la video-grabadora, la máquina filmadora*
view *la vista*
village *el pueblo*
visa *la visa*
tourist visa *visa de turista*
business visa *visa de negociante*
visit *la visita*
visit (to) *visitar*
vocabulary *vocabulario*
volleyball *el volibol*
vote *el voto*
vote (to) *votar*
voter *el/la votante*

W

waist *la cintura*
waiter *el mesero, -a*
walk (to) *caminar, andar*
want (to) *querer*
war *la guerra*
warm *caliente*
wash (to) *lavar*
washing and drying *lavado y secado*
wash oneself (to) *lavarse*
washer *la máquina de lavar*
washing *el lavado*
watch *el reloj*
watch (to) *mirar*
watching TV *mirando la televisión*
water *el agua*
water skiing *el esquí acuático*
way *el lado*
we *nosotros, nosotras (subj. pron.)*
wear out (to) *agotar*
to wear oneself out *agotarse*
weariness *la fatiga*
weather *el tiempo*
wedding *la boda*
Wednesday *el miércoles*
week *la semana*

weekend *el fin de semana*
weigh (to) *pesar*
well *bien*
   . . . well, well then . . . *pues*
what? *¿cómo? ¿cuál? ¿qué?*
where? *¿dónde?*
whether *si*
which *que*
   ¿which? ¿cuál?; ¿qué?
while *mientras*
whim *el capricho*
white *blanco, -a*
who, whom *que; quien, quienes*
wholesale *al por mayor*
whose . . . ? of whom . . . ? *¿de quién . . . ?*
why? *¿por qué?*
wife *la esposa*
wig *la peluca*
win (to) *ganar*
wind *el aire*
window *la ventanilla*
wind *el viento*
windy *ventoso*
wine *el vino*
   red wine *vino tinto*
   white wine *vino blanco*
winner *el ganador, -a*
winter *el invierno*
wish *el deseo*
wish (to) *desear, querer*
with *con*
   with me *conmigo*
   with you *contigo*
   with him, her, you, them *consigo*
withdraw (to) *retirar*
   to withdraw money *retirar dinero*
withdrawal *el retiro*
   to make a withdrawal *hacer un retiro*
without *sin*
witness *el testigo, -a*
woman *la mujer*
wonderful *maravilloso, -a*
wool *la lana*
word *la palabra*
wordprocessor *la procesadora de palabras*
work *la obra, el trabajo*
work (to) *trabajar*
workdays *los días laborables*
world *el mundo*
worldwide *mundial*
worry about (to) *preocuparse por/de*
worse *peor*
worth *el valor*
wound (to) *herir*
wrap (to) *envolver*
wrestler *el luchador*

X

x-ray *la radiografía*
   to take an x-ray *sacar una radiografía*

Y

year *el año*
   all year long *todo el año*
   Happy New Year! *¡Feliz Año Nuevo!*
   last year *el año pasado*
   New Year's Eve *la Nochevieja*
   yearly, annually *por año*
yell (to) *gritar*
yellow *amarillo, -a*
yesterday *ayer*
yet *todavía*
   not yet *todavía no*
yoga *la yoga*
   yoga class *clase de yoga*
you *tú; vosotros, vosotras (pl. subj. pron. Spain); lo, la (fml. sg.); los, las (fml. pl.); te (fam. sg.); ti (prep. obj. pron.)*
young *joven*
   younger *menor*
youngster *el/la joven*

Z

zero *cero*
zone *la zona*

INDEX

ACKNOWLEDGMENTS

This book was nurtured by the Living Language™ staff: Lisa Alpert, Christopher Warnasch, Christopher Medellín, Zviezdana Verzich, Elizabeth Bennett, Helen Tang, Suzanne McGrew, Elyse Tomasello, and Pat Ehresmann. To all of them my thanks. Special thanks also to Ruth Ascencio, Alvin Figueroa, and Cristina Iturrate.

I am particularly indebted to my development editor, Clifford Browder, who understood what I meant and helped me to say it more clearly.